Tourism and Change in Polar Regions

The world's polar regions are attracting more interest than ever before. Once regarded as barren, inhospitable places where only explorers go, the north and south polar regions have been transformed into the latest tourism destinations, increasingly visited by cruise ships as well as becoming accessible with direct flights. Tourism is seen as one of the few economic opportunities in these regions, but at the same time as the polar regions are being opened up to tourism development they are being affected by a number of new factors that are interconnected to travel and tourism. Climate change, landscape and species loss, increasing interest in energy resources and minerals, social changes in indigenous societies, and a new polar geopolitics in which countries disputing boundaries are laying claim to large amounts of seabed under previously international waters bring into question the sustainability of polar regions and the place of tourism within them.

This book provides a contemporary account of tourism and its impacts in polar regions. It reviews the effects of tourism within the broader context of environmental, socioeconomic and political change and uses a range of case studies and examples from northern and southern high latitudes to illustrate the issues arising from the role of tourism in the regions. It is a timely volume and the first attempt to fully explore the relationship between tourism and climate change in both Arctic and Antarctic polar regions by considering the associated environmental, economic, social and political factors in one volume. It draws on a wide range of regional case studies to help illustrate these climate change issues, critically evaluating varying perspectives on polar tourism.

Tourism has become both friend and foe to those seeking to conserve what has been described as the last great wilderness. Tourism is one of the few economic development opportunities in polar regions yet at the same time tourism also contributes to the very changes that are creating concerns for their future; this book proposes action that could be taken by local and global management to achieve a sustainable future for polar regions and development of tourism. This complete and current account of polar tourism issues is written by an international team of leading researchers in this area and will have global appeal to higher level students, researchers, academics in tourism, environmental studies, Arctic/polar studies and conservation enthusiasts alike.

Michael Hall is Professor, Department of Management, University of Canterbury, New Zealand; Docent, Department of Geography, University of Oulu, Finland and Visiting Professor, Baltic Business School, Linnaeus University, Kalmar, Sweden. Co-editor of *Current Issues in Tourism* he has published widely in tourism and mobility, gastronomy and environmental history.

Jarkko Saarinen is Professor of Human Geography at the University of Oulu, Finland. His research interests include tourism development and its impacts and sustainability in peripheries. He is co-author of the book *Nordic Tourism* (2009), with C. Michael Hall and Dieter Muller.

Contemporary Geographies of Leisure, Tourism and Mobility
Series Editor: C. Michael Hall
Professor at the Department of Management, College of Business & Economics,
University of Canterbury, Private Bag 4800, Christchurch, New Zealand

The aim of this series is to explore and communicate the intersections and relationships between leisure, tourism and human mobility within the social sciences.

It will incorporate both traditional and new perspectives on leisure and tourism from contemporary geography, e.g. notions of identity, representation and culture, while also providing for perspectives from cognate areas such as anthropology, cultural studies, gastronomy and food studies, marketing, policy studies and political economy, regional and urban planning, and sociology, within the development of an integrated field of leisure and tourism studies.

Also, increasingly, tourism and leisure are regarded as steps in a continuum of human mobility. Inclusion of mobility in the series offers the prospect to examine the relationship between tourism and migration, the sojourner, educational travel, and second home and retirement travel phenomena.

The series comprises two strands:

Contemporary Geographies of Leisure, Tourism and Mobility aims to address the needs of students and academics, and the titles will be published in hardback and paperback. Titles include:

The Moralisation of Tourism
Sun, sand....and saving the world?
Jim Butcher

The Ethics of Tourism Development
Mick Smith and Rosaleen Duffy

Tourism in the Caribbean
Trends, development, prospects
Edited by David Timothy Duval

Qualitative Research in Tourism
Ontologies, epistemologies and methodologies
Edited by Jenny Phillimore and Lisa Goodson

The Media and the Tourist Imagination
Converging cultures
Edited by David Crouch, Rhona Jackson and Felix Thompson

Tourism and Global Environmental Change
Ecological, social, economic and political interrelationships
Edited by Stefan Gössling and C. Michael Hall

Cultural Heritage of Tourism in the Developing World
Dallen J. Timothy and Gyan Nyaupane

Understanding and Managing Tourism Impacts
Michael Hall and Alan Lew

Routledge Studies in Contemporary Geographies of Leisure, Tourism and Mobility is a forum for innovative new research intended for research students and academics, and the titles will be available in hardback only. Titles include:

1. **Living with Tourism**
   Negotiating Identities in a Turkish Village
   Hazel Tucker

2. **Tourism, Diasporas and Space**
   Edited by Tim Coles and Dallen J. Timothy

3. **Tourism and Postcolonialism**
   Contested discourses, identities and representations
   Edited by C. Michael Hall and Hazel Tucker

4. **Tourism, Religion and Spiritual Journeys**
   Edited by Dallen J. Timothy and Daniel H. Olsen

5. **China's Outbound Tourism**
   Wolfgang Georg Arlt

6. **Tourism, Power and Space**
   Edited by Andrew Church and Tim Coles

7. **Tourism, Ethnic Diversity and the City**
   Edited by Jan Rath

8. **Ecotourism, NGO's and Development**
   A critical analysis
   Jim Butcher

9. **Tourism and the Consumption of Wildlife**
   Hunting, shooting and sport fishing
   Edited by Brent Lovelock

Tourism and Change in Polar Regions

Climate, environments and experiences

C. Michael Hall and Jarkko Saarinen

Routledge
Taylor & Francis Group

LONDON AND NEW YORK

First published 2010
by Routledge
2 Park Square, Milton Park, Abingdon, Oxfordshire OX14 4RN

Simultaneously published in the USA and Canada
by Routledge
711 Third Avenue, New York, NY 10017

First issued in paperback 2014

Routledge is an imprint of the Taylor & Francis Group, an informa business

© 2010 Selection and Editorial matter: C. Michael Hall and Jarkko Saarinen; individual chapters – the contributors

Typeset in Times New Roman by Saxon Graphics Ltd, Derby

British Library Cataloguing in Publication Data
A catalogue record for this book is available from the British Library

Library of Congress Cataloging-in-Publication Data

Tourism and change in polar regions : climate, environment and experiences / [edited by] C. Michael Hall and Jarkko Saarinen.

p. cm. -- (Routledge studies in contemporary geographies of leisure, tourism, and mobility ; 16)

ISBN 13: 978-1-138-88066-5 (pbk)
ISBN 13: 978-0-415-48999-7 (hbk)

1. Tourism--Polar regions. 2. Tourism--Environmental aspects--Polar regions. 3. Tourism--Environmental aspects--Polar regions--Case studies. 4. Polar regions--Environmental conditions. 5. Polar regions--Environmental conditions--Case studies. I. Hall, Colin Michael, 1961- II. Saarinen, Jarkko, 1968-

G155.P713T68 2010

304.20911--dc22

2009045805

Contents

List of Figures

List of Tables

Contributors

Bas Amelung, Maastricht University ICIS, PO Box 616, 6200 MD Maastricht, The Netherlands, b.amelung@icis.unimaas.nl

Jackie Dawson, Department of Geography and Environmental Management, University of Waterloo, 200 University Ave West, Waterloo, Ontario N2L 3G1, Canada, jpdawson@fes.uwaterloo.ca

D. Draper, Department of Geography, Faculty of Social Sciences, University of Calgary, Earth Sciences 356, 2500 University Drive NW, Calgary, Alberta T2N 1N4, Canada, draper@ucalgary.ca

C. Michael Hall, Department of Management, College of Business & Economics, University of Canterbury, New Zealand and Department of Geography, University of Oulu, Oulu, Finland, michael.hall@canterbury.ac.nz

S.E.L. Howell, Foothills Climate Analysis Facility: Centre for Alpine and Arctic Research, Department of Geography, University of Calgary, 2500 University Drive NW, Calgary, Alberta T2N 1N4, Canada, showell@uwaterloo.ca

Margaret Johnston, School of Outdoor Recreation Parks and Tourism, Lakehead University, Thunder Bay, Ontario P7B 5E1, Canada, mejohnst@lakeheadu.ca

Rhonda Koster, School of Outdoor Recreation Parks and Tourism, Lakehead University, Thunder Bay, Canada, rhonda.koster@lakeheadu.ca

Machiel Lamers, Maastricht University ICIS, PO Box 616, 6200 MD Maastricht, The Netherlands, machiel.lamers@icis.unimaas.nl

Raynald (Harvey) Lemelin, School of Outdoor Recreation Parks and Tourism, Lakehead University, Thunder Bay, Ontario P7B 5E1, Canada, harvey.lemelin@lakeheadu.ca

Linda Lundmark, Department of Social and Economic Geography, Umeå University, SE-901 87 Umeå, Sweden, linda.lundmark@geography.umu.se

Norman McIntyre, School of Outdoor Recreation Parks and Tourism,Lakehead University, Thunder Bay, Ontario, P7B 5E1, Canada, nmcintyr@lakeheadu.ca

Patrick T. Maher, Outdoor Recreation and Tourism Management Program,

University of Northern British Columbia, 3333 University Way, Prince George, British Columbia V2N 4Z9, Canada, maherp@unbc.ca

Jamie Noakes, Lakehead University Environmental Studies, Thunder Bay, Ontario P7B 5E1, Canada, jnoakes1@lakeheadu.ca

Mark Nuttall, University of Oulu, Thule Institute, Finland and Department of Anthropology, University of Alberta, Edmonton, Canada, mark.nuttall@oulu.fi; mark.nuttall@ualberta.ca

Ricardo Roura, Arctic Centre, University of Groningen, PO Box 716, 9700 AS Groningen, The Netherlands, ricardo.roura@worldonline.nl; r.m.roura@rug.nl

Jarkko Saarinen, Department of Geography, PO Box 3000, 90014 University of Oulu, Finland jarkko.saarinen@oulu.fi

Daniel Scott, Department of Geography, University of Waterloo, Waterloo, Ontario N2L 3G1, Canada, dj2scott@fes.uwaterloo.ca

Jan H. Stel, Earth and Life Sciences Foundation of the Netherlands Organisation for Scientific Research, NWO, PO Box 93510, 2509 AM The Hague, Netherlands, janstel@skynet.be

Emma Stewart, Department of Geography, Faculty of Social Sciences, University of Calgary, Earth Sciences 356, 2500 University Drive NW, Calgary, Alberta T2N 1N4, Canada, ejstewar@ucalgary.ca

Kaarina Tervo, Department of Geography, PO Box 3000, 90014 University of Oulu, Finland, kaarina.tervo@oulu.fi

Dallen J. Timothy, School of Community Resources and Development, Arizona State University, MC 4020, 411 N Central Ave, Suite 550, Phoenix, AZ 85004, USA, dtimothy@asu.edu

A. Tivy, Foothills Climate Analysis Facility: Centre for Alpine and Arctic Research, Department of Geography, University of Calgary, 2500 University Drive NW, Calgary, Alberta T2N 1N4, Canada, ativy@iarc.uaf.edu

Marisol Vereda, Department of Tourism, Faculty of Humanities and Social Sciences, Universidad Nacional de la Patagonia San Juan Bosco, Ushaia seat, Darwin y Canga s.n°, 9410, Ushuaia, Argentina, marisol.vereda@speedy.com.ar/marisolvereda@infovia.com.ar

Sandra Wilson, Department of Management, University of Canterbury, Christchurch 8140, New Zealand

J. Yackel, Cryosphere Climate Research Group: Centre for Alpine and Arctic Research, Department of Geography, University of Calgary, 2500 University Drive NW, Calgary, Alberta T2N 1N4, Canada, yackel@ucalgary.ca

Preface and Acknowledgements

The polar regions are attracting greater public and scientific interest than probably ever before. A manifestation of the increasing scientific role was the Fourth International Polar Year 2007–08, which provided a focal point for Arctic and Antarctic research activity, including this volume. The polar regions are a major focal point in discussion on global climate change, and in the Arctic there is considerably increased attention on the region's energy resources, which have substantially affected the geopolitics and future prospects of the polar regions. Tourism is significant as it is another form of economic development in the region, and helps reinforce claims to sovereignty as well as being a factor in social and environmental change. Tourism is heavily implicated in this context given that, as research undertaken for this volume illustrates, over five million tourist trips occur in the Arctic and sub-Arctic and more than 40,000 tourists visit Antarctica every year. Thus tourism is deeply embedded in processes of change that are not only environmental or climatic but also economic, social and political.

The volume is broadly divided into four parts. The first two chapters by the editors provide a context for polar tourism. Chapter 1 by Hall and Saarinen defines tourism in polar regions, outlines its significance and also reassesses its extent. This is particularly important in the Arctic as the extent of tourism is likely to be far greater than what many members of the public may imagine. Chapter 2 by Hall provides an overview of the interrelationships between tourism and environmental change in polar regions, highlighting the current state of knowledge with respect to climate change but also indicating the way in which tourism affects biodiversity conservation, especially in biological invasion.

The second series of chapters examine issues of tourism and change in northern polar regions. Chapters by Stewart *et al.* (Chapter 3) and Maher (Chapter 6) discuss the growth of cruise tourism and its implications. Undoubtedly one of the main focal points of public awareness of climate change in the Arctic is attention given to the polar bear by the media and environmental campaigns. Charismatic megafauna such as the polar bear are an important part of nature-based tourism in polar regions and two chapters by Dawson *et al.* (Chapter 4) and Lemelin *et al.* (Chapter 5) examine polar bear viewing in relation to climate change issues. Chapters 7 and 8 then examine tourism and climate change in a Nordic context, with Lundmark discussing longer-term adaptation issues for nature-based tourism as a result of climate change (Chapter 7), and Saarinen and Tervo providing the results of a study of tourism industry knowledge and perceptions of climate change with respect to winter tourism (Chapter 8). The section concludes with a study by Noakes and Johnston of the potential for tourism and mineral development to develop stronger economic connections in northern regions through an examination of the potential development of diamond tourism in the Northwest Territories of Canada (Chapter 9).

The third section examines tourism and change issues in the southern polar regions. Chapter 10 by Roura provides a detailed comparative study of cultural heritage tourism in Antarctica and Svalbard. This chapter not only provides a link between the northern and southern polar regions but also sets the scene for the next three chapters, which capture some of the responses of visitors to the Antarctic and sub-Antarctic. Nuttall (Chapter 11) examines the narratives of expeditioner-tourists in Antarctica, and Maher conveys the results of his studies of visitors' on-site experiences in the Ross Sea region of Antarctica. Chapter 13 by Vereda takes a slightly different slant by focusing on visitor perceptions of Ushuaia (Argentina) as a gateway port, an issue of great economic significance to Ushuaia in gaining greater benefits from tourism to the Antarctic peninsula. Chapter 14 by Lamers *et al.* then provides a different perspective on Antarctic tourism through the conduct of a scenario analysis for tourism in the region. The future orientation of this chapter also sets the scene for the last section of the book, which deals with future issues facing polar tourism. The final chapter in the section, Chapter 15 by Hall and Wilson, provides an overview of tourism management and conservation issues in the sub-Antarctic islands. In Chapter 16 Timothy discusses the growing contestation of place in polar regions, thereby directly relating to the issues raised at the start of the volume, and the way in which tourism may be used to legitimise sovereignty. Finally, in Chapter 17 Hall and Saarinen identify a number of future issues for polar tourism and change as well as tourism research in the regions. As with a number of chapters in this book the conclusion stresses that tourism both contributes to and is affected by change in polar regions, including climate change. The polar regions, and especially the Arctic and the Antarctic Peninsula, appear to be at a point at which continued climate change and environmental change are likely to profoundly alter their environmental and economic state.

The background of this book is twofold. Although the book does not aim to replicate or follow directly the structure and issues laid down in *Polar Tourism*, which Michael coedited with Margaret Johnson in 1995, there are naturally many parallel dimensions. Both of these volumes were generated from International Geographical Union Commission (IGU) activities. While *Polar Tourism* originated from the 1992 IGU meeting in Colorado, this volume grew out of a project on *Tourism and Global Change in Polar Regions* developed by the IGU Commission on the Geography of Tourism, Leisure and Global Change and the Thule Institute and the Department of Geography, University of Oulu as part of the International Polar Year activities. Although this volume is the culmination of the project, it has also involved seminars, meetings, field trips and a graduate workshop.

A number of people and institutions have been influential and assisted us with the editing and publishing of the book. In addition to the authors of the individual chapters the editors would like to thank Kari Laine, Pirjo Taskinen and Jaana Orava from the Thule Institute, who greatly supported the publishing process and its initial phase by collaborating with the organization of the IGU Conference. In addition we would like to thank Emma Travis and Michael P. Jones at Routledge for supporting the project; Irene Edgar, Donna Heslop-Williams and Irene Joseph for printing, photocopying and mail; Mikko Tuomas Tervo for preparing maps; Monica Tennberg from the Arctic Centre for helping with the baseline maps; and Sandra Wilson and Maria Pudas for assisting with gathering visitor and temperature data. Both Jarkko and Michael would also like thank colleagues at the Department of Geography and especially Kaarina Tervo and the rest of the Tourism Geographies research group for collaboration in polar tourism research and co-organising the IGU meeting.

For Michael many colleagues, students and friends have contributed to the evolution of this book. Although he has been undertaking polar-related research since undertaking his PhD, Michael would particularly like to acknowledge the *Polar Tourism* book coedited with Margaret Johnston. Although he has not received any encouragement to carry on working on polar tourism and/or climate change issues in New Zealand, his recent work in issues of impacts and tourism-related environmental, regional and political change in a polar context has been greatly influenced by working with colleagues in the Nordic countries. As well as, of course, Jarkko, he would particularly like to thank Stefan Gössling at Lund University Helsingborg and Kalmar University and Dieter Müller at Umeå University for their accommodation, collaboration and hospitality. In addition, the stimulation of working with Murray Simpson and Tim Coles in the UK; Paul Peeters in the Netherlands; Harvey Lemelin and Daniel Scott in Canada; David Duval, Hannah Jean Blythe, and Nicola van Tiel in New Zealand; and Sandra Wilson in Australia has also greatly contributed to his understanding of polar tourism and environmental change. Finally, he would like to thank Jody, JC and Cooper for coping with time spent on the Mac writing and otherwise being on the road and in the field.

While editing the book Jarkko was staying in Botswana as a visiting scholar. Although polar issues and cold landscapes seemed a bit distant at the time, the University of Botswana and the colleagues there at the Departments of Tourism and Hospitality and Environmental Science supported the work greatly. In addition to many colleagues already acknowledged Jarkko would like to thank Hans Gelter, Enrique del Acebo Ibañez, Gunnar Johannesson, Jari Järviluoma, Outi Rantala, Pirkko Siikamäki, Ola Sletvold and Arvid Viken for the discussions and support over the issues of tourism in polar regions. For Jarkko, Michael has been a very important collaborator as one of the driving actors in polar tourism studies and in the contextualisation of tourism in wider processes and academic fields focusing on global change in the north and south. When visiting and also afterwards Michael has provided a full view of polar tourism in the discussions at the seminar rooms of the 'world's northernmost Department of Geography'. Finally, thanks are due to Satu, Mira, Katlego and nana Dimpho for activating and developing sides of life other than thinking about tourism in polar and other peripheral regions of the south and north.

1 Tourism and Change in Polar Regions

Introduction – definitions, locations, places and dimensions

C. Michael Hall and Jarkko Saarinen

Introduction

The world's polar regions are attracting more public and scientific attention than ever before. The Fourth International Polar Year 2007–08 provided a focal point for Arctic and Antarctic scientific activity; however, probably of greater significance are the issues of climate change and increased interest in the energy resources of the Arctic region, which have substantially affected the geopolitics of the polar regions. Indeed, political and economic change, for example the granting of self-government to Greenland, appears to go hand in hand with environmental and social change. Both the Arctic and Nordic Councils, as well as member governments, have also expressed concerns about the potential changes that may occur as a result of energy exploration and extraction and climate change, particularly with respect to the impact on indigenous peoples (Arctic Climate Impacts Assessment [ACIA] (2005); Anisimov *et al.* 2007). Iconic wildlife, such as polar bears, penguins and whales, have also become standard-bearers for the conservation response to global environmental change.

Tourism is heavily implicated in this context of change. Tourism is regarded as a relatively benign economic development alternative compared with energy and mineral exploration. However, it is also seen as a possible contributor to climate change, with the potential also to contribute directly to environmental change if it is poorly managed. For example, in 2007 a cruise ship sank off the coast of the Antarctic Peninsula. In addition, tourism has been recognised as a potential beneficiary of climate change because of the potential increased access to some locations as well as the extension of the seasons. To further complicate the role of tourism in polar regions, tourism is also potential evidence for claims to polar territory (as a form of economic use) and is therefore part of broader national polar political strategies.

Although visitors to the Antarctic region are probably only just over 40,000 a year, visitors to the Arctic and sub-Arctic are in the millions. Although in the far north of Siberia, Canada and Greenland visitor numbers are more comparable to the Antarctic they still remain significant for the small Arctic communities as a form of economic development, even though tourism is also a contributor to social change. Just as importantly, tourism is also a means of economically and politically justifying the maintenance of transport connections and therefore greatly assists in enhancing the relative accessibility of the polar periphery. Arguably, along with minerals and fisheries, tourism is the most substantial economic driver in high latitudes and, given the current context of change in the region, it demands a comprehensive and accessible analysis to contribute better not only to the scientific and academic understanding of the region but also to the significant policy debates that need to be engaged in with respect to resource management, development and adaptation. This opening chapter provides an introduction to such an analysis first, by outlining the way in which the polar regions have become part of the geographical imagination; second, by defining tourism in a polar context; and third, by providing an overview of the current situation with respect to visitors to the polar regions. The chapter concludes with an outline of the remainder of the book.

The geographies of polar regions

Places can be understood in different ways (Cresswell 2004). As locations – specific points on the earth's surface; as locales – the material and physical settings in which activities, relations and interactions occur; and with respect to a sense of place – the personal and subjective attachments people have to place. Although the last term is usually applied in the context of people who live in a location on a permanent basis and reflects how they feel about its physical and social dimensions it can also apply to the understandings and relationships of people to a location that they have never been to and perhaps have experienced only vicariously but of which they still have an image and a personal understanding: what could be termed the geographical imagination of polar regions. All of these notions of place are significant for understanding the tourism geographies of polar regions.

As locations the polar regions are defined in different ways. The Antarctic is usually defined as south of 60°S latitude (definition used in the 1959 Antarctic Treaty), which includes the continent of Antarctica and its ice shelves, as well as the waters and island territories in the Southern Ocean, or the continent of Antarctica. Another common delineation of the region includes the area south of the Antarctic Convergence, which is an important climatic boundary between air and water masses, and is also used as the approximate boundary of the Southern Ocean that surrounds the Antarctic continent. A broader classification is that of the Antarctic Realm, which is a biogeographical classification (Udvardy 1975, 1987) that includes the provinces of Marielandia (the Antarctic Peninsula and West Antarctica), Maudlandia (the Eastern Antarctic Province that encompasses the majority of mainland Antarctica; the area not covered by ice is often described as the Antarctic Desert), Insulantarctica (primarily the sub-Antarctic islands) and Neozealandia (the North and South Islands of New Zealand and Stewart Island) (Figure 1.1). Tristan da Cunha, the most remote inhabited island group in the world, is the most northerly of the islands usually regarded as sub-Antarctic at 37°7'0"S, 12°17'0"W, a latitude similar to that of Melbourne in Australia.

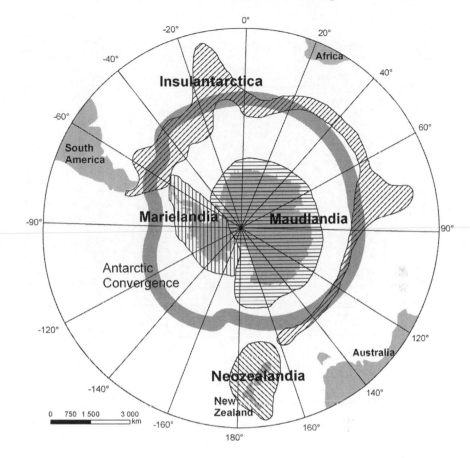

Figure 1.1 Biogeographical zones of the Antarctic region

The Antarctic is the largest transnational space on earth, that is a territory that belongs to no country. A number of countries have claims on Antarctica (Argentina, Australia, Chile, France, Norway, New Zealand and the United Kingdom) (Figure 1.2), with several countries also having expressed a territorial interest (Brazil, Peru, Russia, South Africa, Spain and the USA). However, under the Antarctic Treaty of 1959 and other international agreements that comprise what is referred to as the Antarctic Treaty System, territorial claims are not recognised. As of 2009 the Antarctic Treaty had been signed by 47 countries, with the signatories committing themselves to scientific research and other peaceful purposes on the continent. Although there is no permanent human population in Antarctica, scientific research has led to the establishment of a number of permanent and semi-permanent research stations that are focal points of human visitation, including tourism (Figure 1.3). Some of the sub-Antarctic islands do harbour a permanent population but the number of permanent residents is very small when compared with the Arctic islands. Nevertheless, interest in fisheries

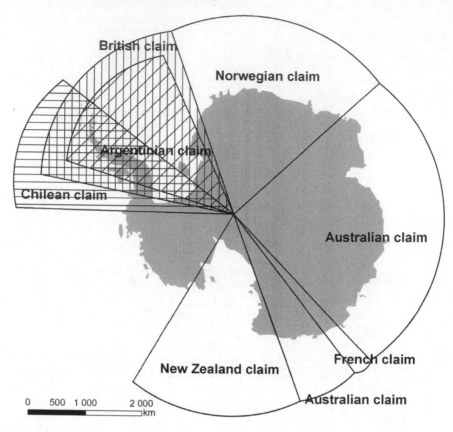

Figure 1.2 Antarctic claims

and mineral resources has meant that a number of countries have sought to extend their territorial waters from their sub-Antarctic territories (British Broadcasting Corporation [BBC] 2007a). For example, in April 2008 Australia added new territorial waters from Macquarie and Heard Islands (BBC 2008) with the Resources Minister, Martin Ferguson, stating, 'I am pleased to announce that Australia, the largest island in the world, has just been dramatically increased in size...The truth of the matter is that they have been hardly explored...This is potentially a bonanza. We have got unknown capacity up there'.

Various delineations of the Arctic also exist; the most common are based on indicators of phytogeography (e.g. the treeline), climate (e.g. the July 10° isotherm), geomorphology (permafrost) or solely on latitude (e.g. north of the Arctic Circle at 66°33'N or 60°N) (Figure 1.4). However, the Arctic concept can be extended even further geographically if a bioregional approach is used, i.e. by including the watersheds of the rivers that drain into the Arctic Ocean, or if a political approach is used. For example, the member states of the Arctic Council include Canada, Denmark (including Greenland and the Faroe Islands), Finland,

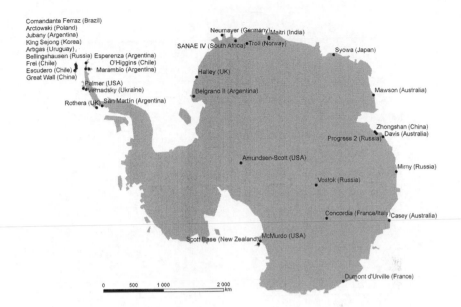

Comandante Ferraz (Brazil)
Arctowski (Poland)
Jubany (Argentina)
King Sejong (Korea)
Artigas (Uruguay)
Bellingshausen (Russia) Esperanza (Argentina)
Frei (Chile)   O'Higgins (Chile)
Escudero (Chile)   Marambio (Argentina)
Great Wall (China)
              Palmer (USA)
              Vernadsky (Ukraine)
Rothera (UK) San Martín (Argentina)

Neumayer (Germany) Maitri (India)
SANAE IV (South Africa) Troll (Norway)
                                    Syowa (Japan)
Halley (UK)
Belgrano II (Argentina)   Mawson (Australia)

                        Zhongshan (China)
                        Davis (Australia)
            Progress 2 (Russia)

Amundsen-Scott (USA)
                                    Mirny (Russia)
            Vostok (Russia)

Concordia (France/Italy) Casey (Australia)

Scott Base (New Zealand) McMurdo (USA)

                        Dumont d'Urville (France)

0   500   1 000   2 000
                        km

Figure 1.3 Antarctic stations

Iceland, Norway, Sweden, the Russian Federation and the USA. In the case of the Arctic Council's (2004) Arctic Human Development Report (AHDR) the region covered a number of areas below 60°N in Canada (southern Nunavik), the USA (parts of Alaska including the Aleutian Islands) and Russia (parts of Kamchatka, Magadan and Sakha (Yakutia) Republic).

Although the Arctic land area is not presently subject to conflicting land claims, with the possible exception of Hans Island (80°49′41″N, 66°27′35″W), which lies in the Nares Strait that separates Ellesmere Island (Canada) from Greenland and is claimed by both Canada and Denmark (DeMille 2005), there is substantial disagreement between Arctic nations over claims to Arctic waters as a result of the increasing fish and mineral importance of the region. Figure 1.5 illustrates some of the current claims to the Arctic Ocean. Arctic claims are based on extension of the Law of the Sea, whereby a signatory coastal state can lay claim to areas of continental shelf beyond the 200 nautical mile norm. Therefore, since the turn of the century there has been increasing interest from claimant states in exploring the geology of the region in order to support its claims, arguably climaxing with the international debate following the placement of a Russian flag made of rust-proof titanium alloy on the Arctic seabed beneath the North Pole by a Russian scientific expedition in August 2007, which served to reinforce Russian claims that the Lomonosov Ridge below the Arctic Sea is an extension of its continental shelf (BBC 2007b).

Both the north and south polar regions are usually portrayed as white and cold, with extreme climates (Pringle 1991; Hall and Johnston 1995; Linneweber *et al.*

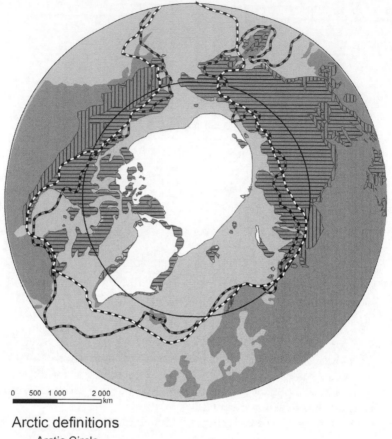

Arctic definitions
—— Arctic Circle
▬▪▬▪ July 10°C isotherm
▪▬▪▬ Phytogeographic Artic boundary
▤ Continous permafrost
▥ Discontinous permafrost

Figure 1.4 Different definitions of the Arctic

2003). However, the reality is that much of the polar regions, particularly in the
Arctic, show far greater variability and have much warmer summer temperatures
than many people believe (Tables 1.1 and 1.2). With the exception of the
continental Antarctic research stations plus-degree temperatures are reached in
the coastal stations, while the sub-Antarctic islands have significantly warmer
temperatures. In the Arctic even high Arctic locations experience positive temperatures in summer, whereas minimum temperatures are usually significantly below
that of the Antarctic except for some areas in Siberia.

The locational dimensions of polar places are not just of interest to

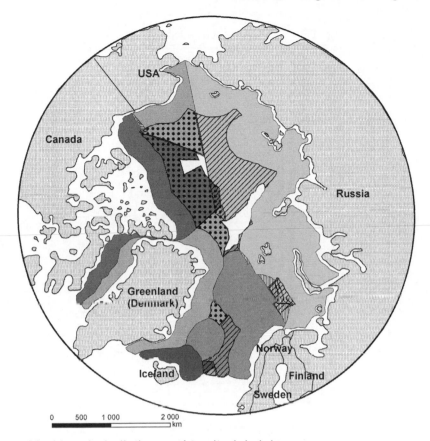

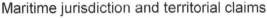

Maritime jurisdiction and territorial claims

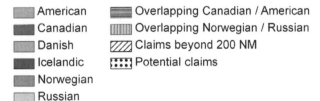

Figure 1.5 Arctic claims

cartographers and geographers. They are important because they also serve to delineate local, national and international boundaries within which law and regulations apply, including tourism activities and the cultural and ecological dimensions of resource management (Dalby 2003). However, such locational aspects of polar tourism also need to be understood in relation to the more personal notions of place that people have, as well as the way in which the polar regions have been portrayed in the media.

Table 1.1 Average Maximum Temperature: Select polar and high latitude locations

Location	J	F	M	A	M	J	J	A	S	O	N	D
Nome, Alaska, USA	-9.6	-11	-8.1	-3.6	5.6	11.6	14.3	13.4	9.3	0.9	-5.3	-9.4
Barrow, Alaska, USA (or Prudhoe Bay)	-21.9	-24.3	-22.8	-15.2	-4.3	3.5	7.2	5.7	1	-7.7	-15.8	-20.7
Whitehorse, Yukon, Canada	-13.3	-8.6	-0.8	6.4	13.1	18.5	20.5	18.5	12.2	4.3	-5.8	-10.6
Inuvik, NWT, Canada	-23.2	-22	-17.5	-7.1	5	17.3	19.8	16.1	7.8	-4.8	-16.8	-21.3
Yellowknife, NWT, Canada	-22.7	-18.6	-11.2	0.4	10.6	18.2	21.1	18.2	10.3	1	-9.9	-19.7
Iqaluit, Nunavut, Canada	-22.5	-23.8	-18.8	-9.9	-0.9	6.8	11.6	10.3	4.7	-2	-8.9	-18.5
Resolute, Nunavut, Canada	-28.8	-29.7	-27.2	-19.1	-7.7	2.2	7.1	3.8	-2.5	-11.8	-20.1	-25.6
Churchill, Manitoba, Canada	-22.7	-20.4	-14.5	-5	3.2	11.4	17.3	16.3	8.8	1.1	-8.9	-18.8
Nain, Newfoundland & Labrador, Canada	-14	-13.6	-7.3	-0.3	5.1	11	15.1	15.6	10.9	4.2	-1.8	-8.8
Nuuk, Greenland	-5	-7	-6	0	3	8	10	9	6	1	-1	-2
Qaanaaq, Greenland	-17	-19	-17	-8	-1	5	8	6	1	-6	-10	-14
Reykjavik, Iceland	2	2	2	6	9	11	13	13	11	7	4	3
Longyearbyen, Svalbard, Norway	5.8	2.4	-2.7	-1.3	3.7	9.6	11.9	11.6	12.4	3.8	3.5	3.7
Tromso, Norway	-2	-1	0	4	8	12	15	14	10	5	1	-1
Kirkenes, Norway	-8	-8	-4	1	6	12	16	14	9	2	-4	-7
Kiruna, Sweden	-10	-8	-4	2	8	14	17	14	9	1	-5	-8
Rovaniemi, Finland	-9	-8	-3	3	10	16	19	16	10	2	-4	-8
Tornio, Finland	-8	-8	-2	4	11	17	20	17	12	5	-2	-6
Ivalo, Finland	-10	-9	-3	2	8	15	18	15	10	2	-5	-9
Oulanka, Kuusamo, Finland	-10	-8	-3	3	10	16	19	16	10	2	-4	-9
Murmansk, Russia	-8	-8	-3	2	7	13	17	14	10	3	-4	-9
Arhangel'sk, Russia	-10	-8	-2	5	12	18	21	17	12	4	-4	-7
Dikson, Russia	-23	-23	-20	-15	-6	2	7	7	3	-6	-16	-21
Tiksi, Russia	-29	-27	-23	-15	-4	6	11	10	4	-9	-22	-26
Yakutsk, Russia	-37	-29	-14	1	13	22	25	21	11	-4	-24	-35
South Pole Station, Antarctica	-25.9	-38.1	-50.1	-54.2	-53.9	-54.4	-55.9	-55.6	-55.1	-48.4	-36.9	-26.5
Dumont d'Urville Station, Antarctica	0.8	-1.8	-6	-8.9	-10.7	-11	-10.5	-10.1	-11.2	-10.5	-4.2	0.4
Mawson Station, Antarctica	2.6	-1.4	-7.2	-11.8	-13.7	-13.6	-15.1	-15.6	-14.4	-10	-2.6	2.1
McMurdo Station, Antarctica	-0.2	-6.3	-14	-17.4	-19	-19.1	-21.7	-22.8	-20.8	-15.5	-6.7	-0.8
Vostok Station, Antarctica	-29	-39.4	-52.9	-60.3	-59.2	-59.3	-56.7	-60.7	-57.5	-53.5	-38.8	-28
Bouvet Island, Norway	3	4	3	2	1	0	-1	-1	-1	0	1	3
Macquarie Island, Australia	8.8	8.6	8	6.9	5.9	5	4.9	5	5.4	5.8	6.5	7.9
Marion Island, South Africa	16.4	16.6	17.1	14.7	13.3	12.3	11.1	11.3	11.9	13.2	15	15.5
Stanley, Falkland Islands	13	13	12	9	7	5	4	5	7	9	11	12
Grytviken, South Georgia, UK	12	12	11	5	7	0	1	0	2	6	7	12

Table 1.2 Average Minimum Temperature: Select polar and high latitude locations

Location	J	F	M	A	M	J	J	A	S	O	N	D
Nome, Alaska, USA	-18.2	-20.3	-17.9	-12.4	-1.6	3.8	7.3	6.7	2.4	-5.4	-12.6	-18.1
Barrow, Alaska, USA	-28.5	-30.9	-29.5	-22.8	-9.8	-1.3	0.9	0.7	-2.8	-12.9	-21.6	-27.3
Whitehorse, Yukon, Canada	-22	-18.7	-12.3	-4.6	0.7	5.1	7.7	6.3	2	-3.1	-13	-19.1
Inuvik, NWT, Canada	-31.9	-31.7	-28.8	-18.4	-4.7	5.3	8.5	5.9	-0.4	-11.6	-25.1	-30.1
Yellowknife, NWT, Canada	-30.9	-28.1	-23.3	-11	0.5	8.7	12.4	10.3	3.8	-4.4	-17.7	-27.7
Iqaluit, Nunavut, Canada	-30.6	-32.2	-28.6	-19.6	-7.8	0.3	3.7	3.3	-0.4	-7.7	-16.7	-26.9
Resolute, Nunavut, Canada	-35.9	-36.6	-34.2	-26.5	-14	-2.5	1.4	-0.8	-6.9	-18	-27	-32.7
Churchill, Manitoba, Canada	-30.7	-28.9	-24.4	-14.5	-4.6	1.7	6.8	7.2	2.5	-4.5	-16.1	-26.8
Nain, Newfoundland & Labrador, Canada	-23.1	-22.9	-17.5	-9.5	-3	1.4	5.2	5.7	3	-2.1	-8.3	-16.8
Nuuk, Greenland	-10	-12	-11	-4	-1	1	3	3	1	-2	-5	-7
Qaanaaq, Greenland	-25	-27	-26	-18	-9	-1	1	0	-4	-10	-15	-20
Reykjavik, Iceland	-2	-3		0	3	6	8	8	5	1	-1	-2
Longyearbyen, Svalbard, Norway	-16.9	-19.1	-23.9	-23.1	-11	-0.1	1.8	0	-4.5	-14	-20.5	-20.7
Tromso, Norway	-5	-5	-4	-2	2	7	9	8	5	1	-2	-4
Kirkenes, Norway	-13	-12	-9	-5	1	6	9	8	4	-1	-7	-11
Kiruna, Sweden	-16	-15	-13	-7	0	6	8	6	2	-4	-10	-15
Rovaniemi, Finland	-14	-13	-9	-4	2	6	12	9	4	-1	-7	-12
Tornio, Finland	-14	-14	-10	-4	2	9	12	10	5	0	-6	-12
Ivalo, Finland	-16	-16	-12	-7	0	6	10	7	3	-2	-10	-15
Oulanka, Kuusamo, Finland	-16	-16	-12	-7	0	7	10	8	3	-2	-8	-14
Murmansk, Russia	-12	-12	-8	-4	1	6	9	8	5	0	-6	-11
Arhangel'sk, Russia	-16	-14	-9	-4	2	8	11	9	5	0	-8	-13
Dikson, Russia	-28	-28	-25	-21	-10	-1	3	4	0	-9	-20	-25
Tiksi, Russia	-34	-32	-30	-24	-10	0	4	4	-1	-14	-27	-31
Yakutsk, Russia	-41	-38	-27	-12	1	9	13	9	1	-12	-31	-40
South Pole Station, Antarctica	-29.4	-42.7	-57	-61.2	-61.7	-61.2	-62.8	-62.5	-62.4	-53.8	-40.4	-29.3
Dumont d'Urville Station, Antarctica	-3.3	-6.7	-11.2	-17.9	-20.7	-22	-20.6	-22.2	-23.5	-16.7	-8.7	-3.8
Mawson Station, Antarctica	-2.6	-7.3	-13.3	-17.3	-19.4	-19.5	-20.8	-21.6	-20.7	-16.5	-8.8	-3.2
McMurdo Station, Antarctica	-5.5	-11.6	-21.1	-24.9	-27.1	-27.3	-30.1	-31.8	-29.4	-23.4	-12.7	-6
Vostok Station, Antarctica	-35.5	-47.4	-63.9	-70.4	-70.5	-70.8	-73.8	-75.4	-71.8	-61.3	-45.4	-35.1
Bouvet Island, Norway	0	0	0	0	-2	-4	-5	-5	-5	-3	-2	-1
Macquarie Island, Australia	5.3	5.3	4.7	3.7	2.5	1.5	1.6	1.5	1.5	2	2.7	4.3
Marion Island, South Africa	1.1	0.9	1	-0.2	-1.1	-2.3	-2.9	-3.3	-3.3	-2.2	-1.2	-0.1
Stanley, Falkland Islands	6	5	4	3	1	-1	-1	-1	1	2	3	4
Grytviken, South Georgia, UK	3	3	4	0	0	-4	-4	-7	-4	0	0	3

Polar landscapes are experienced in different ways by different people. The understanding of a place is always different for those who live there as opposed to those who visit a place or experience it vicariously through the media. Furthermore, the understanding of northern high latitudes, which have a substantial permanent population, is different from that of the south. While the Arctic is an ocean surrounded by continents, the Antarctic is a continent surrounded by oceans.

Northernness has served as an important part of numerous national identities to the point where it has been identified as a common characteristic of northern countries. Hall, Müller and Saarinen (2009) argued that for centuries the north constituted a mythological space, constantly defined and redefined, by centuries of writers, explorers and other image makers (see also Vaughn 2007). Indeed, they felt that the northern or Nordic 'other' was also arguably defined in other European cultures, especially British, French and German, before being defined in Norden itself. Yet even here understanding of Nordic was related to new Romantic nationalist identities, especially in Finland and Norway, that were connected to the northern environment. Significantly, travel played an extremely important role in developing and popularising artistic and intelligentsia understandings of Nordicity both through the travel writing genre and through tourism as a means of extending elite culture into popular culture (Robinson 2007).

Hamelin (1979) argued that the notion of nordicity or degree of northernness, which covered natural and cultural features, was a useful way of capturing the different variables of what the north represented. Hamelin developed an index he called *valeurs polaires* (polar values) or VAPO, in which the North Pole had a VAPO of 1000. The nordicity index had 10 elements:

1   latitude
2   summer heat
3   annual cold
4   types of ice
5   total precipitation
6   natural vegetation cover
7   accessibility by means other than air
8   air service
9   population
10   degree of economic activity

Each component was graded on the scale of 0–100, where 100 represented extreme nordicity, with the VAPO representing the sum of these 10 elements. Canada was then divided into the Extreme North (northern Arctic archipelago), Far North (southern Arctic archipelago, tundra and much of the boreal forest), Middle North (northern parts of most provinces), and Near North, based on their VAPO score. Hamelin's (1979) definition of 'the North' as the area that exists above the tree line that – depending on which northern country you are in – lies between the 55th and 60th parallels has undoubtedly proven influential with respect to issues of northern peripherality and accessibility (Hall *et al.* 2009).

However, as Roth (2005: 43) commented, 'innumerable sources over the centuries indicate that it is not, and never has been, science that has articulated the idea of the North in the North American public imaginary. Rather, it is our own mythical notions of "The North" that circumscribe our views'. For example, with respect to Canada, Shields (1991) wrote of the 'imaginary north' that is 'a frontier, a wilderness, and empty "space" which, seen from southern Canada is white, blank'; and the ideological 'True North Strong and Free' (a line from the Canadian national anthem), which is an 'empty page onto which can be projected images of the essence of "Canadian-ness" and also images to define one's urban existence against' (Shields 1991: 165).

Similar experiences can be identified in the Russian context. According to Makarychev (2002: 46–47), on the negative side, the north 'is associated with remoteness and cultural backwardness':

- the north can be seen as synonymous with vast loosely organised spaces, which have to be somehow preserved or conserved;
- the north is connoted with social conservatism and traditionalism;
- the north is a depopulated area;
- the northern provinces are perceived as prone to [raw] material separatism and even isolationism, and in this capacity they might contribute to the disintegration of the federation;
- the peoples of the north are on their way to emphasising their self-identities, which is a challenge for the federal authorities.

Medvedev (2000: 1, cited in Joenniemi and Sergounin, 2003) in comparing Canadian, Finnish and Russian understandings of the north also argued that 'The North is more often communicated than experienced, imagined rather than embodied'. According to Medvedev (2001: 91), 'Lacking in rationality, the north is rich in mythos and implied meanings. In many traditional mythologies the north is singled out among other parts of the world as essentially being the outer fringe.'

The north is left as 'the last Frontier, the only part of the world that holds the fascination of emptiness, a white space in our mental maps', with the implications of this being substantial for tourism because of the symbolic value of northern-ness. 'Europe's southernmost and easternmost points are hardly known to the public at all; on the contrary, an entire tourist industry has been built around pilgrimages to the Nordkap. The north turns out to be marketable precisely because of its remoteness, relative obscurity and anonymity' (Medvedev, 2001: 91). The north is therefore, 'the emptiness we are filling with our imagination, narratives and texts; a blank sheet of paper on which words are written and erased; an empty snow field on which lonely figures emerge, pass, and disappear' (Medvedev, 2001: 92).

Such comments are significant as they reinforce the notion that the north has been substantially defined by those outside it and who may never even have visited it. As Roth (2005: 44–45) notes, 'the "symbolic north" has been fabricated by non-natives who have talked about it, analysed it, made statements about it, settled it, ruled it, authorized certain views of it, managed it, photographed it, and ultimately produced it as an "exotic" commodity for Southern consumption' (see also Payne 2006; Craciun 2009). Not least of which has been for the benefits of tourists and visitors via the creation of images, myths and place identities, such as Santa Claus and Father Christmas (e.g. Pretes 1994; Grenier 2007; Hall 2008, 2009), representations of northern indigeneity (e.g. Saarinen 1999, 2001; Müller and Pettersson 2001, 2006; Tuulentie 2006; Rosner 2009), wilderness and wild nature, including iconic northern species such as polar bears and reindeer (e.g. Amoamo and Boyd 2005; Saarinen 2005; Lemelin *et al.* 2008), and snow and ice (Hall *et al.* 2009; Hübner 2009). Indeed, in recent years the representation of the region for tourist consumption has become increasingly entwined with the visualisation and representation of the region with respect to climate change (e.g. Clark *et al.* 2008; Hall 2009; Martello 2009).

A number of the themes extant in the representation of the Arctic can also be found in the Antarctic, although, clearly, the role of the south is not so strong with respect to the development of national identity given the lack of large permanent populations as occur in northern high latitudes. That said, the Antarctic has played its part in the development of national mythologies, particularly in connection with the nationalistic 'heroic' portrayals of the age of exploration and Romantic imperialism (which often conveniently ignored the extensive economic exploitation of sea mammal resources in the Antarctic Ocean), and the activities of expeditions lead by Amundsen, Scott and Shackleton (Mickleburgh 1990; Wylie 2002; Dodds 2006; Barwell 2007; Yusoff 2007). As Spufford (2007: 4) observed;

> People usually put quote marks around "heroic", and there is certainly a lot to be sceptical about in the nationalistic fervour that enfolded the great expeditions of the decade leading up to the First World War. But "heroic" is the right word for the role those expeditions have played, ever after, in Antarctic memory. Together, the stories of them make up Antarctica's Iliad – a collective epic, in which figures not quite of human scale struggle and clash and sometimes die.

Such portrayals are significant as, together with the representation of Antarctica as a pristine wilderness with abundant wildlife, they underlie much of present-day tourist interest in the Antarctic. For example, Adventure World's promotion for its Antarctic tours states, 'It is a privilege to visit this awe-inspiring continent and to experience the special magic that has lured explorers, adventurers and scientists for more than two centuries and – most recently – world travellers' (Adventure World 2009). Similarly, the promotional titles of a number of cruises planned for the Austral 2009–10 summer reinforce the exploration dimension by continuing to refer to such cruises as 'expeditions' as well as connecting to specific explorers, e.g. 'In Footsteps of Scott & Shackleton' (Heritage Expeditions), 'Spirit of Shackleton' (GAP Adventures), 'Shackleton Odyssey' (Aurora Expeditions), 'Mawson's Antarctica', 'Scott & Shackleton's Antarctica' (Orion Expedition Cruises) (Fine Cruising 2009).

Apart from the 'heroic' representations of Antarctica, the main portrayals of the region have been conveyed in primarily scientific terms (Dodds 1997). As Pyne (1986: 154) observes with respect to comparing the Romantic art of the Arctic with that of the Antarctic,

> the problem is that Antarctic art–like the rest of Antarctic history–is dominated by Antarctic science. Scientific terms provide a descriptive language; scientific reports substitute for an indigenous art or folktales…The enduring literature of Antarctica consists of exploration memoirs; its principal art, of scientific illustration. Under these circumstances all forms of inquiry tend to become documentary in purpose.

Yet the notion of scientific documentary has itself been transformed. Television documentaries such as the BBC natural history series narrated by naturalist David Attenborough, *Life in the Freezer* (1993), which showed the seasonal cycle of life in Antarctica, and the BBC travel documentary *Pole to Pole* (1992) by former Monty Python member, Michael Palin, have provided vicarious opportunities to experience not only Antarctic science but also its wildlife, landscapes and cultural heritage. However, more recently representations of the Antarctic have also come to be related to issues of environmental change, primarily with respect to climate but also the impacts that tourism can have. For example, the 2006 animated film *Happy Feet,* in which an emperor penguin, Mumble, who dances better than he can sing, has a strong conservation message with respect to human impact on the Antarctic. Penguins have also become the Antarctic icons of campaigns with respect to preventing global warming, in the same way that the polar bear is the northern icon (McCaffrey *et al.* 2006; Poirier 2007–08; Hansen and Machin 2008; Boykoff and Goodman 2009; Manzo 2009). As Leane (2007: 7) notes, 'Animals are central to the human experience of Antarctica; surveys have shown that wildlife is the number one drawcard for tourists. However, most people will never see Antarctic animals in their native habitat. What they will encounter are highly mediated, textual representations of these animals on page and screen'.

The growing public awareness of the polar regions as being at great risk of climate change is now introducing a new set of real and imagined high-latitude geographies in which the Arctic and Antarctic, rather than being portrayed as remote areas of high risk and danger, are being seen as fragile environments all too readily affected by what else happens in the world. The place of the polar regions in the imagination is therefore being inverted. As Kolbert (2007: 8) writes, if climate change continues, 'A landscape that once symbolized the tragic indifference of nature will, for future generations, come to symbolize its tragic vulnerability.' The changing and cumulative perceptions of the Arctic and Antarctic comprise what Sörlin (1998, 1999) describes as the 'articulation of territory', the results of which are symbolic and mental landscapes that are deeply embedded in the image and self-understanding of nations, regions and, of course, individuals. Such articulations serve as major drivers for tourism, creating images of place in the minds of consumers as well as providing motivations for travel. It is therefore perhaps of no great surprise that contemporary environmental change is providing a new set of drivers and promotional possibilities for polar tourism. For example, the Alaskan Office of Economic Development (2008) reports that climate change is an opportunity for Alaskan tourism as 'Global warming or climate change, and the impacts on Alaska – puts Alaska in the spotlight' (2008: 34). Similarly, the front cover of the March 2008 issue of *Destinations of the World News* was entitled 'The Arctic: Tourism's disappearing world' and contained a series of articles on 'paradise lost', with Round (2008: 46) stating

> The wild wonder of the Arctic is one of the hottest destinations of the world. As climate change fuels larger visitor numbers and the cruise industry booms, the race to the top of the world is getting more intense.
>
> The Arctic has got to be one of the most fashionable destinations of the world. Any style magazine worth its weight in off-the-beaten path travel features is featuring the region as this year's must see.
>
> Adding further impetus to Arctic travel are numerous documentaries, websites, pressure groups, photographers and journalists all charting the slow meltdown of global warming led by photogenic polar bears swimming for miles for food and glaciers dramatically cracking into the sea.
>
> The plight of the region has become such a part of our contemporary background that it's no wonder demand for the region has become so high. The message is quite clear: come quickly or you'll miss it.

More recently, Mads Nordlund of Greenland's Tourism and Business Council has told the same magazine a similar story, 'Greenland is always featured in those books that offer 100 Places To Visit Before They Disappear…It's like Kilimanjaro, you can see the change taking place. People want to see it before the ice goes' (in Round 2009). Such accounts illustrate the way that tourism both benefits from and affects climate change, and that its influence is potentially still growing, themes that will be returned to throughout this book. However, as the next section illustrates, tourism is already a significant activity in many of the polar regions.

Polar tourism

Polar tourism is difficult to define. Usually three types of tourism are recognised: (1) domestic tourism, which includes the activities of resident visitors within the country or economy of reference either as part of a domestic or an international trip; (2) inbound tourism, which includes the activities of non-resident visitors within the country or economy of reference either as part of a domestic or an international trip (from the perspective of his/her country of residence); and (3) outbound tourism, which includes the activities of resident visitors outside the country or economy of reference, either as part of a domestic or an international trip (Hall *et al.* 2009).

The United Nations World Tourism Organization (UNWTO) has recommended that an international tourist be defined as: 'a visitor who travels to a country other than that in which he/she has his/her usual residence for at least one night but not more than one year, and whose main purpose of visit is other than the exercise of an activity remunerated from within the country visited'; and that an international excursionist (e.g. a cruise-ship visitor), who are significant in the polar context, be defined as '[a] visitor residing in a country who travels the same day to a country other than which he/she has his/her usual environment for less than 24 hours without spending the night in the country visited and whose main purpose of visit is other than the exercise of an activity remunerated from within the country visited' (UNWTO 1991). Similar definitions have also been developed for domestic tourists, with a domestic tourist having a time limit of 'not more than six months' (United Nations 1994; UNWTO 1991).

More recent statistical recommendations from the UN and UNWTO have focused more on the category of 'visitor' rather than 'tourist' per se, with a number of criteria needing to be satisfied for an international traveller to qualify as an international visitor:

1   The place of destination within the country visited is outside the traveller's usual environment.
2   The stay, or intended stay, in the country visited should last no more than 12 months, beyond which this place in the country visited would become part of his/her usual environment. At which point this would lead to a classification as migrant or permanent resident. The UN and UNWTO recommend that this criterion should be applied to also cover long-term students and patients, even though their stay might be interrupted by short stays in their country of origin or elsewhere.
3   The main purpose of the trip is other than being employed by an organization or person in the country visited.
4   The traveller is not engaged in travel for military service nor is a member of the diplomatic services.
5   The traveller is not a nomad or refugee. According to the UN and UNWTO (2007: 21), 'For nomads, by convention, all places they visit are part of their usual environment so that beyond the difficulty in certain cases to determine their country of residence…For refugees or displaced persons, they have no longer any place of usual residence to which to refer, so that their place of stay is considered to be their usual environment.'

In the Arctic context such definitions work well because there are clearly delineated national jurisdictions in which such definitions can apply, even although some scientists and researchers may not wish to be defined as 'tourists' for statistical purposes. However, in the Antarctic case the UNWTO approaches are not applied for two main reasons. First, the Antarctic is a transnational space. Second, tourism tends to be understood primarily in terms of non-governmental activities (Hall and Johnston 1995; Stewart *et al.* 2005).

The 1959 Antarctic Treaty itself makes no specific reference to tourism (Hall and Johnston 1995). By the time that the Madrid Protocol was finalised in 1991 tourism began to be mentioned, usually in conjunction with respect to all aspects of human activity in Antarctica, but the term was not defined. Indeed, throughout the Antarctic Treaty Consultative Meeting process and the development of the Antarctic Treaty system at no times have the terms 'tourist', 'tourism', 'non-governmental activities', 'adventure tourism', 'expedition', or 'support' been substantively defined, even though there are crucial elements in the management of visitor activities in the Antarctic (Hall and Johnston 1995; Murray and Jabour 2004).

Hall's (1992:4) definition that in the Antarctic context, tourism may be defined 'as all existing human activities other than those directly involved in scientific research and the normal operations of government bases. Such a definition covers the activities of commercial tourism operations, non-government expeditions and the recreational activities of government personnel' has been widely used in Antarctic tourism research (e.g. Bauer 2001; Tracey 2001; Stewart *et al.* 2005), although as Haase (2008) notes, most researchers have tended to exclude the recreational activities of national programme staff. For example, Enzenbacher (1992: 17) defined tourists as 'Visitors who are not affiliated in an official capacity with an established National Antarctic Program. They include both fare-paying passengers, whose numbers are usually reported reliably by tour operators, and private expedition members and adventurers aboard sea or airborne vessels, whose numbers are more difficult to determine'. Similarly, Hasse (2008: 48) defined, Antarctic tourism as 'all human activities either mainly pursuing recreational and/or educational purposes or unequivocally catering for those who engage in recreational and/or educational activities in the Antarctic Treaty area south of 60°S Lat.'

The International Union for Conservation of Nature and Natural Resources (IUCN) (1992: 1) also made a distinction between commercial and private tourism activities for management purposes, because 'Operations by commercial tour companies, whether shipborne or aircraft supported, are usually larger in scale, involve more people, have greater potential for environmental impact or disruption of activities, and, therefore, demand greater management effort.' Similarly, Hemmings *et al.* (1991) also divided tourism in Antarctica into commercial and non-commercial ventures and categorised the principal tourism activities into large group tourism, adventure tourism and recreation. Non-governmental activities such as journalism, science or independent assessment of human activities are not included under the heading of tourism. Such an approach reflects the situation that any discussion of Antarctic tourism by Antarctic Treaty parties is often automatically linked to the management of non-governmental activities. However, Hemmings, Cuthbert and Dalziell (1991: 3) arguably reflect widely long-held views among many Antarctic scientists and government bodies that 'it is tourism, rather than non-governmental activities per se, which has been the publicly acknowledged problem. Yet when it comes to actually drafting something, the terms of reference suddenly become wider than merely tourism.'

The most narrow definition of Antarctic tourism is from Maher *et al.* (2006: 54), who defined Antarctic tourists in terms of 'those who come into physical contact with the continent, but also whose primary activity is simply "being there" (i.e., getting to visit the continent) for educational or recreational purposes.' Such an approach clearly excludes any members of national programmes, who are in Antarctica as scientists or support personnel, tourists taking part in Antarctic overflights, and potentially those visitors who participate in cruise-only tourism and do not leave the ship, as they do not come into physical contact with the continent. Yet such an approach is limiting as it simply does not reflect the effects that such visits can have on the destination, even if they have travelled only to 'watch' and not to land.

The present chapter therefore uses a pragmatic approach to examining tourism in the Antarctic, along the lines of Hall (1992). Data on visitation to Antarctica are limited and therefore the statistics collected by the International Association of Antarctica Tour Operators (IAATO 2003, 2008a, b) remain the main source of information on trends in Antarctic non-government visitation. Although there also appears to be growth in private cruising in the region, especially around the Antarctic Peninsula, it is difficult to collect information on the people involved (Hall 2000; Murray and Jabour 2004). Ideally, the adoption of the UNWTO statistical definition of tourism would provide the clearest basis for collecting information on visitation and its impacts in the Antarctic, especially given that all human visitation to Antarctica contributes to environmental change. However, it is unlikely that Antarctic scientists and Antarctic base staff will wish to see themselves equated to tourists, even if only in a statistical sense, in the foreseeable future. Therefore, it is likely that although signatory states to the Antarctic Treaty and organisations such as IAATO will continue to take positive steps to manage visitor activity in the region, tourism will continue to exist without a clear, agreed-upon definition.

The number of tourist visitors to the Antarctic is difficult to establish with certainty. But the modern period of visitation is usually regarded as having commenced in the late 1950s. Tourists now greatly outnumber the scientists and support staff based in Antarctica during the Austral summer in number of people having landed, but with respect to the amount of time spent on land by people, scientists and support staff still occupy Antarctic space for much longer. Tourism in Antarctica is also highly seasonal. Because of the harshness of the climate and extent of sea ice, access to the continent is restricted to the Austral summer between October and March. This is also the time of year when there are 24 hours of sunlight a day. Such a limited tourist season clearly also has implications for the management of Antarctic tourism given that it means that visitation is constrained in time and also in space (landing/access points). Sea-borne passengers normally make up more than 90% of Antarctic tourists, even including those who travel on overflights.

The majority of Antarctic tourists originate from countries in the northern hemisphere and then assemble in Australasia or South America for transit to Antarctica. Tourism by ship and air began slowly in the late 1950s, when the Chilean and Argentinean governments organised the first tourist expeditions to the Antarctic Peninsula (Brewster 1982). The first tourist cruise was made by an

Table 1.3 Ship and land-based passengers to the Antarctic for Antarctic Austral Summer Seasons

Year	Number	Year	Number	Year	Number
1980–81	855	1990–91	4,698	2000–01	12 248
1981–82	1,441*	1991–92	6,317	2001–02	11 588
1982–83	719	1992–93	6,704	2002–03	13 571
1983–84	834	1993–94	8,016	2003–04	19 886
1984–85	544	1994–95	8,120	2004–05	22 712
1985–86	631	1995–96	9,604	2005–06	26 245
1986–87	1,797	1996–97	10,013	2006–07	28 826P
1987–88	2,782	1997–98	14,762	2007–08	34 354P
1988–89	3,146	1998–99	12,248	2008–09	34 182P
1989–90	2,460	1999–2000	11,588	2009–10	40 000E
Decade totals	15,209		92,060		243 612

Notes:

* In 1981–82 some passengers were both airborne and shipborne.

P Projected

E Authors' estimate

Figures for seabourne passengers from 1980–81 to 1991–92 derived from Enzenbacher and Hall and Johnston.

Figures from 1992–93 on derived from estimated actual numbers of tourists by IAATO. (note that Enzenbacher (1994) provides a figure of 7,037 for 1992–93). IAATO figures from 1997–98 onwards includes commercial yacht activity.

For more detailed profiles of Antarctic tourism consult the IAATO website: http://www.iaato.org/tourism_stats.html

Sources: Enzenbacher 1992, 1994; Hall and Johnston 1995; IAATO 2003, 2008a, b

Argentine vessel, *Les Eclaireus*, to the Antarctic Peninsula in 1958. Ships have the easiest access to Antarctica as aeroplanes are easily affected by changing weather patterns and the difficulty of finding safe landing sites. However, Antarctic shipboard tourism has grown irregularly. In 1974–75, the numbers of passengers rose to a height of more than 3,500, but declined to fewer than 1,000 in 1980 (Stonehouse 1992). Yet as Table 1.3 indicates, tourism has continued to grow since the early 1990s to the point that it is approaching 40,000 tourists a year to Antarctica.

The Antarctic Peninsula is the most frequently visited area of Antarctica because of its proximity to South American ports, with nearly all Antarctic cruises commencing from Punta Arenas (Chile), Puerto Williams (Chile), or Ushuaia (Argentina). The crossing of the Drake Passage to the Antarctic can be made in 48 hours compared with up to 10 days from Hobart (Australia) and Christchurch (New Zealand), which are also traditional departure points for Antarctic expeditions. The Antarctic Peninsula also has a milder climate than anywhere else in Antarctica, relative freedom from pack-ice compared with other parts of the Antarctic coast and access to sub-Antarctic islands such as the Falklands and South Georgia. Furthermore, it has diverse and abundant wildlife, offering photo opportunities, and the largest concentration of Antarctic research stations. Other cruises, often involving the same ships, leave southern ports in New Zealand and Tasmania to visit the McMurdo Sound, Cape Adare, and Commonwealth Bay Sectors, usually including Macquarie Island and some of the southern islands of New Zealand such as Campbell Island. Other areas on the continent are less frequently visited. Antarctic circumnavigation is rare but is increasing. In addition, there appear to be increasing numbers of private yachts visiting the Antarctic and the sub-Antarctic islands, although the exact extent is difficult to determine (Hall 2000).

Northern high latitudes experience far greater tourism visitation as a result of easier air, ship and, to a lesser extent, road access. Tourism has also long been regarded as an important avenue of economic development in northern peripheries, particularly in the absence of resource-extraction industries such as fishing, minerals or timber (e.g. Marsh and Johnston 1984; Marsh 1987; Val 1990; Anderson 1991; Ilyina and Mieczkowski 1992; Downie 1993; Colin 1994; Gusarov and Kempf 1994; Kaltenborn 1996, 2000; Guldbrandsen 1997; Jacobsen 1997; Saarinen 2005; Müller and Jansson 2007; Prokkola 2007; Hall *et al.* 2009). Virtually all state, provincial and national governments of the territories that make up the Arctic Council, an intergovernmental forum for Arctic governments and peoples, for example, have developed tourism strategies.

Alaska receives close to two million visitors a year (Table 1.4). However, like many northern destinations visitation is highly seasonal, with the majority of tourists arriving in the summer months when the cruise season operates, as no cruise ships presently operate in the northern winter (several of the ships operate in the Antarctic at that time) (Tables 1.5, 1.6). Over time the cruise and air markets have become more important than the highway/ferry markets. For 2007 it was estimated that Alaskan summer visitors spent US$1.6 billion, not including travel

Table 1.4 Trends in Full-Year Visitor Volume to Alaska, By Entry/Exit Mode

Mode	2001-02	2002-03	2003-04	2004-05	2005-06	2006-07	2007-08
Air	824,400	831,400	834,400	869,700	1,018,500	1,033,500	1,047,200
Cruiseship	510,000	581,000	620,900	712,400	761,100	758,100	827,800
Highway	100,500	96,800	94,300	94,000	82,000	76,100	74,400
Ferry	18,800	18,400	17,600	17,800	13,600	13,300	12,100
Total	1,453,700	1,527,600	1,567,200	1,693,900	1,875,200	1,881,000	1,961,500
% change	n/a	+5.1%	+2.6%	+8.1%	+10.7%	+0.3%	+4.3%

Notes: 2001-02 to 2004-05 data based on entry mode; 2005-06 to 2007-08 data based on exit mode.
The 2000-01 period is not included because there was no Summer 2000 visitor volume estimate.

Sources: 2001-02 to 2004-05 data from Alaska Visitor Arrivals studies (conducted by Northern Economics, Inc.); 2005-06 to 2007-08 data based on 2006-07 visitor/resident ratios obtained for Alaska Visitor Statistics Program (conducted by McDowell Group, Inc.) in State of Alaska (2008a).

Table 1.5: Trends in Summer Visitor Volume to Alaska, By Entry/Exit Mode

Mode	2001	2002	2003	2004	2005	2006	2007	2008
Air	588,900	594,300	592,900	635,600	786,700	795,900	811,300	800,600
Cruiseship	510,000	581,000	620,900	712,400	761,100	758,100	827,800	836,500
Highway	86,700	82,900	80,400	83,200	72,100	65,800	64,300	59,900
Ferry	17,200	16,800	15,900	16,200	12,100	11,700	10,700	10,400
Total	1,202,800	1,275,000	1,310,100	1,447,400	1,632,000	1,631,500	1,714,100	1,707,400
% change	n/a	+6.0%	+2.8%	+10.5%	+12.8%	0.0%	+5.1%	-0.4%

Note: 2001-04 data based on entry mode; 2005-2008 data based on exit mode.

Sources: 2001-04 data from Alaska Visitor Arrivals studies (conducted by Northern Economics, Inc.); 2005-08 data based on 2006 visitor/resident ratios obtained for Alaska Visitor Statistics Program (conducted by McDowell Group, Inc.) in State of Alaska (2007, 2008b).

to and from the State (Office of Economic Development [OED] 2008). According to the OED (2008: 33), in 2007–08 'Alaska remains a safe "exotic" destination for Americans who would rather not travel to EU countries (and other foreign countries) where the US dollar has lost considerable value' with 'Alaska's reputation for clean water, clean air, and wilderness' and 'healthy wildlife populations' also being regarded as a strength.

Tourism is a significant part of the Yukon economy. In 2008 it was estimated that CAN$194 million of business revenue was directly attributable to non-resident tourism on a yearly basis (Department of Tourism and Culture 2009a). The importance of tourism is indicated when, based on the Yukon Bureau of Statistics 2008 Business Survey, more than one-quarter (27.1%) of all Yukon businesses (797 out of 2,946) and primarily in accommodation and food services and the retail trade, reported that at least a portion of their gross revenue in 2007 was derived from tourism (Department of Tourism and Culture 2009a).

Tourism is highly seasonal in the Yukon, with the majority of tourists visiting in summer, and July and August being the peak months. For example, in 2008 68,519 and 68,449 visitors made the border crossings into the Yukon compared with only 2,820 and 2,678 in January and December, respectively (Department of Tourism and Culture 2009b). As with Alaska, annual border-crossing statistics have remained relatively static in recent years as other modes of access (air in the case of the Yukon) have become more important (Table 1.7). However, the motorcoach market has increased in significance as a proportion of border crossings and now accounts for almost 30% of visitors. The annual number of border crossings made by non-motorcoach (e.g. cars, campers, recreational vehicles) visitors into the Yukon fluctuates each year but has consistently declined since 2003. This is of significance to the Yukon, as non-motorcoach visitors 'spend more time in the Yukon, spend more per person and also have more flexibility during their trip, when compared to motorcoach travellers' (Department of Tourism and Culture 2009a: 7). The growth of air passenger arrivals in the Yukon is indicated in Table 1.8, which shows an increase of almost 40% between 2003 and 2008. European air charters have shown a much more moderate growth over the same period and as Table 1.9 illustrates, the pattern of charter arrivals serves only to reinforce the seasonal nature of tourism in the Yukon.

Tourism is the Northwest Territories' (NWT) third largest export behind mining and petroleum products. In 2007–08, it was estimated that 79,000 vacationers and business travellers spent CAN$138 million on NWT goods and services, of which just over CAN$60 million is attributable to the accommodation and food services sector (Government of the Northwest Territories Industry, Tourism and Investment [GNWTITI] 2009). 'Contributing more to the economy than the combined sales of agriculture, forestry, fishing and trapping, tourism is [the] largest renewable resource industry. Tourism provides an excellent market for local arts and crafts, utilising many traditional skills and contributing to the preservation of local cultures, and is compatible with the principles of sustainable development' (GNWTITI 2009: 1).

NWT tourism has shown marginal annual increases since 2000 (Table 1.10),

Table 1.6: Trends in Fall/Winter Visitor Volume to Alaska, By Entry/Exit Mode

Mode	2000–01	2001–02	2002–03	2003–04	2004–05	2005–06	2006–07	2007–08
Air	238,700	235,500	237,100	241,500	234,100	231,800	237,600	235,900
Highway	14,000	13,800	13,900	13,900	10,800	9,900	10,300	10,100
Ferry	1,500	1,600	1,600	1,700	1,600	1,500	1,600	1,400
Total	254,200	250,900	252,600	257,100	246,500	243,200	249,500	247,400
% change	n/a	-1.3%	+0.7%	+1.8%	-4.1%	-1.3%	+2.6%	-0.8%

Note: 2000-01 to 2003-04 data based on entry mode; 2004-05 to 2007-08 data based on exit mode.

Sources: 2000-01 to 2003-04 data from Alaska Visitor Arrivals studies (conducted by Northern Economics, Inc.); 2004-05 to 2007-08 visitor/resident ratios obtained for Alaska Visitor Statistics Program (conducted by McDowell Group, Inc.) in State of Alaska (2008a).

Table 1.7: Yukon border crossing statistics by origin

	1995	1996	1997	1998	1999	2000	2001	2002	2003	2004	2005	2006	2007	2008
Canada	66 336	68 425	66 577	72 858	65 183	61 299	59 607	62 053	62 454	64 893	64 960	60 218	60 676	62 045
United States	220 195	206 628	206 715	225 024	236 459	218 390	200 608	229 000	217 946	224 897	230 655	228 279	238 946	206 878
Mexico	67	82	156	157	309	242	364	395	421	525	582	553	668	683
Total North America	286 598	275 135	273 448	298 039	301 951	279 931	260 579	291 448	280 821	290 315	296 197	289 050	300 290	269 606
Europe	20 309	22 637	21 050	23 262	22 500	22 832	18 895	17 456	18 571	19 375	20 831	18 785	20 155	21 360
Asia/Pacific	3 854	4 387	5 190	4 814	5 543	4 952	3 429	3 875	3 750	5 493	6 476	7 015	7 794	8 120
Other	658	539	705	731	978	742	573	511	590	714	780	654	887	783
Grand Total	311 419	302 698	300 393	326 846	330 972	308 457	283 476	313 290	303 732	315 897	324 284	315 504	329 203	299 860
Arrive by motor coach					65 528	59 266	43 838	49 546	56 802	80 150	95 936	109 470	125 871	112 891

Notes

All figures represent total annual visitation.

Passenger totals do not include train visitors, those in commercial vehicles, visitors arriving by air, or marine arrivals (Dawson City).

The Canadian Citizens category includes Yukon residents.

Source: Yukon Bureau of Statistics and Canada Border Service Agency (2009); Department of Tourism and Culture (2009b, c).

Table 1.8: Annual Erik Nielsen Whitehorse International Airport Passenger Traffic and European Air Charter Arrivals

Year	2003	2004	2005	2006	2007	2008
Depart	79,750	88,924	93,067	93,463	114,990	113,744
Arrive	79,511	85,600	99,620	98,517	113,033	112,307
European air charter passengers	4,319	4,640	4,324	4,314	4,655	4,744

Source: Derived from Department of Tourism and Culture (2005, 2007, 2009b).

Table 1.9: Whitehorse Seasonal European Air Charter Statistics

	May	Jun	Jul	Aug	Sep	Oct	Total
2007 Flights	7	8	9	9	8	6	47
2008 Flights	6	8	10	8	9	2	43
+/- Flights	-1	0	1	-1	1	-4	-4
% Change	-14%	0%	11%	-11%	13%	-67%	-9%
2007 Passengers	468	897	1189	1428	504	169	4655
2008 Passengers	487	848	1358	1207	708	136	4744
+/- Passengers	19	-49	169	-221	204	-33	89
% Change	4%	-5%	14%	-15%	40%	-20%	2%

Source: Adapted from Department of Tourism and Culture (2009b).

and Table 1.11 indicates some of the main travel markets for the territory. Business travellers are the most important market by expenditure, with many of the visitors related to the mineral sector. Other segments are facing increased competition from other northern destinations. For example, for the first time since 2001–02, there was a decline in 2006–07 in visitors to see the aurora, which was attributed to the additional direct flights to Fairbanks, Alaska from Japan. According to InterVISTAS and Ile Royale Enterprises Limited (2008: 41) 'The direct Air Canada flight from Vancouver helps, but it cannot totally offset the direct flights from Japan to Fairbanks; the strength of the Canadian dollar (cost advantage for Alaska); and the high cost of airfares to the NWT'.

Only recently have baseline data been published regarding tourist visitation to Nunavut (Datapath 2007). The data revealed that approximately 9,300 tourists visited the Territory between June and October 2006, with 2,100 visiting on a cruise. The majority of visitors were male (62%) and mainly from Canada (79%). One-half of the visitors visit for business purposes, one-third for a vacation and the remainder either were visiting friends or family (VFF) or participating in an educational trip. Visitors from the USA are most likely to be the vacationers, and vacation travel is highest in the Baffin Region, while VFF was highest in the

Table 1.10: Northwest Territories Visitation

Year	Number of Visitors
2000–01	56,644
2001–02	53,917
2002–03	62,111
2003–04	64,251
2004–05	65,340
2005–06	67,803
2006–07	63,461

Source: Government of Northwest Territories, Northwest Territories Industry, Tourism and Investment (2007) *Visitor Markets Strategic Overview: Northwest Territories*, in InterVISTAS and Ile Royale Enterprises Limited (2008)

Table 1.11: Changes in visitation to Northwest Territories by segment

Activity	2000–01	2001–02	2002–03	2003–04	2004–05	Average Annual Change
VFR	6,126	6,175	7,410	7,599	7,780	6.9%
Fishing	4,355	4,311	4,268	4,225	4,183	−1.0%
Outdoor Adventure North American	1,480	1,552	1,965	1,841	1,725	4.8%
General Touring North American	6,737	7,068	11,984	11,229	10,522	13.5%
European	1,896	3,727	2,400	3,221	2,957	7.4%
Hunters	1,300	1,400	1,380	1,117	1,279	−2.6%
Aurora Tours	13,000	6,500	9,000	9,990	10,245	−0.5%
Total Leisure	34,894	30,733	38,407	39,223	38,691	4.5%
Business	16,876	18,313	19,014	20,725	22,591	7.1%
Grand Total	51,770	49,046	57,421	59,948	61,282	5.4%

Source: Department of Industry, Tourism and Investment (2005).

Kivalliq Region. Iqaluit, the territory's capital, attracted the most visitors (30%), which is not surprising given the prevalence of business tourism. The report suggests that the summer tourism industry accounts for nearly CAN$4.4 million dollars to Nunavut, with over half being spent in the Baffin Region. Of this total, cruise tourism was estimated to generate CAN$2.1 million dollars to the territory (Datapath 2007).

As with all northern high-latitude regions, Greenland is also seeking to develop tourism as part of its economic diversification strategy as it seeks to reduce its dependence on Danish subsidies. Although commencing from a low base, Greenland tourism is growing rapidly and arguably serves to encourage neighbouring Nunavut's development of tourism. Cruise-passenger numbers jumped by 30% from 22,051 in 2006 to 28,891 in 2008 and in 9 years the total number of travellers to Greenland had more than doubled from 26,410 in 1999 to 57,223 in 2008 (see Table 1.12). As with many coastal polar areas, much of the tourism growth comes from cruise tourism. The number of cruise ships operating in Greenland waters has grown from 13 in 2003 to 39 in 2008, with the number of port arrivals increasing from 164 to 375 in the same period (Greenland Port Statistics; Greenland Tourism & Business Council in Snyder 2009). A number of authors, including ACIA (2005) and Anisimov *et al.* (2007), suggested that such growth was potentially likely to occur, but they perhaps did not expect climate change to be a specific promotional factor of Greenland cruises (Greenland.com 2009; Round 2009).

Tourism is also of great significance to Iceland's economy, particularly in rural areas. In 2008 tourism represented 11% of Iceland's export of goods and services (73.061 million Icelandic krona [ISK]) (after marine/fish products and aluminium and ferrosilicone products). Iceland markets itself strongly in Europe and the USA for a variety of tourism products that range from the wilderness and rural tourism (especially horse trekking), which are regarded as more typical high-latitude experiences, to urban tourism and weekend breaks. More than 70% of summer visitors and 50% of winter visitors cite Icelandic nature as the main reason for coming to Iceland. The main markets are other Nordic countries, the USA and Canada, Germany and the UK. As with other Nordic countries there is

Table 1.12: International Visitors to Greenland

year	Number of tourists per year (flight passenger statistics)	Number of overnight stays per year	No. of cruise guests
2000	31,331	212,434	
2001	34,039	189,463	
2002	29,366	179,349	
2003	29,712	192,774	approx 10,000
2004	31,524	190,755	approx 15,000
2005	33,082	215,916	approx 16,500
2006		225,667	22 051
2007		234,604	
2008	57,223		28 891

Greenland Tourism and Business Council (2007); Round 2009

also a relatively high degree of seasonality in visitation, although greater attempts are being made to boost winter tourism.

The economic downturn and financial crisis of 2008 and 2009 have served only to increase the importance of tourism to the Icelandic economy, particularly as the value of the ISK dropped considerably against the euro and the currencies of their main Nordic markets. Table 1.13 illustrates that the number of overnight stays in Iceland has continued to increase and, like elsewhere in the Arctic region, cruise tourism is continuing to grow, with Iceland being part of itineraries that include Norway, the Faroe Islands and the Shetland Islands by some operators (e.g. P&O), and Greenland and Labrador by others (e.g. Hurtigruten).

The mainland European Nordic countries of Finland, Sweden and Norway all receive large numbers of tourists to their Arctic and sub-Arctic areas (Tables 11.14, 11.15, 11.16). Promotion of nature-based and wilderness tourism is extensive across the northern regions of all three countries, and Sami tourism is also prominent (Hall et al. 2009). Natural attributes such as the 'Midnight Sun' are an important part of the attractiveness of the area, and the North Cape is a major tourist destination. Although portrayed as the northernmost point of Europe in the popular imagination, that title belongs to a neighbouring promontory, Knivskjellodden, which is low and therefore less striking than the 300-m cliffs of North Cape. The headland is a principal attraction for many of the international visitors to Northern Scandinavia. Annually, more than 200,000 people come to see the Cape, primarily during the never-ending Arctic summer day, the Midnight Sun period, from 11 May to 31 July (Jacobsen 2009).

The social construction of the North Cape as a major tourist attraction has been accompanied by other efforts to promote tourism to the region. In an effort to overcome some of the issues of seasonality in the region there has been a

Table 1.13: Tourism in Iceland

| Year | Number of overnight stays all accommodation | | | Passengers through Keflavik airport | Passenger ship arrivals in Faxaflóa-harbour |
	Total	*Domestic*	*International*		
1996	1 292 000	459 000	832 000		51
1997	1 387 000	499 000	887 000		46
1998	1 541 000	524 000	1 016 000		42
1999	1 685 000	582 000	1 102 000		37
2000	1 736 000	589 000	1 147 000		48
2001	1 743 000	559 000	1 184 000		49
2002	1 861 000	604 000	1 256 000		50
2003	1 985 000	608 000	1 377 000	600 369	58
2004	2 134 000	655 000	1 479 000	693 883	70
2005	2 189 000	668 000	1 521 000	747 534	79
2006	2 457 000	737 000	1 719 000	830 158	74
2007	2 645 000	777 000	1 868 000	927 689	
2008	2 716 000	792 000	1 925 000	879 122	

Note: Figures for 1994-2004 show the total number of ship arrivals in Reykjavík harbours only and luxury liners only arriving in the outer harbour.

Source: Statistics Iceland (2006, 2008, 2009).

Table 1.14: Visitors to Finland (Overnight stays)

Year	National			Lapland			Oulu Region		
	Total	Domestic	Int.	Total	Domestic	Int.	Total	Domestic	Int.
1995	14 388 689	11 004 194	3 384 495	1 576 795	1 097 907	478 888	910 138	801 789	108 349
1996	14 520 476	11 151 658	3 368 818	1 472 598	1 057 079	415 519	887 316	785 052	102 264
1997	15 301 209	11 586 699	3 714 510	1 524 068	1 110 345	413 723	974 822	863 862	110 960
1998	15 767 063	11 982 611	3 784 452	1 643 995	1 188 079	455 916	958 036	835 033	123 003
1999	16 048 747	12 205 535	3 843 212	1 654 243	1 180 300	473 943	1 062 410	916 706	145 704
2000	16 484 938	12 356 012	4 128 926	1 690 286	1 150 851	539 435	1 128 051	969 738	158 313
2001	16 714 455	12 445 473	4 268 982	1 702 178	1 123 025	579 153	1 184 142	1 018 743	165 399
2002	16 462 350	12 092 585	4 369 765	1 739 700	1 088 314	651 386	1 189 094	977 692	211 402
2003	16 508 254	12 086 636	4 421 618	1 864 936	1 138 109	726 827	1 193 157	998 851	194 306
2004	16 626 590	12 243 392	4 383 198	1 912 440	1 174 700	737 740	1 216 278	1 026 458	189 820
2005	17 259 037	12 760 402	4 498 635	2 004 649	1 212 733	791 916	1 315 321	1 125 472	189 849
2006	18 168 869	13 165 119	5 003 750	2 119 353	1 289 996	829 357	1 358 757	1 121 985	236 772
2007	19 036 665	13 708 450	5 328 215	2 247 164	1 355 655	891 509	1 460 428	1 199 800	260 628

Source: Statistics Finland PX-Web data bank. Arrivals and over-night visits (2008). http://pxweb2.stat.fi/database/StatFin/lii/matk/matk_fi.asp . 4.12.2008.

Table 1.15: Visitors to Sweden (Overnight stays)

Year	Sweden Total	Domestic	Inter.	Norrbotten Total	Domestic	Inter.	Västerbotten total	Domestic	Inter.
1995	38 188 000			1 823 000			1 309 000		
1996	37 449 000	18 407 000	5 407 000	1 686 000			1 230 000		
1997	36 929 000	29 270 000	7 659 000	1 605 000	1 157 000	448 000	1 282 000	1 027 000	255 000
1998	37 498 000	29 469 000	8 029 000	1 687 000	1 183 000	504 000	1 196 000	950 000	246 000
1999	39 855 000	31 254 000	8 601 000	1 638 000	1 097 000	541 000	1 302 000	1 051 000	251 000
2000	39 810 000	31 155 000	8 655 000	1 614 000	1 145 000	469 000	1 272 000	1 035 000	237 000
2001	41 195 000	32 061 000	9 134 000	1 700 000	1 149 000	551 000	1 323 000	1 090 000	233 000
2002	42 895 000	33 128 000	9 767 000	1 753 000	1 144 000	609 000	1 360 000	1 086 000	274 000
2003	44 054 000	34 339 000	9 715 000	1 768 000	1 232 000	536 000	1 378 000	1 109 000	269 000
2004	42 666 000	32 942 000	9 724 000	1 719 000	1 148 000	571 000	1 305 000	1 020 000	285 000
2005	44 939 000	34 862 000	10 077 000	1 771 000	1 217 000	554 000	1 395 000	1 115 000	280 000
2006	47 706 000	36 754 000	10 952 000	2 003 000	1 305 000	698 000	1 405 000	1 077 000	328 000
2007	48 605 000	37 405 000	11 200 000	2 051 000	1 397 000	654 000	1 500 000	1 114 000	386 000

Source: Regionfakta.com. Over-nights in hotels and camping. Norrbotten/ Västerbotten. (2008). http://www.regionfakta.com/dynamiskPresentation.aspx?id=533 5.12.2008; Regionfakta.com. Over-nights in 1997–2007 based on nationalities. Norrbotten/ Västerbotten. (2008). http://www.regionfakta.com/dynamiskPresentation. aspx?id=535 5.12.2008.

Table 1.16: Visitors to Norway (Overnight stays)

Year	Norway Total	Domestic	Internat.	Finnmark total	Domestic	Internat.	Tromso total	Domestic	Internat.	Nordland total	Domestic	Internat.
1995				343 945	206 119	137 826	451 002	343 094	107 908	682 020	488 243	193 777
1996	19 740 000	12 503 000	7 236 000	314 263	195 007	119 256	495 133	395 673	99 460	701 063	510 228	190 835
1997	20 199 000	12 956 000	7 243 000	320 564	196 579	123 985	492 550	391 513	101 037	699 286	522 219	177 067
1998	24 383 000	16 513 000	7 869 000	324 193	198 241	125 952	537 708	411 197	126 506	744 866	547 382	197 484
1999	24 443 000	16 628 000	7 815 000	329 253	209 959	119 294	539 875	421 254	118 621	762 059	566 998	195 061
2000	24 271 000	16 802 000	7 469 000	323 375	201 671	121 704	534 478	414 332	120 146	747 091	564 772	182 319
2001	24 333 000	17 010 000	7 322 000	311 198	188 900	122 298	558 620	435 156	123 464	740 587	560 610	179 977
2002	24 384 000	17 109 000	7 276 000	308 925	202 266	106 659	549 975	427 971	122 004	713 623	539 966	173 657
2003	23 808 000	16 853 000	6 956 000	303 348	206 889	96 459	568 702	455 804	122 898	723 114	540 177	182 937
2004	25 274 000	17 832 000	7 442 000	309 305	193 515	115 790	592 495	474 993	117 502	714 387	537 220	177 167
2005	26 272 000	18 628 000	7 644 000	334 596	121 208	121 208	603 682	487 322	116 360	765 851	559 243	206 608
2006	27 489 000	19 567 000	7 922 000	359 772	124 070	124 070	605 185	489 115	116 070	765 005	578 455	186 550
2007	28 643 000	20 338 000	8 306 000	347 012	124 881	124 881	644 251	519 105	125 146	793 861	590 775	203 086

Source: Statistics Norway (2008), Eurostat (2008).

substantial attempt in recent years to encourage winter tourism. In Sweden this is perhaps best recognised internationally in the development of the Ice Hotel, and other developments include snowcastle and icebreaker trips with ice dips in Kemi (Finland) and dining on ice in Luleå (Sweden). Originally the Ice Hotel in Jukkasjärvi in Swedish Lapland started off as a summer tourism destination in the 1970s, but by the end of the 1980s the activities were reorganised based on using the dark and cold winter as an advantage. In 1990 the exhibition igloo for ice- and snow-based small art was used for 'voluntary' guest accommodation. In the following years facilities made out of ice were built to serve as more exotic accommodation, and place promotion has been undertaken in cooperation with internationally known products such as Sweden's Absolut vodka, one of the world's best known vodka brands. However, perhaps the most significant winter tourism development is the growth of Santa Claus tourism, which has become most associated with Finnish Lapland and the Rovaniemi area in particular, although Greenland, Iceland, Norway and Sweden have also attempted to promote themselves in association with Christmas tourism (Hall 2008). The Ice Hotel and Santa tourism are extremely significant in the polar tourism context as they provide examples of how the unique elements of the Arctic winter environment have become to be regarded as an asset (Hall *et al.* 2009) and therefore overcome some of the issues of seasonality that plague northern high-latitude tourism.

The large numbers of tourists to the region also reflect, of course, the relative ease of accessibility to the region from the rest of Europe. For example, North Cape is the end point of three EuroVelo bicycle routes: route 1 via Norway to Sagres in Portugal, route 7 via Sweden to Malta, and route 11 via Finland to Athens. Similarly, the northern Nordic region has excellent road and aviation access as well as railway access. Nevertheless, despite such clear advantages the region remains peripheral in the European context, with tourism likely to remain an economic mainstay in the immediate future.

The northernmost part of Norway is the archipelago of Svalbard, which lies midway between mainland Norway and the North Pole. Although also having a Russian mining town the islands became part of Norway following the signing of the Spitsbergen Treaty in 1920. The economy is founded on coal mining and fisheries, with tourism becoming increasingly important in terms of cruise ship visitation and nature-based tourism (Tables 1.17 and 1.18). The islands provide relatively easy access to view Arctic wildlife, such as polar bears, birds and marine mammals. Like Greenland, travel to the islands is also becoming increasingly connected to growing awareness of the effects of climate change, particularly with respect to biodiversity conservation, and the attractiveness of iconic Arctic species.

Accurate statistics are difficult to obtain in northern Russia despite increasingly being opened up for tourism. Although not providing any hard data, Snyder (2007: 62) commented that 'Russia's entry into the polar tourism market represents the single largest geographic expansion of tourism in the Arctic'; in January 2007 the Russian Ministry of Transport in coordination with regulations from the Ministry of Defence and the Federal Customs Service granted permission to open six

Table 1.17: Tourism in Svalbard

Year	Number of tourists	No overnight stays in Longyearbyen	Domestic	International
1998	13,800	46,201	37,211	8,990
1999	13,900	43,577	33,666	9,911
2000	20,000	61,277	49,522	11,755
2001	23,100	76,154	61,034	15,120
2002	27,300	74,433	56,704	17,729
2003	26,100	71,049	52,382	18,667
2004	27,700	77,926	58,574	19,352
2005	23,900	75,570		
2006	26,900	83,049		
2007	31,152	86,097		
2008	35,140	88,951		

Source: Sysselmannen på Svalbard (2006, 2008).

Table 1.18: Number of overseas cruise ships and number of passengers to Svalbard

Year	No. of ships	No of sailings	No. of passengers	No. of crew	Total on board
1997	24		15,437	9,057	24,494
1998	21		17,463	9,505	26,968
1999	31		17,763	8,150	25,913
2000	29		16,404	8,964	25,368
2001	25		20,069	9,922	29,991
2002	22	33	16,892	8,771	25,663
2003	28	43	19,736	10,238	29,974
2004	28	45	21,206	11,384	32,590
2005	34	50	29,224	15,460	44,684
2006	29	41	28,787	14,598	43,385

Source: Sysselmannen på Svalbard (2006)

Russian ports to foreign tourists. Specific tourism data for the Russian Arctic are difficult to obtain, although the Barents region and Kamchatka are major areas for ecotourism development, whereas ship tourism is available in Murmansk, the White Sea, Arkangel, Wrangel Island World Heritage site and the North Pole (Lemelin and Johnston 2008). Although the global focus on economic development in the Russian Arctic tends to be on oil and gas, the encouragement of tourism is continuing to grow. For example, in June 2009 Russian Prime Minister Vladimir Putin announced that Russia would create a new 1.5-million-hectare 'Russian Arctic' park located on the northern part of the island of Novaya Zemlya, a central area for the Barents and Kara Sea polar bear populations, as well as some adjacent marine areas. The tourism significance of the project is indicated by the fact that when announcing the park, Prime Minister Putin said that he hoped it would be a major attraction for tourism and announced that he personally planned to vacation there (World Wildlife Fund [WWF] 2009). Undoubtedly, a major factor in the development of tourism in northern Russia is the gradual improvement in aviation connectivity as well as the development of cross-border travel, especially in the

Barents region. Most significant of all, though, will be the potential opening up of summer sea routes through the Russian Arctic Sea – the Northern Sea Route – as a result of climate change, as well as an overall increase in year-round access (Brigham 2007), with the first cruise ship passage through the Northern Sea Route being conducted in 2008. It should also be recognised that the infrastructure required for oil, gas and other mineral development in the Russian Arctic with respect to transport connectivity and accommodation is the same infrastructure that is also used by commercial tourism.

Conclusions

This chapter has provided an introduction with respect to tourism in polar regions. It has sought to accomplish three main goals. First, to identify the way in which high-latitude areas are as much a part of the geographical imagination of place as they are actual locations. For visitors from most of the world, it is this imagined place with its associated images and history that acts as a major driver for the desire to travel to the far north and south. Yet, at the same time, it must be remembered that, especially in the Arctic and sub-Arctic, we are dealing with places in which people live and work and their understanding and senses of place will be different from that of the tourist and even the researcher. Second, the chapter has sought to define polar tourism in a manner that is consistent with international tourism statistics, although it has noted that, particularly in Antarctica, data collection may not follow standard definitions, and numerous gaps remain in our knowledge base. Finally, it has provided detailed statistics on polar tourism that indicate that the number of visitors to high latitudes is substantial, especially in the Arctic, and is continuing to grow. Given the more than 40,000 tourists to Antarctica and the well over 5 million tourist trips that occur in the Arctic and sub-Arctic every year it is therefore no surprise that tourism is deeply embedded in processes of change that are occurring in the world's polar regions. Such changes are therefore not just environmental or climatic but also economic and social.

Table 1.19 provides something of the overall context within which polar tourism occurs. Although the northern and southern polar regions share much in common there are also significant differences between them, not just with respect to the actual numbers of tourists who visit them, but also their system of governance, tourism management regimes, level of development and degree of accessibility. Nevertheless, what happens in one region also influences what happens in the other as a result of similarities in climate as well as the sensitivity of the environment to change. The following series of chapters therefore may inform debate and discussion of polar tourism not just with respect to their specific case studies and issues but in the broader context of polar tourism development and its relationship to change.

The next chapter provides an overview of tourism's relationship with environmental change, including climate change, in high-latitude regions. The book is then divided into a series of chapters on the northern and southern polar regions.

Table 1.19: Comparative context of tourism and change within the Antarctic and Arctic regions

Factor	Antarctic and Sub-Antarctic	Arctic and Sub-Arctic
Terrestrial Sovereignty	Disputed sovereignty over continental lands	Relatively clear sovereignty over land
	Sub-Antarctic islands relatively clear sovereignty with exception of the Falkland Islands and dependencies	
Maritime sovereignty	Growth in claims for extension of rights to exclusive economic zones under the Law of the Sea	Dispute exists over definition of international waters
	Contestation between claimants where terrestrial sovereignty is unclear	Increased contestation for extension of rights to exclusive economic zones under the Law of the Sea
Scientific bases and sovereignty	Used as a means of reinforcing territorial claims	Used as a means of reinforcing territorial claims
Tourism and sovereignty	Historically used as a means of reinforcing territorial claims	Used as a means of reinforcing territorial claims
Conservation	Conservation primarily operates under international management regime except on sub-Antarctic islands	Conservation primarily operates under a national management regime, including designation of national park and reserve areas; growing international cooperation
Military presence	Minor military presence	Significant military presence
Minerals	Mineral resource exploration and mining under moratorium	Substantial mineral resource exploration and mining
Fishing and whaling	Significant fishing and whaling in international and national waters	Significant fishing and whaling in international and national waters
Grazing and hunting	None	Significant for indigenous people and growing as a tourism attraction
Indigenous peoples	None	Indigenous peoples seeking greater economic and political self-determination
Legal context for tourism	Tourism operates in a legislative vacuum, effective laws can only be made by countries with respect to their own citizens although tourism activities are increasingly incorporated within the Antarctic Treaty System	Tourism is clearly subject to national and regional legislative control except in disputed international waters
Tourist access	Tourist access is extremely difficult, sea and air only	Tourist access though difficult is available by air, land and sea. Northern regions of North America and Europe have well established air networks and a good Subarctic road network
Climate	Extremely harsh; realistically accessible only through Austral Summer	Harsh climate but a relatively mild Summer (other than High Arctic)
Sensitivity of physical environment to human impact	Extremely high	Extremely high
Nature-based tourism	Ecotourism; limited adventure tourism	Hunting and fishing; ecotourism (extensive wildlife focus); wilderness tourism
Cultural tourism	Historic and industrial heritage sites; current scientific and government sites	Indigenous tourism; historic and industrial heritage sites; museums and arts and crafts; industrial tourism; some urban tourism; growth of staged tourism attractions
Tourism infrastructure	Ship-based	Extensive land-based accommodation and retail infrastructure; cruise ships growing in importance

As can be expected, climate change remains a significant theme throughout many of the chapters, as are biodiversity and heritage conservation, visitor expectations and their management, and the development of new forms of tourism. The book then concludes with two chapters that discuss issues that affect both polar regions: the relationship between tourism and the legitimisation of sovereignty, and potential future issues facing the high latitudes and the development of appropriate policy responses.

This book is being written at a new crossroads in polar regional policy, not only with respect to how the global challenge of climate change is met, and how therefore the Arctic and Antarctic may continue to undergo anthropogenic change, but also how polar regions are managed and developed, particularly in light of those people who live there. It is therefore to be hoped that this book will make one further contribution to understanding how tourism is embedded in such processes and cannot be ignored as both a contributor to change but also being heavily affected by it.

References

Adventure World (2009) Antarctica. Online. Available HTTP: http://www.adventure-world.co.nz/Country.asp?country = 55&gclid = CNzA7LrFh5wCFRZCagod-gfP-A (accessed 1 August 2009).

Amoamo, M. and Boyd, S. (2005) 'Shifting images: an historical and contemporary view of tourism development in the Northwest Territories of Canada', *Tourism and Hospitality Planning & Development*, 2(1): 1–15.

Anderson, M.J. (1991) 'Problems with tourism in Canada's eastern Arctic', *Tourism Management*, 12(3): 209–20.

Anisimov, O.A., Vaughan, D.G., Callaghan, T.V., Furgal, H., Marchant, H., Prowse, T.D., Vilhjálmsson, H. and Walsh, J.E. (2007) Polar regions (Arctic and Antarctic). In M.L. Parry, O.F. Canziani, J.P. Palutikof, P.J. van der Linden and C.E. Hanson (eds) *Climate Change 2007: Impacts, Adaptation and Vulnerability*, Cambridge: Cambridge University Press.

Arctic Climate Impacts Assessment (ACIA) (2005) *Impacts of a Warming Arctic: Arctic Climate Impacts Assessment*, Cambridge: Cambridge University Press.

Arctic Council (2004) *Arctic Human Development Report*, Akureyri: Stefansson Arctic Institute.

Barwell, C. (2007) 'Frozen memories: unthawing Scott of the Antarctic in cultural memory', *Visual Communication*, 6(3): 345 – 57.

Bauer, T.G. (2001) *Tourism in the Antarctic: Opportunities, Constraints, and Future Prospects*, New York: Haworth Press.

Boykoff, M.T. and Goodman, M.K. (2009) 'Conspicuous redemption? Reflections on the promises and perils of the "celebritization" of climate change', *Geoforum*, 40(3): 395–406.

Brewster, B. (1982) *Antarctica – Wilderness at Risk*, Wellington: Friends of the Earth/A.H. & A.W. Reed.

Brigham, L.W. (2007) 'Arctic Marine Shipping Assessment (AMSA): Status for the Senior Arctic Officials, 29 November 2007', paper presented at Arctic Council SAO Meeting, Narvik, Norway, November 2007.

British Broadcasting Corporation (BBC) (2007a) UK looks to make Antarctica claim, *BBC News*, Wednesday, 17 October 2007, Online. Available HTTP: http://news.bbc.co.uk/2/hi/uk_news/7048237.stm .

— (2007b) Arctic seabed 'belongs to Russia'. *BBC News*, Thursday, 20 September 2007, Online. Available HTTP: http://news.bbc.co.uk/2/hi/europe/7005483.stm .

— (2008) Australia extends rights over sea, *BBC News*, Monday, 21 April 2008, Online. Available HTTP: news.bbc.co.uk/1/•hi/world/asia-pacific/7358432.stm .

Clark, D., Tyrell, M., Dowsley, M., Foote, A.L., Freeman, M. and Clark, S.G. (2008) 'Polar bears, climate change, and human dignity: disentangling symbolic politics and seeking integrative conservation policies', *Meridian*, Fall/Winter: 1–6.

Colin, M. (1994) 'Ecotourism and conservation policies in Canada'. In C. Kempf and L. Girard (eds) *Le tourisme dans les régions polaires/Tourism in polar regions, Proceedings of the Symposium*, Colmar, France, 21–23 April, 1992.

Craciun, A. (2009) 'The scramble for the Arctic', *Interventions*, 11(1): 103–14.

Cresswell, T. (2004) *Place: A Short Introduction*, Oxford; Blackwell.

Dalby, S. (2003) 'Geopolitical identities: Arctic ecology and global consumption,' *Geopolitics*, 8(1): 181–202.

Datapath (2007) 'Nunavut Exit Study 2006', Unpublished presentation: January 15, 2007.

DeMille, D. (2005) 'Denmark "goes Viking" in Canada's Arctic islands – strategic resources of the high Arctic entice the Danes,' *Canadian American Strategic Review*, March, Online. Available HTTP: http://www.casr.ca/id-arcticviking1.htm (accessed 1 August 2009).

Department of Industry, Tourism and Investment (2005) *Tourism 2010: A Tourism Plan for the Northwest Territories, Tourism and Parks*, Yellowknife: Department of Industry, Tourism and Investment, Government of the Northwest Territories & Northwest Territories Tourism.

Department of Tourism and Culture (2005) *2004 Yukon Visitor Statistics: Year End Report*, Whitehorse: Department of Tourism and Culture, Government of Yukon.

— (2007) *2006 Yukon Visitor Statistics: Year End Report*. Whitehorse: Department of Tourism and Culture, Government of Yukon.

— (2009a) *2009–2010 Tourism Yukon Situation Analysis*, Whitehorse: Department of Tourism and Culture, Government of Yukon.

— (2009b) *2008 Yukon Visitor Statistics: Year End Report*, Whitehorse: Department of Tourism and Culture, Government of Yukon.

— (2009c) *Yukon Border Crossing Statistics: By Origin 1995-2008*, Whitehorse: Department of Tourism and Culture, Government of Yukon.

Dodds, K.J. (1997) 'Antarctica and the modern geographical imagination', *Polar Record*, 33: 47–62

— (2006) 'Post-colonial Antarctica: an emerging engagement', *Polar Record*, 42(1): 59–70.

Downie, B. (1993) 'Katannilik Territorial Park: an Arctic tourism destination'. In M.E. Johnston and W. Haider (eds) *Community, Resources and Tourism in the North*, Thunder Bay: Lakehead University Centre for Northern Studies.

Enzenbacher, D.J. (1992) 'Tourists in Antarctica: numbers and trends', *Polar Record*, 28: 17–22.

— (1994) 'Antarctic tourism: an overview of 1992/93 season activity, recent developments, and emerging issues', *Polar Record*, 30(173): 105–16.

Eurostat (2008) *Data Navigation tree. Nights spent in hotels and similar establishments & nights spent in other collective accommodation establishments*. Online. Available

HTTP: http://epp.eurostat.ec.europa.eu/portal/page?_pageid = 1996,45323734&_dad = portal&_schema = PORTAL&screen = welcomeref&open = /&product = REF_TB_ tourism&depth = 2 (accessed 8 December 2008).

Fine Cruising (2009) Antarctica, Online. Available HTTP: http://finecruising.cruisefactory.net/destinations/antarctica/findacruise/?date_from=&date_to=&gclid= CJ7Y8rzIh5wCFRwpawode0Q0-g (accessed 1 August 2009).

Government of the Northwest Territories Industry, Tourism and Investment (GNWTITI) (2007) Visitor Markets Strategic Overview: Northwest Territories, Yellowknife. Government of Northwest Territories, Northwest Territories Industry, Tourism and Investment.

Government of the Northwest Territories Industry, Tourism and Investment (GNWTITI) (2009) 'Tourism within the economy'. *Economic Trends*, Summer: 1.

Greenland.com (2009) 09.05.12 – Climate changes with the FRAM and Dr. David Holland. Greenland.com, News, 9 May, Online. Available HTTP: http://www.greenland.com/content/english/tourist/news/news_archive/climate_changes_with_the_fram_and_dr_david_holland (accessed 1 August 2009).

Greenland Tourism and Business Council Council (2007) *Greenland Tourism Statistics*, Online. Available HTTP: http://www.greenland.com/content/english/business_and_investment/travel_trade/greenlands_tourism_statistics (accessed 26 November 2008; 1 August 2009).

Grenier, A.A. (2007) The diversity of polar tourism: some challenges facing the industry in Rovaniemi. *Polar Geography*, 30(1/2): 55–72.

Guldbrandsen, C. (1997) 'A holistic approach to the evaluation of publicly assisted tourism projects in Greenland'. In L. Lyck (ed.) *Socio-economic Developments in Greenland and in Other Small Nordic Jurisdictions*, Revised conference papers of a meeting held in January, 1996, sponsored by Nordic Arctic Research Forum, Frederiksberg: Forlaget Samfundslitteratur.

Gusarov, S. and Kempf, C. (1994) 'Tourism and science in Siberia: the 1991 experience'. In C. Kempf and L. Girard (eds) *Le tourisme dans les régions polaires/Tourism in polar regions*, Proceedings of the Symposium, Colmar, France, 21–23 April, 1992.

Haase, D. (2008) 'Tourism in the Antarctic: modi operandi and regulatory effectiveness', unpublished PhD thesis, University of Canterbury, Christchurch.

Hall, C.M. (1992) 'Tourism in Antarctica: activities, impacts, and management,' *Journal of Travel Research*, 30(4): 2–9.

— (2000) 'The tourist and economic significance of Antarctic travel in Australian and New Zealand Antarctic gateway cities', *Tourism and Hospitality Research: The Surrey Quarterly Review*, 2(2): 157–69.

— (2008) 'Santa Claus, place branding and competition', *Fennia: International Journal of Geography*, 186(1): 59–67.

— (2009) 'Changement climatique, authenticité et marketing des régions nordiques : conséquences sur le tourisme finlandais et la « plus grande marque au monde » ou « Les changements climatiques finiront-ils par tuer le père Noël? »', *Téoros*, 28(1): 69–79.

Hall, C.M. and Johnston, M.E. (1995) 'Introduction: Pole to Pole: tourism issues, impacts and the search for a management regime in the polar regions'. In C.M. Hall and M.E. Johnston (eds) *Polar Tourism: Tourism in the Arctic and Antarctic Regions*, Chichester: John Wiley & Sons.

Hall, C.M., Müller, D. and Saarinen, J. (2009) *Nordic Tourism*, Clevedon: Channel View Publications.

Hamelin, L-E. (1979) *Canadian Nordicity: It's Your North, Too*. Montreal: Harvest House.

Hansen, A. and Machin, D. (2008) 'Visually branding the environment: climate change as a marketing opportunity', *Discourse Studies* 10(6): 777–94.

Hemmings, A.D., Cuthbert, A. and Dalziell, J. (1991) Non-governmental activities and the protection of the Antarctic environment, a paper for the government of New Zealand, Antarctic and the Southern Ocean Coalition (NZ), Wellington.

Hübner, A. (2009) 'Tourist images of Greenland and the Arctic: a perception analysis', *Polar Record*, 45: 153–66.

Ilyina, L. and Mieczkowski, Z. (1992) 'Developing scientific tourism in Russia', *Tourism Management*, 13(3): 327–31.

International Association of Antarctic Tour Operators (IAATO) (2003) *1992–2002 Antarctic Tourist Trends*, Online. Available HTTP: http://www.iaato.org/tourism_stats.html (accessed 1 August 2009).

— (2008a) *1992–2007 Antarctic Tourist Trends*, Online. Available HTTP: http://www.iaato.org/tourism_stats.html (accessed 1 August 2009).

— (2008b) *1992–2007 Antarctic Tourist Trends – Landed*, Online. Available HTTP: http://www.iaato.org/tourism_stats.html (accessed 1 August 2009).

International Union for Conservation of Nature and Natural Resources (IUCN) (1992) Tourism in Antarctica, XVII ATCM/INFO 18, 11 November, IUCN, Gland.

InterVISTAS and Ile Royale Enterprises Limited (2008) *International Air Travel, Tourism and Freight Opportunity Study, prepared for Investment and Economic Analysis Division of Industry, Tourism and Investment (ITI)*, Yellowknife: Government of the Northwest Territories. Online. Available HTTP: http://www.iti.gov.nt.ca/publications/index.shtml#tourismparks (accessed 1 August 2009).

Jacobsen, J.K.S. (1997) 'The making of an attraction: the case of North Cape', *Annals of Tourism Research*, 24: 341–56.

— (2009) 'Prominent promontory: the social construction of North Cape'. In C.M. Hall, D. Müller and J. Saarinen, *Nordic Tourism*, Clevedon: Channel View Publications.

Joenniemi, P. and Sergounin, A.A. (2003) *Russia and the European Union's Northern Dimension: Encounter or clash of civilisations?* Nizhny Novgorod: Nizhny Novgorod Linguistic University Press.

Kaltenborn, B.P. (1996) 'Tourism in Svalbard: planned management or the art of stumbling through?' In M. Price (ed.) *People and Tourism in Fragile Environments*, Chichester: John Wiley & Sons.

— (2000) Arctic-Alpine environments and tourism: Can sustainability be planned? Lessons learned on Svalbard. *Mountain Research and Development*, 20(1): 28–31.

Kolbert, E. (2007) 'Introduction'. In E. Kolbert (ed.) *The Ends of the Earth: An Anthology of the Finest Writing on the Arctic and the Antarctic*, Vol.1 *The Arctic*, London: Granta Books.

Leane, E. (2007) 'Culture creatures: Antarctic animals in popular culture', *Australian Antarctic Magazine*, 13: 10–11.

Lemelin, R.H., Fennell, D. and Smale, B. (2008) 'Polar bear viewers as deep ecotourists: how specialised are they?' *Journal of Sustainable Tourism*, 16(1): 42–62.

Lemelin, R.H. and Johnston. M. (2008) 'Arctic tourism'. Iin M. Lück (ed.) *Encyclopedia of Tourism and Recreation in Marine Environments*, New York: Cognizant Communication.

Linneweber, V., Hartmuth, G. and Fritsche, I. (2003) 'Representations of the local environment as threatened by global climate change: toward a contextualized analysis of environmental identity in a coastal area'. In S. Clayton and S. Opotow (eds) *Identity and the Natural Environment: The Psychological Significance of Nature*. Cambridge, MA: MIT Press.

Maher, P.T., McIntosh, A.J. and Steel, G.D. (2006) 'Examining dimensions of anticipa-
    tion: inputs prior to visiting the Ross Sea region, Antarctica', *Tourism in Marine
    Environments*, 2(2): 51–63.
Makarychev, A.S. (2002) *Ideas, Images, and Their Producers: The Case of Region-Making
    in Russia's North West Federal District*, Copenhagen Peace Research Institute Working
    Papers, Copenhagen: Copenhagen Peace Research Institute.
Manzo, K. (2009) 'Imaging vulnerability: the iconography of climate change', *Area*, 42(1):
    96–107. 10.1111/j.1475–4762.2009.00887.x
Marsh, J.S. (1987) 'Tourism and conservation: case studies in the Canadian north'. In J.G.
    Nelson, R. Needham and L. Norton (eds) *Arctic Heritage: Proceedings of a Symposium*,
    Ottawa: Association of Canadian Universities for Northern Studies.
Marsh, J.S. and Johnston, M.E. (1984) 'Conservation, tourism and development in the
    north: case studies in northern Canada'. In F. Duerden (ed.) *Applied Research in the
    Canadian North*, Occasional paper, Toronto: Department of Geography, Ryerson
    Polytechnical Institute.
McCaffrey, M., Salmon, R. and Jeffries, M. (2006) 'Polar bears and penguins are the tip of
    the iceberg: education, outreach, and communication strategies for the International
    Polar Year and beyond III posters'. *Eos Transactions American Geophysical Union*,
    87(52), Fall Meeting Supplement, Abstract ED23B.
Martello, M.L. (2008) 'Arctic indigenous peoples as representations and representatives of
    climate change', *Social Studies of Science*, 38(3): 351–76.
Medvedev, S. (2000) 'Glenn Gould, Russia, Finland and the North', Paper presented at
    ISA Congress in Los Angeles, March 14–18, 2000.
— (2001) '[the_blank_space] Glenn Gould, Russia, Finland and the North', *International
    Politics*, 38(1): 91–102.
Mickleburgh, E. (1990) *Beyond the Frozen Sea: Visions of Antarctica*, London: Paladin.
Müller, D.K. and Jansson, B. (eds) (2007) *Tourism in Peripheries: Perspectives from the
    Far North and South*, Wallingford: CABI International.
Müller, D.K. and Pettersson, R. (2001) 'Access to Sami tourism in Northern Sweden',
    Scandinavian Journal of Hospitality and Tourism, 1: 5–18.
— (2006) 'Sami heritage at the Winter Festival in Jokkmokk, Sweden', *Scandinavian
    Journal of Hospitality and Tourism*, 6: 54–69.
Murray, C. and Jabour, J. (2004) 'Independent expeditions and Antarctic tourism policy',
    Polar Record, 40(215): 309–17.
Office of Economic Development (OED) (2008) *Alaska Economic Performance Report
    2007*. Anchorage: Office of Economic Development, Department of Commerce,
    Community and Economic Development.
Payne, C. (2006) 'Lessons with Leah: Re-reading the photographic archive of nation in the
    National Film Board of Canada's Still Photography Division', *Visual Studies*, 21(1):
    4–22.
Poirier, M.P. (2007–8) 'A very clear blue line: behavioural economics, public choice,
    public art and sea level rise', *Southeastern Environmental Law Journal*, 16: 83–112.
Pretes, M. (1994) 'Postmodern tourism: The Santa Claus industry', *Annals of Tourism
    Research*, 22(1): 1–15.
Pringle, T.R. (1991) 'Cold comfort: the polar landscape in English & American popular
    culture 1845–1990', *Landscape Research*, 16(2): 43–48.
Prokkola, E. (2007) 'Cross-border regionalization and tourism development at the Swedish-
    Finnish border "Destination Arctic Circle"', *Scandinavian Journal of Hospitality and
    Tourism*, 7(2): 120–38.

Pyne, S. (1986) *The Ice: A Journey to Antarctica*, New York: Ballantine Books.

Robinson, M.F. (2007) *The Coldest Crucible: Arctic Exploration and American Culture*. Chicago: University of Chicago Press.

Regionfakta.com (2008) *Overnights in hotels and camping/Overnights in 1997–2007 based on nationalities Norrbotten/ Västerbotten*. Available HTTP: http://www.regionfakta.com/dynamiskPresentation.aspx?id=533 (accessed 5 December 2008).

Rosner, V. (2009) 'Gender and polar studies: mapping the terrain', *Signs: Journal of Women in Culture and Society*, 34(3): 489–93.

Roth, L. (2005) *Something New in the Air: The Story of First Peoples Television*, Montreal: McGill-Queen's University Press.

Round, A. (2008) 'Frozen assets', *Destinations of the World News*, issue 21(March): 46.

—— (2009) On top of the world. *Destinations of the World News*, July, Online. Available HTTP: http://www.dotwnews.com/tabid/129/default.aspx (accessed 1 August 2009).

Saarinen, J. (1999) 'Representations of indigeneity: Sami culture in the discourses of tourism'. In P.M. Sant and J.N. Brown (eds) *Indigeneity: Constructions and Re/ Presentations*. New York: Nova Science Publishers.

—— (2001) *The Transformation of a Tourist Destination: Theory and Case Studies on the Production of Local Geographies in Tourism in Finnish Lapland*. Oulu: Oulu University Press.

—— (2005) 'Tourism in the northern wilderness: wilderness discourses and the development of nature-based tourism in northern Finland'. In C.M. Hall and S. Boyd (eds) *Nature-based Tourism in Peripheral Areas: Development Or Disaster?* Clevedon: Channel View Publications.

Shields, R. (1991) *Places on the Margin: Alternative Geographies of Modernity*, London: Routledge.

Snyder, J.M. (2007) 'Economic roles of polar tourism'. In J. Snyder and B. Stonehouse (eds) *Prospects for Polar Tourism*, Wallingford: CABI.

—— (2009) 'Arctic Tourism: A Growing Presence in an Ice Diminishing Region', paper presented at 3rd Symposium on the Impacts of an Ice-Diminishing Arctic on Naval and Maritime Operations, June 9–11, 2009, US Naval Academy, Alumni Center, Annapolis, Maryland.

Sörlin, S. (1998) 'Monument and memory: landscape imagery and the articulation of territory', *World Views: Environment, Culture, Religion*, 2(3): 269–79.

—— (1999) 'The articulation of territory: landscape and the constitution of regional and national identity', *Norsk Geografisk Tidsskrift Norwegian Journal of Geography*, 53(2–3): 103–12.

Spufford, F. (2007) 'Introduction'. In F. Spufford (ed.) *The Ends of the Earth: An Anthology of the Finest Writing on the Arctic and the Antarctic*, Vol.2 *The Antarctic*, London: Granta Books.

State of Alaska (2007) *Alaska Visitor Statistics Program V. Interim Visitor Volume Report Summer 2007*. Prepared for State of Alaska, Department of Commerce, Community and Economic Development, Office of Economic Development by McDowell Group. Anchorage: Office of Economic Development.

—— (2008a) *Alaska Visitor Statistics Program V: Interim Visitor Volume Report Fall/Winter 2007–2008*. Prepared for State of Alaska, Department of Commerce, Community and Economic Development, Office of Economic Development by McDowell Group. Anchorage: Office of Economic Development.

—— (2008b) *Alaska Visitor Statistics Program V. Interim Visitor Volume Report Summer 2008*. Prepared for State of Alaska, Department of Commerce, Community and

Economic Development, Office of Economic Development by McDowell Group. Anchorage: Office of Economic Development.

Statistics Finland (2008) Statistics Finland PX-Web data bank. Arrivals and over-night visits (2008). http://pxweb2.stat.fi/database/StatFin/lii/matk/matk_fi.asp (accessed 4 September 2009).

Statistics Iceland (2006). *Iceland in figures 2006–2007*. Online. Available HTTP: http://www.iceland.is/media/Utgafa/Iceland_in_figures_2006–07.pdf (accessed 26 November 2008).

— (2008) *Tourist industry: Number of overnight stays by foreigners, all accomodation*, Online. Available HTTP: http://www.statice.is (accessed 26 November 2008).

— (2009) Statistics » Tourism, transport and information technology, Online. Available HTTP: http://www.statice.is (accessed 1 August 2009).

Statistics Norway (2008) *StatBank. Hotels and similar establishments. Guest nights by nationality*. Online. Available HTTP: http://statbank.ssb.no/statistikkbanken/Default_FR.asp?PXSid = 0&nvl = true&PLanguage = 1&tilside = selecttable/hovedtabellHjem. asp&KortnavnWeb = overnatting (accessed 9 December 2008).

Stewart, E.J., Draper, D. and Johnston, M.E. (2005) 'A review of tourism research in the polar regions', *Arctic*, 58(4): 383–94.

Stonehouse, B. (1992) 'Monitoring shipborne visitors in Antarctica: a preliminary field study', *Polar Record*, 28(166): 213–18.

Sysselmannen På Svalbard (2006) *Tourism Statistics for Svalbard 2006*. Online. Available HTTP: www.sysselmannen.no/Tourism_statistics_1997–2006_iX9sq.pdf.file (accessed 27 November 2008).

— (2008) *Reiselivstatistikk for Svalbard*. Online. Available HTTP: //www.sysselmannen. no/enkel.aspx?m = 46070 (accessed 20 September 2009)

Tracey, P.J. (2001) 'Managing Antarctic tourism', Unpublished PhD thesis, University of Tasmania, Hobart, Tasmania.

Tuulentie, S. (2006) 'The dialectic of identities in the field of tourism: the discourses of the indigenous Sami in defining their own and the tourists' identities', *Scandinavian Journal of Hospitality and Tourism*, 6: 25–36.

Udvardy, M.D.F. (1975) *A Classification of the Biogeographical Provinces of the World*. IUCN Occasional Paper no. 18. Morges, Switzerland: IUCN.

— (1987) 'The biogeographical realm Antarctica: a proposal', *Journal of the Royal Society of New Zealand*, 17:187–94.

United Nations (1994) *Recommendations on Tourism Statistics*, New York: United Nations.

United Nations and United Nations World Tourism Organization (UN and UNWTO) (2007) *International Recommendations on Tourism Statistics (IRTS) Provisional Draft*, United Nations and United Nations World Tourism Organization: New York/Madrid.

Val, E. (1990) 'Parks, aboriginal peoples and sustainable tourism in development regions: the international experience and Canada's Northwest Territories'. In J. Vining (ed.) *Social Science and Natural Resource Recreation Management*, Boulder: Westview Press.

Vaughn, R. (2007) *The Arctic: A History*. Chalford: Sutton Publishing.

World Tourism Organization (WTO) (1991) *Resolutions of International Conference on Travel and Tourism, Ottawa, Canada*, Madrid: World Tourism Organization.

World Wildlife Fund (WWF) (2009) *New Russian Arctic Park to Protect Key Polar Bear Habitat*, WWF Press Release June 16, 2009. Online. Available HTTP: http://www.world-wildlife.org/who/media/press/2009/WWFPresitem12722.html (accessed 1 August 2009).

Wylie, J. (2002) 'Becoming-icy: Scott and Amundsen's south polar voyages 1910–13', *Cultural Geographies*, 9(3): 249 – 65.

Yukon Bureau of Statistics and Canada Border Service Agency (2009) *Yukon border crossing statistics by origin 1995–2008*, Department of Tourism and Culture, Government of Yukon. Online. Available HTTP: http://www.tc.gov.yk.ca/765.html (accessed 1 August 2009).

Yusoff, K. (2007) 'Antarctic exposure: archives of the feeling body', *Cultural Geographies*, 14(2): 211–33.

2 Tourism and Environmental Change in Polar Regions

Impacts, climate change and biological invasion

C. Michael Hall

Introduction

The polar regions and their species are regarded by many commentators as the proverbial canaries in the coal mine with respect to global environmental change (GEC), and climate change in particular (e.g. Natural Resources Defense Council 2005; *An Inconvenient Truth* 2006; National Wildlife Federation 2008; Union of Concerned Scientists 2008). Although climate change receives considerable attention in both academic and popular media, climate change is only a part of the broader issue of GEC. As Slaymaker and Kelly (2007: 1, 2) comment with respect to cryospheric change, 'a single focus on climate is likely to be counterproductive in the interpretation of environmental change...In fact, any surface cover change, whether natural or anthropogenic, causes changes in energy and mass balance that can have dramatic effects on the landscape.'

The global environment is always changing, although change is never uniform across time and space. Nevertheless, 'all changes are ultimately connected with one another through physical and social processes alike' (Meyer and Turner 1995: 304). However, what is most significant with respect to present environmental change is that it is not due to natural processes, but rather the scale and rates of change have increased dramatically as a direct result of human action related to the consumption of natural resources, the creation of new habitat for humans, and the waste products of human consumption and production. Human impacts on the environment can be regarded as having a global character in two ways. First, 'global refers to the spatial scale or functioning of a system' (Turner *et al.* 1990: 15), e.g. the climate and the oceans have the characteristic of a global system. Second, GEC occurs if a change is cumulative, 'occurs on a worldwide scale, or represents a significant fraction of the total environmental phenomenon or global resource' (Turner *et al.* 1990: 15–16), e.g. desertification. Tourism is regarded as significant for both types of change (Gössling 2002; Gössling and Hall 2006; UNWTO–UNEP–WMO 2008; Hall and Lew 2009; Gössling *et al.* 2010).

Although environmental change occurs at a global scale, regional and even local analyses are essential (Kasperson 1992). Changes find different expression and have different consequences in different regions (Meyer and Turner 1995). Many significant studies of environmental change are also organised on a regional basis so as to reflect geographical, political and even economic and social commonalities and associated responses (e.g. AHDR 2004; Huntington *et al*. 2007). This chapter outlincs some of the key environmental changes occurring in the polar regions and their relationship to tourism. However, one of the most significant points to emphasise is that tourism both contributes to and is affected by environmental change. The notion of tourism impact that is widely used in the academic and popular literature therefore needs to be understood as a multidimensional concept rather than as a unidimensional framework in which tourism is regarded as affecting the environment in a one-sided fashion.

The nature of impacts

An impact is a change in a given state over time as the result of an external stimulus. However, understanding of the environmental impacts of tourism in polar regions (along with economic and social impacts) remains fragmented for a number of reasons, including

- different scales of analysis in space and time;
- the limited locations at which research has been undertaken;
- the use of different and inconsistent research methods;
- a lack of longitudinal studies;
- few genuinely comparative studies of different locations;
- a lack of baseline data, i.e. what existed before tourism commenced;
- the paucity of information on the adaptive capacities of ecosystems, communities and economies;
- the difficulty of distinguishing between changes induced by tourism and those induced by other human activities;
- the concentration of researchers upon particular types of tourism;
- a lack of an effective ergodic hypothesis for tourism (see Hall and Lew 2009).

Furthermore, 'rapid expansion of humans during the twentieth century has left few opportunities to implement comprehensive conservation plans for the mitigation of cumulative effects of existing, proposed, and future developments across broad geographic areas that encompass ecosystems' (Johnson *et al*. 2005: 4).

One of the historical difficulties in examining the effects of tourism is that studies have tended to examine impacts only in terms of one element of the tourism system, usually the destination, rather than examining the environmental effects of a tourism system as a whole. Nevertheless, there are a number of ways in which tourism affects the environment of polar regions. Figure 2.1 identifies several of the ways in which tourism contributes to environmental change. These include the more obvious point sources of impact and pollution such as tourism infrastructure (e.g. resorts, roads, attractions), the demands of tourism on local resources such as water and energy, and the subsequent effects of tourism on habitats. However, significant impacts may also occur with respect to the affects of tourism on animal behaviour as a result of nature-based tourism/ecotourism

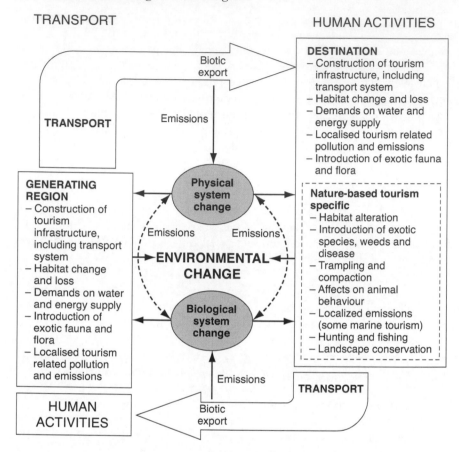

Figure 2.1 The contribution of tourism to environmental change

activities (Williams and Crosbie 2007). A critical dimension of understanding the impacts of tourism is that some of the most significant impacts occur as a result of the mobility required to travel between a tourism source area and the destination. Such mobility acts to transfer biotic material, including not only fauna and flora but also disease, and the transport that enables such mobility is a major source of emissions and pollution.

One of the difficulties in assessing the impacts of tourism is the time lag between the initial tourism stimulus and recognition that change has occurred. Change is clearly quickly recognisable with respect to the development of infrastructure and even trampling, but the introduction of exotic flora, for example, may take some time before it is recognised. Changes in landscape and climate may also take many years before they become noticed (Figure 2.2). Yet, such changes may have profound economic and social effects on the environment and even its relative attractiveness as a tourist destination.

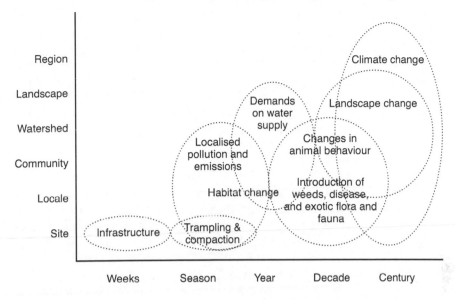

Figure 2.2 Time and space in the observation of the impacts of tourism on the polar environment

The contribution of tourism to climate change

Climate change is undoubtedly the major focal point for environmental change in polar regions. Before discussing the implications of climate change for polar tourism it is important to note the contribution of tourism to global climate change.

It is estimated that tourism's share of global emissions of CO_2 was of the order of 5% in 2005 (UNWTO-United Nations Environment Programme [UNEP]-World Meteorological Organization [WMO] 2008) (Table 2.1). While this share may appear minor, it should be noted that the sector's contribution to radiative forcing, a measure considering the warming caused by all greenhouse gases (GHG), is probably higher; in the order of 4.4–9.0%, when including

Table 2.1: Distribution of global emissions from tourism by sector

Sector	CO2 (Mt)	Per cent
Air transport	522	40
Car transport	418	32
Other transport	39	3
Accommodation	274	21
Activities	52	4
TOTAL	1,307	100
Total World (IPCC 2007)	26,400	
Tourism contribution		4.95%

Source: UNWTO-UNEP-WMO 2008

aviation-induced cirrus clouds (UNWTO-UNEP-WMO 2008). Transport is the sector that makes the greatest contribution to tourism emissions, with aviation accounting for 40% of tourism's contribution to CO_2, and up to 75% of the sector's contribution to radiative forcing. However, Gössling *et al.* (2010) note that this estimate is conservative, as the role of aviation in radiative forcing has been revised upwards from 2–8% (best estimate: 3%; Intergovernmental Panel on Climate Change [IPCC] 2007b) to 2–14% (best estimate: 4.9 %; Lee *et al.* 2009). Tourism's contribution to climate change is therefore, on a global level, substantial. If tourism were a country, its emissions would come fifth, after the USA, China, the European Union, and Russia (Hall 2010), although, if the upper estimate of radiative forcing effects were used, tourism would rank only behind the USA and China in terms of its contribution to climate change.

At a regional level the relative contribution of tourism to GHG emissions in polar regions is likely greater than for many other regions because of the reliance on aviation and cruise ships. Amelung and Lamers (2007) in examining the emissions from Antarctic tourism in the 2004–05 season reported that the average per capita emissions from travelling to the gateway ports of Ushuaia/Punta Arenas and Christchurch by Antarctic-bound tourists were 8.58 and 8.48 tonnes per capita respectively. Total ship-based CO_2 emissions were estimated at 169,666 tonnes. Average per-capita emissions were 6.16 tonnes per passenger, but the contribution varied widely depending on the ship, ranging from 2.09 tonnes per passenger for the *Alexander Humboldt* to 22.63 tonnes per passenger for the *Spirit of Enderby*. The per-capita emissions of land-based tourism in Antarctica were estimated as being just under 50 tonnes per tourist, including transport between gateway cities and Antarctica. Cruising provided the largest single source of emissions, although because aviation is important in terms of radiative forcing, air travel contributes close to 60% of emissions when calculated in CO_2 equivalents (see Table 2.2). From their research Amelung and Lamers (2007) estimated that the total contribution of Antarctic tourism to GHG emissions for 2004–05 was 425 ktons of CO_2-equivalents. In absolute terms such an amount is negligible. However, on a per-capita basis the 14.97 tonnes of GHG produced during the typical 2-week travels of the Antarctic tourist is equal to the total emissions produced by an average European in 17 months.

No comprehensive studies have been conducted of the GHG emissions associated with tourism in northern polar regions. However, as highlighted in chapter 1, the scale of Arctic tourism is substantial and growing, with air and cruise ship the dominant modes of travel to Alaska (over 90% of all visitors), NWT, Nunavit, Greenland, Iceland, and Svalbard. Even in mainland Arctic Europe the contribution of aviation to international tourist arrivals is substantial. For example, it is estimated that over half of Finnish Lapland's international tourist arrivals come by air (see Halpern 2008). Dawson and colleagues in chapter 4 calculated that the emissions of tourists participating in a polar bear viewing experience in Churchill, Manitoba range from 1.54 to 58.61 t/CO_2e per person. This means that a polar bear viewing experience is 6 to 34 times higher than an average global tourist experience, depending on the distance flown between an

Table 2.2: Estimated total CO_2 emissions resulting from Antarctic tourism 2004/05

Activity	CO2 (tonnes)	Emissions CO2-equivalent (tonnes)	CO2-equivalent tonnes per capita
Origin-destination aviation transport – South America	87,005	234,906	8.58
Origin-destination aviation transport – Australia / New Zealand	1,738	4,690	8.48
Expedition cruises	142,559	142,559	6.33
Cruise-only	27,105	27,105	5.40
Land-based (Antarctic Logistics and Expeditions)	3,423	9,182	48.32
Land-based (Aerovias DAP)	139	375	0.57
Overflights – Qantas	1,890	5,102	3.25
Overflights - Lanchile	263	710	1.54
Total	264,122	424,629	
Total (excluding overflights and DAP)	261,830	418,442	14.97

Notes: The land-based figures refer to the activities of two private companies. The Aerovias DAP figures were not included because the country of origin of tourists was not known.

Source: Derived from Lamers 2009

individual's place of residence and Churchill. Compared with other tourist activity-based studies, the maximum carbon footprint estimated for a polar bear viewing long-haul tourist is amongst the highest, second only to the energy-intensive cruise-based journeys to Antarctica discussed earlier (Amelung and Lamers 2007), although for polar bear viewing tourists coming from North America, emission levels are much lower. Based on a sample of 3,000 tourists Dawson and colleagues estimate that the total emissions for the entire polar bear-viewing network of industries, including transportation, accommodation and activities, are approximately 7,830 t/CO_2e per 6-week season (accommodation and activity emissions for 3,000 tourists ~ 495.6 t/CO_2e + air transportation ~7,325 t/CO_2e).

Cruise ships can be a major source of GHG emissions at destinations in which the sea provides major access point. Glacier Bay National Park in Alaska is both a focal point for climate change education and research as a result of glacier decline and a major tourist destination. In 2004 Glacier Bay received 353,686 recreational visitors. In that year the park's total GHG emissions were 13,747 t/CO_2e. As Table 2.3 demonstrates, marine vessels represent the greatest source of GHG emissions (97% of total), followed by stationary combustion (2% of total). Of marine vessel GHG emissions, 63% (8,360 t/CO_2e) result from operating cruise ships within park boundaries, visitors entering the park in private marine vessels account for approximately 24% (3,179 t/CO_2e) of marine vessel GHG emissions, while charter and tour vessels operated by concessionaires other than Glacier Bay Lodge & Tours account for approximately 12% (1,654 t/CO_2e) of marine vessel GHG emissions (Climate Friendly Parks 2005).

Table 2.4 presents the results of Glacier Bay's criteria air pollutant (CAP) emission inventory. Nitrous oxide (NO_x) is the most emitted gas. Of NO_x emissions 60.3% result from cruise ships, which are also the largest source of CO_2, the second

Table 2.3: Glacier Bay National Park and Preserves's greenhouse gas emissions (tonnes) by source and emitting entity

Emitting Entity	Stationary Combustion	Highway Vehicles & Non-road Equipment	Wastewater Treatment	Waste	Marine Vessels	Gross Emissions
Park Operations	222	30	1	2	65	320
Visitors	NA	NE	NA	NA	3,179	3,179
Glacier Bay Lodge & Tours	111	6	NA	NA	116	234
Other Concessionaires	NA	NA	NA	NA	1,654	1,654
Cruise Ships	NA	NA	NA	NA	8,360	8,360
Gross Emissions	333	36	1	2	13,375	13,747

NE=not estimated. NA=not applicable

Source: Climate Friendly Parks 2005

Table 2.4: Glacier Bay National Park and Preserves's Criteria Air Pollutant (CAP) emissions (lbs) by gas and emitting entity

Emitting entity	Sulphur dioxide (SO2)	Nitrogen oxide (NOx)	Volatile organic compounds (VOC)	Particulate matter $<=10\mu m$ (PM10)	Particulate matter $<=2.5\mu m$ (PM2.5)	Carbon Dioxide (CO2)
Park operations	308	47,831	19,450	378	72	43,470
Visitors	12,369	380,500	9,285	NA	9,684	60,110
Glacier Bay Lodge & Tours	635	37,132	2,857	195	351	2,126
Other concessionaires	6,460	198,224	4,578	NA	5,034	30,509
Cruise ships	33,324	1,009,645	16,770	NA	25,361	130,518
Gross emissions	53,096	1,673,332	52,939	573	40,502	266,733

(NA=not applicable)

Source: Climate Friendly Parks 2005

most emitted gas, and SO_2, the third most emitted gas. Most of the remaining emissions of these gases occur through the operation of other marine vessels in the park. Park operations are responsible for the highest level of volatile organic compound (VOC) emissions, which result primarily from fuel storage tanks, with cruise ships responsible for almost 32% (Climate Friendly Parks 2005).

Arctic cruise tourism appears to be continuing to grow, with its expansion being encouraged by the opening up of new cruising areas and extended seasons as a result of climate change. Indeed, both ACIA (2005) and Anisimov *et al.* (2007) note the potential economic benefits of reduced sea ice for the lengthening of the ship navigation season and increased marine access, including the opening up of new sea routes along the Northwest Passage and the Northern Sea Route. Instanes *et al.* (2005) suggest that by 2050, the Northern Sea Route will have 125 days/year with less than 75% sea ice cover, which represents favourable conditions for navigation by ice-strengthened ships. However, while this is regarded as a potentially positive benefit of climate change, other aspects are seen as having a far more serious impact.

The implications of polar climate change for tourism

The 2007 IPCC report provides a benchmark from which to evaluate the potential implications of climate change for polar regions and for tourism. Table 2.5 provides a summary of IPCC findings with respect to climate change in the polar regions (Anisimov *et al.* 2007). The IPCC has highlighted the extent to which sub-regions of the Arctic (the interior portions of northern Asia and northwestern North America) and Antarctic (the Antarctic Peninsula) have demonstrated the most rapid rates of warming over the last century (Turner *et al.* 2007).

Serreze and Francis (2006) concluded that the Arctic is manifesting the early stages of a human-induced greenhouse signature. Surface air temperatures in the Arctic have warmed at approximately twice the global rate (McBean *et al.*, 2005), with a figure of 1–2°C representing the areally averaged warming north of 60°N since a temperature minimum in the 1960s and 1970s. The most recent (1980 to present) warming of much of the Arctic is greatest (about 1°C/decade) in winter and spring, and weakest in autumn; it is strongest over the interior portions of northern Asia and northwestern North America (McBean *et al.* 2005). The extent of recent warming is such that it has been recognised as the warmest period in the Arctic for the last 2,000 years, with four of the five warmest decades in that period occurring in the past 50 years (Kaufman *et al.* 2009). Precipitation in the Arctic has increased at about 1% per decade over the past century, although the trends are spatially highly variable and highly uncertain because of deficiencies in the meteorological record (McBean *et al.* 2005).

Consistent with the observed increases in Arctic surface air temperatures, there is widespread evidence of reductions of Arctic sea ice and glaciers (see Lemke *et al.* 2007), reductions in the duration of river and lake ice in much of the sub-Arctic (Prowse *et al.* 2004; Walsh *et al.* 2005), and since the 1980s warming of permafrost (Romanovsky *et al.* 2002; Walsh *et al.* 2005). Arctic sea ice has also shown a substantial reduction since the 1950s. Sea ice in the Arctic shrank to its smallest size on record in September 2007, when it extended across an area of just 4.13 million km^2 (1.59 million m^2), beating the previous low of 5.32 million km^2, measured in 2005 (Giles et al. 2008). Using previously classified submarine data Kwok and Rothrock (2009) indicate that the average thickness at the end of the melt season has decreased by 1.6 m or some 53% from 1958 to 2008. The peak winter thickness of 3.64 m in 1980 (from submarine data) decreased to 1.89 m by the winter of 2008 (in satellite data), a net decrease of 1.75 m or 48% in thickness. On 12 September 2009 the Arctic sea ice reached a minimum ice extent of 5.1 million km^2. Although the 2009 minimum was almost one million square kilometers, around twice the size of Spain, above that for 2007, and less than 2008, the second-lowest year on record, when the minimum sea ice extent was 4.52 million km^2, there is no indication that the long-term trends are reversing (Schiermeier 2009).

All meteorological stations on the Antarctic Peninsula have shown strong and significant warming over the last 50 years, with the peninsula becoming a focus of media attention on global climate change. However, over the wider Antarctic

Table 2.5 Summary of IPCC findings with respect to climate change in the polar regions

	Confidence level			
	Low	Medium	High	Very high
Both polar regions				
Strong evidence of the ongoing impacts of climate change on terrestrial and freshwater species, communities and ecosystems				X
– that such changes will continue			X	
– with implications for biological resources and globally important feedbacks to climate		X		
Surface albedo is projected to decrease and the exchange of greenhouse gases between polar landscapes and the atmosphere will change				X
Components of the terrestrial cryosphere and hydrology are increasingly being affected by climate change				X
– these changes will have cascading effects on key regional bio-physical systems and cause global climatic feedbacks, and in the north will affect socio-economic systems			X	
Changes to cryospheric processes are modifying seasonal runoff and routings				X
Continued changes in sea-ice extent, warming and acidification of the polar oceans are likely to further impact the biomass and community composition of marine biota as well as human activities			X	
Acidification of polar waters is predicted to have adverse effects on calcified organisms and consequential effects on species that rely upon them			X	
Arctic				
Strong evidence exists of changes in species' ranges and abundances and in the position of some tree lines			X	
Increase in greenness and biological productivity has occurred in parts			X	
A small net accumulation of carbon will occur in Arctic tundra during the present century	X			
Higher methane emissions responding to the thawing of permafrost and an overall increase in wetlands will enhance radiative forcing		X		
Increased Eurasian river discharge to the Arctic Ocean, and continued declines in the ice volume of Arctic and sub-Arctic glaciers and the Greenland ice sheet				X
Combined effects of changes to cryospheric and hydrological processes will impact freshwater, riparian and near-shore marine systems			X	
Economic benefits, such as enhanced hydropower potential, may accrue, but some livelihoods are likely to be adversely affected			X	
Adaptation will be required to maintain freshwater transportation networks with the loss of ice cover			X	

Statement		
Impact of climate change on Arctic fisheries will be regionally specific; some beneficial and some detrimental. The reduction of Arctic sea ice has led to improved marine access, increased coastal wave action, changes in coastal ecology/biological production and adverse effects on ice-dependent marine wildlife, and continued loss of Arctic sea ice will have human costs and benefits		X
Human communities are adapting to climate change, but both external and internal stressors challenge their adaptive capabilities		X
Benefits associated with climate change will be regionally specific and widely variable at different locations	X	
Impacts on food accessibility and availability, and personal safety are leading to changes in resource and wildlife management and in livelihoods of individuals (e.g., hunting, travelling)		X
The resilience shown historically by Arctic indigenous peoples is now being severely tested		X
Warming and thawing of permafrost will bring detrimental impacts on community infrastructure		X
Substantial investments will be needed to adapt or relocate physical structures and communities		X
The benefits of a less severe climate are dependant on local conditions, but include reduced heating costs, increasing agricultural and forestry opportunities, more navigable northern sea routes, and marine access to resources	X	

Antarctic

Statement		
Some parts of the Antarctic ice sheet are losing significant volume		X (Very high)
Combined effects of changes to cryospheric and hydrological processes will impact freshwater, riparian and near-shore marine systems on sub-Antarctic islands		X
Further decline of sea-ice extent will impact the predators and ecosystems of krill		X

Source: Derived from Ansimov et al. (2007).

Description of confidence (IPCC 2007a: 4):

Terminology	Degree of confidence in being correct
Very high confidence	At least 9 out of 10 chance of being correct
High confidence	About 8 out of 10 chance
Medium confidence	About 5 out of 10 chance
Low confidence	About 2 out of 10 chance
Very low confidence	Less than a 1 out of 10 chance

there is considerable variability in temperature trends. Anisimov *et al.* (2007) noted that if the individual station records are considered as independent measurements, then the mean trend is warming at a rate comparable with mean global warming (Vaughan *et al.*, 2003), but observed that there is no evidence of a continent-wide 'polar amplification' in Antarctica. Since 1978 (from when satellite data provided reliable data) there has been no general trend in duration of Antarctic sea ice, but there have been strong regional trends, with duration increasing in the Ross Sea and decreasing in the Amundsen and Bellingshausen Seas (Parkinson 2002). Such patterns strongly reflect trends in atmospheric temperatures in those regions (Vaughan *et al.* 2003). Walsh (2009) notes that the ongoing climate variations in the Arctic and Antarctic pose an apparent paradox because Antarctic temperatures and sea ice show little change, except for the Antarctic Peninsula, in stark contrast to the large warming and loss of sea ice in the Arctic (although see de la Mare [2009], who argues that there can be little doubt that a substantial shift in the extent of sea ice occurred from the 1930s to the 1980s, which corresponds to a 20–30% reduction in sea ice). Walsh (2009) suggests that Antarctic changes of recent decades appear to be shaped by ozone depletion and an associated strengthening of the southern annular mode of the atmospheric circulation and although the signature of greenhouse-driven change is projected to emerge in Antarctica from the natural variability during the present century, the emergence of a statistically significant greenhouse signal may be slower than in other regions.

Climatic conditions are extremely important for tourism because of the extent to which they influence the accessibility and attractiveness of a given location. Climate change will therefore influence the seasonality of a location as a tourist attraction by the extent to which access is economically feasible in a polar environment as well as determining the local environmental conditions that may prove appealing to visitors. For example, climate change is also regarded as having enabled the lengthening of the northern polar cruise season as well as providing access to hitherto inaccessible locations. However, in the polar context climate change is also important because of the way it affects polar terrestrial and marine ecosystems and their biodiversity, including iconic species such as penguins, albatross, reindeer and polar bears (see chapter 1).

As Anisimov *et al.* (2007) emphasised many polar species are particularly vulnerable to climate change because they are highly specialised and have adapted to their environment in ways that are likely to make them poor competitors with potential immigrants from environmentally more benign regions as conditions change (e.g. Callaghan *et al.* 2005; Peck *et al.* 2006). Furthermore, stress brought about by increased human contact via tourism may only add to a series of anthropogenic impacts, including not only climate change but also increasing contaminant loads, increased ultraviolet-B radiation, and further habitat loss and fragmentation. Polar ecosystems are also particularly vulnerable to environmental change as their species richness prior to the current period of anthropogenic-induced change is low, with correspondingly low levels of redundancy, making it easier for new species to outcompete existing species in the same ecological niche. (See later discussion with respect to the role of tourism as a vector for invasive species.)

'The adaptive capacity of current Arctic ecosystems is small because their extent is likely to be reduced substantially by compression between the general northwards expansion of forest, the current coastline and longer term flooding of northern coastal wetlands as the sea level rises, and also as habitat is lost to land use' (Anisimov *et al.* 2007: 659). The general vulnerability of Arctic ecosystems to warming and the lack of adaptive capacity of Arctic species and ecosystems are therefore likely to lead to, where possible, relocation rather than rapid adaptation to new climates.

In the Antarctic there is also substantial evidence that indicates that major regional changes are occurring in terrestrial and marine ecosystems in areas that have experienced warming. These include increasing abundance of shallow-water sponges and their predators, and declining abundances of krill, Adelie and Emperor penguins and Weddell seals (Ainley *et al.* 2005). Of longer-term significance is the acidification of the Southern Ocean as a result of increased draw-down of CO_2, which will have considerable consequences for a number of marine species as well as the wider food web (Orr *et al.* 2005; Royal Society 2005; Fabry *et al.* 2008). On the Antarctic continent the abundance and distribution of the only two species of native flowering plant, the Antarctic pearlwort (*Colobanthus quitensis*) and the Antarctic hair grass (*Deschampsia antarctica*), are increasing as the amount of ice-free habitats expands (Fowbert and Smith 1994). Similarly, climate change is also affecting Antarctic algae, lichens and mosses, with further changes expected as temperature, water and nutrient availability increase (Robinson *et al.* 2003). In the sub-Antarctic islands the decline of sphagnum moss beds in number and size has also been associated with climate change (Whinam and Copson 2006). The simplicity of Antarctic terrestrial ecosystems makes them extremely vulnerable to the introduction of exotic species, particularly as climate change creates more opportunities for successful introductions. Historically, the introduction of new species was usually as a result of human industrial and extractive activities, such as whaling, but the expansion of Antarctic tourism provides the possibility that tourists will become significant vectors of non-indigenous plant seeds and disease.

Climate change will also have implications for human populations, including tourists. Environmental change is already substantially affecting traditional lifestyles and economies in the Arctic, particularly with respect to hunting, herding, fishing and gathering (Nuttal *et al.* 2005; Huntington *et al.* 2007). As well as being culturally important to Arctic peoples, traditional activities also serve as significant tourism resources for culturally oriented tourism, whereas hunting and fishing are important motivations for tourism in a number of Arctic regions. Other important environmental issues include the extent to which freshwater resources and permafrost are affected by climate change. In the former, potential impacts on tourism include changes to water availability as well as ice-road construction and open-water transportation, although potential changes in freshwater ecology may also be significant for ecotourism and fishing (e.g. Prowse *et al.* 2006; Reist *et al.* 2006; Schindler and Smol 2006). The thawing of permafrost (defined as sub-surface earth materials that remain at or below 0°C continuously for 2 or more years) is increasing in Alaska, northern Canada, northern Scandinavia, and Siberia, with substantial negative impacts on the infrastructure that is built upon it, necessitating new construction. In broader terms one of the greatest concerns of the thawing of permafrost is the extent to which it releases GHG, therefore further affecting climate change. Given the extent to which Arctic human settlement is based in coastal areas or on river systems there is widespread concern about riverbank and coastal erosion, which is among the highest anywhere (Brown *et al.* 2003). Coastal stability in high latitudes is affected by factors common to all areas (exposure, relative sea-level change, climate and coastal geomorphology), and by specific polar factors (low temperatures, ground ice and sea ice). The most severe erosion occurs in areas of rising sea level, where warming coincides with areas that are subject to wave erosion that are seasonally free of sea ice or where there is widespread ice-rich permafrost, such as in the western Canadian Arctic, northern Alaska and along much of the Russian Arctic coast (Forbes 2005). For example, in Shishmaref (Alaska, USA) and Tuktoyaktuk (NWT, Canada), the combined effects of reduced sea ice, thawing permafrost, storm surges and wave erosion have led to significant loss of property, with subsequent relocation or abandonment of homes, facilities and other infrastructure (Instanes *et al.* 2005).

Overall, the potential effects of climate change on human populations in the polar regions are so great that, as Anisimov *et al.* (2007: 661) concluded, 'Currently we do not know the limits of adaptive capacity among Arctic populations, or what the impacts of some adaptive measures will be'. Indeed, tourism should also be understood as being one particular form of economic adaptation to the broader economic and social change brought about by climate change, especially with respect to the shift from subsistence to commercial economies (ACIA 2004, 2005; Chapin *et al.* 2004, 2006). Another area in which tourism may play a major role is in providing a financial justification for the conservation of polar biodiversity. For example, Einarsson (2009) notes how Icelandic fishing communities have shifted in their perspectives on whales so that they become regarded as 'good to watch' as well as 'good to eat'. Table 2.6 details some of the ways in which tourism supports biodiversity conservation strategies in the polar region. The role that tourism plays in providing an economic rationale for the establishment and maintenance of national parks and conservation areas is arguably the most important, what may be regarded as an economic 'ecosystem service' (Wookey 2007), and tourism is also a significant justification for conservation efforts of iconic species (e.g. Lemelin and Wiersma 2007; Lemelin *et al.* 2008; Ragen *et al.* 2008; Rayfuse 2009) (see also chapter 4). However, at the same time, tourism either via infrastructure, transport or human visitation may also negatively affect individual species as well as the overall ecology of an area via various means, including disturbance of breeding sites (e.g. Ellenberg *et al.* 2006; Trathan *et al.* 2008; Wojczulanis-Jakubas *et al.* 2008), changes in animal behaviour (e.g. Eckhardt 2005; Otley 2005; Walker *et al.* 2005; Mallory 2006; Burger and Gochfield 2007; Wheeler *et al.* 2009), trampling or even picking of vegetation (e.g. Ayres *et al.* 2008; Tejedo *et al.* 2009; Tin *et al.* 2009), soil

Table 2.6 Tourism in relation to major strategies of polar biodiversity conservation

Strategy	Element	Role of Tourism	Examples
In situ conservation (On site)	Establish protected area network, with appropriate management practices, corridors to link fragments; restore degraded habitats within and outside protected areas	Tourism economic justification for protected area framework given their role as attractions; volunteer tourism may also assist in protected area management. Tourism also important for development of environmental knowledge	National parks and protected areas throughout the Arctic region, e.g. Sør-Spitsbergen National Park in the Svalbard archipelago, Norway. In the Antarctic, Sites of Special Scientific Interest.
Ex situ conservation (Off site)	Establish botanical and zoological gardens, conservation stands; banks of germplasm, pollen, seed, seedlings, tissue culture, gene and DNA	Botanical and zoological gardens are significant tourism attractions; volunteer tourism also significant; significant educational tourism function	The Polar-Alpine Botanic Garden near Kirovsk on the Kola Peninsula in Russia and the Arctic-alpine Botanic Garden, in Tromsø, Norway.
Reduction of anthroprogenic pressure	Reduce anthropogenic (human) pressure on natural species populations by altering human activities and behaviours. May also include cultivating species elsewhere	Species populations can have a role as tourism attractions; some species which can be sustainably harvested may also be used for hunting and fishing	Use of voluntary codes of conduct by Arctic and Antarctic cruise ships as well as the development of visitor codes (e.g. AECO, IAATO, WWF); State of Alaska's Sport Fishing Guide License Program.
Reduction of biotic pressure	Removal or reduction of invasive exotic species and pests that compete with indigenous species	Ensure good biosecurity practice; interpretation programmes to support eradication of invasive species and pests	South Georgia and South Sandwich Islands biosecurity measures; Volunteer tourism programmes
Rehabilitation	Identify and rehabilitate threatened species; launch augmentation, reintroduction or introduction programmes	Species may become tourism attractions; volunteers also significant in management	Volunteer tourism programmes

Source: Modified from Hall and Lew (2009: 205)

compaction (e.g. Tejedo *et al*. 2009; Tin *et al*. 2009) and short- or long-term changes to habitat, e.g. pollution, infrastructure development and site disturbance (e.g. Pfeiffer and Peter 2004; Tejedo and Benayas 2006; Pfeiffer *et al*. 2007; Tin *et al*. 2009).

Tourism and biological invasion of polar regions

Arguably one of the most significant potential effects on tourism in polar regions is via acting as a vector for biological invasion by alien microbes, fungi, plants and animals that can act as drivers for ecosystem change (Barnes and Convey 2005; Frenot *et al*. 2005; Crowl *et al*. 2008). In the Antarctic, cruise ships and yachts (Lewis *et al*. 2003, 2005), as well as site visitation, may be particularly significant avenues of species introduction. For example, the green alga *Entero-morpha intestinalis* that grows in dense mats in the intertidal zone at Half Moon Island (62°37'W 59°57'S), may have been introduced via the hulls of visiting vessels (Clayton *et al*. 1997). Tavares and De Melo (2004) reported the discovery of the North Atlantic majid spider crab (*Hyas araneus*) in the Antarctic Peninsula marine waters. This is the only record of a non-indigenous marine species in Antarctic seas and it may have arrived in Antarctica via the sea-chests or ballast water of ships. According to Frenot *et al*. (2005) four trends in Antarctic tourism are of significance to the potential for the introduction and spread of alien organisms to and in the region:

1   Tourists are disproportionately attracted to sites of high/medium diversity (Navareen *et al*., 2001).
2   The intensity of visitor use is increasing (see chapter 1).
3   Sites of high popularity are not consistent over time. The 25 most visited sites in the Antarctic Peninsula region changed between 1989 and 1999 (Navareen *et al*., 2001), meaning that the potential for human impact is not contained to a number of specific sites but varies as a result of tourist trends and changing fashions.
4   The range of tourist activities is expanding. In addition to being able to land on beaches and observe immediately accessible wildlife, options now include extensive walks, kayaking trips and even a marathon on King George Island (South Shetland Islands) (Frenot *et al*. 2005).

The Arctic is regarded as being especially vulnerable to the introduction of invasive species via increased international trade and tourism. In the northern part of mainland Europe and in some parts of Canada and Alaska road transport will provide a major mechanism for the introduction of new species. However, in much of the Arctic the growth in shipping, including cruise ships, is expected to play a major role in introducing marine and terrestrial invasives (Molnar *et al*. 2008; Pyke *et al*. 2008). Hull fouling (Drake and Lodge 2007) and ballast water (Endresen *et al*. 2004) are identified as major sources of alien maritime species. As in the Antarctic Peninsula, new locations are opening up to tourist visitation, creating opportunities for the introduction of alien species. For example, on Svalbard 'warming has allowed access to areas that were once impossible to reach' (Round 2008: 47).

Although it is not completely within the Arctic region, Hall (2009) identified the potential threat of alien species to the natural capital that underlies tourism in the Nordic context. Drawing on the NOBANIS alien species database (European Network on Invasive Alien Species), Hall noted not only the role of greater transport connectivity for species transfer, especially for agricultural, horticultural, industrial and leisure purposes, but also the direct potential of tourism to act as a vector for alien species (Tables 2.7 and 2.8). Such species movement may be a significant threat for the conservation of national parks and nature reserves with high natural ecological value as well as the maintenance of marine and landscape values. However, despite the acknowledged impacts of invasive species on biodiversity, Hall (2009) reported that Nordic ecotourism businesses generally appeared to have little knowledge of biosecurity issues and the threats posed by tourism as a potential vector for alien species. Hall (2009) also observed that even in the case of cruise lines and expedition operators who already had substantial experience with biosecurity in the Antarctic and sub-Antarctic context, where such measures were often a requirement of being able to land at some locations (see chapter 15 [this volume]), many of them did not take such stringent precautions during Arctic and Nordic cruises, with only limited advice being available to their customers.

Table 2.7 Number of alien species in Nordic countries

Country	Invasive	Potentially invasive	Not invasive	Not known
Denmark	17	63	2015	561
Faroe Islands	2	–	–	144
Finland	98	66	32	44
Greenland	–	–	–	131
Iceland	7	17	83	19
Norway	28	59	752	15
Svalbard	–	4	7	–
Sweden	174	60	827	1020

Source: Derived from NOBANIS 2009 in Hall 2009

Table 2.8 Tourism related species introduction pathways in Nordic countries

Country	Ballast water & sediments	Hull fouling	Hunting	Angling/sport	Transport
Denmark	51	3	7	6	61
Faroe Islands	2	–	1	–	2
Finland	10	5	5	1	21
Greenland	1	–	–	2	3
Iceland	2	–	–	–	21
Norway	23	3	2	4	4
Svalbard	–	–	–	–	2
Sweden	80	18	9	8	58

Source: Derived from NOBANIS 2009 in Hall 2009

The combination of climate change and increased tourism and transport, especially shipping, is therefore presenting itself as a major challenge to the polar environment, with consequent implications for the different pathways that invasive species may take and locations in which they may potentially establish themselves (Hellmann *et al.* 2008). Figure 2.3 seeks to illustrate the key stages in the process by which a new species becomes established and indicates that tourism is not only a significant vector in overcoming distance or barriers to dispersal but

STAGE

TRANSPORT
Major filters: Distance and barriers to long-distance dispersal, e.g. oceans
Physical factors in recipient ecosystem: na
Tourists and transport represent a way of overcoming distance and barriers

COLONIZATION
Major filters: Abiotic barriers to colonization, eg temperature, moisture
Physical factors in recipient ecosystem: climate, soil, resource availability, disturbance regime

ESTABLISHMENT
Major filters: Biotic filters to population growth and establishment, eg pathogens, competition, herbivores
Physical factors in recipient ecosystem: climate, soil, resource availability, disturbance regime

SPREAD
Major filters: Landscape filters to dispersal and new establishment in new areas, eg dispersal ability, habitat connectivity, dispersal vectors
Physical factors in recipient ecosystem: disturbance regime, patch attributes, presence of suitable patches for colonization and establishment, dispersal corridors, heterogeneity of landscape

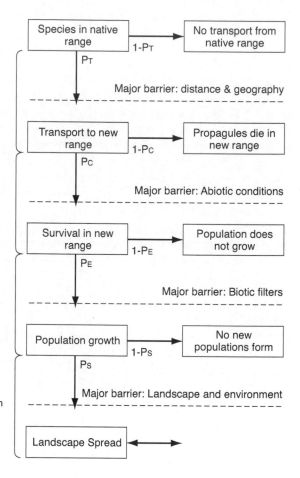

Conceptual model of the process of nonindigenous plant species invasion. Transition probabilities between four distinct stages of invasion are marked Pi. All transitions could be affected by climate change.

Source: Derived from Theoharides and Dukes 2007; Hellmann *et al.* 2008; Rahel and Olden 2008; Hall and Lew 2009

Figure 2.3 Stages in the process of species invasion

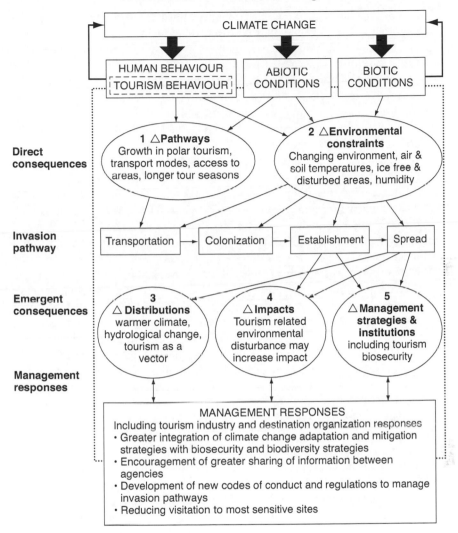

Source: Derived from Hall 2006a, b; Hellmann *et al.* 2008; Hall and Lew 2009

Figure 2.4 Consequences for invasive species in polar regions under climate change

can also serve to create a disturbance regime that may enable species to become established (Theoharides and Dukes 2007). Figure 2.4 highlights the five possible consequences of climate change for invasive species in polar regions (Hellmann *et al.* 2008):

1   Altered mechanisms of transport and introduction, e.g. new polar shipping routes, provide opportunities for the introduction of species in ballast water

and on ship hulls, whereas the growth in polar tourism also increases the opportunities and likelihood of the dispersal of invasive species outside their natural range. For example, in September 2009 two German merchant ships sailed the Northeast Passage from Asia to Europe via Russia's Arctic coast as part of a promotion of the safety and efficiency of the route as a commercial alternative to the Suez Canal in summer. By avoiding the Suez Canal and using the northern route, the trip from Asia to Europe was shortened by almost 5,000 km (3,100 miles) and saved about US$300,000 per vessel (BBC 2009).

2   Altered climatic and environmental constraints on invasive species, e.g. climate change, may provide more favorable environmental conditions, such as increased temperature, for species survival. In the polar context climate change will also increase the area of ice-free land and sea in time and space, therefore also providing opportunities for invasive species. For example, newly ice-free areas in Glacier Bay National Park and Preserve have high numbers of invasive plant species (Rapp 2008), with the park having the highest number of invasive species of any Alaskan national park.

3   Altered distribution of existing invasive species, e.g. cold-temperature constraints on invasive species, will be reduced at their higher-latitude or upper-elevation range limits, whereas conversely warm-temperature constraints on invasive species will increase at their lower-latitude or lower-elevation range limits. One example in which the decline of a northern species appears to be due to interactions with an expanding southern species involves northern pike (*Esox lucius*) and Arctic char (*Salvelinus alpinus*), with recent warming allowing northern pike to migrate upstream in a watershed and colonise a subarctic lake in Sweden through predation of Arctic char (Byström *et al.* 2007);

4   Altered impact of existing invasive species, e.g. climate change, may alter invasive species impacts as a result of changes in range, abundance and per-capita (or per-unit biomass) impact. Byers (2002) argues that the speed, persistence and ubiquity of anthropogenic habitat alterations may suddenly put even previously well-adapted native species at a competitive disadvantage with alien species as anthropogenic disturbance may so drastically alter environments that a native species finds itself in an environment that is in many key ways just as novel as it is to an invasive species. Extreme disturbances, such as those arising from climate change or other forms of anthropogenic change, may thereby erase a native species' prior advantage of local environmental adaptation accrued during its long-term incumbency over evolutionary time (Byers 2002); and

5   The altered effectiveness of management strategies and the institutions, e.g. laws and regulations, agencies and international agreements, that seek to manage or eliminate invasive species. Hellmann *et al.* (2008) focus on the altered effectiveness of management strategies primarily in the context of control. However, strategies should also be understood in a wider context of the regulatory and institutional context that may affect the invasion pathways

of alien species. The invasion pathway, and the five consequences for invasive species under climate change, will therefore all influence management responses, which will in turn feed back into the system, particularly with respect to tourism behaviour, biosecurity strategies and adaptation and mitigation of climate change.

Conclusions

This chapter has highlighted how tourism is implicated in environmental change in polar regions and contributes substantially to both climate change and biological invasions. The growth of high-latitude tourism, and even the use of tourism as an adaptive economic response to climate change in the Arctic (chapter 1), suggest that the role of tourism in polar environmental change will continue to expand in the transition of high-latitude environments to new sets of conditions (Figure 2.5). The notion of transition is important because it needs to be recognised that the polar environment has often shifted from one relatively stable state to another over geological time. The concept of transition therefore helps address the sense in which environmental and landscape change 'is not merely chronological and linear, or simply a "lagged" response to climatic and tectonic changes' (Slaymaker and Kelly 2007: 7). 'There are diachronous episodes of (incomplete) readjustment to the cessation of past conditions, and towards later conditions, of which those present are only one set. There are distinctive spatial and temporal patterns of adjustment, including self adjustment specific to the earth surface processes at work' (Hewitt 2002: 2). To Hewitt (2002: 6) temporal transitions in cold regions have two important geographical aspects. First, there is a change in environments through the expansion and contraction of climatic, tectonic, biotic, abiotic and anthropogenic conditions. Second, past cold conditions remain to a greater or lesser extent, imprinted on the high-latitude landscape to the present day and they will remain so for much of the foreseeable future, even allowing for the physical effects of climate change, and will continue to act as constraints on present-day developments, given that 'few aspects of landscape respond instantaneously to climatic and geological conditions' (Hewitt 2002: 7).

The concept of transition in high latitudes in landscape and geomorphological terms has significant parallels to understanding how ecosystems adapt or fail to adapt to disturbance and particularly the concept of transformability, which is 'the capacity to create a fundamentally new system when ecological, economic, or social (including political) conditions make the existing system untenable. Transformability means defining and creating new stability landscapes by introducing new components and ways of making a living, thereby changing the state variables, and often the scale, that define the system' (Walker *et al.* 2004). As this chapter has suggested – and as illustrated in Figure 2.5 – the polar regions are in the process of transitioning to a new state. This is one in which polar ecosystems are transformed by a combination of climate change, biological invasion and anthropogenic change, in which tourism is deeply embedded. Increasing transport and tourism connectivity and frequency, growing numbers of

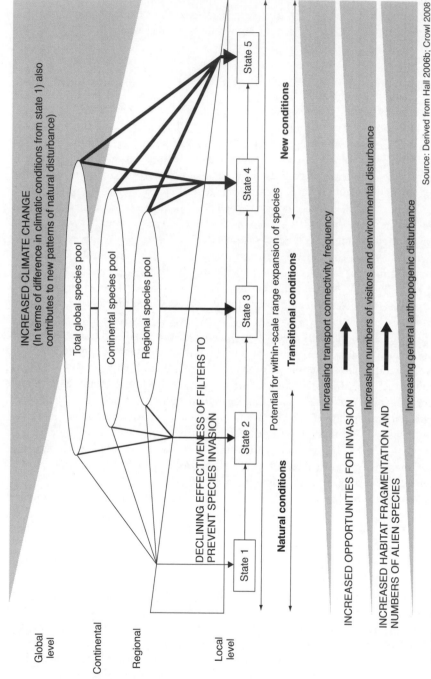

Figure 2.5 The changing state of polar environments as a result of climate change, biological invasion, and toursim

Source: Derived from Hall 2006b; Crowl 2008

visitors, and associated environmental disturbance all appear to be contributing to a new ecosystem state that will be marked by new climatic conditions as well as new sets of ecological relationships with the arrival of invasive biota and disease.

Tourism will not be the only source of anthropogenic change, but there is mounting evidence that it will be a major one, especially because it is going to be a major element of the socioeconomic adaptation of polar regions to GEC, primarily in the Arctic, where there is a substantial permanent population, but also in the Antarctic and sub-Antarctic, where is provides, along with fishing, the major economic use of the region, and also because it provides a substantial rationale for conservation. This situation reflects the findings of the ACIA that as 'existing adaptation strategies become obsolete, new adaptations to climate impacts must develop as northern communities adjust to the many social, institutional, and economic changes related to land claim settlements, changes in job opportunities, and the creation of new political and social structures in the North' (Weller *et al.* 2005: 1014). Yet, as this chapter has stressed, it is also vital that tourism in polar regions is understood within an assessment of the 'vulnerabilities of coupled human-environment systems in the Arctic' with vulnerability being understood as 'the degree to which a system is susceptible to or unable to cope with adverse effects of multiple and interacting stresses' (Weller *et al.* 2005: 1014). This chapter has therefore highlighted the importance of the interaction between climate change, biodiversity, biological invasions and tourism in developing an understanding of environmental change in high latitudes. However, while sources of stress on the capacity of systems to adapt are increasingly recognised, knowledge of the consequences of such stresses and their interactions is only at an early stage (ACIA 2005; Slaymaker and Kelly 2007). Much greater research efforts are therefore needed for assessing the vulnerabilities or degrees of susceptibility to adverse multiple interacting stresses, including the critical role of tourism as a contributor, vector and response to change.

References

Ainley, D.G., Clarke, E.D., Arrigo, K., Fraser, W.R., Kato, A., Barton, K.J. and Wilson, P.R. (2005) 'Decadal-scale changes in the climate and biota of the Pacific sector of the Southern Ocean, 1950s to the 1990s', *Antarctic Science*, 17: 171–82.

Amelung, B. and Lamers, M. (2007) 'Estimating the greenhouse gas emissions from Antarctic tourism', *Tourism in Marine Environments*, 4(2–3): 121–33.

An Inconvenient Truth (2006) directed by Davis Guggenheim. Released May 24, 2006. Paramount Classics.

Anisimov, O.A., Vaughan, D.G., Callaghan, T.V., Furgal, H., Marchant, H., Prowse, T.D., Vilhjálmsson, H. and Walsh, J.E. (2007) 'Polar regions (Arctic and Antarctic)', in M.L. Parry, O.F. Canziani, J.P. Palutikof, P.J. van der Linden and C.E. Hanson (eds) *Climate Change 2007: Impacts, Adaptation and Vulnerability*, Cambridge: Cambridge University Press.

Arctic Climate Impacts Assessment (ACIA) (2004) *Impacts of a Warming Arctic: Arctic Climate Impacts Assessment*. Cambridge: Cambridge University Press.

— (2005) *Arctic Climate Impacts Assessment*. Cambridge: Cambridge University Press.

Arctic Human Development Report (AHDR)(2004) *Arctic Human Development Report*, Akureyri: Stefansson Arctic Institute.

Ayres, E., Nkem, J.N., Wall, D.H., Adams, B.J.; Barrett, J.E.; Broos, E.J., Parsons, A.N., Powers, L.E., Simmons, B.L. and Virginia, R.A. (2008) 'Effects of human trampling on populations of soil fauna in the McMurdo dry valleys, Antarctica', *Conservation Biology*, 22(6): 1544–51.

Barnes, D.K.A. and Convey, P. (2005) 'Odyssey of stow-away noctuid moths to southern polar islands', *Antarctic Science*, 17(3), 307–11.

British Broadcasting Company (BBC) (2009) German ships blaze Arctic trail, BBC News, 11 September. Online. Available HTTP: http://news.bbc.co.uk/2/hi/europe/8251914.stm (accessed 11 September 2009).

Brown, J., Jorgenson, M.T., Smith, O.P., and Lee, W. (2003) 'Long-term rates of coastal erosion and carbon input, Elson Lagoon, Barrow, Alaska', in M. Phillips, S.M. Springman and L.U. Arenson, (eds) *Proceedings, 8th International Conference on Permafrost*, Lisse: A.A. Balkema.

Burger, J. and Gochfield, M. (2007) 'Responses of Emperor Penguins (*Aptenodytes forsteri*) to encounters with ecotourists while commuting to and from their breeding colony', *Polar Biology*, 30(10): 1303–13.

Byers, J.E. (2002) 'Impact of non-indigenous species on natives enhanced by anthropogenic alteration of selection regimes', *Oikos*, 97: 449–58.

Byström, P., Karlsson, J., Nilsson, P., Van Kooten, T., Ask, J. and Olofsson, F. (2007) 'Substitution of top predators: effects of pike invasion in a subarctic lake', *Freshwater Biology*, 52: 1271–80.

Chapin, F.S., III, Hoel, M., Carpenter, S.R., Lubchenko, J., Walker, B., Callaghan, T.V., Folke, C., Levin, S.A., Mäler, K.-G., Nilsson, C., Barrett, S., Berkes, F., Crépin, A.-S., Danell, K., Rosswall, T., Starrett, D., Xepapadeas, A. and Zimov, S.A. (2006) Building resilience and adaptation to manage Arctic change. *AMBIO: A Journal of the Human Environment*, 35(4): 198–202.

Chapin III, F.S., Peterson, G. Berkes, F., Callaghan, T.V., Angelstam, P., Apps, M., Beier, C., Bergeron, Y., Crépin, A.-S., Danell, K., Elmqvist, T., Folke, C., Forbes, B., Fresco, N., Juday, G., Niemelä, J., Shvidenko, A. and Whiteman, G. (2004) 'Resilience and vulnerability of northern regions to social and environmental change', *AMBIO: A Journal of the Human Environment*, 33: 342–47.

Clayton, M.N., Wiencke, C. and Klöser, H. (1997) 'New records and sub-Antarctic marine benthic macroalgae from Antarctica', *Polar Biology*, 17: 141–49.

Climate Friendly Parks (2005) *Glacier Bay National Park & Preserve Action Plan*, Produced by the NPS Environmental Leadership Program, with technical assistance from EPA's Office of Air and Radiation/Office of Atmospheric Programs Climate Change Division/Program Integration Branch and NPS's Natural Resources Stewardship and Science Division. Washington DC: National Park Service.

Crowl, T.A., Crist, T.O., Parmenter, R.R., Belovsky, G. and Lugo, A.E. (2008) 'The spread of invasive species and infectious disease as drivers of ecosystem change', *Frontiers of Ecology and Environment*, 6(5): 238–46.

De la Mare, W.K. (2009) 'Changes in Antarctic sea-ice extent from direct historical observations and whaling records', *Climatic Change*, 92: 461–93.

Drake, J.M. and Lodge, D.M. (2007) 'Hull fouling is a risk factor for intercontinental species exchange in aquatic ecosystems', *Aquatic Invasions*, 2: 121–31.

Eckhardt, G. (2005) The effects of ecotourism on polar bear behavior. Unpublished masters thesis, Department of Biology, University of Central Florida, Orlando, Florida.

Einarsson, N. (2009) 'From good to eat to good to watch: whale watching, adaptation and change in Icelandic fishing communities', *Polar Research*, 28: 129–38.

Ellenberg, U., Mattern, T., Seddon, P.J. and Luna, G. (2006) 'Physiological and reproductive consequences of human disturbance in Humboldt penguins: The need for species-specific visitor management', *Biological Conservation*, 133(1): 95–106.

Endresen, O., Behrens, H.L., Brynestad, S., Anderson, A.B. and Skjong, R. (2004) 'Challenges in global ballast water management', *Marine Pollution Bulletin*, 48: 615–23.

Fabry, V.J., Seibel, B.A., Feely, R.A. and Orr, J.C. (2008) 'Impacts of ocean acidification on marine fauna and ecosystem processes', *Journal of Marine Sciences*, 65: 414–32.

Forbes, D.L. (2005) 'Coastal erosion', in M. Nutall (ed.) *Encyclopedia of the Arctic*, New York: Routledge.

Fowbert, J.A. and R. Smith, R. (1994) 'Rapid population increases in native vascular plants in the Argentine Islands, Antarctic Peninsula', *Arctic and Alpine Research*, 26: 290–96.

Frenot, Y., Chown, S.L. Whinam, J., Selkirk, P.M., Convey, P., Skotnicki, M. and Bergstrom, D.M. (2005) 'Biological invasions in the Antarctic: extent, impacts and implications', *Biological Review*, 80: 45–72.

Giles, K.A., Laxon, S.W. and Ridout, A.L. (2008) 'Circumpolar thinning of Arctic sea ice following the 2007 record ice extent minimum', *Geophysical Research Letters*, 35, L22502, doi:10.1029/2008GL035710.

Gössling, S. (2002) 'Global environmental consequences of tourism', *Global Environmental Change*, 12: 283–302.

Gössling, S. and Hall, C.M. (eds) (2006) *Tourism and Global Environmental Change*, London: Routledge.

Gössling, S., Hall, C.M., Peeters, P. and Scott, D. (2010) 'The future of tourism: a climate change mitigation perspective', *Tourism Recreation Research*, 35(2), accepted.

Hall, C.M. (2006a) 'Tourism, disease and global environmental change: The fourth transition', in S. Gössling and C.M. Hall (ed.) *Tourism and Global Environmental Change: Ecological, Economic, Social and Political Interrelationships*, London: Routledge.

— (2006b) 'Tourism, biodiversity and global environmental change', in S. Gössling and C.M. Hall (ed.) *Tourism and Global Environmental Change: Ecological, Economic, Social and Political Interrelationships*, London: Routledge.

— (2009) Changing Environments in Changing Times: Sustaining the Natural Capital of Nordic Tourism, presentation at Nordic Symposium in Tourism and Hospitality Research, University of Southern Denmark, Ejsberg, October. Online. Available: HTTP: http://canterbury-nz.academia.edu/CMichaelHall (accessed 1 November 2009)

— (2010) 'Changing paradigms and global change: from sustainable to steady-state tourism', *Tourism Recreation Research*, 35(2): (in press).

Hall, C.M. and Lew, A. (2009) *Understanding and Managing Tourism Impacts: An Integrated Approach*. London: Routledge.

Halpern, N. (2008) 'Lapland's airports: facilitating the development of international tourism in a peripheral region', *Scandinavian Journal of Hospitality and Tourism*, 8(1): 25–47.

Hellmann, J.J., Byers, J.E., Bierwagen, B.G. and Dukes, J.S. (2008) 'Five potential consequences of climate change for invasive species', *Conservation Biology*, 22(3): 534–43.

Hewitt, K. (2002) 'Introduction: landscape assemblages and transitions in cold regions', in K. Hewitt, M-L, Byrne, M. English and G. Young (eds) *Landscapes of Transition: Landform Assemblages and Transformations in Cold Regions*. Dordrecht: Kluwer

Academic.

Huntington, H.P., Hamilton, L.C., Nicolson, C., Brunner, R., Lynch, A., Ogilvie, A.E.J. and Voinov, A. (2007) 'Toward understanding the human dimensions of the rapidly changing Arctic system: insights and approaches from five HARC projects', *Regional Environmental Change*, 7: 173–86.

Instanes, A., Anisimov, O., Brigham, L., Goering, D., Ladanyi, B., Larsen, J.O. and Khrustalev, L.N. (2005) 'Infrastructure: buildings, support systems, and industrial facilities', in C. Symon, L. Arris and B. Heal (eds) *Arctic Climate Impact Assessment* Cambridge: Cambridge University Press.

Intergovernmental Panel on Climate Change (IPCC) (2007a) *Climate Change 2007: Impacts, Adaptation and Vulnerability. Contribution of Working Group II to the Fourth Assessment Report of the Intergovernmental Panel on Climate Change*, Cambridge: Cambridge University Press.

— (2007b) 'Summary for Policymakers', in *Intergovernmental Panel on Climate Change Fourth Assessment Report Climate Change 2007: Synthesis Report*. Cambridge: Cambridge University Press.

Johnson, C.T., Boyce, M.S., Case, R.L., Cluff, H.D., Gau, R.J., Gunn, A. and Mulders, R. (2005) 'Cumulative Effects of Human Developments on Arctic Wildlife', *Wildlife Monographs*, 160(July): 1–36.

Kasperson, R.E. (1992) 'Human response to environmental degradation in endangered areas', *Acta Universitatis Carolinae Geographica*, 1: 29–36.

Kaufman, D.S., Schneider, D.P., McKay, N.P., Ammann, C.M., Bradley, R.S., Briffa, K.R., Miller, G.H., Otto-Bliesner, B.L., Overpeck, J.T., Vinther, B.M., and Arctic Lakes 2k Project Members (2009) 'Recent warming reverses long-term Arctic cooling', *Science*, 325(5945): 1236–39.

Kwok, R. and Rothrock, D.A. (2009) 'Decline in Arctic sea ice thickness from submarine and ICESat records: 1958–2008', *Geophysical Research Letters*, 36(15), L15501 doi:10.1029/2009GL039035.

Lamers, M. (2009) The future of tourism in Antarctica: challenges for sustainability, PhD Thesis, University of Maastricht.

Lee, D.S., Fahey, D.W., Forster, P.M., Newton, P.J., Wit, R.C.N., Lim, L.L., Owen, B., and Sausen, R. (2009) 'Aviation and global climate change in the 21st century', *Atmospheric Environment*, 43(22-23): 3520–3537.

Lemelin, R.H. and Wiersma, E.C. (2007) 'Gazing upon Nanuk, the polar bear: the social and visual dimensions of the wildlife gaze in Churchill, Manitoba', *Polar Geography*, 30(1): 37–53.

Lemelin, R.H., Fennell, D. and Smale, B. (2008) 'Polar bear viewers as deep ecotourists: how specialised are they?' *Journal of Sustainable Tourism*, 16(1): 42–62.

Lemke, P., Ren, J., Alley, R., Allison, I., Carrasco, J., Flato, G., Fujii, Y., Kaser, G., Mote, P., Thomas R., and Zhang, T. (2007) Observations: change in snow, ice and frozen ground. Climate Change 2007: The Physical Science Basis. Contribution of Working Group I to the Fourth Assessment Report of the Intergovernmental Panel on Climate Change, S. Solomon, D. Qin, M. Manning, Z. Chen, M. Marquis, K.B. Averyt, M. Tignor and H.L. Miller (eds), Cambridge: Cambridge University Press.

Lewis, P.N., Hewitt, C.L., Riddle, M. and McMinn, A. (2003) 'Marine introductions in the Southern Ocean: an unrecognized hazard to biodiversity', *Marine Pollution Bulletin*, 46: 213–23.

Lewis, P.N., Riddle, M.J. and Smith, S.D.A. (2005) 'Assisted passage or passive drift: a comparison of alternative transport mechanisms for non-indigenous coastal species into the Southern Ocean', *Antarctic Science*, 17(2), 183–91.

McBean, G., Alekseev, G., Chen, D., Førland, E., Fyfe, J., Groisman, P.Y., King, R., Melling, H., Vose, R. and Whitfield, P.H. (2005) 'Arctic climate: past and present', in C. Symon, L. Arris and B. Heal (eds) *Arctic Climate Impact Assessment,* Cambridge: Cambridge University Press.

Mallory, M.L. (2006) 'The Northern fulmar (*Fulmarus glacialis*) in Arctic Canada: ecology, threats, and what it tells us about marine environmental conditions', *Environmental Reviews*, 14(3): 187–216.

Meyer, W.B. and Turner II, B.L. (1995) 'The Earth transformed: trends, trajectories, and patterns', in R.J. Johnston, P.J. Taylor and M. Watts (eds) *Geographies of Global Change: Remapping the World in the Late Twentieth Century*. Oxford: Blackwell.

Molnar, J.L., Gamboa, R.L., Revenga, C. and Spalding, M.D. (2008) 'Assessing the global threat of invasive species to marine biodiversity', *Frontiers of Ecology and Environment*, 6(9): 485–92.

Natural Resources Defense Council (2005) Global Warming Puts the Arctic on Thin Ice. Online. Available HTTP: http://www.nrdc.org/globalwarming/qthinice.asp (accessed 1 August 2009).

National Wildlife Federation (2008) *The Polar Bear: The Canary in the Coal Mine*. Fact Sheet. National Wildlife Federation.

Navareen, R., Forrest, S.C., Dagit, R.G., Blight, L.K., Trivelpiece, W.Z. and Trivelpiece, S.G (2001) 'Zodiac landings by tourist ships in the Antarctic Peninsula region, 1989–99', *Polar Record*, 37: 121–32.

NOBANIS (European Network on Invasive Alien Species) (2009) Country statistics. Online. Available HTTP: http://www.nobanis.org/ (accessed 1 November 2009).

Nuttall, M., Berkes, F., Forbes, B., Kofinas, G., Vlassova, T. and Wenzel, G. (2005) 'Hunting, herding, fishing and gathering: indigenous peoples and renewable resource use in the Arctic', in C. Symon, L. Arris and B. Heal (eds) *Arctic Climate Impact Assessment*, Cambridge: Cambridge University Press.

Orr, J. C., Fabry, V.J., Aumont, O., Bopp, L., Doney, S.C., Feely, R.A., Gnanadesikan, A., Gruber, N., Ishida, A., Joos, F., Key, R.M., Lindsay, K., Maier-Reimer, E., Matear, R., Monfray, P., Mouchet, A., Najjar, R.G., Plattner, G-K., Rodgers, K.B., Sabine, C.L., Sarmiento, J.L., Schlitzer, R., Slater, R.D., Totterdell, I.J., Weirig, M-F., Yamanaka, Y. and Yool., A. (2005) 'Anthropogenic ocean acidification over the twenty-first century and its impact on calcifying organisms', *Nature*, 437: 681–86.

Otley, H.M. (2005) 'Nature-based tourism: experiences at the Volunteer Point penguin colony in the Falkland Islands', *Marine Ornithology*, 33: 181–87.

Parkinson, C.L. (2002) 'Trends in the length of the Southern Ocean sea ice season, 1979–99', *Annals of Glaciology*, 34: 435–40.

Peck, L.S., Convey, P. and Barnes, D.K.A. (2006) 'Environmental constraints on life histories in Antarctic ecosystems: tempos, timings and predictability', *Biological Reviews,* 81: 75–109.

Pfeiffer, S. and Peter H.U. (2004) 'Ecological studies toward the management of an Antarctic tourist landing site (Penguin Island, South Shetland Islands)', *Polar Record*, 40: 1–9.

Pfeiffer, S., Buesser, C., Mustafa, O. and Peter, H.U. (2007) 'Tourism growth and proposed management solutions in the Fildes Peninsula region (King George Island, Antarctica)', *Tourism in Marine Environments*, 4(2–3): 151–65.

Prowse, T.D., Wrona, F.J. and Power, G. (2004) Dams, reservoirs and flow regulation, in *Threats to Water Availability in Canada*. National Water Resource Institute, Scientific

Assessment Report No. 3, Ottawa: Environment Canada.

Prowse, T.D., Wrona, F.J., Reist, J., Hobbie, J.E., Lévesque, L.M.J. and Vincent, W. (2006) 'General features of the Arctic relevant to climate change in freshwater ecosystems', *Ambio*, 35(7): 330–38.

Pyke, C.P., Thomas, R., Porter, R.D., Hellmann, J.J., Dukes, J.S., Lodge, D.M. and Chavarria, G. (2008) 'Current practices and future opportunities for policy on climate change and invasive species,' *Conservation Biology*, 22: 585–92.

Ragen, T.J., Huntington, H.P. and Hovelsrud, G.K. (2008) 'Conservation of Arctic marine mammals faced with climate change', *Ecological Applications*, 18 (Supplement: Arctic Marine Mammals): S166–S174.

Rahel, F.J. and Olden, J.D. (2008) 'Assessing the effects of climate change on aquatic invasive species', *Conservation Biology*, 22(3): 521–33.

Rapp, W. (2008) Exotic Plant Management in Glacier Bay National Park and Preserve Gustavus, Alaska, Summer 2007 Field Season Report. Gustavus: National Park Service.

Rayfuse, R. (2009) 'Protecting marine biodiversity in polar areas beyond national jurisdiction', *Review of European Community & International Environmental Law*, 17(1): 3–13.

Reist, J., Wrona, F.J., Prowse, T.D., Power, M., Dempson, J.B., Beamish, D., King, J.R., Carmichael, T.J. and Sawatsky, C.D. (2006) 'General effects of climate change on arctic fishes and fish populations', *Ambio*, 35(7): 370–80.

Robinson, S.A., Wasley, J. and Tobin, A.K. (2003) 'Living on the edge: plants and global change in continental and maritime Antarctica', *Global Change Biology*, 9: 1681–1717.

Romanovsky, V.E., Burgess, M., Smith, S., Yoshikawa, K. and Brown, J. (2002) 'Permafrost temperature records: indicators of climate change', *EOS Transactions*, 83: 589–94.

Round, A. (2008) 'A Question of Perspective', *Destinations of the World News*, issue 21(March): 47–49.

Royal Society (2005) *Ocean Acidification Due to Increasing Atmospheric Carbon Dioxide*. Policy Document 12/05, London: The Royal Society.

Schiermeier, Q. (2009) Arctic sea ice levels third-lowest on record, *Nature*, 18 September, doi:10.1038/news.2009.930. Online. Available HTTP: http://www.nature.com/news/2009/090918/full/news.2009.930.html (accessed 19 September 2009).

Schindler, D.W. and Smol, J.P. (2006) 'Cumulative effects of climate warming and other human activities on freshwaters of Arctic and Subarctic North America', *AMBIO: A Journal of the Human Environment*, 35(4): 160–68.

Serreze, M.C. and Francis, J.A. (2006) 'The Arctic amplification debate', *Climatic Change*, 76: 241–64.

Slaymaker, O. and Kelly, R.E.J. (2007) *The Cryosphere and Global Environmental Change*. Oxford: Blackwell.

Tavares, M. and De Melo, G.A.S. (2004) 'Discovery of the first known benthic invasive species in the Southern Ocean: the North America spider *Hyas araneus* found in the Antarctic Peninsula', *Antarctic Science*, 16: 129–31.

Tejedo, P. and Benayas, J. (2006) Is maritime Antarctic ready for the impacts of commercial tourism? In D. Siegrist, C. Clivaz, M. Hunziker and S. Iten (eds) *Exploring the Nature of Management. Proceedings of the Third International Conference on Monitoring and Management of Visitor Flows in Recreational and Protected Areas*. University of Applied Sciences, Rapperswil, Switzerland, 13–17 September 2006.

Tejedo, P., Justel, A., Benayas, J., Rico, E., Convey, P. and Quesada, A. (2009) 'Soil trampling in an Antarctic Specially Protected Area: tools to assess levels of human impact', *Antarctic Science*, 21(3): 229–36.

Theoharides, K.A. and Dukes, J.S. (2007) 'Plant invasion pattern and process: factors affecting plant invasion at four spatio-temporal stages', *New Phytologist*, 176: 256–73.

Tin, T., Fleming, Z.L., Hughes, K.A., Ainley, D.G., Convey, P., Moreno, C.A., Pfeiffer, S., Scott, J. and Snape, I. (2009) 'Impacts of local human activities on the Antarctic environment', *Antarctic Science*, 21(1): 3–33.

Trathan, P.N., Forcadaa, J. Atkinson, R., Downie, R.H. and Shears, J.R. (2008) 'Population assessments of gentoo penguins (Pygoscelis papua) breeding at an important Antarctic tourist site, Goudier Island, Port Lockroy, Palmer Archipelago, Antarctica', *Biological Conservation*, 141(12): 3019–28.

Turner, B.L., Clark, W.C., Kates, R.W., Richards, J.F., Mathews, J.Y. and Meyer, W.B. (eds) (1990) *The Earth as Transformed by Human Action*, Cambridge: Cambridge University Press.

Turner, J., Overland, J. and Walsh, J. (2007) 'An Arctic and Antarctic perspective on recent climate change', *International Journal of Climatology*, 27: 277–93.

Union of Concerned Scientists (2008) Federal Science Agencies Release Annual Temperature Predictions, Statement by UCS Climate Scientist Melanie Fitzpatrick, Union of Concerned Scientists, 16 December, 2008. Online. Available HTTP: http://www.ucsusa.org/news/press_release/federal-science-agencies-1077.html (accessed 1 August 2009).

United Nations World Tourism Organization, United Nations Environment Programme and World Meteorological Organization (UNWTO–UNEP–WMO)(2008). *Climate Change and Tourism: Responding to Global Challenges*. Madrid: UNWTO, UNEP and WMO.

Vaughan, D.G., Marshall, G.J., Connolley, W.M., Parkinson, C.L., Mulvaney, R., Hodgson, D.A., King, J.C., Pudsey, C.J. and Turner, J. (2003) 'Recent rapid regional climate warming on the Antarctic Peninsula', *Climatic Change*, 60: 243–74.

Walker, B., Holling, C.S., Carpenter, S.R., and Kinzig, A. (2004) 'Resilience, adaptability and transformability in social–ecological systems', *Ecology and Society*, 9(2): 5. [online] URL: http://www.ecologyandsociety.org/vol9/iss2/art5/

Walker, B.G., Boersma, P.D. and Wingfield, J.C. (2005) 'Physiological and behavioral differences in Magellanic penguin chicks in undisturbed and tourist-visited locations of a colony', *Conservation Biology*, 19(5): 1571–77.

Walsh, J.E. (2009) 'A comparison of Arctic and Antarctic climate change, present and future', Antarctic Science, 21 (3): 179–188.

Walsh, J.E., Anisimov, O., Hagen, J.O.M., Jakobsson, T., Oerlemans, J., Prowse, T.D., Romanovsky, V., Savelieva, N., Serreze, M., Shiklomanov, I. and Solomon, S. (2005) 'Cryosphere and hydrology', in C. Symon, L. Arris and B. Heal (eds) *Arctic Climate Impact Assessment,* Cambridge: Cambridge University Press.

Weller, G., Bush, E., Callaghan, T.V., Corell, R., Fox, S., Furgal, C., Hoel, A.H., Huntington, H., Källén, E., Kattsov, V.M.,.Klein, D.R., Loeng, H., Martello, M.L., MacCracken, M., Nuttall, M., Prowse, T.D., Reiersen, L.-O., Reist, J.D., Tanskanen, A., Walsh, J.E., Weatherhead, B. and Wrona, F.J (2005) 'Summary and synthesis of the ACIA', in C. Symon, L. Arris and B. Heal (eds) *Arctic Climate Impact Assessment*, Cambridge: Cambridge University Press.

Wheeler, M., de Villiers, M.S. and Majiedt, P.A. (2009) 'The effect of frequency and nature of pedestrian approaches on the behaviour of wandering albatrosses at sub-Antarctic Marion Island', *Polar Biology*, 32(2): 197–205.

Whinam, J. and Copson, G. (2006) 'Sphagnum moss: an indicator of climate change in the sub-Antarctic', *Polar Record*, 42: 43–49.

Williams, R. and Crosbie, K. (2007) 'Whales and Antarctic tourism', *Tourism in Marine Environments*, 4(2/3): 195–202.

Wojczulanis–Jakubas, K., Jakubas, D. and Stempniewicz, L. (2008) 'Avifauna of Hornsund area, SW Spitsbergen: present state and recent changes', *Polish Polar Research*, 29(2): 187–97.

Wookey, P.A. (2007) 'Climate change and biodiversity in the Arctic–Nordic perspectives', *Polar Research*, 26: 96–103.

3 Cruise Tourism in Arctic Canada

Navigating a warming climate

E.J. Stewart, S.E.L. Howell, D. Draper, J. Yackel and A. Tivy

Introduction

Consistent with cruise-ship activity in other polar locations, the number of cruise vessels visiting the Canadian Arctic has increased substantially since 2006, when the number of cruise ships doubled from 11 cruises in 2005 to 22 cruises in 2006 (Buhasz 2006). This trajectory of growth was expected to continue during the 2008 summer cruise season, when the Canadian Arctic was projected to host 26 separate cruises. These figures illustrate considerable and sustained growth in this niche cruise sector. The number of anticipated cruises in 2008 is particularly impressive given the absence of the MS *Explorer*, the veteran polar cruise vessel who before her sinking off the Antarctic Peninsula in the 2007 Austral summer was a regular visitor to Arctic Canada. This growth of the cruise sector in Arctic Canada confirms observations from elsewhere that the ocean environment has become one of the fastest-growing areas of the world's tourism industry (Miller and Auyong 1991; Orams 1999; Hall 2001).

Given the ever-expanding body of scientific and indigenous knowledge indicating that climate-induced changes are likely to open up shipping activity in the Arctic region, some commentators suggest decreased sea ice within the Canadian Arctic promotes better ship access, and despite reduced opportunities to see ice-dependent wildlife, cruise tourism will inevitably continue to increase (Pagnan 2003; ACIA 2004; Johnston 2006). While the evidence continues to mount pertaining to a changing climate, it is still uncertain if the observed change is the result of anthropogenic forcing or natural variability (Serreze and Francis 2006), but what is certain is that Arctic regions are expected to exhibit the first signs of change (IPCC 2001, 2007). The reported increases in Arctic surface air temperatures (Rigor *et al.* 2000; Wang and Key 2003) that are accompanied with reported decreases in Arctic sea ice extent (Serreze *et al.* 2007) and thickness (Rothrock *et al.* 2008) are reflective of this polar amplification.

The objective of this chapter is to examine ice regimes in the Canadian Arctic to help understand past, present and possible future cruise activity in the region. We begin with a brief description of the sea ice regimes of the Canadian Arctic, followed by a review of past and current trends in cruise tourism in Arctic Canada. Using the Canadian Ice Service digital ice charts, we examine changes in sea conditions over the past 39 years in order to provide the basis for a discussion about the future of cruise tourism in these regions.

Sea ice regimes in the Canadian Arctic

The Canadian Arctic is often divided into western and eastern sub-regions, both of which contain the Queen Elizabeth Islands and span the Northwest Passage (Figure 3.1). The eastern and western regions also both contain a mix of seasonal first-year ice and multiyear ice but are governed by different ice regimes. First-year sea ice grows and decays seasonally, whereas multiyear sea ice has survived at least one summer's melt. In the absence of ridging, the thickness of first-year ice is typically no more than 2 m, whereas multiyear sea ice can range between 3 and 4 m thick (Maykut and Untersteiner 1971). During the winter, land-fast seasonal first-year ice and multiyear ice cover most of the Canadian Arctic until break-up commences in July only to refreeze again in October (Falkingham *et al.* 2001; Falkingham *et al.* 2002; Melling 2002).

Regions in the western Canadian Arctic can contain as much as 50% multiyear ice because of the influx from the Canadian Basin and in situ formation (McLaren *et al.* 1984; Falkingham *et al.* 2002; Howell *et al.* 2006; Kwok 2006). In contrast, sea ice in the eastern Canadian Arctic is mainly seasonal first-year ice (Falkingham *et al.* 2001). Sea ice in the Queen Elizabeth Islands is a mix of first-year ice and multiyear ice and in a typical year, less than 20% of multiyear ice and 50% of first-year ice melts; thus, sea ice concentrations are high during summer (Melling 2002). Sea ice within the Canadian Basin adjacent to the western Canadian Arctic is not land-fast; instead this perennial multiyear ice circulates according to the predominately anticyclonic circumpolar gyre (also known as the Beaufort Gyre) centered about 80′N, 155′W (Thorndike 1986). As a result, sea ice is forced up continuously against the Queen Elizabeth Islands and is ridged heavily, creating some of the oldest and thickest sea ice in the world, potentially reaching over 6–8 m high (Bourke and Garrett 1987; Agnew *et al.* 2001; Melling 2002).

Cruise ships have travelled through these varying ice regimes of the Canadian Arctic in the past, and are expected to continue to do so, in increasing numbers, into the future. Drawing on desk-based reviews of literature and computer-based reviews of polar travel websites (the reviewed sites in 2006 and 2008 include Polar Cruises, Hapag-Lloyd, Cruise North, Adventure Canada, Polar Star Expeditions and Zegraham Expeditions), we now turn to an overview of past and current cruise tourism activity in the Canadian Arctic.

Cruise tourism in the Canadian Arctic

Compared with other Arctic locations, the cruising phenomenon started later in Arctic Canada, and currently, cruise tourism there is a great deal smaller by volume of cruise passengers. For example, in Arctic Scandinavia cruising can be traced to as early as 1845, when regular steamship tours were conducted from Norway's most northerly town, Hammerfest, to North Cape (Stewart *et al.* 2005).

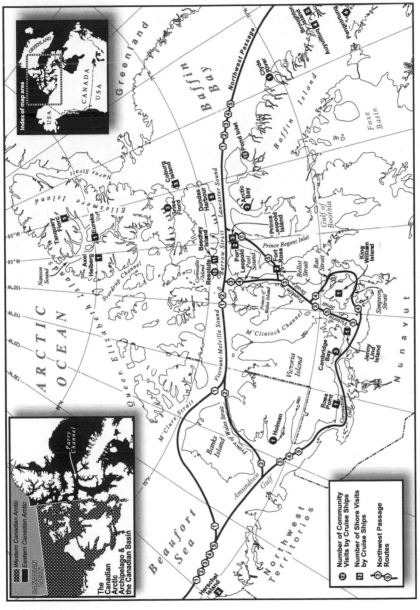

Figure 3.1 The Canadian Arctic archipelago: routes through the Northwest Passage and planned toursim cruises for 2006

Since then, Norway has established a stable cruise industry, with approximately 324,000 passengers visiting by cruise ship in 2005 (Cruise Norway 2008). In Greenland cruise tourism first began in the 1930s (Kaae 2006), with the number of cruise passengers increasing rapidly since 2005. Greenland's cruise statistics for 2006 show 33 cruise ships, making a total of 116 calls at port with approximately 22,000 guests onboard, a 33% increase in cruise passengers from 2005 (Greenland Statistics 2008). However, the number of cruise passengers visiting Alaska eclipses, by far, all other polar cruise locations (including Antarctica) with 876,000 cruise passengers recorded in 2004 (Snyder 2007) (see also chapter 1 [this volume]).

Cruise tourism in Arctic Canada started in 1984 when the MS *Explorer* traversed the Northwest Passage. With 98 passengers on board, the cruise ship traversed the Passage in 23 days, only the 33rd full passage ever (Marsh and Staple 1995; Jones 1999). There was sufficient tourist interest in the historically important Northwest Passage to warrant similar crossing attempts. However, only two transits were successful during the next 4 years (Marsh and Staple 1995), but from 1992 to 2004 a more regular pattern of cruise activity emerged, with between one and three successful voyages being completed each year (Table 3.1). A turning point came in 2006, when the number of cruises in Arctic Canada doubled to 22 (Buhasz 2006). In 2007, an overall stabilisation of cruise activity in the Canadian Arctic was observed, but in 2008, six vessels were projected to operate in the Canadian Arctic and carry passengers on 26 separate cruises (although four of these cruises were either repositioning tours or cruises predominately based in the Newfoundland and Labrador region). From 2006 to 2008 the length of the cruise season in Arctic Canada increased by 4 weeks (Stewart *et al.* 2008). In 2006, the season was 95 days in length (26 June to 28 September) but in 2008 the season was planned to start on 11 June and finish on 14 October (126 days). This means that the cruise season was starting 2 weeks earlier, and finishing 2 weeks later than it did in 2006. This finding is remarkable given this increase has occurred in a short 3- year period. However, despite overall growth, there is a slight decline in cruise activity in some parts of Arctic Canada, and a small increase in activity elsewhere in the region. In part, this variability is due to the absence of the MS *Explorer* who, before her sinking in Antarctica, was a regular visitor to Arctic Canada.

Of the variety of existing routes through the Northwest Passage (Figure 3.1), by far the most commonly traversed route for tourism vessels is route 3 (see Table 3.1). This route passes through Lancaster Sound and Barrow Strait then southward through Peel Sound, along Franklin Strait and Victoria Strait before heading west into the Coronation Gulf and Amundsen Gulf. Depending on the chosen route through the Passage, cruise-ship passengers have visited communities and other places of natural, historic or cultural interest. Along the Northwest Passage, passengers have taken part in excursions to the communities of Holman, Cambridge Bay, Resolute and Pond Inlet, as well as shore landings to places such as Beechey Island, Hershel Island and King William Island (Figure 3.1). The route through the Coronation Gulf and Amundsen Gulf is popular as there is an

Table 3.1 Cruise ship transits through the Northwest Passage (1984-2004) (after Headland, 2004)

No.	Year	Ship	Vessel type	Route through Northwest Passage[1]	Ship registry
1	1984	*Explorer*	Ice-strengthened	4	Sweden
2	1985	*World Discoverer*	Ice-strengthened	4	Singapore
3	1988	*Society Explorer* (formerly *Explorer*)	Ice-strengthened	3	Bahamas
4	1992	*Frontier Spirit*	Ice-strengthened	3	Bahamas
5	1992	*Kapitan Khlebnikov*	Ice-breaker	3	Russia
6	1993	*Kapitan Khlebnikov*	Ice-breaker	3	Russia
7	1993	*Frontier Spirit*	Ice-strengthened	3	Bahamas
8	1994	*Kapitan Khlebnikov*	Ice-breaker	2	Russia
9	1994	*Kapitan Khlebnikov*	Ice-breaker (return voyage)	2	Russia
10	1994	*Hanseatic*	Ice-strengthened	3	Bahamas
11	1995	*Kapitan Khlebnikov*	Ice-breaker	5	Russia
12	1996	*Kapitan Dranitsyn*	Ice-breaker	5	Russia
13	1996	*Hanseatic*	Ice-strengthened (grounded in Simpson Strait)	3	Bahamas
14	1997	*Hanseatic*	Ice-strengthened (escorted to Victoria Strait)	3	Bahamas
15	1997	*Kapitan Khlebnikov*	Ice-breaker	3	Russia
16	1998	*Kapitan Khlebnikov*	Ice-breaker	3	Russia

Table 3.1 continued

No.	Year	Ship	Vessel type	Route through Northwest Passage[1]	Ship registry
17	1998	*Hanseatic*	Ice-strengthened (escourted to Victoria Strait)	3	Bahamas
18	1999	*Kapitan Dranitsyn*	Ice-breaker	3	Russia
19	2000	*Hanseatic*	Ice-strengthened	3	Bahamas
20	2000	*Kapitan Dranitsyn*	Ice-breaker (cirumnavigated Arctic)	3	Russia
21	2001	*Kapitan Khlebnikov*	Ice-breaker	1	Russia
22	2001	*Kapitan Khlebnikov*	Ice-breaker (return voyage)	1	Russia
23	2002	*Kapitan Khlebnikov*	Ice-breaker	3	Russia
24	2002	*Hanseatic*	Ice-strengthened	3	Bahamas
25	2003	*Bremen* (formerly *Frontier Spirit*)	Ice-strengthened	3	Bahamas
26	2003	*Bremen* (formerly *Frontier Spirit*)	Ice-strengthened	3	Bahamas
27	2004	*Kapitan Khlebnikov*	Ice-breaker	5	Russia

Route 1: traverses the more northerly sections of the Northwest Passage passing through Viscount Melville Sound, McClure Strait and into the Beaufort Sea (has been traveled in an easterly and westerly direction).

Route 2: also passes through Viscount Melville Sound but veers in a south-westerly direction into the Prince of Wales Strait before emerging in the Beaufort Sea via the Amundsen Gulf (has been traveled in an easterly and westerly direction).

Route 3: vessels travel through Lancaster Sound and Barrow Strait then southward through Peel Sound, and then south-west along Franklin Strait and Victoria Strait before heading west into the Coronation Gulf and Amundsen Gulf (has been traveled in an easterly and westerly direction).

Route 4: (a variation of route 3) takes vessels along the Rae and Simpson Straits, around King William Island, and was successfully navigated by Explorer on the maiden voyage through the Northwest Passage in 1984.

Route 5: takes a course along the Prince Regent Inlet and through the narrow Bellot Strait into the Franklin and Victoria Straits, and out into the Coronation and Amundsen Gulfs.

opportunity to visit the historically important community of Cambridge Bay.

More favorable ice conditions, allied with spectacular scenery, good wildlife viewing and opportunities to also visit Greenland, mean that the eastern Canadian Arctic has continued to receive the most cruises in the Canadian Arctic. For example, Baffin Island has been circumnavigated multiple times and communities on Baffin Island, such as Pangnirtung and Pond Inlet, host cruise passengers on a regular basis (Figure 3.1). By contrast, the ice-congested conditions of the Queen Elizabeth Islands usually deter cruise ship travel. Since the Beaufort Sea is considered the entry/exit point into and out of the Northwest Passage, shore visits are uncommon along Canada's northern coast. Although Herschel Island has hosted cruise vessels in the past, ships passing through this region usually are inbound or outbound to Alaska via the Bering Strait.

As Figure 3.1 illustrates, the frequency of community and shore visits varies throughout the region. During the 2006 cruise season, three traverses of the Northwest Passage were made. The *Akademik Ioffe*, an ice-strengthened vessel built in Finland in 1989, sailed the Passage via Peel Sound, as did the *Bremen*. The *Kapitan Khlebnikov* cruised through the Passage from west to east, but because of heavy ice conditions near Barrow, Alaska, its arrival into Cambridge Bay, the first scheduled community visit, was delayed significantly. During the 2006 cruise season, communities such as Pond Inlet on Baffin Island hosted 12 cruise ships over a 41-day period, including the Germany-based ship, the *Hanseatic* (Figure 3.2). Resolute on Cornwallis Island is an entry/exit point into or out of the Canadian High Arctic, and regularly scheduled flights operate between Resolute, Cambridge Bay, Iqaluit and Ottawa. During the 2006 season, Resolute hosted 10 cruise ships. The community of Pangnirtung hosted four cruise ships; the hamlet of Arctic Bay hosted three cruise ships; and Grise Fiord, the most northerly community in Canada, located on the southern shore of Ellesmere Island, hosted three cruise ships. Also in 2006, the *Kapitan Khlebnikov* (Figure 3.3) ventured as far north as Tanquary Fiord on her Ellesmere Island tour.

In 2008, the Northwest Passage anticipated five passenger cruises, with the *Akademik Ioffe* and *Orlova* both making two sailings each, and the *Bremen* making one crossing. For the 2008 cruise season, Pond Inlet expected to host nine cruise vessels (although anecdotal evidence suggests that the community also receives at least one unexpected cruise ship every year), Pangnirtung anticipated six cruise ships, and Qikiqtarjuaq expected three cruise ships. The planned itinerary of the *Kapitan Khlebnikov* included visits to Quttinirpaaq National Park on two occasions, first via Tanquary Fjord and, immediately following this cruise the icebreaker transited passengers along the east coast of Ellesmere Island to Fort Conger (Stewart *et al.* 2008).

This brief overview of cruise tourism in Arctic Canada (1984–2008) reveals that the industry has moved beyond its infancy, and is now entering a maturing phase with increased numbers of vessels, a lengthening season, more demanding routes, and more regular and predictable patterns of activity. A range of factors is likely to support this maturing phase of the industry, including increasing tourist

Figure 3.2 The *Hanseatic* cruise ship visiting Pond Inlet, Nunavut (August 2006)
            (photograph by Emma J. Stewart)

Figure 3.3 The *Kapitan Khlebnikov* cruise ship visitng Cambridge Bay, Nunavut
            (photograph by Emma J. Stewart)

demand for travel to remote places, overall popularity of cruising worldwide, more sophisticated promotional activities by tour agencies, and increasing awareness at the political and community levels about the benefits of cruise tourism. But, the extent, condition and behaviour of sea ice may well be crucial in dictating where cruise ships travel in the Canadian Arctic in the future. We now review sea ice variability in the Canadian Arctic as a basis for discussion about future Arctic cruise activity.

Sea ice variability in the Canadian Arctic: 1968–2007

Improving our understanding of future patterns of cruise activity in the Canadian Arctic requires an examination of the historical variability of sea ice in this region. One of the primary climatological products issued by the Canadian Ice Service is regional digital ice charts that provide sea ice information for Canadian Arctic waters. We used these charts to examine changes in sea ice conditions from 1968 to 2007. These charts are derived weekly through the integration of data from a variety of sources including surface observations and aerial and satellite reconnaissance; they represent the best estimate of ice conditions based on all available information at the time (Canadian Ice Service Archive Documentation Series 2007). In order to accommodate the cruise-shipping season, we confined our study period to a 17-week time window from 25 June to 15 October each year from 1968 to 2007. This 17-week time window represents the optimal period for the navigation season (Falkingham et al. 2001; Howell and Yackel 2004). From this time window, the total accumulated sea ice coverage (km^2) was calculated by summing total sea ice coverage for each of the weekly ice charts. This was also calculated for the multiyear ice coverage component of the total sea ice. These parameters provide an indicator of the amount of total sea ice and multiyear sea ice present each year and are relatively insensitive to anomalies on individual ice charts and are the most stable and robust parameter in the database to represent long-term climate change (Crocker and Carrieres 2000; Falkingham et al. 2001; Falkingham et al. 2002; Canadian Ice Service Archive Documentation Series 2007).

From 1968 to 2007 the western Canadian Arctic has experienced decreases in total sea ice coverage at −3.7% decade[-1] and the multiyear ice component has decreased at −5.1% decade[-1] (Figure 3.4). During the same time period, total sea ice coverage within the eastern Canadian Arctic has decreased at −6.8% decade[-1] and the multiyear ice component has decreased at −2.4% decade[-1] (Figure 3.5). All decreases are significant at the 99% confidence level except multiyear ice in the eastern Canadian Arctic, which is not significant at any meaningful confidence level. Despite these observed decreases in both total and multiyear sea ice, light ice years are still interspersed with heavy ice years, which points out the cyclic nature of sea ice within the Canadian Arctic. For nearly four decades the heavy ice conditions within the western Canadian Arctic have persisted because following years of light ice conditions there is always a period of recovery from dynamically imported multiyear ice from the

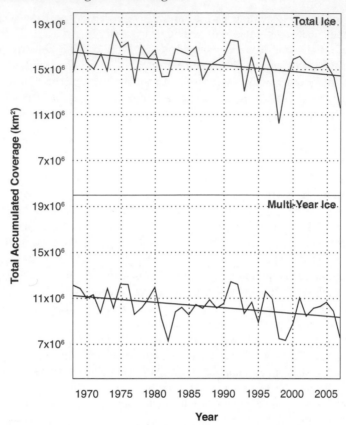

Figure 3.4 Total accumulated ice coverage for toal sea ice (top) and multi-year sea ice
(bottom) from June 25 to October 15 within the western Canadian Arctic,
1968–2007

Arctic Ocean and/or from seasonal first-year ice surviving the melt season and
being promoted to multiyear sea ice (Howell *et al.* 2008b). Multiyear ice does not
accumulate so much in the eastern Canadian Arctic because it transits more
quickly through Queen Elizabeth Islands into the warmer waters of Baffin Bay,
where it subsequently melts (Melling 2002). Indeed, the eastern and western
Canadian Arctic regions are experiencing decreases in sea ice but the cyclic nature
of multiyear sea ice within these regions has important implications for cruise-ship
operations throughout the Canadian Arctic. This highlights the major pitfall of
ships successfully navigating through Canadian Arctic waters: multiyear ice
invasions from high latitudes into the cruise channels of the Canadian Arctic
(Falkingham *et al.* 2001; Melling 2002; Howell and Yackel 2004; Howell *et al.*
2006). Multiyear ice is thicker, stronger, and takes longer to break up than seasonal
first-year ice and thus presents a serious navigation threat to transiting ships.

Decreases in total sea ice have been observed in Baffin Bay during the
1979–2004 period (Moore 2007), suggesting that entrance to the Canadian Arctic

via the Northwest Passage from Baffin Bay likely would be feasible. However, difficulties arise in the vicinity of Lancaster Sound; there has been an observable increase in multiyear ice in this region from 1968 to 2005 (see Stewart *et al.* 2007). Once in the Canadian Arctic these multiyear ice navigation hazards or 'choke points' become more abundant as the Northwest Passage is traversed. The northerly islands of the Queen Elizabeth Islands contain high concentrations of thick multiyear ice and when warming perturbations reach this region, multiyear ice can flow into the Parry Channel and subsequently into the lower latitude regions of the Canadian Arctic, creating more choke points (Melling 2002; Howell and Yackel 2004; Howell *et al.* 2006). These choke points first present themselves at Barrow Strait, southern Peel Sound, and Franklin Strait, as these regions are susceptible to multiyear ice invasions from the Queen Elizabeth Islands (Howell and Yackel 2004; Howell *et al.* 2006).

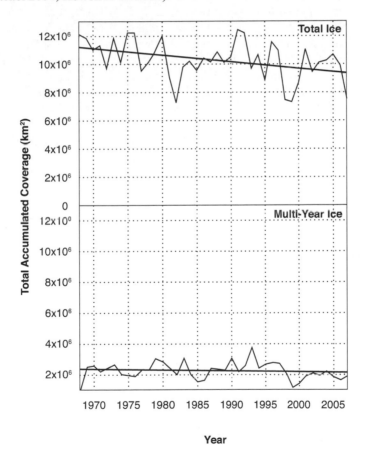

Figure 3.5 Total accumulated ice coverage for total sea ice (top) and multi-year sea ice (bottom) from June 25 to October 15 within the eastern Canadian Arctic, 1968–2007

The most direct route through the Canadian Arctic uses the Northwest Passage via Viscount Melville Sound on into M'Clure Strait and around the coast of Banks Island. This route is marred with difficult ice, particularly in the M'Clure Strait and Viscount Melville Sound, as large quantities of multiyear ice have been found in this region (Howell *et al.* 2008b). Considerable amounts of multiyear ice also are present off the western coast of Banks Island (Howell *et al.* 2008b; Galley *et al.* 2008). Cruise ships could use the Prince of Wales Strait to avoid the choke points on the western coast of Banks Island, but the strait is typically plugged with multiyear ice (Howell and Yackel 2004). The Northwest Passage route through the M'Clure Strait was open briefly during 2007, marking the second-lowest year of multiyear conditions in the western Canadian Arctic (Figure 3.4), but the cyclic nature of multiyear ice makes it difficult to suggest that this will become a regular occurrence. Moreover, it is noteworthy that very little multiyear ice was dynamically imported or formed in situ within the M'Clure Strait and Viscount Melville Sound since 2004 (Howell *et al.* 2008a). Most of the ice within these regions was seasonal first-year ice, hence the temporary clearing of the Northwest Passage in 2007, although significant, was perhaps not unexpected. Following removal of this seasonal ice in 2007, a net positive dynamic import of multiyear ice into the region was observed and the region also is conditioned to facilitate more dynamic import of multiyear ice in the upcoming years (Howell *et al.* 2008a).

An alternative, longer route through the Canadian Arctic passes through either Peel Sound or Bellot Strait. The latter route could avoid hazardous multiyear ice in Peel Sound but its narrow passageway makes it unfeasible for use by larger vessels. Regardless of which route is selected, a choke point remains in the vicinity of Victoria Strait. This Strait acts as a drain trap for multiyear ice, facilitating its slow southward movement from the high-latitude regions of the Canadian Arctic (Howell and Yackel 2004; Howell *et al.* 2006). Although Howell and Yackel (2004) showed slightly safer navigation conditions from 1991 to 2002 compared with 1969 to 1990, they attributed this improvement to the anomalous warm year of 1998, which removed most of the multiyear ice in the region. Multiyear ice increases are then apparent after 1998 as the drain-trap begins to fill again only to become full again in 2005 (Figure 3.4). The region was cleared of multiyear ice following 2007 and movement is expected to re-initialise once again (Howell *et al.* in press). The implications of sea ice variability for cruise travel in the Canadian Arctic are discussed in the following section.

Implications for cruise tourism

Based on findings drawn from the 39-year observational record identified in the previous section, there is little to no evidence to support the claims that climate change is affecting sea ice conditions in the Canadian Arctic enough to facilitate the possibility of increased ship traffic through the waters of Arctic Canada. While some increases in open water have been recognised, the navigable areas through the Northwest Passage have exhibited increases in hazardous ice conditions;

navigation choke points remain, principally because of the influx of multiyear ice into the channels of the Northwest Passage. Thus, cruise operators working in the Canadian Arctic face considerable uncertainty in the future. Rather than widespread accessibility, as some have claimed, there is likely to be much more variability of ice conditions across this region.

A key concern in what seems to be the most likely scenario of increased cruise traffic, combined with increased interannual variability in sea ice hazards, is the availability of short-term and long-range sea ice forecasts to aid in safe vessel transits, route planning and long-term planning. The National Ice Center in the USA and the Canadian Ice Service in Canada are the government departments responsible for relaying ice information to the public. Both agencies run short-term (12–24 hour) ice forecasting models (Sayed and Carrieres 1999; Van Woert *et al.* 2004). Both models were developed for the open ocean and neither model incorporates sufficient sea ice processes specific to the narrow channels of the Canadian Arctic Archipelago (such as ice bridges, fast ice, and the dynamics of ice flowing through narrow channels), to generate skillful forecasts. This is, however, an area of active research (Sayed *et al.* 2002).

Recent advances in seasonal forecasting have been incorporated into operations at both the National Ice Center and the Canadian Ice Service. Simple statistical models that exploit the long-term memory in the climate system have been successful at predicting the length of the shipping season along the northern coast of Alaska (Drobot 2003, 2005) and the start date of the shipping season in Hudson Bay (Tivy *et al.* 2007). Further research would be required to adapt these models to meet the specific needs of the tourism industry. In general, the current state of short-term and long-range sea ice forecasting is insufficiently advanced to deal with a major increase in ship traffic in Canada's ice-infested waters, particularly through the narrow channels of the Canadian Arctic Archipelago.

The consequences of climate change for prediction of tourist flows has been the subject of considerable debate in the tourism literature (see literature reviewed by Gössling and Hall 2006). Researchers have warned that destinations may experience simultaneous losses and gains in their attractiveness. Similarly, in the Canadian Arctic the changing nature of sea ice is likely to be double-edged for the cruise-tourism industry (Stewart and Draper 2006). On the one hand, an ice-free summer presents opportunities for improved ship access to some places in the Canadian Arctic. As presented previously, cruise operators may be forced to reduce their activities in the Northwest Passage and to focus more heavily on the eastern Canadian Arctic, where ice conditions are likely to continue to be more favorable for safe navigation. This is beginning to occur around Baffin Island, where communities such as Pond Inlet are emerging as favored destinations for cruise operators. In contrast, we speculate that land-based tourism activities such as sport hunting, eco/nature tourism, retreat tourism, conference tourism and winter-based tourism activities could play a more prominent role in western Canadian Arctic communities in the future.

On the other hand, the absence of ice presents significantly reduced opportunities to view ice-dependent wildlife. Predicted changes to tundra across Arctic

Canada could signal extinction of some and movement further north of other key species and biomes (Scott and Suffling 2000; Lemieux and Scott 2005). Since tourism in the Canadian Arctic is built on the expectation of viewing ice-dependent species, some commentators have suggested that cruise-ship itineraries may alter in the future, to track the changing ranges of key wildlife (ACIA 2004). Evidence from cruise tourists to Nunavut in 2006 suggested that tourists were disappointed by the small number and variety of wildlife viewed (Maher and Meade 2008). Given that tourism in Arctic Canada relies on wildlife in particular but also on snow, ice, mountains and glaciers to sell cruise experiences, a key question emerges: would people really continue to visit Arctic Canada if charismatic fauna such as bears and whales have moved elsewhere? Some tour operators might speculate that the variability of wildlife sightings from cruise vessels is all part of the charm, and thrill, of Arctic cruising. But, how long can tour agencies continue to sell Arctic cruises based on images of polar bears, narwhal and beluga whale without delivering on those promises?

The momentum of this growth in Arctic cruise tourism presents many challenges to Arctic Canada particularly because, to date, there has been little coordinated, trans-regional planning for the sustained development of cruise tourism in Arctic Canada (Stewart and Draper 2006). As has been the experience elsewhere in the world, cruise operators often are responsible for planning cruise itineraries, with the result being sporadic development of cruise activity (Liburd 2001). Evidence suggests that communities and agencies in Arctic Canada need to take a long-term view toward adoption of holistic, integrated planning approaches for tourism. As Johnson (2002) suggests, operators need to continue to invest in good environmental practice (such as implementing biosecurity measures), and both operators and communities need to raise current levels of environmental awareness and to practise environmentally responsible activities. Not only is political will required to safeguard Arctic destinations, greater profit-sharing must occur between shareholders and destination communities. There is a sense of urgency to address these issues because changes ushered in by climate change are likely to accelerate the development of cruise tourism in some regions, while decelerating development in other regions of the Canadian Arctic (Stewart and Draper 2006).

Conclusion

Arguably, global climate change is the most pressing environmental concern for tourism (Patterson *et al*. 2006). The changing global climate has significant implications for the key land, sea and ice resources of Arctic tourism and for the people and wildlife that inhabit the region (ACIA 2004). The sensitivity of tourism to climate change is evident especially in the polar cruise sector, and this is particularly the case considering recent evidence that finds that the transition to a summertime sea ice-free Arctic may occur much earlier than originally forecast (Stroeve *et al*. 2007). However, as we have illustrated, cruise operators must still exercise caution in their activities in the Canadian Arctic because the mechanisms in place can still facilitate the continued presence of thick multiyear ice during the transition to a summertime sea ice-free Arctic.

With a trajectory of growth in mind for the cruise industry in Arctic Canada, we suggest that decision-makers be mindful of the explosive pattern of cruise activity development in Antarctica and be aware of the implicit dangers associated with commercial travel through polar waters, shown by the disastrous impact by hazardous ice of the MS *Explorer* along the Antarctic Peninsula. The sinking of this veteran cruise ship in 2007 gave global focus to the growth of polar cruising, and the implicit dangers associated with cruise vessels operating in remote polar waters (Stewart and Draper 2008). Individual, cultural and environmental safety issues need to remain at the forefront of planning efforts so that tourists can continue to enjoy and learn from the Arctic Canada environment and that Inuit people can benefit from the economic possibilities cruise tourism presents (Stewart and Draper 2006).

Acknowledgements

An earlier version of this chapter appeared in the journal *Arctic* (see Stewart *et al.* 2007) and the authors are grateful to Karen McCullough for her advice on the development of this work. We would like to express our gratitude to S.D. Drobot, A.A. Grenier, P.T. Maher and one other anonymous reviewer for their insight and valuable suggestions on the earlier paper. Respectively, Emma Stewart and Stephen Howell would like to acknowledge the Pierre Elliot Trudeau Foundation and the Natural Sciences and Engineering Research Council (NSERC) for supporting their research.

References

Agnew, T., Alt, B., Abreu, R. and Jeffers, S. (2001) *The loss of decades old sea ice plugs in the Canadian Arctic Islands.* Paper presented at the 6th Conference on Polar Meteorology and Oceanography, May 14–18 2001, San Diego.

Arctic Climate Impacts Assessment (ACIA) (2004) *Arctic climate impact assessment: impacts of a warming Arctic.* Cambridge: Cambridge University Press.Bourke, R.H. and Garrett, R.P. (1987) 'Sea ice thickness distribution in the Arctic Ocean', *Cold Regions Science and Technology,* 13: 259–80.

Buhasz, L. (2006) Northern underexposure. *Globe & Mail,* 1 July 2006.

Canadian Ice Service Archive Documentation Series (2007) *Regional charts: history, accuracy, and caveats.* Online. Available HTTP: http://ice.ec.gc.ca/IA_DOC/cisads_no_001_e.pdf (accessed 9 April 2007).

Crocker, G. and Carrieres, T. (2000) *Documentation for the Canadian Ice Service digital sea ice database* (No. Contract Report 00–02): Ballicater Consulting Ltd.

Cruise Norway (2008) *Number of cruise passengers to Norway 1997–2005.* Online. Available HTTP: http://www.cruise-norway.no/cda/storypg.aspx?id = 921&zone = 48%20&parentzone = 0&version = 1 (accessed 29 July 2008).

Drobot, S.D. (2003) 'Long-range statistical forecasting of ice severity in the Beaufort/ Chukchi Sea', *Weather and Forecasting,* 18: 1161–76.

— (2005) A seasonal outlook for the opening date of navigation to Prudhoe Bay, 1979–2000. Paper presented at the 18th International Conference on Port and Ocean Engineering Under Arctic Conditions (POAC), 26–30 June 2005, Potsdam, NY.

Falkingham, J., Chagnon, R. and McCourt, S. (2001) Sea ice in the Canadian Arctic in the 21st century. Paper presented at the 16th International Conference on Port and Ocean Engineering under Arctic Conditions (POAC), 12–17 August 2001, Ottawa, Ontario.

— (2002) Trends in sea ice in the Canadian Arctic. Paper presented at the 16th International Symposium on Ice, 2–6 December 2002, Dunedin, New Zealand.

Galley, R., Key, E., Barber, D.G., Hwang, B.J. and Ehn, J.K. (2008) 'Spatial and temporal variability of sea ice in the Southern Beaufort Sea and Amundsen Gulf: 1980–2004', *Journal of Geophysical Research*, 113, C05S95, doi:10.1029/2007JC004553.

Gössling, S. and Hall, C.M. (2006) 'Uncertainties in predicting tourist flows under scenarios of climate change', *Climatic Change,* 79: 163–73.

Greenland Statistics (2008) *Greenland's tourism statistics*. Online. Available HTTP: http://www.greenland.com/media(1468,1033)/Tourism_2006 – Statistics_Greenland. pdf.pdf (accessed 29 July 2008).

Hall, C.M. (2001) 'Trends in ocean and coastal tourism: the end of the last frontier?', *Ocean and Coastal Management,* 44: 601–18.

Headland, R. (2004) 'Northwest Passage voyages', in L. Brigham and B. Ellis (eds) *Arctic Marine Transport Workshop*. Cambridge: Scott Polar Research Institute, University of Cambridge.

Howell, S.E.L., Tivy, A., Yackel, J.J., Else, B.G.T. and Duguay, C. R. (2008a) 'Changing sea ice melt parameters in the Canadian Arctic Archipelago: implications for the future presence of multi-year ice', *Journal of Geophysical Research*, 113, C09030, doi:10.1029/2008JC004730.

Howell, S.E.L., Tivy, A., Yackel, J.J. and McCourt, S. (2008b) 'Multi-year sea ice conditions in the Western Canadian Arctic Archipelago section of the Northwest Passage: 1968–2006', *Atmosphere-Ocean,* 46: 229–42.

Howell, S.E.L., Tivy, A., Yackel, J.J. and Scharien, R. (2006) 'Application of a SeaWinds/ QuikSCAT sea ice melt algorithm for assessing melt dynamics in the Canadian Arctic Archipelago', *Journal of Geophysical Research,* 111: 1–21.

Howell, S.E.L. and Yackel, J.J. (2004) 'A vessel transit assessment of sea ice variability in the Western Arctic, 1969–2002: implications for ship navigation', *Canadian Journal of Remote Sensing,* 30: 205–25.

Intergovernmental Panel of Climate Change (IPCC) (2001) *Intergovernmental Panel on Climate Change. Climate change 2001 – The science of climate change*. Cambridge: Cambridge University Press.

— (2007) *Intergovernmental Panel on Climate Change. Climate Change 2007: the physical science basis: summary for decision makers*. Cambridge: Cambridge University Press.

Johnson, D. (2002) 'Environmentally sustainable cruise tourism: a reality check', *Marine Policy,* 26: 261–70.

Johnston, M.E. (2006) 'Impacts of global environmental change on tourism in the Polar regions', in S. Gössling and C.M. Hall (eds) *Tourism and Global Environmental Change,* London: Routledge.

Jones, C.S. (1999) 'Arctic ship tourism: an industry in adolescence', *The Northern Raven,* 13: 28–31.

Kaae, B.C. (2006) 'Greenland/Kalaallit Nunaat', in G. Baldacchino (ed.), *Extreme Tourism: Lessons from the world's coldwater destinations,* London: Elsevier.

Kwok, R. (2006) 'Exchange of sea ice between the Arctic Ocean and the Canadian Arctic Archipelago', *Geophysical Research Letters,* 33(16): L16501.1

Lemieux, C.J. and Scott, D.J. (2005) 'Climate change, biodiversity conservation and protected area planning in Canada', *The Canadian Geographer,* 49: 384–99.

Liburd, J.J. (2001) 'Cruise tourism development in the south of St. Lucia', *Tourism: An International Interdisciplinary Journal,* 49: 215–28.

McLaren, A.S., Wadhams, P. and Weintraub, R. (1984) 'The sea ice topography of M'Clure Strait in winter and summer of 1960 from submarine profiles', *Arctic,* 37: 110–20.

Maher, P.T. and Meade, D. (2008) *Cruise tourism in Auyuittuq, Sirmilik, and Quttinirpaaq National Parks: Project technical report (2007 season) – Draft.* Iqaluit: Parks Canada.

Marsh, J. and Staple, S. (1995) 'Cruise tourism in the Canadian Arctic and its implications', in C.M. Hall and M.E. Johnston (eds) *Polar Tourism: Tourism and the Arctic and Antarctic regions,* Chichester: John Wiley and Sons.

Maykut, G.A. and Untersteiner, N. (1971) 'Some results from a time dependent thermodynamic model of sea ice', *Journal of Geophysical Research,* 76: 1550–75.

Melling, H. (2002) 'Sea ice of the northern Canadian Arctic Archipelago', *Journal of Geophysical Research,* 107: PAGEPAGESPAGES

Miller, M.L. and Auyong, J. (1991) 'Coastal zone tourism: a potent force affecting environment and society', *Marine Policy,* 15: 75–99.

Moore, G.W.K. (2006) 'Reduction in seasonal sea ice conditions surrounding southern Baffin Island 1979-2004'. *Geophysical Research Letters,* 33: L20501.

Orams, M. (1999) *Marine tourism: development, impacts and management.* London: Routledge.

Pagnan, J.L. (2003) *Climate change impacts on Arctic tourism.* Paper presented at the 1st International Conference on Climate Change and Tourism, 9–11 April, Djerba, Tunisia.

Patterson, T., Bastianoni, S. and Simpson, M. (2006) 'Tourism and climate change: two-way street, or vicious/virtuous circle?' *Journal of Sustainable Tourism,* 14: 339–48.

Rigor, I.G., Colony, R.L. and Martin, S. (2000) 'Variations in surface air temperature observations in the Arctic 1979–97', *Journal of Climate,* 13: 896–914.

Rothrock, D.A., Percival, D.B. and Wensnahan, M. (2008) 'The decline in arctic sea-ice thickness: separating the spatial, annual, and interannual variability in a quarter century of submarine data', *Journal of Geophysical Research,* 113: 1–9.

Sayed, M. and Carrieres, T. (1999) Overview of a new operational ice forecasting model. Paper presented at the 9th International Offshore and Polar Engineering Conference (ISOPE), 30 May – 4 June, Brest, France.

Sayed, M., Carrieres, T., Train, H. and Savage, S. (2002) Development of an operational ice dynamics model for the Canadian Ice Service. Paper presented at the 12th International Offshore and Polar Engineering Conference (ISOPE), Kitakyushu, Japan.

Scott, D. and Suffling, R. (eds) (2000) *Climate Change and Canada's National Park System: a screening level assessment.* Hull: Environment Canada – Parks Canada.

Serreze, M.C., and Francis, J.A. (2006) 'The Arctic amplification debate', *Climatic Change,* 76: 241–64.

Serreze, M.C., Holland, M.M. and Stroeve, J.C. (2007) 'Perspectives on the Arctic's shrinking sea-ice cover', *Science,* 316: 1533–36.

Snyder, J.M. (2007) 'The polar tourism markets', in J.M. Snyder and B. Stonehouse (eds) *Prospects for polar tourism,* Wallingford: CABI.

Stewart, E.J. and Draper, D. (2006) 'Sustainable cruise tourism in Arctic Canada: an integrated coastal management approach', *Tourism in Marine Environments,* 3: 77–88.

Stewart, E.J., and Draper, D. (2008) 'The sinking of the MS Explorer: implications for cruise tourism in Arctic Canada', *Arctic (InfoNorth),* 61: 224–31.

Stewart, E.J., Draper, D., and Johnston, M.E. (2005) 'A review of tourism research in the Polar regions', *Arctic,* 58: 383–94.

Stewart, E.J., Howell, S., Draper, D., Yackel, J., and Tivy, A. (2008) *Cruise tourism in a warming Arctic: implications for northern National Parks.* Paper presented at the Parks for Tomorrow conference, May 8–13, University of Calgary, Canada.

Stewart, E.J., Howell, S. E. L., Draper, D., Yackel, J., and Tivy, A. (2007) 'Sea ice in Canada's Arctic: implications for cruise tourism', *Arctic,* 60: 370–80.

Stroeve, J., Holland, M.M., Meier, W., Scambos, T. and Serreze, M. (2007) 'Arctic sea ice decline: faster than forecast', *Geophysical Research Letters,* 34: 1–5.

Thorndike, A.S. (1986) *Kinematics of sea ice.* No. NATO ASI Series B 146.

Tivy, A., Alt, B., Howell, S., Wilson, K., and Yackel, J. (2007) 'Long-range prediction of the shipping season in Hudson Bay: a statistical approach', *Weather and Forecasting,* 22: 1063–75.

Van Woert, M.L., Zou, C., Meier, W.N., Hovey, P.D., Preller, R.H. and Posey, P.G. (2004) 'Forecast verification of the Polar Ice Prediction System (PIPS) sea ice concentration fields', *Journal of Atmospheric and Oceanic Technology,* 21: 944–57.

Wang, X. and Key, J.R. (2003) 'Recent trends in Arctic surface, cloud, and radiation properties from space', *Science,* 299: 1725–28.

4 Climate Change and Polar Bear Viewing

A case study of visitor demand, carbon emissions and mitigation in Churchill, Canada

Jackie Dawson, Emma Stewart and Daniel Scott

Introduction

Climate change represents one of the most significant challenges to humanity in the 21st century and is anticipated to have profound consequences for the highly climate-sensitive tourism sector (UNWTO-UNEP 2008). Because polar regions are expected to exhibit the first signs of environmental change associated with a warming climate (IPCC 2007), tourism destinations in these regions are thought to be particularly vulnerable to climate change. Global average temperature increased by 0.74°C between 1906 and 2005 (IPCC 2007), while Arctic regions are experiencing the most dramatic changes in climate (ACIA 2004; Overpeck *et al.* 2005; Bonsal and Prowse 2006; Richter-Menge *et al.* 2006; Furgal and Prowse 2008), with temperatures increasing at almost twice the rate of the global average (ACIA 2004; IPCC 2007). Between 1950 and 1998 mean annual temperature trends showed warming of 1.5 to 2°C in the western Canadian Arctic, 0.5°C in the central Canadian Arctic and cooling in the extreme northeast. More recent trends show warming across the entire Canadian Arctic, which is strongest in the winter and spring seasons (Furgal and Prowse 2008).

In Arctic Canada, the changing climate is likely to have significant implications for the people and wildlife that live there (Stewart and Draper 2007); as the popular and scientific press report, this is particularly the case for mega fauna such as the polar bear. More than any other species, the polar bear has become an evocative symbol of global climate change, exemplified by images in the popular media of polar bears 'struggling' to survive in a warming Arctic climate. Although some of these images may be misleading, it is clear that across the Arctic, many polar bear populations are under threat from significant decreases in sea ice extent, thickness and increased variability (see Johannessen *et al.* 1999; Vinnikov *et al.* 1999; Serrenze *et al.* 2000; ACIA 2004; Comiso and Parkinson, 2004; Derocher *et al.* 2004; Howell *et al.* 2006; Richter-Menge *et al.* 2006; Zhang and Walsh, 2006; Furgal and Prowse, 2008).

Polar bear viewing in Churchill

The community of Churchill (population 923) is located on the western shore of Hudson Bay in northern Manitoba and is known as 'the polar bear capital of the world'. It was estimated in 2003 that up to 3,000 tourists visit in the autumn to view the abundant polar bears in the region. Recent visitor number estimates reported in newspaper outlets are higher, although numbers are unconfirmed (Bruemmer 2008). In 2003, the polar bear viewing industry was calculated to have added CAN$2 million to the Churchill economy in a 6-week time period (Lemelin 2004); however, revenues in recent years are likely to be higher considering the estimated increased visitor numbers. Between October and November each year, polar bears gather along the western shore of Hudson Bay while they await the formation of sea ice (Stirling and Derocher 1993; Stirling *et al.* 1997). In essence, tourism operators have capitalised on this 'waiting period' when polar bears are relatively inactive but highly visible, providing tourists with an opportunity to view polar bears in their natural habitat with relative ease, and in relative safety (Lemelin 2005).

Polar bear viewing typically occurs 21 km east of Churchill in two protected areas: mainly in the Churchill Wildlife Management Area (CWMA), created in 1978, and to a lesser extent in Wapusk National Park, created in 1996 (see Figure 4.1). These protected areas were established to protect polar bear staging and denning areas, nesting grounds for geese, and habitat for caribou (Teillet 1988; Manitoba Conservation 2008).

Tourists view polar bears and other Arctic wildlife in this area from the comfort of 'tundra vehicles', which are essentially converted buses, widened and elevated, allowing for easy mobility along the uneven tundra landscape (see Figure 4.2). There are currently 18 tundra vehicles licensed to operate in the region. In

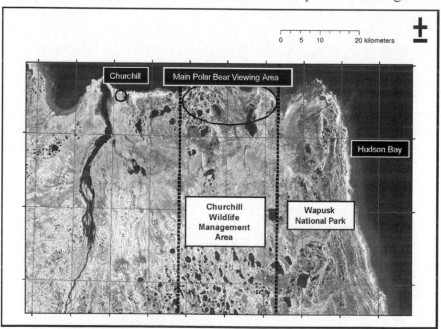

Figure 4.1 Polar bear viewing in protected areas neighbouring Churchill

Figure 4.2 Tundra vehicle used for polar bear viewing in Churchill, Manitoba

addition, 'the polar bear viewing industry' in Churchill is comprised of two helicopter companies, two dog sledding companies, one local museum, a research centre, multiple souvenir and tourist shops, two tundra lodges (tundra-based hotels), and several local hotels and bed-and-breakfasts that provide accommodation that is in excess of 300 rooms.

Resident concerns in Churchill

In an attempt to understand local perspectives on the implications of climate change for the community of Churchill, 75 interviews were conducted with local residents between 2005 and 2006 (see Stewart and Draper 2007). One of the key findings to emerge was that many residents identified climate change as the most important issue facing future development of tourism in Churchill. For example: 'there is a lot of talk about the polar bears because of global warming, about whether the bears are eating enough, going onto the ice too early or too late. It's going to be hard on the bears, and tourism will drop off, will be gone for ever' (Churchill resident: 17) and similarly 'We need to manage the bears, but with climate change they might not be here. To survive, the bears will have to shift. It's unpredictable' (Churchill resident: 23). Other respondents identified that, 'The polar bears won't last forever and that in itself may heighten interest in them because they are on the path to virtual extinction with climate change' (Churchill resident: 50) (see Table 4.1 for selection of other quotes).

Resident concerns, scientific research projecting the significant and increasing vulnerability of the polar bear species, particularly in Western Hudson Bay (WHB), along with increasing public awareness of the impact of climate change

Table 4.1: Selection of quotes from residents regarding the implications of climate change for Churchill

Churchill resident #	Comment on climate change
Churchill resident: 03	"Need to manage the bears, but with climate change they might not be here. To survive the bears will have to shift. It's unpredictable. The ice is not as thick, and the currents are changing"
Churchill resident: 18	"With global warming there goes our tourism, especially the bears…"
Churchill resident: 22	"I think we will see more Europeans coming and in fifty years the bears will be gone, it will kill [tourism] here…"
Churchill resident: 26	"With the bears it all depends on global warming. The season time might change, it might be earlier. Its risky for the town too, we need to protect the locals. It might also mean that the bears will be here for longer, which will be better for the tourists"
Churchill resident: 27	"So long as the polar bears stay there is a future here"
Churchill resident: 51	"Climate change will happen over a long period of time…it'll be progressive. I can't see aggressive changes happening. But we will have a lot less people"
Churchill resident: 55	We know polar bears have only about 50 years left with climate change…"
Churchill resident: 42	"Global warming will affect all mammals, but I don't think we'll be free of ice. It'll be okay for me! Down the road we'll have to watch out. Last year they recorded the largest ice hole at the Pole…it will affect the bears"

on tourism resources in the polar regions, together raise important questions about (1) the future sustainability of the polar bear viewing industry in Churchill, (2) the impact the industry has in perpetuating climate change and (3) the role that tourists, local people and the tourism industry could play in helping reduce the negative consequences of change on the community of Churchill. This chapter outlines the potential demand shift in Churchill's polar bear viewing industry under future warming scenarios, highlighting plausible behavioural adaptation of tourists. In addition, we estimate the GHG emissions created by the industry and suggest some mitigation strategies for reducing emissions and potentially enhancing the industry's marketability as an eco-friendly, or even carbon-neutral, option.

The impact of climate change on polar bears

One of the most significant changes currently occurring in the Arctic is decreasing sea ice extent and thickness caused by increasing temperature and changes in other climatic variables (see Johannessen *et al.* 1999; Vinnikov *et al.* 1999; Serrenze *et al.* 2000; ACIA 2004; Comiso and Parkinson 2004; Zhang and Walsh 2006; Howell *et al.* 2006; Richter-Menge *et al.* 2006; Furgal and Prowse 2008; chapters 2 and 17 [this volume]). Polar bears predominantly feed on ringed seals

(Phoca hispida), which depend on sea ice on which to give birth and nurse their pups (Stirling and Derocher 1993; Ferguson *et al.* 2005). Reductions in sea ice make polar bears and seals particularly vulnerable (Stirling and Derocher 1993; Derocher *et al.* 2004; Stirling and Parkinson 2006). Polar bears also depend on sea ice to travel, sometimes long distances, in search of other food sources and to access maternity denning areas (Stirling and Derocher 1993).

Polar bear populations in WHB (see Figure 4.3) consistently travel long distances to and from the shores near Churchill, for both terrestrial maternity denning purposes and also because of the complete annual sea ice melt in the region (Stirling *et al.* 1997; Parkinson *et al.* 1999; Gagnon and Gough 2005). Polar bears in this region spend late July to early November on shore near the southwestern region of Hudson Bay because advection of ice as a result of winds and ocean currents makes the area one of the last regions to experience ice break-up, therefore allowing polar bears to maximise the amount of time spent on the ice each year (Etkin 1991; Stirling *et al.* 1997). While on land polar bears decrease their metabolic rates and subsist on stored fat reserves, allowing them to conserve energy over the warm summer and early autumn months until they return to the ice again, where they can hunt seals (Derocher and Stirling 1996; Stirling *et al.* 1997).

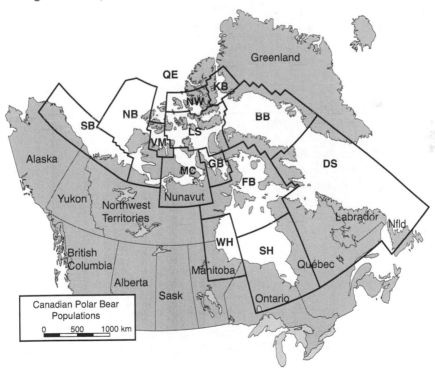

Figure 4.3 Polar bear subpopulations of Canada, USA and Greenland

Decreasing sea ice has a direct relationship with the overall health of polar bears. For example, the longer the bears have to feed on seals while they are on the ice, the healthier they are when they come off and the better they are able to survive the fasting period (Stirling *et al.* 1999). The amount of time that WHB polar bears are forced to fast each year while waiting for freeze-up has been increasing with the decline of annual and multiyear ice in the region (Gough *et al.* 2004; Stirling *et al.* 2004; Gagnon and Gough 2005). Stirling and Parkinson (2006) found that on average spring ice break-up has been occurring 7–8 days earlier each decade. This estimation concurs with Gagnon and Gough (2005), who found that sea ice in the Hudson Bay region is breaking up 3 weeks earlier than it did 30 years ago. Gough and Wolfe (2001) suggested that ice might be completely gone from the Hudson Bay region by the middle of the present century.

If average Hudson Bay regional temperatures were to increase by 1°C, this would cause a longer ice-free season (approximately 2+ weeks) and female polar bears would lose approximately 22 kg per season (Stirling and Derocher 1993). Recent studies project a 2°C temperature increase in the Canadian Arctic as early as the 2020s (Furgal and Prowse 2008), suggesting that the impact on female polar bears is likely to be even greater than originally projected. Continuous weight loss at this rate will have negative impacts on reproduction and cub survival rates (Derocher *et al.* 1993; Stirling and Derocher 1993; Atkinson and Ramsay 1995; Derocher and Stirling 1996). Because polar bears have a slow breeding rate (i.e. females have one or two cubs every 3 years) this could significantly accelerate population decline.

Population decline is already evident despite protected habitat and strict hunting quotas. Between 1988 and 2004 the WHB polar bear population declined by 22% (Stirling and Parkinson, 2006). Stirling and Parkinson (2006) believe it is possible that female polar bears in the WHB region may stop producing cubs within the next 20–30 years. Not only would this tragedy be an ecological catastrophe, it would significantly impact the tourism industry in Churchill, and its residents who depend on tourism for their livelihood.

Methodology

Within the climate change and tourism literature two major knowledge gaps are apparent including: (1) the limited understanding of the implications of climate change for tourist demand and (2) a lack of studies examining the emission contribution from different tourism activities. There are very few studies that examine climate change as an influence on tourist demand (e.g. König and Abegg 1998; Behringer *et al.* 2000; Richardson and Loomis 2004; Uyarra *et al.* 2005; Hamilton *et al.* 2005; Jones and Scott 2006; Scott *et al.* 2007; Amelung *et al.* 2007), and even fewer that attempt to understand activity-specific behavioural responses (e.g. König 1998; Behringer *et al.* 2000). Several studies are beginning to emerge examining the emission contribution of tourism (UNWTO-UNEP 2008); however, there remain a limited number that estimate carbon emissions for specific tourism activities (e.g. Becken and Simmons 2002; Becken *et al.* 2003; Gossling et al. 2005; Amelung and Lamers 2007).

In order to address these knowledge gaps, a visitor survey was conducted during the 2007 polar bear viewing season in Churchill. The shifting demand patterns under future warming scenarios were examined and carbon emissions estimated. The survey was designed to be self-completed and focused on four key areas:

- trip and activity characteristics (for GHG emission calculations)
- response to climate-change scenarios
- individual perception of climate change
- sociodemographics and tourist type.

A total of 334 surveys were collected during the 2007 polar bear viewing season (October–November) in Churchill, representing just over 11% of the polar bear tourism market. In addition to these self-completed surveys the researcher engaged a smaller number of visitors in more in-depth interviewing (*n* = 15).

Behavioural adaptation of tourists

Typical polar bear viewing tourists include older adults who are generally retired, exhibit higher than average levels of education (72% hold undergraduate university degrees) and reside in the USA, Canada, the United Kingdom, Australia or Europe. Visitors on average stay in Churchill for 5 days, participate in 2 full-day trips on a tundra vehicle, visit the local museum, go dog sledding, go on a helicopter tour, eat several meals at local restaurants and go souvenir shopping. The majority of visitors to Churchill would return to the region again to see either polar bears (50%) or beluga whales (59%), suggesting that there is a strong repeat visitation market in the town despite the limited tourism products available (i.e. wildlife viewing of polar bears, beluga whales, nature-based tours of wildflowers and tundra vegetation, and aurora borealis viewing).

Polar bear viewing tourists seem resilient to change and are willing to continue to visit Churchill to view the bears under varying future change scenarios, all of which project declining abundance and appearance of the species. Over 82% of respondents indicated that even if environmental conditions altered the population dynamics of polar bears so much that they were able 'to view only a quarter of the number of bears they actually saw on a 2007 visit', they would still visit Churchill in the future. If visitors were 'not guaranteed to see any bears' (i.e. they may or may not see them), the percentage of visitors indicating that they would still visit remains just above 50%. If in the future, polar bear populations were to 'appear unhealthy' (i.e. very skinny), which is already beginning to occur and is expected to continue, over 60% of visitors would still visit Churchill to see polar bears. The majority of visitors indicated that if they 'could not view polar bears in Churchill', for example, if the WHB subpopulation was locally extirpated, 72% of visitors 'would be willing travel somewhere else so they could view polar bears'. Of the individuals who are motivated to view polar bears despite the potentially negative consequences of climate change, 70% 'would be willing to pay more' than they did during their 2007 trip, which cost tourists on average between CAN$5,000 and CAN$8,000 per person.

These findings indicate that the market for polar bear viewing is strong. It is likely that because the polar bear species is particularly vulnerable to climatic and other environmental changes, and often used as the 'poster species' for climate change in the media, there will be an even greater increase in demand for the product in the short to medium term (i.e. next 20–30 years). This phenomenon has been labeled in popular media as 'last chance tourism' or 'doomsday tourism', which involves a desire to view wildlife, and landscapes such as glaciers, ice bergs or coral reefs, before they are gone forever (see chapter 17). This behavioural adaptation is important, not only for Churchill's polar bear viewing industry, but all tourism markets capitalising on this recent phenomenon. Although there is great potential in the short and medium term, in the long term, sustainability is of great concern, particularly if operators and visitors are unaware of how their presence and participation contribute to the perpetuation of negative change.

Polar bear viewing tourists are largely unaware of the contribution of tourism to global climate change and therefore the declining health of polar bears. The vast majority of respondents (88%) understood and agreed that humans contribute to changes in the global climate; however, just 69% believed that air travel contributes to climate change (according to UNWTO-UNEP [2008] air travel is estimated to be responsible for 40% of all GHG emissions). This perception in part explains why just 12% of respondents strongly agreed that they would, in the future, be willing to pay to offset carbon emission in addition to the price of an airline ticket. Reasons respondents were not willing to participate in air travel carbon offset schemes included a lack of understanding of what a carbon tax is (n = 41) and what the money would be used for (n = 70), not knowing which company to trust (n = 39), and a perception that it would be too expensive (n = 12). Of those respondents who would be willing to pay more to offset their carbon emissions from air travel, the majority would pay 5–10% of the price of their airline ticket on top of the ticket price (43%).

Of the polar bear viewing tourists, 60% were able to make the connection between climate change and declining abundance and health of polar bears, meaning that 40% of visitors do not understand the potential impact climate change has for the species. This is not surprising considering the indirect and non-linear dynamics of a changing climate. For example, it is difficult for people to make the connection between, for example, flying in an airplane to go snorkeling on the Great Barrier Reef (which contributes to GHG emissions, climate change and declining health of polar bears) and climate change impacts occurring on the other side of the world. Environmental issues of the past have been more linear and easier for people to understand. For example, the reduce, reuse and recycle campaigns of the 1980s showed us that by following the 3 Rs we can reduce material ending up in landfills. Even earlier, thanks in part to Rachel Carson (i.e. *Silent Spring*, Carson 1962) we learned that if we spray harmful pesticides on agriculture products, run-off affects the quality of our drinking water. These direct relationships are much easier to grasp than the indirect global phenomenon of climate change.

Educating and communicating the causes, impacts and 'solutions' to climate change remains a significant challenge for the future. Operator and tourist interviews conducted in Churchill found some scepticism around climate change and the related changes to polar bear populations. For example:

'...nothing is going to happen to the bears...I've lived here all my life you see, and the bears were here when I was born and they will be here long after I die'

(tourism stakeholder number 2).

'...oh yeah...that climate change stuff...the media sure is taking hold of that hogwash...that is for sure'

(tourist number 12).

However, local government officials and many community members hold a different view (as indicated in Table 4.1) and are highly concerned about the future impacts of climate change, including negative impacts on polar bear populations. Implementing more interpretation and education programs on polar bear viewing tours could help increase understanding of the relationship between climate change and polar bears. During the 2007 season only 65% of tourists reported receiving any environmental information during their tundra vehicle tour, much of which was descriptive in nature and very little of which discussed climate change or species vulnerability. There remains much room for improvement in this area; however, it is not clear that tourism operators want to provide this sort of information for fear of decreasing demand.

Estimating Carbon Emissions

The paradox of climate change and polar bear tourism lies in the fact that tourists travelling long distances to view polar bears before they are gone, are disproportionately responsible, on a per capita basis, for increased GHG emissions, which ironically impact the health of the very resource they are there to see: the polar bear. In estimating the GHG emissions of a typical polar bear viewing tourist it quickly becomes evident that this tourism market is highly carbon intensive. Visitors often travel long distances to Churchill, which is not accessible by road. There is rail access to Churchill from Winnipeg, with trains scheduled approximately every 3 days; however, because the journey takes between 24 and 36 hours depending on regular delays the majority of tourists choose to fly: 80% in this study.

A global average tourist journey is estimated to generate 0.25 tonnes of CO_2 (UNWTO-UNEP 2008). According to our calculations a polar bear viewing experience in Churchill is well above this average, ranging from 1.54 to 58.61 tonnes/CO_2-e per person. This means that a polar bear viewing experience is 6 to

34 times higher than a globally average tourist experience, depending on the distance flown between an individual's place of residence and Churchill. Compared with other tourist activity-based studies, the maximum carbon footprint estimated for a long-haul polar bear viewing tourist is amongst the highest, second only to energy-intensive cruise-based journeys to Antarctica (Amelung and Lamers 2007). However, for shorter-haul polar bear viewing tourists coming from North America, emission levels are much lower.

Lemelin (2004) estimated that during the 2003 polar bear viewing season 3,000 tourists visited Churchill during the short 6-week viewing season. Although more recent estimates of polar bear tourist numbers, quoted in newspaper articles, are higher (Bruemmer 2008), we have used Lemelin's (2004) estimate for the purpose of this study as it represents the only methodologically sound study of the visitor numbers. Based on a sample of 3,000 tourists the total emissions for the entire industry, including transportation, accommodation and activities, indicate that this tourism market emits approximately 7,830 tonnes/CO_2e per 6-week season (accommodation and activity emissions for 3,000 tourists ~ 495.6 tonnes/CO_2e + air transportation ~7 325 tonnes/CO_2e).

The main barrier to GHG emission reduction for the polar bear viewing industry is currently the disconnect between people's understanding that climate change is occurring (and is human induced), exactly how tourists themselves contribute to change through their travel-related emissions, and what impacts those changes have for resources they depend upon or value. Becken (2007) found that as people become more aware of the impact of aviation and the impact of GHG on climate change it is likely that more people will be willing to pay to offset their travel, indicating that education may be the first step towards mitigating climate change.

Mitigation strategies

The Tourism Industry Association of Canada (2008) recently urged Canadian tourism operators to measure and monitor carbon emissions, emphasising the vital need for carbon reduction to keep Canadian tourism competitive in an increasing carbon-aware marketplace. The polar bear viewing industry has several emission mitigation options including increased marketing to closer markets (i.e. Canada and northern USA) rather than international regions, investing in renewable energy sources (i.e. solar panels, wind, geothermal), burning friendlier sources of fuel, substituting emission intensive activities with less consumptive activities, ensuring vehicle tours are filled to capacity, promoting education and interpretation programs, improving train transportation (schedule, tracks and service) and promoting train travel from Winnipeg.

After measures have been taken to reduce carbon emission wherever feasible, it is possible to offset the remainder or a portion of tourist's travel emissions. This can be done through the offsetting market, which provides central locations for people to donate money toward carbon sequestration or renewable energy generation projects. In this way travellers can offset the amount of carbon they have emitted. This market has grown substantially over the past few years from

Table 4.2: Cost to offset emissions to Churchill

	Atmosfair (CDN $)	CarbonNeutral (CDN $)	Zerofootprint (CDN $)	Average (CDN $)
From New York	75	18	27	40
From Los Angeles	90	24	34	49
From Toronto	56	16	22	31
From Vancouver	62	18	29	36
From London (UK)	200	54	77	110
From Frankfurt (Germany)	214	57	77	116
From Sydney (Australia)	399	97	126	207

just a few in 2000–01 to approximately 40 in 2006 (Gössling 2007; Gössling *et al.* 2007). There are large differences evident between companies regarding the cost to offset emissions (Gössling 2007; Gössling *et al.* 2007). This is likely due to differing calculation methodologies (i.e. sometimes because of the inclusion or exclusion of radiative forcing index [RFI]) and discrepancy in cost for carbon sequestion/carbon offsetting schemes. For example, some offsetting companies focus on tree-planting incentives to help offset carbon, whereas others invest in research or production of renewable energy incentives (see Table 4.2).

If Churchill's polar bear viewing industry were to offset all of its emissions (i.e. not including any reductions that may occur by implementing mitigation strategies), it would cost the sector approximately CAN$140,264 (estimated using the average cost per tonne of CO_2 from three offsetting companies: Atmosfair, Carbon Neutral and Zerofootprint (Atmosfair 2008; Zerofootprint 2008). When this estimation is divided among the 3,000 visitors who come to Churchill during the 6-week viewing season the cost totals less than CAN$47 per person or approximately 0.7% of the average cost of a polar bear viewing vacation. This dollar value represents a small percentage of the costs tourists incur during their visit to Churchill. A small donation to offset carbon, either by tourists or tour operators, could lead to Churchill claiming to be the first carbon neutral destination in North America. Not only is this gesture environmentally responsible (as well as feasible) it provides Churchill with the opportunity to market itself as a truly carbon responsible destination and in addition it is in Churchill's best interest considering the vulnerable resources they rely on.

Conclusion

This chapter has outlined some of the changes that may occur to Churchill's polar bear viewing industry under future climate change scenarios. Polar bears have become one of the most heartbreaking, yet politicised species of climate change. The species is particularly vulnerable to warming regimes because of its dependence on sea ice. As the ice declines, so do polar bear populations, which is a tragedy not only for Canadians, who have come to identify with the species as a national symbol of pride, but also for the rest of the world, who have come to love this charismatic mega-fauna.

The loss of the polar bear subpopulation in WHB spells disaster for Churchill's tourism industry, which relies heavily on polar bear viewing. However, with declining health reported in polar bear populations there appears to have been an increase in demand from tourists wishing to view polar bears in their natural environment before they are gone from the area forever. As this chapter reveals, tourists are interested in viewing polar bears despite declining numbers and ailing species health, and are in fact willing to pay more to view fewer bears in the future; however, long-term sustainability of the industry is impossible under current climate change projections. It is likely that in the future the polar bear viewing industry in Churchill will experience an inverse relationship between demand and supply; meaning that as supply decreases (polar bear abundance and health) demand will increase at least temporarily until polar bear populations decline significantly, which could occur as early as 2060. This relationship is a common response, and will likely become even more frequent as climate change impacts vulnerable Arctic resources, such as Arctic wildlife and landscapes. As we outline in this chapter, this activity has become known as 'last chance tourism'.

Given the amplification of environmental change in the Arctic region, it is vital that decision-makers, local residents, tour operators and tourists understand the potential impacts and behavioural adaptation of tourists. It is a matter of urgency that all stakeholders adapt appropriately, for example, through emission reduction programs and educational campaigns. With integrated, collaborative and multi-sectoral management, mitigation measures could be implemented that could make Churchill the first carbon neutral destination in North America. This would be a triumph for local residents and tour operators who depend on nature-based tourism for their livelihood; for tourists who come to learn about the environment; and most importantly, for the polar bears themselves.

Acknowledgements

The authors thank the staff at the Churchill Northern Research Centre for their ongoing support and funding of this research through the Northern Research Fund. Thanks go to various agencies, individuals and participants who have so willingly given of their time to this project. Acknowledgement also goes to Harvey Lemelin for sharing his expertise in the area. Jackie Dawson would like to acknowledge her support from the Social Sciences and Humanities Research Center, the Northern Scientific Training Program and the Canadian Wildlife Federation and Emma Stewart would like to acknowledge her support from the Pierre Elliot Trudeau Foundation.

References

Aars, J., Lunn, N. and Derocher, A.E. (2006) *Polar Bears,* Proceedings of the 14th Working Meeting of the IUCN/SSC Polar Bear Specialist Group, 20–24 June 2005, Seattle, Washington, USA. Occasional Paper of the IUCN Species Survival Commission. Gland: IUCN.

Amelung, B. and Lamers, M. (2007) 'Estimating the greenhouse gas emissions from Antarctic tourism', *Tourism in Marine Environments*, 4: 121–33.

Amelung, B., Nicholls, S. and Viner, D. (2007) 'Implications of global climate change for tourism flows and seasonality', *Journal of Travel Research*, 45: 285–96.

Arctic Climate Impacts Assessment (ACIA) (2004) *Arctic Climate Impact Report: impacts of a warming Arctic*, Cambridge: Cambridge University Press.

Atmosfair (2008) Atmosfair Home. Online. Available HTTP. www.atmosfair.de (accessed 8 June 2008).

Atkinson, S.N. and Ramsay, M.A. (1995) 'The effects of prolonged fasting on the body composition and reproductive success for female polar bears (Ursus martimus)', *Functional Ecology*, 9: 559–67.

Becken, S. (2007) 'Tourists' perception of international air travel's impact on the global climate and potential climate change policies', *Journal of Sustainable Tourism*, 15: 351–68.

Becken, S. and Simmons, D.G. (2002) 'Understanding energy consumption patterns of tourist attractions and activities in New Zealand', *Tourism Management*, 23: 343–54.

Becken, S., Simmons, D.G. and Frampton, C. (2003) 'Energy use associated with different travel choices', *Tourism Management*, 24: 267–77.

Behringer, J., Buerki, R. and Fuhrer, J. (2000) 'Participatory integrated assessment of adaptation to climate change in alpine tourism and mountain agriculture', *Integrated Assessment*, 1: 31–338.

Bosnal, R.G. and Prowse, T.D. (2006) 'Regional assessment of GCM-simulated current climate over northern Canada', *Arctic*, 59: 115–28.

Bruemmer, F. (2008) Churchill is known as the polar bear capital: as the habitat of these great hunters shrinks, so will their numbers. *Ottawa Citizen*, Online. Available HTTP. www.canada.com/ottawacitizen/news/travel/story.html?id=a38ade9c-c110–4619-bacc-0dd68ca1a137 (accessed 12 November 2008).

Carbon Neutral (2008) Online. Available HTTP. www.carbonneutral.com.au (accessed 8 June 2008).

Carson, R. (1962) *Silent Spring*, Boston: Riverside Press.

Comiso, J.C. and Parkinson, C.L. (2004) 'Satellite-observed changes in the Arctic', *Physics Today*, 22: 38–44.

Derocher, A.E., Andriashek, D. and Stirling, I. (1993) Terrestrial foraging by polar bears during the ice-free period in western Hudson Bay', *Arctic*, 46: 251–54.

Derocher, A.E., Lunn, N.J. and Stirling, I. (2004) 'Polar bears in a warming climate', *Integrative and Comparative Biology*, 44: 163–76.

Derocher, A.E. and Stirling, I. (1996) 'Aspects of survival in juvenile polar bears', *Canadian Journal of Zoology*, 74: 1246–52.

Etkin, D.A. (1991) 'Break-up in Hudson Bay: its sensitivity to air temperatures and implications for climate warming', *Climatological Bulletin*, 25: 21–35.

Ferguson, S.H., Stirling, I. and McLoughlin, P. (2005) 'Climate change and ringed seal (*Phoca hispida*) recruitment in western Hudson Bay', *Marine Mammal Science*, 21: 121–35.

Furgal, C. and Prowse, T.D. (2008) 'Northern Canada', in D.S. Lemmen, F.J. Warrent, J. Lacroix and E. Bush (eds) *From Impacts to Adaptation: Canada in a changing climate*, Ottawa: Government of Canada.

Gagnon, A.S. and Gough, W.A. (2005) 'Trends in the dates of ice freeze-up and breakup over Hudson Bay, Canada', *Arctic*, 58: 370–82.

Gössling, S. (2007) 'It does not harm the environment! An analysis of industry discourses on tourism, air travel and the environment', *Journal of Sustainable Tourism*, 15: 402–17.

Gössling, S., Peeters, P., Ceron, J.P., Dubois, G., Patterson, T. and Richardson, R.B. (2005) 'The eco-efficiency of tourism', *Ecological Economics*, 54: 417–34.

Gough, W.A., Gagnon, A.S. and Lau, H.P. (2004) 'Interannual variability of Hudson Bay ice thickness', *Polar Geography*, 28: 222–38.

Gough W.A. and Wolfe, E. (2001) 'Climate change scenarios for Hudson Bay, Canada, from general circulation models', *Arctic*, 54: 142–50.

Hamilton, J.M., Maddison, D., and Tol, R.S. (2005) 'Effects of climate change on international Tourism', *Climate Research*, 29: 245–54.

Howell, S.E.L., Tivy, A., Yackel J.J. and Scharien, R. (2006) 'Application of seawinds/ quickSCAT sea ice melt algorithm for assessing melt dynamics in the Canadian Arctic Archipelago', *Journal of Geophysical Research*, 111: 1–21.

Intergovernmental Panel on Climate Change (IPCC) (2007) 'Summary for policymakers', in M.L. Parry, O.F. Canziani, J.P. Palutikof, P.J. van der Linden and C.E. Hanson (eds) *Climate Change 2007: impacts, adaptation and vulnerability.* Contribution of Working Group II to the Fourth Assessment Report of the Intergovernmental Panel on Climate Change. Cambridge: Cambridge University Press.

Johannessen, O.A. Shalina E.V. and Miles M.W. (1999) 'Satellite evidence for an Arctic sea ice cover in transformation', *Science*, 286: 1937–39.

Jones, B. and Scott, D. (2006) 'Climate change, seasonality and visitation to Canada's national parks', *Journal of Parks and Recreation Administration*, 24: 42–62.

König, U. and Abegg, B. (1997) 'Impacts of climate change on tourism in the Swiss Alps', *Journal of Sustainable Tourism*, 5: 46–58.

Lemelin, H. (2004) The integration of human dimensions with the environmental context: a study of polar bear observers in the Churchill Wildlife Management area, Churchill, Manitoba, unpublished thesis, University of Waterloo.

— (2005) 'Wildlife tourism at the edge of chaos: complex interactions between humans and polar bears in Churchill, Manitoba', in F. Berkes, R. Huebert, H. Fast, M. Manseau and A. Diduck (eds) *Breaking Ice: Renewable Resource and Ocean Management in the Canadian North,* Calgary: University of Calgary Press.

Manitoba Government (2008) *Manitoba designates polar bears as threatened.* Online. Available HTTP: www.gov.mb.ca/chc/press/top/2008/02/2008-02-07-131000-3044. html (accessed 21 June 2008).

Overpeck, J.T. Strum, M., Francis, J.A., Perovich, D.K., Serrenze, M.C., Benner, R., Carmack, E.C., Chapin III, F.S., Gerlach, S.C., Hamilton, L.C., Hinzman, L.D., Holland, M., Huntington, H.P., Key, J.R. Loyd, A.H., MacDonald, G.M., McFadden, J., Noone, D., Prowse, T.D., Schlosser, P. and Vörösmarty, C. (2005) 'Arctic system on trajectory to new, seasonally ice-free state', *EOS Transactions, Geophysical Union,* 86: 309–16.

Parkinson, C.L., Cavalierei, D.J., Gloersen, P., Zwally, H.J. and Comiso, J.C. (1999) 'Arctic sea ice extents, areas, and trends: 1978–96', *Journal of Geophysical Research,* 104: 20837–56.

Richardson, B.R. and Loomis, J.B. (2004) 'Adaptive recreation planning and climate change: A contingent visitation approach', *Ecological Economics,* 50: 83–99.

Richter-Menge, J., Overland, J., Proshutinsky, A., Romanovsky, V., Bengtsson, L., Bringham, L., Dyurgerov, M., Gascard, J.C., Gerland, S., Gravenersen, R., Haas, C., Karcher, M., Kuhry, P., Maslanik, J., Melling, H., Maslowski, W., Morision, J., Perovich, D., Przybylak, R., Rachold, V., Rigor, I., Shiklomanov, A., Stroeve, J.,

Walker, D. and Walsh, J. (2006) *State of the Arctic Report*, NOAA OAR Special Report, Seattle: NOAA/OAR/PMEL.

Scott, D., Jones, B., and Konopek, J. (2007) 'Implications of climate and environmental change for nature-based tourism in the Canadian Rocky Mountains: a case study of Waterton Lakes National Park', *Tourism Management*, 28: 570–79.

Serrenze, M.C., Walsh, J.E., Chapin III, F.S., Osterkamp, T., Dyurgerov, M., Romanovsky, V., Oechel, W.C., Morison, J., Zhang, T. and Barry, R.G. (2000) 'Observational evidence of recent change in the northern high-latitude environment', *Climatic Change*, 46: 159–207.

Stewart, E.J. and Draper, D. (2007) 'A collaborative approach to understanding local stakeholder perceptions of tourism in Churchill, Manitoba (Canada)', *Polar Geography*, 30: 7–35.

Stirling, I., Clark, D.A. and Calvert, W. (1997) 'Distribution, characteristics and use of earth dens and related excavations by polar bears on the western Hudson Bay lowlands', *Arctic*, 50: 158–66.

Stirling, I. and Derocher, A.E. (1993) 'Possible impacts of climatic warming on polar bears', *Arctic*, 46, 240–45.

Stirling, I., Lunn, N.J. and Iacozza, J. (1999) 'Long-term trends in the population ecology of polar bears in western Hudson Bay', *Arctic*, 52: 294–306.

Stirling, I., Lunn, J.J., Iacozza, J., Elliot, C. and Obbard, M. (2004) 'Polar bear distribution and abundance on the southwestern Hudson Bay coast during open water season, in relation to population trends and annual ice patterns', *Arctic*, 57: 15–26.

Stirling, I. and Parkinson, C.L. (2006) 'Possible effects of climate warming on selected populations of polar bears (*Ursus maritimus*) in the Canadian Arctic', *Arctic*, 59: 261–75.

Teillet. D.J. (1988) *The Churchill Wildlife Management Area: Management guidelines*. Report produced for the Manitoba Department of Natural Resources, Winnipeg, MB.

Tourism Industry Association of Canada (2008) *The report on Canada's tourism competitiveness: a call for action for Canadian Tourism by the Tourism Industry Association of Canada*, June 2008. Online. Available HTTP: www.tiacaitc.ca/english/documents/ ReportonTourismCompetitivenessFINAL.pdf (accessed 20 May 2008).

United Nations World Tourism Organization, United Nations Environment Programme (UNWTO-UNEP) (2008) *Climate Change and Tourism: responding to global challenges* (prepared by Scott, D., Amelung, B., Becken, S., Ceron, J.P., Dubois, G., Gössling, S., Peeters, P. and Simpson, M.C.), UNWTO, Madrid, and UNEP, Paris.

Uyarra, M., Cote, I., Gill, J., Tinch, R., Viner, D., and Watkins, R. (2005) 'Island-specific preferences of tourists for environmental features: implications of climate change for tourism-dependent states', *Environmental Conservation*, 32: 11–19.

Vinnikov, K.Y., Robock, A., Stougger, R.J., Walsh, J.E., Parkinson, C.L., Cavalieri, D.J., Mitchell, J.F.B., Garrett, D. and Zakharov, V.F. (1999) 'Global warming and northern hemisphere sea ice extent', *Science*, 286: 1934–37.

Zerofootprint (2008) Zerofootprint. Online. Available: www.zerofootprint.net (accessed 8 June 2008).

Zhang, X. and Walsh, J.E. (2006) 'Toward a seasonally ice-covered Arctic ocean: Scenarios from the IPCC AR4 model simulations', *Journal of Climate*, 19: 1730–47.

5 Climate Disruption and the Changing Dynamics of Polar Bear–Human Interactions in Northern Ontario

A case study of polar bear management in Polar Bear Provincial Park, Ontario, Canada

Raynald Harvey Lemelin, Norman McIntyre, Rhonda Koster and Margaret Johnston

Introduction

The polar bear, or *Wabusk* in Cree, figures prominently on the town logos of the Washeo/Fort Severn First Nation (hereafter Washeo) and the Weenusk First Nation at Peawanuck (hereafter Weenusk) in Northern Ontario. This should come as no surprise, since the *Muskekowuck Athinuwick*, the original people of the Hudson Bay Lowlands of Northern Ontario, Quebec and Manitoba, have been interacting with *Wabusk* for several millennia (Lytwyn 2002; Bird 2005).

> Polar bears were unique to the coastal environment, and valued by the Lowland Cree for their flesh and fat. […] The Indians likewise eat the flesh of all [polar bears] they kill, and mixed the fat with cranberries, pounded venison [ruhiggan] which constitutes one of their greatest dainties
>
> (Lytwyn 2002: 110).

The relationship between the Cree and *Wabusk* in Northern Ontario was often utilitarian. But, as the Cree elder and scholar Louis Bird explains, polar bears are also important icons in Cree lore for they are 'the very closest to the Native way of behaviour. They follow the seasons – they have their routine. There is a time when they are dangerous and there are times where they are not so powerful' (Bird 2007: 102). *Wabusk* is also a critical sociocultural symbol. For example, it plays an important role during certain vision quest ceremonies, where its spirit will often be summoned (Bird 2007). Because of these differing roles, the Cree have always recognised the polar bear as an important member of northern ecosystems. Recent studies of the two polar bear populations in Hudson and James Bays suggest that the health and distribution of these animals and their habitat (eg. dens, staging areas) are being affected by climate change including increasing temperatures, declining sea ice quality, melting permafrost, and increasing precipitation such as springtime rains (Scott *et al*. 2002; Obbard 2006; Stirling and Parkinson 2006; Obbard *et al*. 2007).

The term climate change is often used in the literature, but the people of Nunavik (Northern Quebec, Canada) argue that 'change' implies the ability to adapt to resulting social, economic and ecological alterations; because this is not reflected in their experience of climate change, climatic disruption may be a more appropriate term in this context because it encapsulates sudden and abrupt variations in climatic factors (Kendall 2006). The unexpectedness and rapidity of these variations provide little or no transition period for adaptation, and can in some cases compromise traditional activities and even render less effective existing knowledge systems (Holdren *et al.* 2007). These issues are of serious concern in communities such as Washeo and Weenusk, which still largely depend on traditional activities for sustenance. Complicating these processes are governance issues involved with management policies and legislation (e.g. the *Species at Risk Act* in Canada, the *Endangered Species Act* in the USA) pertaining to polar bears (Lunn *et al.* 2006; Barringer & Revkin 2007). Despite having constitutional and treaty rights and recognition in the co-management plan for the Polar Bear Provincial Park (PBPP), which in Ontario includes the right to harvest a small number of polar bears, Cree First Nations in Northern Ontario have rarely, if ever, exercised their legislative rights (see Fidler *et al.* 2008; Lemelin *et al.* 2008).

The goal of this chapter is to discuss the human dimensions of polar bear management with particular reference to protected areas and parks, and the role of First Nations within the context of climatic disruption and sociopolitical change. The chapter begins by describing polar bears and their management in Ontario, followed by a community profile of the Washeo and Weenusk First Nations. It then provides an overview of the Southern Hudson Bay (SHB) bioregion, its polar bears and their protection (i.e. PBPP). Finally, key issues with climate disruption and polar-bear management affecting Washeo and Weenusk are discussed.

Wabusk – polar bears

There are approximately 20,000 to 25,000 polar bears in the world, with approximately two-thirds of them located in Canada. Two of these polar bear populations inhabit Northern Ontario: the Western Hudson Bay (WHB) population, on the western edge of the province, is co-managed by Ontario, Manitoba and Nunavut; and the SHB population is co-managed by Ontario, Quebec and Nunavut. Both populations are protected in two of Canada's largest parks: PBPP in Ontario, and Wapusk National Park in Manitoba (see Figure 5.1). Most of the attention regarding climate change and climate disruption and polar bears has, until recently, been focused on the WHB (i.e. the 'Churchill' polar bears) (see chapter 4 for further information). This is changing, though, as concerns over climate change and the 'world's most southerly population of polar bear' attract increasing attention from environmental groups (e.g. WWF, Canadian Parks and Wilderness Society), the media (Lambert 2007; Ontario Ministry of Natural Resources [OMNR] 2007a,b), and researchers and First Nations (Fidler *et al.* 2008; Lemelin *et al.*, 2008).

Figure 5.1 Polar bear management zones in Ontario

Since the Hudson and James Bays are located at the southernmost extent of the range of polar bears, climate disruptions here may be a forewarning of changes to come in other areas of the Arctic. According to researchers, climate-related effects are already evident in the declining WHB polar bear population (Regehr *et al.* 2007). Recent studies indicate that SHB polar bears in this population have been experiencing significant declines in body condition since the mid-1980s, which, when combined with satellite data on sea ice reductions, increasing precipitation, and increasing rises in temperatures (Gagnon and Gough 2005), suggests that population declines may follow (Obbard 2006; Obbard *et al.* 2007).

   Polar bears are currently protected internationally under the *Agreement on the Conservation of Polar Bears* (1976). The IUCN, the agency responsible for overseeing the agreement on polar bear conservation, has recently upgraded polar bears from 'lower risk' (i.e. least concern) to 'vulnerable' (Lunn *et al.* 2006). In Ontario, polar bears are protected through various approaches, including protected area strategies (i.e. PBPP, Cape Henrietta-Maria Wilderness Area), management guidelines (e.g. the proposed *Wabusk Co-Management Agreement*), and legislation (*Fish and Wildlife Conservation Act*). The *Fish and Wildlife Conservation Act* (FWCA) (Statutes of Ontario, 1997, Chapter 41) states that there is no official hunting season for polar bears, although traditional hunters can harvest a limited number of them. Individuals wishing to sell the pelt of a polar bear must acquire authorisation from the OMNR (Lunn *et al.* 2002). These conservation and protection measures are discussed later in the section on PBPP.

Broadly similar protection is afforded to polar bears in Manitoba, including in protected areas (i.e. the Churchill Wildlife Management Area, Wapusk National Park), through management activities (e.g. the Polar Bear Alert Program), guidelines, policies and legislation (the *Manitoba Wildlife Act*, the *Polar Bear Protection Act*, the *Resource Tourism Operators Act*). In the winter of 2008, the province listed polar bears as threatened under the *Endangered Species Act of Manitoba* (Manitoba Government 2008); a few months later, polar bears were listed as a threatened species in the USA under the *Endangered Species Act* (US Department of the Interior 2008a, 2008b). The 2008 report released by the Committee on the Status of Endangered Wildlife in Canada (COSEWIC) noted that climate change, the reduction of sea ice, and northern development projects pose threats to polar bears, especially in the southern portions of their ranges (i.e. WHB, SHB). Despite this report, and comments made by the Environment Minister, John Baird, that a reexamination of some of the polar bear subpopulations may be warranted under the *Species at Risk Act* in Canada might be warranted (Lunn *et al.* 2006; CBC 2008), the federal status of polar bears as a species of Special Concern or Vulnerable has not changed (COSEWIC 2008). None of these decisions or discussions has, to date, included the First Nations of Weenusk and Washeo.

The new designations for polar bears in the USA and Manitoba increase the protection of these animals, especially with co-managed populations, and bring the traditional harvest of these animals under greater scrutiny. In addition, listing the bears as a threatened species means that their environment (i.e. the sea ice and coastal zones) will theoretically be protected from exploration, shipping and contaminants (US Department of Interior 2008a, 2008b). How such decisions will affect the management of endangered species between provincial and federal agencies is still open to debate.

Washeo and Wenenusk

The residents of the remote communities of Washeo and Weenusk, located in the Hudson Bay Lowlands, have lived with, interacted with and depended on various wildlife species, including polar bears, for millennia (Lytwyn 2002). In terms of polar bear management, both communities and their traditional rights to harvest polar bears are recognised by the Province of Ontario, and highlighted in the PBPP Management Plan. A small harvest of polar bears occurs in Washeo and Weenusk, and both communities offer commercial opportunities to visitors to view polar bears (Figure 5.2).

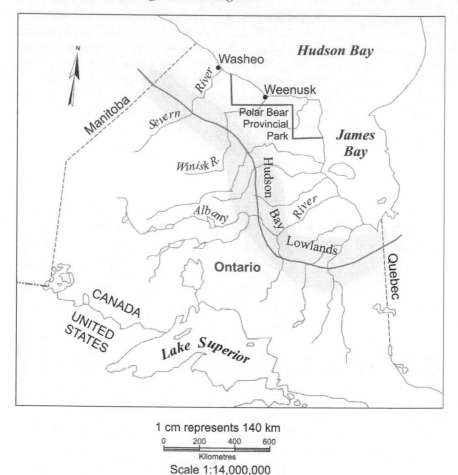

1 cm represents 140 km

0   200   400   600
Kilometres

Scale 1:14,000,000

Figure 5.2 The Hudson Bay Lowlands

Washeo is the most northerly and westerly community in the province of Ontario. This small (3,959 hectares), remote Cree community of approximately 578 people (449 living on the reserve, and 129 living off the reserve), is situated in the Hudson Bay Lowlands, 9 km from the mouth of the Severn River where it drains into Hudson Bay. Like many communities along the shores of Hudson Bay, Washeo was established by the Hudson's Bay Company in the 17th century, about 5 km up river from the modern settlement (Pilon 1982). The settlement lies within the boundaries of the territory described by the *1929–30 Adhesion to the James Bay Treaty of 1905 – Treaty No. 9*. The community was relocated to its present site in 1973 (Pilon 1982).

The Weenusk ('ground hog' in Cree) Cree First Nation once traded with the Hudson's Bay Company along the length of the Hudson Bay and James Bay coastlines from York Factory in the west to Fort George in the east (Graham

1988). The establishment of the trading post on the Weenusk River in the late 18th century made some of the Cree families more sedentary and dependent on manufactured goods (Graham 1988). Members of Weenusk First Nation formerly resided at Winisk but they were forced to move 30 km southwest to Peawanuck ('the land where the flint is found' in Cree) in May 1986, when spring floods swept away much of the original settlement (Feherty 2006). The present Weenusk First Nation at Peawanuck (5,310 hectares) is located on the site where the Asheweig River drains into the Winisk River within an excluded zone of PBPP. The current population is 266 (Feherty 2006).

PBPP

PBPP is Ontario's largest provincial park (2,355,200 ha or 24,087 km^2), and one of Canada's largest protected areas. It also incorporates one of Canada's major wetlands of international significance (2,408,700 ha), designated under the Ramsar Convention on Wetlands in 1971 (Usher 1993; Obbard and Walton 2004). Because there are no fees, no on-site staff, and limited infrastructure, PBPP is considered a non-operational wilderness park. The park, administered by the OMNR, was established in 1970 with the support of members of the Weenusk First Nation (Lemelin and McIntyre in press) and includes the majority of Ontario's tundra region, and over a third of Ontario's Arctic coastline (Beechey and Davidson 1999). A number of archeological and historical sites are found in the park (OMNR 1977a; Usher 1993).

Since 1963, the OMNR has conducted an annual aerial census of polar bears along the Ontario coast of Hudson and James Bays (Prevett and Kolenosky 1982). These annual observations, combined with other studies, make this particular population of polar bears one of the most researched in Canada (Kolenosky and Prevett 1983; Obbard *et al.* 2007). The park also provided a rationale for the protection of two critical habitat elements for the SHB polar bear population: coastal staging habitat (e.g. Cape Henrietta-Maria) used by all types of polar bears, and inland maternity denning habitat used by pregnant females (e.g. along the Winisk River). It is estimated that over 70% of the maternity dens for the SHB are located within the park (Richardson *et al.* 2006).

The initial goals for PBPP as identified in the park master plan were threefold: (1) to protect its environment for the benefit of present and future generations from significant alterations by humans; (2) to provide quality, low-intensity wilderness recreational opportunities; and (3) to provide opportunities for scientific research (OMNR 1980). Of particular importance is the role of Weenusk in the initial creation of the park, and the subsequent consultative process with three First Nations located near the park (Washeo, Weenusk, Attawapiskat) that occurred prior to the park's establishment, and the proposed *Wabusk Co-Management Agreement*. Although the polar bear co-management agreement was never signed, it continues to provide direction regarding polar bear management in the province.

Polar bears can be hunted by Aboriginal people in Ontario on a subsistence basis only. The hunting season is closed in summer when polar bears are in dens and, unlike in Nunavut, no trophy hunts are permitted (OMNR 1994). Concerns regarding the polar bear harvest within and around PBPP were voiced in 1977, and again in 1994 by representatives of environmental not-for-profit groups (OMNR 1977a, 1977b, 1994). Although not directly referring to polar bear harvest by Cree members in Ontario, similar concerns arose in the discussions over the listing of polar bears as a 'threatened' species under the *Endangered Species Act* in the USA (WWF 2007; Fidler *et al.* 2008; Lemelin et al. 2008). These concerns were raised by researchers and environmental groups (often the latter are significant financial supporters of the former) over traditional harvest and sport hunting (also referred to as conservation hunting) in Nunavut.

The background document for PBPP (OMNR 1977a) estimated that about 10 to 30 polar bears were harvested annually by Cree members from Washeo, Weenusk and Attawapiskat, and a quota system for the entire SHB population was devised based on these records. The harvesting quota for Ontario and Quebec animals was suggested in the 1970s by researchers from the OMNR. The quota is reviewed by the OMNR in Ontario and presented to the IUCN/SCC Polar Bear Specialist Group. No information is provided as to how the communities were involved, if they were, in these decisions. The current annual quota for the SHB population in Ontario and Quebec is 90 animals, 30 of which are allocated to Ontario, and 60 to Quebec. Nunavut also set a quota of 13 polar bears on the Belcher Islands, which are home to some of the SHB population. Northern Cree communities in Ontario harvest around 13 polar bears annually (note there are no Inuit communities in Ontario), whereas in Quebec about 38 polar bears are harvested each year by Aboriginal peoples. In Quebec, no distinction is made between Cree and Inuit harvests. These numbers are well under the established quota of 90. Yet, the latest document produced by the IUCN/SSC Polar Bear Specialist Group reported that the total harvest of polar bears may be beyond a sustainable harvest level of 40 animals (Lunn *et al.* 2006). Research (see Fidler *et al.* 2008; Lemelin *et al.* 2008) and informal discussions with community elders and leaders in Washeo and Weenusk did not indicate that these concerns had been brought to their attention.

Further complicating wildlife management strategies in this region of the province are the contentious issues surrounding the creation of protected areas in Northern Ontario. For example, ideas about what constitutes consultation, preservation and traditional activities often differ among the parties involved (Buscher and Whande 2007; Nishnawbe Aski Nation [NAN] 2007). Although the OMNR was one of the first natural resource agencies in Canada to involve local First Nations in discussions and negotiations concerning park designation or management, a number of concerns regarding PBPP exist.

They can stop us from hunting. They can stop us shooting the polar bear permanently. They can do that. The conservation officers in that Ministry of Natural Resources have that authority. Regardless if they have said in the treaty that we can still live upon the surface of the land, regardless of the

Polar Bear Provincial Park that has been created in the James Bay-Hudson Bay district – that can be erased with one stroke of the pen.

(Bird 2005: 229).

This quote from Cree elder Louis Bird, a community member from Weenusk, highlights the concerns of Cree leaders and elders regarding the creation of protected areas, and wildlife management in the north (NAN 2007; Fidler *et al.* 2008). To some Cree leaders and elders, the roles of foreign governments and environmental non-governmental organisations (ENGOs) in what they consider local, regional, and provincial issues further weaken their sovereignty and their quest for self-governance (NAN 2007; Fidler *et al.* 2008; Lemelin *et al.* 2008).

Tourism in PBPP

Recreational and tourism opportunities were addressed in the original park planning proposal (OMNR 1977b) and subsequently reviewed in the 1980 Master Plan, the *Polar Bear Provincial Park Tourism Development Study* (1988), the *Goose Camp Action Plan* (1990), and the Management Plan Review of 1994. In these plans, Weenusk was named the 'gateway' community to PBPP and the role of Washeo was also recognised. The majority of the discussion surrounding tourism in the park pertained to the hunting and fishing camps that were established in the 1960s, all of which are owned by Cree entrepreneurs located in Weenusk. Some camps operate on a seasonal basis (i.e. during hunting season), and all are small and rustic. Traditionally, visitors to the camps were mostly anglers, but, more recently, operators have diversified by offering wildlife viewing opportunities (Usher 1993; Lemelin and McIntyre in press). One of the most popular attractions is the polar bear. Although both consumptive and non-consumptive polar bear uses were contemplated, 'a study examining the economic viability of an Indian-guided sport hunt for polar bears recommended against such a program. Partly, this was because the hides are of poor quality in the fall when the bears are accessible' (Calvert *et al.* 1991: 5).

At the time of writing viewing polar bears in northern Ontario is limited to two local operators: Wild Wind Tours, which offers day and overnight tours up the Winisk River, and Polar Bear Park Expeditions (formerly known as Ice Bear Tours), which offers polar bear viewing excursions from a tourism camp located near the mouth of the Sutton River within PBPP. Although polar bear viewing opportunities are available in Washeo, they are not offered within PBPP.

Management of tourism access in PBPP is provided through the park management plan and various revisions of this plan. The plan currently identifies five access zones where aircraft landing is permitted. The OMNR requires that aircraft landing permits be obtained for any visitors flying into PBPP. Generally these permits are obtained by outfitters who are transporting visitors, although a few private individuals also obtain permits each year. Currently, the park does not have a tracking system to determine how many trips are made annually (Ontario

Parks management personnel, communication with author, June 2006). No permits are required for water-based travel (i.e. kayakers, canoeists, motor boaters).

Usher (1993) estimated that as many as 1,300 tourists were visiting the area in the late 1980s and early 1990s. The majority of these visitors were hunters, anglers and canoeists. These estimates are high compared with the figures provided by the OMNR, which suggest that annual visitation ranges from less than 50 (OMNR 1977a) to 350 visitors (OMNR 1994). Estimates provided by one tourism outfitter indicated that in 2005, 38 specialised adventurers undertook excursions offered in PBPP. If we combine these numbers with other visitors, there are still only a few hundred people visiting the park on an annual basis (tourism outfitter, personal communication with the first author, December 2006).

Discussion with community members in Washeo and Weenusk suggest that both First Nations have benefited little from the park. There are several reasons for this, including the remoteness and isolation of the park, and the agency's reluctance to promote tourism developments within a wilderness park like PBPP. This has been exacerbated by decreasing budget allocations to the OMNR in the late 1980s and 1990s and in particular, the small budget allocation to the park, resulting in inadequate infrastructure and staffing to support the development of tourism and recreation (Lemelin & McIntyre in press).

The changing face of governance in the north

The initial development of PBPP indicated a progressive relationship between the OMNR and local First Nations. This relationship appears to have been developed in the early phases of the park development when community members of Weenusk first approached the OMNR to establish a protected area, then consulted other local First Nations before the establishment of PBPP, and recognised the traditional rights of Aboriginal people. These consultative processes continued throughout the creation of the master plan (OMNR 1980) and management plan reviews (OMNR 1994). More recent developments include the amendment to the PBPP management plan permitting the construction of a new winter road route from Fort Severn to Weenusk, with 123 km of this road within PBPP. However, this development came with some restrictions: 'The road is intended to provide the two communities with critical supplies' and is not intended to provide public access to the park (Ontario Parks 2005). What is further evident is that the OMNR has also exhibited some degree of flexibility regarding such issues as hunting, fishing, trapping and polar bear hunts in the park.

One of the conditions outlined in the plan is 'that no changes will be made to the master plan by the Ministry without first consulting with the bands. If such an agreement is possible, it will be incorporated into the master plan during its first five year review' (OMNR 1977b: 6). Since neither the master plan nor the management plans have been revised since the early 1980s, some dissatisfaction regarding the infrequency of these revisions remains. The delays associated with revising the management plans for PBPP according to Wilkinson and Wilkinson

(2005) are not unusual in Ontario parks, given that a great number of provincial parks in Ontario have outdated or no management plans at all.

The co-management of natural resources, in particular wildlife, has gained increased acceptance as an effective means by which First Nations can participate in the management of their natural resources (Christian *et al.* 1996; Lemelin 2005). This principle includes an awareness of the value of traditional ecological knowledge and an understanding of aboriginal self-governance (Lemelin et al. 2008). Furthermore, the provincial government of Ontario has demonstrated a new sensitivity and respect for Aboriginal treaty rights in the revision to the *Endangered Species Act* (OMNR 2007b), the *Provincial Parks and Conservation Act* (2007) (Government of Ontario 2007), and the Far North Initiative. This acceptance indicates an interest by the provincial government to consider implementing collaborative management approaches that would apparently be supportive of initiatives such as the proposed *Wabusk Co-Management Agreement*.

It was stated in the conclusion of the 1994 report that the *Wabusk Co-Management Agreement* will be updated and presented to the Chiefs and Council of the three First Nations, and to the Minister of Natural Resources for ratification. In this way, the 'new co-management committee can become involved in the development and review of the management plan and begin the process of co-managing' (OMNR 1994: 44). However, the proposed *Wabusk Co-Management Agreement* for PBPP to create a Co-Management Committee that would oversee the management of resources and activities in the park was never signed. This omission and the oversights noted above are important issues for these Cree communities, especially with the revised status of polar bears in other parts of North America. This revision in status and proposed management plan reviews of PBPP could have significant implications for traditional Cree practices. Appropriate levels of consultation and involvement are essential, therefore, if the changing circumstances of Washeo and Weenusk (i.e. climate disruption) are to be included and their needs with respect to traditional practices and economic and social development recognised.

Conclusion

Although a great proportion of Northern Ontario (above the 57th parallel) in the Hudson Bay Lowlands bordering both the Hudson and James Bays shares two polar bear populations with the provinces of Quebec and Manitoba and with the territory of Nunavut, it is often excluded from various definitions of the Canadian Arctic and even the sub-Arctic. As such, the people, the flora and fauna, and stressors affecting climate disruption in the area, are frequently overlooked. This oversight is somewhat surprising, considering that this region is recognised as one of the most vulnerable to climate-induced change in Canada (Scott *et al.* 2002). This chapter provides some insight into this situation by providing perspectives on the situation of Cree communities located in this area, the management of a major provincial park dedicated to the protection of polar bears, and the potential impacts of climate disruption on the world's most southerly population of polar bears.

For some time PBPP because of its size and geographic isolation was considered too remote for forestry and hydroelectric developments. Consequently, most of the concerns pertaining to anthropogenic impacts in the region centred on traditional uses, and recreational and tourism activities (OMNR 1997; Wiersma *et al.* 2005). However, the north of Ontario is changing dramatically in response to increased mineral exploration, Ontario's first diamond mine near the First Nation of Attawpiskat, and ongoing considerations of hydroelectric generation in Ontario. Back-country recreation and tourism are ever-growing industries, challenging wider access to remote regions, often increasing encounters between humans and some species. In addition, the potential impacts from climate disruption on community well-being and ecosystem health present a threat to northern ecosystems, the magnitude of which is not yet understood (Scott *et al.* 2002; Suffling and Scott 2002; Galley 2004).

The creation of PBPP was partly justified because it did not compromise traditional harvesting activities, it provided options for co-management, and it highlighted tourism potential. Although the park does attract some visitors, including specialised polar bear tourists, it still lacks a polar bear management plan and comprehensive tourism and research strategies. Thus the support for the park from local First Nations is minimal at best. This last factor is particularly important because the provision of direct economic opportunities to and the active involvement of rural people in management help to foster and sustain a high level of trust, cooperation, and understanding between natural resource managers and local residents (Christian *et al.* 1996). Such a relationship is critical for long-term national conservation efforts, as well as for providing justification for the use of wildlife tourism as one of the primary strategies to protect unique ecosystems and species, such as the Hudson Bay Lowlands and polar bears (Christian *et al.*, 1996).

The management of Wabusk has traditionally been dominated by a particular Western approach to wildlife management, with certain actors and stakeholders consciously or unconsciously vying for control. For example, polar bear management has tended to emphasise either a conservationist utilitarian approach to game species management, or a preservationist approach emphasising the need for protection of endangered species. This somewhat Eurocentric and expert-driven approach to wildlife management, although effective in some areas of North America, may be myopic given the recognition of 'newer' approaches to wildlife management, which include multidisciplinary research, collaborative management, integration of traditional ecological knowledge in wildlife management, and the emergence of new stakeholders in these sociopolitical arenas. Consideration of collaborative approaches in wildlife management is fundamental to the appropriate development of PBPP, and the potential stresses from climate disruption; if polar bear management is to benefit from these new opportunities, then a reflexive reexamination of the dominant wildlife management paradigm in PBPP and polar bear management in Ontario in general will be required.

The recognition of the interplay between social values and research will occur only when all crucial stakeholders and their knowledge systems are equally acknowledged, and when polar bear management incorporates multidisciplinary approaches (i.e. ecosystem sciences and social sciences) with traditional ecological knowledge. Ironically, the PBPP master plan, management plan, and *Wabusk Co-Management Agreement* provide templates for how such strategies can be implemented. What is now required is a revision of these strategies, and written confirmation by all parties, so that these management plans become active management strategies, in which a systematic approach to monitoring the effects of implementation on social and ecological circumstances ensures the health of all beings in the Hudson Bay Lowlands.

References

Barringer, F. and Revkin, A.C. (2007) Agency proposes to list polar bears as threatened. *New York Times*. On-line document. Available HTTP: http://www.nytimes. com/2006/12/28/science/28polar.html (accessed 16 October 2007).

Beechey T.J. and Davidson, R.J. (1999) 'The Hudson Bay lowland', in L. Labatt and B. Littlejohn (eds) *Ontario's Parks and Wilderness: Islands of Hope*, Willowdale: Firefly Books.

Bird, L. (2005) *Telling Our Stories : Omushkego Legends and Histories from Hudson Bay*. Peterborough: Orchard Park.

— (2007) *The Spirit Lives in the Mind : Omushkego Stories,Lives, and Dreams*. Montreal: McGill-Queen's University Press.

Buscher, B. And Whande, W. (2007) 'Whims of the winds of time? Emerging trends in biodiversity conservation and protected area management', *Conservation and Society*, 5: 22–43.

Calvert, W., Stirling, I., Taylor, M., Lee, L.J., Kolenosky, G.B., Kearney, S., Crete, M., Smith, B. and Luttich, S (1991) 'Polar bear management in Canada 1985–87', in S.C. Amstrup and O. Wiig (eds) *Polar Bears: Proceedings of the Tenth Working Meeting of the IUCN/SSC Polar Bear Specialist Group, October 25–29, 1988, Sochi, USSR*. Gland, SW: Occasional Papers of the IUCN Species Survival Commission (SSC) No. 7.

Canadian Broadcast Corporation (CBC) News Service. (2008) U.S. lists polar bears as threatened species. On-line document. Available HTTP: http://www.cbc.ca/world/story/2008/05/14/polar-bear.html (accessed 15 May 2008.)

Christian C.S., Potts, T.D. Burnett, G.W. and Lacher. T.E. (1996) 'Parrot conservation and ecotourism in the Windward Islands', *Journal of Biogeography*, 23, 287–393.

The Committee on the Status of Endangered Wildlife in Canada (COSEWIC) (2008) Polar Bear and other Species at Risk Assessed by Independent Canadian Science Body: The Committee on the Status of Endangered Wildlife in Canada (COSEWIC) met in Yellowknife, Northwest Territories from April 20 to 25, 2008. On-line PDF document. Available HTTP: http://www.cosewic.gc.ca/rpts/sct7_3_11_e.pdf (accessed 26 April 2008).

Feherty, B. (2006) *Peawanuck The Promised Land*. Charleston: Book Surge.

Fidler, A., Lemelin, R.H., Peerla, D. and Walmark, B. (2008) 'Hearing the voices of all parties', WWF Arctic Bulletin, 1/08, 16–17.

Gagnon, A.S. and Gough, W.A. (2005) '*Trends in the dates of ice freeze-up and breakup over Hudson Bay, Canada*', *Arctic*, 58(4): 370–382.

Galley, K.E.M. (ed.) (2004) *Global Climate Change and Wildlife in North America*.

Technical Review 04–2. Technical Review Committee on Global Change and Wildlife. The Wildlife Society. Bethesda, MD.

Graham, J.E. (1988) *The Weenusk Cree: A Preliminary Background Report of Locals, Locations and Relocations, for Technology Assessment in Subarctic Ontario.* TASO Research Report # 30. Hamilton: McMaster University Research: Research Program for Technoloy Assessment in Subarctic Ontario.

Government of Ontario (2007) Provincial Parks and Conservation Reserves Act. On-line legal document. Available HTTP: http://www.e-laws.gov.on.ca/html/statutes/english/elaws_statutes_06p12_e.htm (accessed 14 October 2007).

Holdren, J.P., Heinz, T. and Heinz, J. (2007) Global Climate Disruption What Do We Know? What Should We Do? On-line PDF document. Available HTTP: http://belfer-center.ksg.harvard.edu/files/uploads/2007_11–16_Forum_(NXPowerLite).pdf (accessed 26 June 2008).

Kendall, C. (2006) 'Life on the edge of a warming world', *The Ecologist*, 36: 26–29.

Kolenosky, G.B. and Prevett, J.P. (1983) Productivity and maternity denning of polar bears in Ontario. *International Conference on Bear Research and Management,* 5: 238–45.

Lambert, S. (2007) Harper pledges money for northern research, improvements to port of Churchill. Available HTTP: http://origin.www.cbc.ca/cp/national/071005/n100590A.html (accessed October 14, 2007).

Lemelin, R.H. (2005) 'Wildlife tourism at the edge of chaos: complex interactions between humans and polar bears in Churchill, Manitoba', in F. Berkes, R. Huebert H. Fast, M. Manseau and A. Diduck (eds) *Breaking Ice: Renewable Resource and Ocean Management in the Canadian North,* Calgary: University of Calgary Press.

Lemelin, R. H. and McIntyre, N. (in press) 'Resiliency and Tourism in Ontario's Far North: The Social Ecological System of the Weenusk First Nation at Peawanuck', in P. Maher, E. Stewart, and M. Lück (eds) *Polar Tourism: Human, Environmental and Governance Dimensions*. Elmsford: Cognizant Communication Corporation.

Lemelin, R.H., Peerla, D. and Walmark, B. (2008) 'Voices from the Margins: The Muskekowuck Athinuwick/Cree People of Northern Ontario and the Management of Wapusk/Polar Bear', *Arctic* 61: 101–3.

Lunn, N.J., Atkinson, S., Branigan, M., Calvert, M., Clark, D., Doidge, B., Elliot, C., Nagy, I., Obbart, M., Otto, R., Stirling, I., Taylor, M., Vandal, D. and Wheatley, P. (2002) 'Polar bear management in Canada 1997–2000', in N.J. Lunn, S. Schliebe, and E.W. Born (eds) *Polar Bears: Proceedings of the 13th Working Meeting of the IUCN/SSC Polar Bear Specialist Group, 23–28 June 2001, Nuuk, Greenland.* Gland, SW: Occasional Paper of the IUCN Species Survival Commission.

Lunn, N.J., Branigan, M., Carpenter, E.L., Chaulk, K., Doidge, B., Galipeau, J., Hedman, D., Huot, M., Maraj, R., Obbard, M., Otto, R., Stirling, I., Taylor, M. and Woodley, S. (2006) 'Polar bear management in Canada 2001 – 2004', in J. Aars, N.J. Lunn, and A.E. Derocher (eds) *Polar Bears: Proceedings of the 14th Working Meeting of the IUCN/SSC Polar Bear Specialist Group, 20–24 June 2005, Seattle, Washington, USA.* Gland, SW: Occasional Paper of the IUCN, 32, Species Survival Commission.

Lytwyn, V.P. (2002) *Muskekowuck Athinuwick : Original People of the Great Swampy Land.* Winnipeg: Manitoba, Press.

Nishnawbe Aski Nation (NAN) (2007) NAN grand chief demands responsible land use planning. On-line news release. Available HTPP: http://www.nan.on.ca/upload/documents/comm-nan-release-land-use-planning-oct-3-2007-lh.pdf (accessed 19 October 2007).

Obbard, M.E. (2006) Temporal trends in the Body Condition of Southern Hudson Bay

Polar Bears. Climate Change Research Information Note Number 3. Government of Ontario, Applied Research and Development Branch. On-line report. Available HTTP: sit.mnr.gov.on.ca (accessed 3 August 2007).

Obbard, M.E., Mcdonald, T.L., Howe, E.J., Regehr, E.V. and Richardson, E.S. (2007) *Polar Bear Population Status in Southern Hudson Bay, Canada*. Reston, Virginia: US Department of the Interior, US Geological Survey.

Obbard, M.E. and Walton, L.R. (2004) 'The importance of Polar Bear Provincial Park to the southern Hudson Bay polar bear populations in the context of future climate change', in C.K. Rehbein J.G. Nelson, T.J. Beechey and R.J. Payne (eds) *Planning Northern Parks and Protected Areas: Proceedings of the Parks Research Forum of Ontario (PRFO), Annual General Meeting May 4–6, 2004, Lakehead University*. Waterloo, ON: Parks Research Forum of Ontario.

Ontario Ministry of Natural Resources (OMNR) (1977a) *Background Information: Polar Bear Provincial Park*. Toronto: Ministry of Natural Resources.

— (1977b) *Planning Proposal: Polar Bear Provincial Park*. Toronto: Ministry of Natural Resources.

— (1980) *Polar Bear Provincial Park: Master Plan*. Toronto: Ministry of Natural Resources.

— (1994) *Polar Bear Provincial Park Management Plan Review: Public Comments and Co-planning Team Responses Concerning the "Summary of Issues and Options Discussion Paper (November 1991)*. Toronto: Ministry of Natural Resources.

— (2007a) Addressing climate change: Research on the polar bears of southern Hudson Bay. On-line article. Available HTTP: http://www.mnr.gov.on.ca/MNR/csb/news/2007/jul19bg2_07.html (accessed 16 October 2007).

— (2007b) Ontario introduces proposed endangered species act, 2007: Backgrounder. On-line article. Available HTTP: http://www.mnr.gov.on.ca/MNR/Csb/news/2007/mar20bg1_07.html (accessed 19 October 2007).

Ontario Parks (2005) *Polar Bear Provincial Park. Master Plan – Proposed Amendment – November 2005*. On-line document. Available HTTP: http://www.ontarioparks.ca/english/planning_pdf/pola_plan_ammend.pdf (accessed 22 February 2007).

Pilon, J.L. (1982) 'Fort Severn land use and occupancy study', unpublished thesis, University of Toronto.

Prevett, J.P. and Kolenosky, G.B. (1982) 'The status of polar bears in Ontario', *Le Naturaliste Canadien*, 109: 933–39.

Regehr, E.V., Lunn, N.J., Amstrup, S.C. and Stirling, I. (2007) Effects of earlier sea ice breakup on survival and population size of polar bears in western Hudson Bay, *Journal of Wildlife Management*, 71, 2673–83.

Richardson, E.M., Branigan, W., Calvert, M., Cattet, M., Derocher, A.E., Doidge, W., Hedman, D., Lunn, N.J., McLoughlin, P., Obbard, M.E., Stirling, I. and Taylor, M. (2006) 'Polar bear management in Canada 2001–4' in J. Aars, N.J Lunn and A.E. Derocher (eds) *Polar Bears: Proceedings of the 14th Working Meeting of the IUCN/SSC Polar Bear Specialist Group, 20–24 June 2005, Seattle, Washington, USA*, 117–32, Gland, SW: Occasional Paper of the IUCN, 32, Species Survival Commission.

Scott, D., Malcolm J.R. and Lemieux, C. (2002) 'Climate change and modeled biome representation in Canada's National park system: implications for system planning and park mandates', *Global Ecology and Biogeography*, 11: 475–85.

Stirling, I., and Parkinson, C.L. (2006) 'Possible effects of climate warming on selected populations of polar bears (*Ursus maritimus*) in the Canadian Arctic', Arctic, 59: 261–75.

Suffling, R. and Scott, D. (2002) 'Assessment of climate change effects on Canada's national park system', *Environmental Monitoring and Assessment,* 74: 117–39.

US Department of the Interior (2008a) Remarks By Secretary Kempthorne: Press Conference On Polar Bear Listing May 14, 2008. On-line document. Available http: http://www.doi.gov/secretary/speeches/081405_speech.html (accessed 26 June 2008).

— (2008b) Endangered and threatened wildlife and plants: determination of threatened status for the polar bear (*Ursus maritimus*) throughout its range. On-line PDF document. Available HTTP:http://www.doi.gov/issues/polar_bears/Polar%20Bear%20Final%20 Rule_to%20FEDERAL%20REGISTE%20-Final_05-14-08.pdf (accessed 26 June 2008).

Usher, A.J. (1993) 'Polar Bear Park and area: community-oriented tourism development in Ontario's arctic, in M.E. Johnston and W. Haider (eds.) *Communities, Resources and Tourism In The North*, Thunder Bay; Lakehead University Centre for Northern Studies, Northern and Regional Studies Series.

Wiersma, Y.F., Beechey, T.J., Oosenbrug, B.M. and Meikle, J.C. (2005) *Protected Areas in Northern Canada: Designing for Ecological Integrity*. Gatineau: Canadian Council on Ecological Areas.

Wilkinson, P. and Wilkinson, C. (2005) 'Planning in the wind: the current planning status of Ontario's provincial parks', Proceedings from the 11th Canadian Congress on Leisure Research. *The Two Solitudes: Isolation or Impact?* Nanaimo: Malaspina University-College.

World Wildlife Fund (WWF) (2007) WWF-Canada statement on polar bears. PDF document. Available http : http://wwf.ca/NewsAndFacts/NewsRoom/RESOURCES/ PDF/WWF-Canada_Statement_PolarBears.pdf (accessed 19 October 2007).

6 Cruise Tourist Experiences and Management Implications for Auyuittuq, Sirmilik and Quttinirpaaq National Parks, Nunavut, Canada

Patrick T. Maher

Introduction

Tourism in the polar regions is a rapidly growing industry in terms of visitor, research, and political interest (see Maher 2007a; Maher and Stewart 2007; Snyder 2007; Snyder and Stonehouse 2007). The first of these (visitor interest) is likely brought about by growing media interest in the polar regions because of recent events, both positive (the International Polar Year) and negative (the sinking of the MS *Explorer* and other recent cruise ship groundings). Specific to Canada's Arctic, visitor numbers appear to be strong and in many cases growing (see Table 6.1) (see chapter 1).

Table 6.1: Estimates of visitor numbers to the Canadian Arctic by Province/Territory.

Location	Estimates	Study reference
Nunavut	• 13,000 visitors • 33,000 visitors • 9,323 summer visitors	• Buhasz, 2006 • Milne, 2006 • Datapath, 2006
Yukon	• 8049 visitors (North Yukon tourism region figures for 2004)	• Yukon Department of Tourism and Culture, 2006
Northwest Territories	• 62,045 non-resident travellers to the entire territory (visited in 2006-2007)	• Northwest Territories Industry, Tourism and Investment, 2007
Northern Manitoba	• 2100-3000 visitors to the Churchill Wildlife Management Area (CWMA) • 6300-9000 actual visits into the CWMA	• Lemelin, 2005 • Lemelin and Smale, 2007
Nunavik (Northern Quebec)	• 25,000 (Nord du Quebec, which in 2004 included both the Nunavik and James Bay regions)	• Tourisme Quebec, 2004
Nunatsiavut (Northern Labrador)	• 565 visitors to Torngat Mountains National Park in 2008 (272 in 2006; 484 in 2007) • 21,000 adventure tourists to all of Labrador in 2001	• Lemelin and Maher, in press • Hull, 2001

Modified and updated by author from: Dawson, Stewart, Maher and Slocombe (2009).

Cruise tourism is a sector of the Canadian industry that is undergoing considerable growth, and while volume does not yet compare with cruise activities elsewhere some predict the rate of growth will rapidly accelerate in the near future (Dawson *et al*. 2009). Cruise tourism is also a concerning activity for researchers (see Maher 2007a; Stewart *et al*. 2005), and for policy-makers/management (see Stewart and Draper 2006; Marquez and Eagles 2007) (see also chapter 3).

Nunavut's cruise product is a style of 'expedition cruising', in which cruising aboard smaller vessels is combined with brief shore visits (including community visits) and extensive education components (Dawson et al. 2009) (see Figure 6.1). The first 'expedition' cruise in Nunavut took place in 1984 by the MS *Lindblad Explorer* (Jones 1999); in the spotlight more recently as the cruise ship that sank off the Antarctic Peninsula in November 2007.

Figure 6.1 The *Prince Albert II* expedition cruise ship on a 2008 voyage. Pictured here in Torngat Mountains National Park, Labrador

Currently, the Baffin Bay region of Nunavut seems to receive the most cruises (see Joint Task Force North 2007), likely because of its quintessential 'Arctic' scenery, and its good wildlife viewing opportunities (Dawson *et al.* 2009). This region is also close to Greenland, which has an established cruise industry (see Association of Arctic Expedition Cruise Operators [AECO] 2007). As a result Baffin Island has been circumnavigated multiple times and many communities on Baffin Island regularly host cruise passengers. These realities thus affect all three parks covered by this chapter: Auyuittuq, Sirmilik and Quttinirpaaq (see Figure 6.2).

Cruise visitors to Nunavut are thought to be like most Arctic cruise tourists: generally well educated, well travelled, in their more advanced years and having high levels of disposable income (Jones 1999; Grenier 2004). The proposed itinerary generated by the government of Nunavut for 2007 listed 23 separate cruises run by six different companies (Nunavut Department of Economic Development and Transportation 2007). Based on maximum occupancies, an estimate would be 2,113 visitors in 2007 (Dawson *et al.* 2009). This estimate matches that collected through Nunavut's first visitor exit survey, when a total of 2,096 cruise tourists were accounted for on 22 cruise vessels in 2006 (Datapath 2006). Many communities across Nunavut are visited and information for Pond Inlet would thus have direct impacts for Sirmilik National Park. Pond Inlet received 10 cruise visits between 29 July and 8 September 2007. All of the cruise ships had between 110 and 150 passenger berths (Parks Canada 2007). Anecdotal evidence from Pond Inlet suggests that the community also receives at least one 'surprise' cruise ship visit every year.

According to data from the Joint Task Force North (2007), the busiest three weeks of cruising in 2007 were 26 July–22 August, when five separate vessels navigated the waters off Baffin, Devon and Ellesmere Islands. August was also the leading month for cruise travel to Nunavut according to the 2006 Nunavut visitor exit survey (Datapath 2006). The exit survey also reveals that cruise passengers participate in a wide variety of activities (more so than other types of tourists), including shopping, hiking, visits to cultural centres, wildlife viewing, visits to Territorial and/or National Parks, special events and kayaking. In Nunavut it is estimated that cruise tourists spend on average CAN$134 per person per night, contributing a total of CAN$2,124,000 to the Nunavut economy (Datapath 2006).

As a comparison, cruise tourism in other Arctic destinations is at higher levels. In Svalbard, 2003 numbers indicate that there were 69,691 landings made by 28,190 passengers (Geitz 2004). In 1998 numbers were at 19,341 and stabilised until the millennium, and then have been approximately 10,000 higher in the years since 2001 (Geitz 2004). Karlsdóttir (2004) noted that 53 ships made a port call in Akureyri, Iceland on their route between Europe and northern Norway, Svalbard and Greenland. These ships carried 32,500 passengers.

In Haines, Alaska (at the north end of Southeast Alaska's panhandle) there were 50,000 cruise visitors in 1994, and more than 187,000 in 2000 (Cerveny 2004). Of Southeast Alaska's 800,000 visitors in 2000, it is estimated that upwards of three-quarters (or 600,000) of these visitors arrive aboard large cruise ships

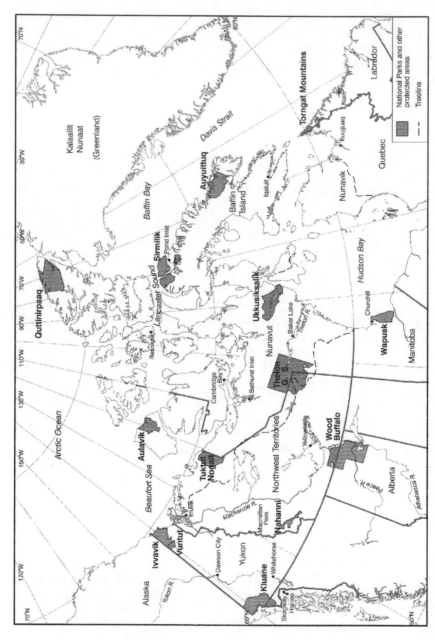

Figure 6.2 National Parks and Protected Areas in Canada's north

(Cerveny 2004). Linked to Alaska's cruise industry is its effect on Canada's Yukon territory and Kluane National Park. Sandiford (2006) reports that from Skagway, Alaska's 12,000 each Wednesday of the 2005 season, a single dog sled operator in the Yukon hosted 10,000 tourists. Kluane National Park reported 200 tourists/Wednesday hiking in the park, and in Parks Canada's eyes they were reaching a new audience with which to share their ecological messages (Sandiford 2006). Spin-offs from the park tours were felt in the park's gateway, Haines Junction, and the entire Alaskan cruise industry generated CAN$175 million and 2,000 jobs for the Yukon in 2000 (Sandiford 2006).

Methods

Surveys for this study were developed in cooperation between the University of Northern British Columbia (UNBC) and Parks Canada for the 2007 season. Advice on specific potential questions was sought from experts throughout the Nunavut Field Unit of Parks Canada, and questions were included to compare with previous related works (see Lachapelle *et al*. 2004, 2005; Maher *et al*. 2006; Maher 2007b).

Surveys were distributed to cruise vessels entering Nunavut's three cruise-accessible national parks (Auyuittuq, Sirmilik and Quttinirpaaq) by Parks Canada staff. Surveys were returned to Parks Canada by the cruise operators and were at season's end sent on to UNBC for data entry and analysis. The assumption is that every cruise guest and staff entering the three parks in 2007 was given a survey, as it was linked to their visitor registration process. Overall there were 323 respondents to the survey, with 2 couples replying on a single survey.

The survey was made available in both French and English, so it was hoped that language was not a major barrier to survey non-completion. As some cruises may have entered multiple parks, there is the presumption that some individuals may have answered the survey more than once. Overall it is important to note that this project was implemented as a pilot to potentially larger projects in the future. It was implemented to gather some important baseline data on a park visitor, the cruise tourist, whose numbers were rapidly increasing, but about whom relatively little was known by Parks Canada, the national parks' management agency.

Results

The results section of this chapter follows two main themes: a demographic profile of the respondents and their trip information, and the specific dimensions of their experience. This breakdown is based on the set-up of the survey; further details can be found in Maher and Meade (2008).

Demographic profile and trip information

The first section of the survey profiled the cruise passengers. Respondents provided their country, state/territory/province and city. The majority of the passengers came from either Canada (34.6%) or Denmark (35.0%). The remaining visitors came from the USA (10.2%), other European countries – notably France (4.6%) and Germany (4.3%) – and Australia (2.1%). The only populated continent that did not have passengers represented was Asia, and South America (0.9%) and Africa (0.3%) were poorly represented. Of the Canadian passengers, most hailed from the provinces of Ontario (57%) and Quebec (29%).

Visitors were also profiled based on age and gender. Passengers spanned many different age-groups. Responses indicate 51% were over the age of 60 years, 30% were between the ages of 40 and 59 years, 8% were between 20 and 39 years and 3% were under the age of 20 years. The remaining 8% gave no response. Gender was represented almost evenly, with females having a slightly higher representation (50%) than males (47%).

As the survey was included in the parks' visitor registration process, the survey asked about the passenger's role on the ship; 83% of passengers were paying guests, 7% were ship/expedition staff and 2% were 'other', usually media or public relations representatives of the cruise operators.

Trip information included asking about the National Park visited by each passenger, as well as the ship, company and sailing origin of the passengers. Of passengers surveyed, 215 visited Sirmilik National Park, 83 visited Auyuittuq National Park and 25 visited Quttinirpaaq National Park. The *Lyubov Orlova* had 168 passengers surveyed, *Ocean Nova* had 92 and the *Kapitan Khlebnikov* had 23. The *Kapitan Khlebnikov* was the only ship surveyed at Quttinirpaaq. The *Lyubov Orlova* had visitors surveyed at Auyuittuq and Sirmilik and *Ocean Nova* was surveyed only for Sirmilik.

Specific information regarding experiences

Prior experience travelling in the Canadian Arctic or on cruises

Passengers were asked if they had prior experience travelling in the Canadian Arctic: 60% of passengers indicated they had not, 33% indicated they had and 7% gave no response. When broken down for the countries with the most passengers, Americans were the most likely to have experienced the Canadian Arctic before (49%); this was higher than those who had not (45%). Of Canadian respondents, only 30% had travelled in the Canadian Arctic before and 66% had not (4% no response). Of European respondents; 14% of Germans, 13% of French, and 8% of Danish reported previous experience in the Canadian Arctic. Respondents were given an opportunity to describe where they had been and responses ranged from the Yukon in the west to Labrador in the east, as far south as Niagara Falls and Whistler (neither of which is in the Canadian Arctic by most people's definitions) to Eureka in the north; and virtually everywhere in between.

Passengers were asked if they had ever travelled on a cruise in the Arctic or Antarctic before. Of all responses, 33% had been on a cruise in the Arctic or Antarctic before, 60% had not and 7% gave no response. When broken down for the countries with the most passengers, 43% of Germans, 40% of French, 37% of

Danish, and 33% of Americans had been on an Arctic/Antarctic cruise before. Only 21% of Canadians had been on an Arctic/Antarctic cruise before and for 73%, this cruise was their first in either the Arctic or the Antarctic. Again, respondents were given an opportunity to describe where they had been in the past and responses varied from Svalbard, to Northeast and Northwest Greenland, Arctic Canada previously, the Russian Arctic and the Antarctic Peninsula.

Hope to experience

Passengers were asked what they hoped to experience during their trip. Of the 289 respondents who answered the question, there were 2,329 responses (as multiple responses were permitted for this question). Table 6.2 outlines both the total number of responses and relative percentage for each response category.

For the 17 'Other' responses, items that respondents stated that they hoped to experience were:

- Plants
- Inuit
- Glaciers
- Art
- Geology/Paleontology
- Peace and untouched nature
- Walrus (mentioned 3 times)
- Arctic fox
- Walk the tundra
- Spies at Eureka
- Native plants
- International experience with guests from around the world
- Friends (mentioned twice)
- Meet people

Trip planning

Passengers were asked how they learned about this specific trip. Those who gave responses frequently cited newspapers (52 responses), the internet (42 responses), the cruise company (36 responses) and word of mouth (31 responses). They also cited, less frequently, brochures, magazines, radio and staff. When asked how they learned about the specific tour company they had chosen, of those who responded, newspapers (45 responses), the internet (42 responses) and word of mouth (33 responses) were most frequently cited. Respondents also cited learning about the company from previous trips with them, travel agencies, the cruise company and brochures, but much less frequently than the first three media.

Passengers were asked how they learned about National Parks in Nunavut before leaving home. Of those who gave responses (174) most reported getting information about Nunavut's National Parks from the internet (28 responses),

Table 6.2: What visitors hope to experience during the trip.

Hope to Experience	Total	%
Wildlife	251	10.8
Birds	191	8.2
Whales	245	10.5
Polar Bears	258	11.1
Icebergs	241	10.3
Inuit Culture	224	9.6
Archaeological Sites	96	4.1
24 hour daylight	67	2.9
Mountains	140	6.0
Evidence of global climate change	87	3.7
Canadian National Park	120	5.2
Solitude	75	3.2
Silence	103	4.4
Lack of crowds	90	3.9
Pristine Scenic Vistas	124	5.3
Other	17	0.8

Lonely Planet and other guidebooks (24 responses), or the cruise company (24 responses).

Expectations met

Passengers were asked if their expectations of the experience had been met. Overall, the majority 197 (61%) of passengers felt their expectations were met. No response was given by 89 (28%) and 36 (11%) felt expectations were not met; one answer was illegible.

When broken down by country, 75% of Canadian respondents felt their expectations were met and only 4% felt they were not. Similarly, 67% of Danish expectations were met and 12% were not. Americans were split: 43% had expectations met, 24% did not and 33% gave no response. Conversely, 35% of German respondents indicated their expectations were met and 42% felt the experience did not meet their expectations. French respondents most frequently gave no response (80%). By age-group, 20–39 and 40–59-year-olds were the most satisfied that their expectations were met (70% each). Indications that expectations were not met increased with age, 0% for < 20, 7% for 20–39, 9% for 40–59 and 13% for 60+. In terms of prior experience there was little difference in whether expectations were met or not based on either Canadian Arctic experience or Arctic/Antarctic cruise experience.

When broken down by National Park visited, 68% of Sirmilik visitors felt their expectations were met and only 7% felt they were not. Of Quittinirpaaq visitors 60% felt their expectations were met and 40% felt they were not. Visitors of Auyuittuq often gave no response (45%) but had expectations usually met by the remaining group of respondents (43%).

Comments as to why or why not their expectations were met resulted in 19% no response, 25% were disappointed with the amount of wildlife seen (specifically polar bears, whales and narwhals), 19% felt it was too early in their trip to tell if expectations were met, 14% were disappointed with the amount of ice/ icebergs and wildlife, 8% were disappointed with the amount of ice, and 6% were disappointed with the ship. Notably, one person commented about park permits, and another about Inuit participation.

Categories with the most 'no' responses (country, age group and National Park) all shared comments citing 'the amount of wildlife' and 'the amount of wildlife and ice' as to why expectations were not met.

Mood

Passengers were asked to pick three words from a list that best describe the trip. These words relate to the visitor's mood on the trip, and are comparable with the dimension of mood studied in Maher *et al.* (2006) or Maher (2007b). For this question there were 499 responses from 209 respondents. This was out of a total of 627 possible responses, as each respondent had the opportunity to choose 3 unranked responses. Numbers and percentages of responses are shown in Table 6.3; 114 respondents left this question blank.

The list of mood descriptors is from the circumplex work of Russell (1980, 2003) and expressed similarly to the work of Maher *et al.* (2006) and Maher (2007b). The two dimensions of the circumplex are plotted as two perpendicular lines with mood descriptors being arranged in a 360° circle from the right-hand

Table 6.3: Full list of mood attributes and their corresponding degree (out of 360°), total responses and percentage of total.

Degree (out of 360°)	Mood title	Total	%
25°	Delightful	74	14.8
49°	Exciting	131	26.4
70°	Astonishing	68	13.6
97°	Alarming	0	0
100°	Infuriating	0	0
112°	Frightening	2	0.4
140°	Frustrating	3	0.6
180°	Unpleasant	3	0.6
189°	Miserable	0	0
210°	Depressing	4	0.8
245°	Boring	0	0
272°	Sleepy	3	0.6
316°	Calm	33	6.6
320°	Satisfying	67	13.4
329°	Serene	38	7.6
353°	Pleasant	73	14.6
——	Other	0	0

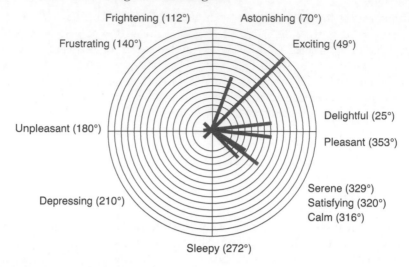

Figure 6.3 Mood attributes plotted on a circumflex

side around the circumplex. The assumption is that a dimension is not independent, but rather that for example 'exciting' is a dimension in its own right, but also a combination of arousing and pleasant. In this study visitors were given the choice of 16 descriptors (as was the case with Maher *et al.* 2006 and Maher 2007b) and asked to choose up to three. They were also given the option of choosing an 'other' category if the 16 descriptors listed did not cover their moods.

Mood descriptors, as chosen by respondents, have been approximated in Figure 6.3. Each band of the circumplex (bullseye) represents 10 responses. Thus, the longer the line the greater the number of respondents who chose it, the particular quadrant of the circumplex that the line falls in indicates a group of related moods.

Landings and impacts

Passengers were asked if they had made any landings so far on their trip, and if so the amount of money they had spent on each one. A total of 192 visitors mentioned making a landing and 130 visitors wrote in a dollar amount for how much they had spent. The amount spent ranged from CAN$0 to CAN$900.00 and for the 80 responses that included a dollar above $0.00 amount for a landing, a total of CAN$8,618.00 was spent in communities or CAN$107.74 per response/landing.

Passengers were asked if they noticed any negative impacts associated with cruise ship visits. Most visitors who landed did not notice any negative impacts; however, 20 people (6%) did. They were also asked to comment about the impacts they saw. Of those who did notice negative impacts, the main concern was that the tourists overwhelm the communities, i.e. the tourists cause the population to double and there is much disorder. These respondents also identified cultural impacts, selling of narwhal tusks, garbage and the town still appearing poor despite tourism as other impacts.

Specific climate change impacts

Passengers were asked if they had heard about or noticed any effects of global climate change. The majority of respondents indicated that they had noticed effects of climate change on their trip (52%). Of the remainder 15% indicated that they had not noticed any effects of climate change and 33% gave no response.

When broken down by country the French had the highest 'Yes' responses (71%) and zero 'No' responses. Americans were also highly likely to indicate that they had noticed effects of climate change; 64% 'Yes', 3% 'No'. Similarly, 60% of Canadians had noticed effects while 14% had not. The Danish responded differently, with no majority response: 44% 'Yes' and 24% 'No'. The majority of German respondents gave no response (66%).

This question also asked those who did notice effects of climate change if experiencing the northern ecosystem (both nature and culture) had inspired them to make changes to their lifestyle when they returned home. Most passengers noted that they were inspired to make changes to their lifestyle (71%).

When broken down by age group, the youngest passengers all indicated they were inspired to make changes (100%). This inspiration to make changes decreased with age; age 20–39 (85%), age 40–59 (79%), age 60+ (62%).

When broken down by country, although the French had the highest percentage of 'Yes' responses for effects of climate change they had the highest percentage of 'No' responses for lifestyle changes (50%), whereas Canadians had the highest percentage of respondents who indicated a desire to implement a change in lifestyle (84%).

Respondents were also given an opportunity to comment on the changes; 21 comments were made by those who were inspired by the northern ecosystem. There were eight who 'have decided to make a change', and seven who have 'already made changes–reinforced' comments. Two comments reflected the scale of the changes beyond the individual and two comments related to the fact that they were expecting to hear about climate change, but had not so far in their cruise.

Specific experience in Nunavut's National Parks

The last question asked passengers to classify the experience they desire in Nunavut's National Parks. For those who used one response, 'Arctic Experience' made up 49% of the responses. 'Learning/Appreciation' made up 22%, 'Naturalness' 14%, 'Challenge/Adventure' 8% and 'Serenity/Freedom' 6%. Only one person (< 1%) indicated 'Spirituality' as their desired experience.

Some respondents indicated more than one desired experience, but 51% of the responses were some combination of 'Arctic Experience' and another. Responses that included both 'Naturalness' and 'Arctic Experience' made up 27%, 'Serenity' in some combination made up 11% and 'Naturalness' in combination made up 7%. Some respondents desired all experiences (2%).

Conclusions

The data analysed in this study (Maher and Meade 2008) have revealed some interesting and potentially useful information for management regarding cruise tourism experiences in Auyuittuq, Sirmilik and Quttinirpaaq National Parks. Specific to the individual portions of the study, some key findings are as follows:

Demographic profile

Cruise tourists in Auyuittuq, Sirmilik and Quttinirpaaq National Parks are from similar countries to other polar cruise tourists, i.e. developed nations. Of note is the potential effect on results that having certain operators visiting certain places has; e.g. the high proportion of Danes links to the uniquely marketed voyages of the *Ocean Nova*.

The high proportion of Ontario and Quebec passengers within the Canadian contingent is likely in direct connection with the air transport linkages between southern Canada and Nunavut; the economic capacity of individuals in those provinces; and probably also connected by simple geography (south of Nunavut), whereas western Canadians may choose to visit NWT or the Yukon.

Age is also similar to other polar cruise tourist statistics: still primarily an older crowd, but not exclusively, and in many destinations getting younger. The gender split amongst respondents is as expected and 'guest' being the primary role for respondents was also as expected.

Trip information

The split of visitors amongst the three parks is interesting. The overwhelming number of respondents visiting Sirmilik National Park matches the concern shown by Parks Canada in implementing this study, especially as Sirmilik was left out of other recent studies (Lachapelle *et al*. 2004, 2005).

Low response numbers from Quttinirpaaq National Park are not surprising given the park location and limited number of cruises that visit it each year. Low response numbers from the *Kapitan Khlebnikov* match the fact that it is the vessel used to visit Quttinirpaaq National Park.

Ocean Nova's visits to only Sirmilik National Park, with a primarily Danish population, may have some interesting management implications for Parks Canada, especially in light of the sovereignty concerns between Canada and Denmark over even the smallest points of land between Baffin Island and Greenland.

Specific information regarding experiences

Respondents' limited travel experience in the Canadian Arctic in the past may have some interesting implications for management in that more generic information and interpretation may be necessary. This may also influence the respondent's ability to accurately answer some of the questions further along on the survey.

The relatively high percentage of US respondents who had travelled to the Canadian Arctic points to how heavily such a market has already traveled in the polar regions (the USA has always been the primary market for Antarctic cruises since their inception). The increase in Danish and other European tourists, however, may point to the future.

Travel across the Canadian Arctic was varied and included some interesting answers, e.g. Whistler and Niagara Falls. The number of respondents who had travelled on a polar cruise in the past may link to the growing importance of this sector as a way to experience such remote areas. In the past, the overall percentage that the cruise sector occupied for Canada's Arctic was likely much lower. The percentage of certain nationalities to have taken a polar cruise is an interesting finding; the reason for such numbers, however, is unclear.

The items respondents hoped to experience are highly skewed towards natural features of wildlife (especially iconic ones such as polar bears and whales) and scenery (icebergs), with culture (Inuit), being only the fifth ranked choice. This is likely a result that could have been expected, given the highly visual, versus experiential, manner in which the cruises may have been advertised. Respondents' reliance on newspapers and the internet as a source of information is interesting, newspaper advertising being the traditional source of the past and the internet being the source of the future.

Expectations being met and exceeded is not surprising. The region where all three parks are located is spectacular, has unique cultural attributes and operators strive to offer excellent experiences given the cost of tours. Because of the nature of the question on the survey it is, however, unclear whether respondents are responding to the overall experience on the cruise or the specific National Park where they were surveyed. It is interesting to note that expectations not being met increased with age.

Again because of the non-specific nature of the question, it is interesting to examine the relation between expectation met and National Park visited; is Quttinirpaaq National Park not meeting expectations, or does this 'No' response translate to the operator or perhaps the price of a tour to that even more remote location? From the note as to why expectations were not met, it is interesting that the main reason 'Lack of wildlife' is out of everyone's control (park management, operators). The highly positive mood is similar to results from other polar tourism studies (Maher *et al*. 2006; Maher 2007b), but the link between mood and expectation is an area for further examination in this instance and elsewhere.

The limited amount of money spent in local communities is an important result. This is an area that needs to be worked on if the potential benefit of cruise tourism to the parks (and nearby communities) is to be fully realised. It is interesting to note the lack of negative impacts on communities seen by cruise tourists; this contradicts findings from recent community-based studies on tourism in the Arctic (see Stewart and Draper 2007).

Comments on climate change are interesting, but again it should be noted that it may be difficult for cruise tourists to truly 'notice' changes given how many have not visited before. Perhaps there is a sense of noticing the changes after having been told about them beforehand by the operator and the media. 'Arctic experience', however classified by respondents, is of much higher importance to cruise tourists than to the more recreational type of visitors studied by Lachapelle *et al.* (2004, 2005). For Parks Canada, figuring out exactly what this entails is a key management strategy, especially given their recently revised mandate that now focuses on creating memorable visitor experiences as well as maintaining ecological integrity.

Acknowledgements

The data presented in this chapter are a result of a research project conducted with funding from a UNBC seed grant for 2007. The project was supported in its implementation by the Nunavut Field Unit of the Parks Canada Agency. Specific acknowledgment for their input to the project goes to Christian Kimber, Andrew Maher, Carey Elverum, Pauline Scott and Kristy Frampton of Parks Canada; Dani Meade, an undergraduate research assistant at UNBC; Pam Schaus of Wilfrid Laurier University for creating the map in Figure 2; the cruise ship operators; and the cruise ship visitors themselves for all the valuable information they provided.

References

Association of Arctic Expedition Cruise Operators (AECO) (2007) *AECO'S guidelines for Expedition Cruise Operations in the Arctic.* Longyearbyen, Svalbard: AECO.
Buhasz, L. (2006) Northern underexposure. *Globe & Mail,* July 1.
Cerveny, L.K. (2004) *Preliminary research findings from a study of the sociocultural effects of tourism in Haines, Alaska.* General technical report PNW-GTR-612. Portland, OR: USDA Forest Service, Pacific Northwest Research Station.
Datapath (2006) Nunavut Exit Survey. Marsh Lake.
Dawson, J., Maher, P.T. and Slocombe, D.S. (2007) 'Climate change, marine tourism and sustainability in the Canadian Arctic: contributions from systems and complexity approaches', *Tourism in Marine Environments,* 4(2–3): 69–83.
Geitz, M. (ed.) (2004) Cruise Tourism on Svalbard – A risky business? Oslo: WWF.
Grenier, A.A. (2004) *The Nature of Nature Tourism,* Acta Universitatis Lapponiensis 74, Rovaniemi: University of Lapland.
Hull, J.S. (2001) 'Opening up the big land to the world: the role of the public sector in adventure tourism development in Labrador', in B. Sahlberg (ed.) *Going North: Peripheral Tourism in Canada and Sweden,* Östersund: European Tourism Research Institute.
Joint Task Force North (2007) *Shipping Activity Brief-2007 JTFN J2 Section.* Unpublished Report.
Jones, C.S. (1999) 'Arctic ship tourism: an industry in adolescence', *The Northern Raven,* 13(1): 28–31.
Karlsdóttir, A. (2004) *Cruise Tourists in Iceland: Survey on the economic significance of cruise tourism,* Project Report, Reykjavik: University of Iceland Tourism Unit.
Lachapelle, P.R., McCool, S.F. and Watson, A.E. (2004) *Developing an Understanding of*

Landscape Interactions, Experiences and Meanings: Auyuittuq and Quttinirpaaq National Parks of Canada, Nunavut, Technical completion report, Missoula, MT: The University of Montana and the Aldo Leopold Wilderness Research Institute.

— (2005) *Auyuittuq and Quttinirpaaq National Parks summer 2004 visitor experience study,* Missoula: The University of Montana and the Aldo Leopold Wilderness Research Institute.

Lemelin, R.H. (2005) 'Wildlife tourism at the edge of chaos: complex interactions between humans and polar bears in Churchill, Manitoba', in F. Berkes, R. Huebert, H. Fast, M. Manseau and A. Diduck (eds) *Breaking Ice: Renewable Resource and Ocean Management in the Canadian North,* Calgary: University of Calgary Press.

Lemelin, R.H. and Maher, P.T. (2009) 'Nanuk of the Torngats: human-polar bear interactions in Torngat Mountains National Park, Labrador, Canada', *Human Dimensions of Wildlife,* 14(2): 152–55.

Lemelin, R.H. and Smale, B. (2007) 'Wildlife tourist archetypes: are all polar bear viewers in Churchill, Manitoba ecotourists?' *Tourism in Marine Environments,* 4(2–3): 97–111.

Maher, P.T. (2007a) 'Arctic tourism: a complex system of visitors, communities, and environments', *Polar Geography,* 30(1–2): 1–5.

— (2007b) Footsteps on the ice: visitor experiences in the Ross Sea region, Antarctica, unpublished Doctor of Philosophy thesis, Lincoln University.

Maher, P.T., McIntosh, A.J. and Steel, G.D. (2006) 'Examining dimensions of anticipation: inputs for experience prior to visiting the Ross Sea region, Antarctica', *Tourism in Marine Environments,* 2(2): 51–63.

Maher, P.T. and Meade, D. (2008) *Cruise Tourism in Auyuittuq, Sirmilik and Quttinirpaaq National Parks,* Technical Report – ORTM Publication Series 2008–02, Prince George: UNBC ORTM Program.

Maher, P.T. and Stewart, E.J. (2007) 'Polar tourism: research directions for current realities and future possibilities', *Tourism in Marine Environments,* 4(2–3): 65–68.

Marquez, J.R. and Eagles, P.F.J. (2007) 'Working towards policy creation for cruise ship tourism in parks and protected areas of Nunavut', *Tourism in Marine Environments,* 4(2–3): 85–96.

Milne, S. (2006) 'Baffin Island, Nunavut, Canada', in G. Baldacchino (ed.) *Extreme Tourism: Lessons from the World's Cold Water Islands,* Oxford: Elsevier.

Northwest Territories Industry, Tourism and Investment. (2007) *Canada's Northwest Territories: Tourism & Parks: Tourism research and statistics.* Online. Available: HTTP: http://www.iti.gov.nt.ca/parks/tourism/research_and_statistics.htm (accessed 28 September 2007).

Nunavut Department of Economic Development and Transportation. (2007) *2007 Nunavut cruise ship itinerary list,* Unpublished report.

Parks Canada (2007) *Cruise ships to Pond Inlet, NU,* Unpublished listing for Sirmilik National Park.

Russell, J.A. (1980) 'A circumplex model of affect', *Journal of Personality and Social Psychology,* 39(6): 1161–78.

— (2003) 'Core affect and the psychological construction of emotion', *Psychological Review,* 110(1): 145 – 172.

Sandiford, K. (2006) 'Cruise control', *Up Here* (May/June): 38–43, 73.

Snyder, J. (2007) *Tourism in the Polar Regions: The Sustainability Challenge,* Paris: United Nations Environment Program.

Snyder, J.M. and Stonehouse, B. (eds) (2007) *Prospects for Polar Tourism,* Wallingford: CABI.

Stewart, E.J. and Draper, D. (2006) 'Sustainable cruise tourism in Arctic Canada: an integrated coastal management approach', *Tourism in Marine Environments,* 3(2): 77–88.

— (2007) 'A collaborative approach to understanding local stakeholder perceptions of tourism in Churchill, Manitoba (Canada)', *Polar Geography*, 30(1–2): 7–35.

Stewart, E.J., Draper, D. and Johnston, M.E. (2005) 'A review of tourism research in the Polar Regions', *Arctic*, 58(4): 383 – 394.

Tourisme Québec (2004) *Tourisme en chiffres 2004 – version finale*, Québec: Gouvernement du Québec.

Yukon Department of Tourism and Culture (2006) *2004 visitor exit survey: Klondike region*, Whitehorse: Government of Yukon.

7 A Holiday on Ice on Hold? Nature-based Tourism and Climate Change in the Nordic North

Linda Lundmark

Introduction

Outdoor recreation and nature-based tourism have been and still are of great importance for people in the Nordic countries (Hall *et al.* 2009) (Figure 7.1). Skiing, hiking, bird watching and dog sledging are only some examples of activities that are enjoyed. Natural resources and amenities are therefore an essential part of the tourism product. Tourism, being a business dependent on many factors that the entrepreneur does not control, is constantly affected by demographic, economic, market and technological changes. Furthermore, political decisions and regulations play an important role for the tourism entrepreneur. As climate and weather are resources used by tourism entrepreneurs, climate change will affect the entrepreneurs' opportunities, possibilities and constraints for development and change (Bürki *et al.* 2003; Dewar 2005; Saarinen and Tervo

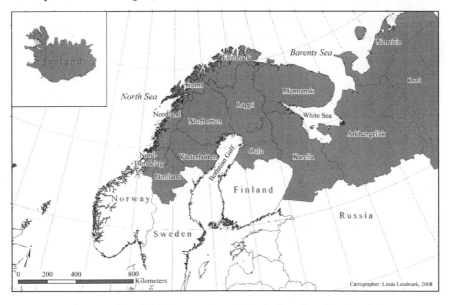

Figure 7.1 The countries of the European north (excluding Greenland) and the administrative areas of the polar region

2006; chapter 8 [this volume]). Nature-based tourism is more vulnerable than other types of tourism because it requires outdoor activities in turn dependent on good climate conditions and weather (Scott *et al*. 2007a, 2007b; Sievänen *et al*. 2005).

This chapter outlines the possible effects of climate change on nature-based tourism in sparsely populated areas in the north of the Scandinavian peninsula. Some of the most important factors for adaptation and vulnerability are discussed as well as some of the difficulties facing nature-based tourism research and climate change.

Nature-based tourism

Nature-based tourism in its widest sense incorporates all tourism that takes place in areas rich in natural amenities as well as activities connected to nature. It also includes related concepts such as wilderness tourism, ecotourism and adventure tourism (Hall *et al*. 2009). Furthermore, indigenous tourism, being a combination of both nature and culture tourism, is included (Notzke 1999). In the polar region of the European North nature-based tourism is an important part of the tourism industry. The most common commercial activities that people engage in are winter skiing, ice fishing and snowmobiling; in summer, fishing and hiking in the mountains are common as well as hunting. More specialised tourism attractions are whale safaris in the North Sea and trips to Svalbard. Using a broad definition, however, most nature-based tourism falls outside regular commercial activities unless undertaken as guided tours. Examples are such activities as walking in the forest, sunbathing, picking mushrooms and berries and bird watching. However, although not contributing directly to activity-based tourism, business tourists still contribute to the local economy. It is therefore difficult to estimate the economic value of nature for tourism. However, in Finland as much as 40% of the adult population is involved in nature-based tourism, with an average of 9 trips per year per person. This amounts to around 14 million trips annually (Sievänen 2007). Nature is cited by foreign visitors as the most important reason for choosing Finland as their travel destination. In 2004 almost 5 million foreign visitors came to Finland, of which 25% participated in outdoor activities. In the late 1990s nature-based tourism was estimated to account for 1,700 year-round jobs and 1,450 part time/seasonal jobs, or around 200 million Euro in Finland (Rinne and Saastamoinen 2005). This is equivalent to 20% of the total turnover of foreign tourism on a national level. A modest estimation of the economic value of nature-based tourism in Sweden is around 2.5 million euro (Fredman *et al*. 2008), based on visitor attractions in the country and thus not including several important tourism segments such as second home tourism, fishing and hunting.

The landscapes that people encounter in the polar region of the European North are varied and include lakes, forests, mountains, sea and other dramatic environments as well as towns and villages. Environmental and climate-related factors important for nature-based tourism include snow, ice and cold in the winter, with short days in terms of sunlight. In summer a pleasant climate (albeit with mosquitoes), short nights, reindeer and wildlife such as moose are also part of the natural assets.

Climate change predictions

There are numerous studies in which the expected impacts of climate change at different geographical levels are estimated (e.g. Ministry of the Environment 2001: 71; Keup-Thiel *et al*. 2005). Climate change predictions for Sweden made by Sykes and Prentice (1999) for the Swedish Environmental Protection Agency built on the European Center Hamburg Model (ECHAM3) climate model and the Hadley Climate Centre forecasts predict increased mean temperatures in central Sweden of 1–2° to 5–6°C by the end of the century. 2008 was the warmest winter ever recorded in most parts of Norway, Sweden and Finland (McMullen and Jabbour 2009). More recent IPCC forecasts have suggested that depending on the capacity to control anthropogenic emissions then the figures for high latitudes may be even higher (McMullen and Jabbour 2009; also see chapter 2 [this volume]). The ACIA (2005), focusing on the climate change and variability in polar areas, shows that in region 1 (which includes eastern Greenland, North Atlantic, Northern Scandinavia, northwestern Russia) the temperature is likely to rise between 2° and 3°C in eastern Greenland and northern Scandinavia, and as much as 3–5°C in northwestern Russia. Even the more modest climate change estimations would entail a drastic and serious cause for concern for society as a whole as well as for tourism (McMullen and Jabbour 2009).

The most immediate and direct impact on vegetation in the north will be on biomass, where an increase in annual growth rate is expected (IPCC 2007). A warmer climate in combination with increased precipitation stimulates biomass growth, including shrubs and a more rapid growth of seedlings and young forest. Climatic changes will also increase the potential for the introduction of new species as well as the movement of existing ones to the north and to higher altitudes (see also chapter 2). The area considered in this paper is geographically located within the Arctic region, where the temperature will most likely increase even more than on average. Greater intensive precipitation, shorter snow periods and longer vegetation periods are to be expected. The coastal areas are expected to suffer from higher water levels, with flooding, an increased area of wetlands, and greater erosion levels. The prediction is also that seasonal changes will intensify. Increased precipitation and seasonal flooding will likely cause disruption of transportation networks and the long-term spreading of wetlands (Keup-Thiel *et al*. 2005).

Changes in demand and supply of nature-based tourism

There is no doubt that climate change as described above will affect both the supply of and demand for nature-based tourism. However, exactly how this will happen is still uncertain (Bigano *et al*. 2006; Gössling and Hall 2006). Before any attempt to estimate the economic impact of climate change on tourism, an understanding of the differences within the industry is vital. For tourism, changes in climate can have more or less immediate effects on travel patterns that do not appear to be the case for other economic activities in the area, for example, with respect to forest-related activities (Lundmark 2005). This means that tourism is more sensitive to climate change at the local and regional business level. Impact of climate change is generally considered to increase with time so depending on the time frame considered there are different conclusions to be drawn. According to Berrittella *et al.* (2006) there could be positive effects on tourism in the European Union until 2030, but by 2050 such changes will have turned negative, with Western Europe as net losers, especially in the Mediterranean region.

The general effects of climate change on demand and supply are difficult to foresee, but it is expected that the volume of travellers, when people travel during the year, the choice of destination and type of holiday experience tourists seek will all change (Aall and Höyer 2005). However, supply side effects are not only related to the tourist behaviour but also to the quality and nature of the attraction.

With respect to demand, there are three ways in which climate can change behaviour and experience of a destination (Richardson and Loomis 2004; Saarinen and Tervo 2006):

1   The *direct effects* of weather condition and climate. Temperature, precipitation and snow depth can become important for tourists' motivation to visit and revisit a destination, for the number of days they spend at a destination or whether they visit at all.
2   Climate change also has some *indirect effects* via changes to flora and fauna and thus the landscape and environment in which tourism occurs. These effects may have the same results as the direct effects on visitation.
3   The direct and indirect effects of climate change do not only impact the destination. The origin of the potential tourist is also changing with potential impact on preference and demand on destinations.

Studies on climate change and tourism have indicated a relationship between travel patterns and climate (e.g. Berrittella *et al.* 2006; Hamilton *et al.* 2005). Since climate is strongly connected to temperature, temperature is often used as a parameter to establish demand in many studies (e.g. Gómez Martín 2005). Research has indicated that climate affects well-being and that precipitation, temperature, wind and sun are factors that affect temporary and permanent migration (Richardson and Loomis 2004; Gössling and Hall 2006). This means that an increase in temperature potentially could be positive for colder areas. However, higher temperatures in combination with increased precipitation and humidity may increase the incidence of pests and disease, which may also spread more easily; if this occurs then it could hamper the potential benefits of any temperature increases for tourism development (see chapter 2).

The relationship between increasing temperatures and travel flows is not linear, however (Maddison 2001; Hamilton *et al.* 2005; Gössling and Hall 2006), and could be influenced by different sources of information. The available information about destinations from direct contact between people, general media and through guidebooks is important as well (Bigano *et al.* 2006; Zillinger 2007). Information on how climate change is affecting a region and also how it is received is also important from a supply-side perspective. There are studies that have used interviews or surveys in order to see how stakeholders perceive and handle climate change in tourism and tourism demand. These studies show that while most stakeholders recognise climate change to be a problem, they do not think it is as severe as the media want them to believe (e.g. Bürki *et al.* 2003; Sievänen *et al.* 2005). Most actors thought that snowmaking techniques would be sufficient to mitigate the negative impact of climate change (Bürki *et al.* 2003). In a study by Sievänen *et al.* (2005) half of the interviewees did not think that climate change is occurring, and many of the others had little information on how climate change would affect them.

Some of the implications of climate change are general to tourism on a global scale. Pleasing and dramatic landscapes attract both active and passive visitors, which means that not only those tourists directly motivated by or dependent on nature and nature-based activities for their trip will be affected by climate change and weather conditions. Factors to consider include transport, accessibility and security issues. Unreliable nature conditions, which increase the element of risk, thus decrease the interest for visiting among tourists in general.

Changes in tourism flows on a global scale entail changes in overall consumption patterns, both spatially and in terms of expenditure on different consumer goods and services related to tourism. There is a relocation of expenditures because changes in preferences among tourists influence patterns of consumption. Assuming that the size of the global demand stays the same there should be an increase in one place consistent with a decrease somewhere else and climate change is also believed to affect the number of people who prefer to travel domestically rather than to go abroad (Berrittella *et al.* 2006). Several studies have concentrated on travel patterns for different nationalities. Maddison (2001), for example, concentrates on British travellers whereas Hamilton (2003) focuses on German travellers. These studies also take into account the economic aspects of climate change and tourism, although not from an economics perspective.

Winter tourism, and especially ski tourism, is likely to be adversely affected by rising temperatures, because of its high level of dependence on reliable snow conditions (IPCC 2001, 2007; Sievänen *et al.* 2005; Saarinen and Tervo 2006; Hall 2009; chapter 8 [this volume]). One study has shown that during periods of snow scarcity, 49% of tourists choose to go to another destination and 32% ski less (Bürki 2000). As major destinations for winter tourism northern areas are identified as vulnerable to climate change. The Alps as well as more northern destinations have already experienced decreasing snow depth and shorter snow periods (Moen and Fredman 2007). As an activity, skiing is important for many destinations in Sweden, Finland and Norway. The vulnerability of the local context is therefore dependent on the flexibility in other areas of economic activity and government structures.

Recognising that a core factor for economic development in tourism is entrepreneurship (Lordkipanidze *et al.* 2005) does not mean that entrepreneurship is the only important factor for development. The vulnerability of businesses depends on externalities independent of the entrepreneur such as institutionalized vacation times, disposable incomes, cost for travel and mobility and restrictions on travel within and between countries and regions. These will in turn be the drivers for future demand and travel patterns (Sievänen *et al*. 2005; Bigano *et al*. 2006).

Climate change, vulnerabilities and adaptation in tourism

Nature-based tourism is sensitive to changes in climate and subsequent impact on flora and fauna as well as the activities offered at the destination (Richardson and Loomis 2004; Gössling and Hall 2006). Demand is affected by climate change, especially because the tourists experience climate as weather (Gómez Martín 2005). Tourism studies on climate change so far have concentrated on a limited number of topics (Hall 2008). Gössling and Hall (2006) identify two 'branches of publications' within tourism and climate change research. One strand of research focuses on the impact of climate change on destinations and the industry within a national framework, whereas the other focuses on tourist responses and preferences in relation to climate and climate change. Hamilton *et al*. (2005) divide the studies into three categories in which statistical analysis of behaviour, scenarios and weather as an attraction are counted. Adaptation to and mitigation of climate change in the tourism system from a supply-side point of view is a field of study that has been poorly investigated, with some notable exceptions, most of which focus on the winter tourism industry (Bürki *et al*. 2003; Sievänen *et al*. 2005; Moen and Fredman 2007; Scott *et al*. 2007a, 2007b). Because of the rapid changes that are predicted, especially in the polar areas, there is clearly a need for more in-depth studies.

Two general concepts that are widely used in climate change studies are vulnerability and adaptive capacity. In its simplest form, as interpreted by the IPCC, 'Vulnerability is the degree to which a system is susceptible to, or unable to cope with, adverse effects of climate change, including climate variability and extremes' (IPCC 2001: 6). According to Viner and Agnew (1999: 46)'the most vulnerable tourist resorts and regions are a function of the likely magnitude and extent of the climate impact and the importance of tourism to the local economy'. However, this interpretation excludes basic information about the local and national circumstances and structures that support or impede adaptation. O'Brien *et al*. (2004) claim that three basic assumptions are required to understand vulnerability: vulnerability varies geographically and among social groups, it is scale dependent and it is dynamic. The connection between social, economic and political characteristics and trends and the ability to respond to environmental stress is universal, although the response and adaptation strategies vary with time and space (Kelly and Adger 2000). Adaptive capacity and vulnerability thus change with other socioeconomic processes occurring at the local to the global scale. Overall structures and characteristics are also important because of the supply of labour and services to the industry. These circumstances may either facilitate or constrain adaptation for individuals, businesses, communities, regions and nations. An example of future change that is important for tourism is demographic change. Lundgren (2005) models the trends for travel in Sweden departing from individual characteristics of a future population in Sweden. According to his research, the ageing population could be a potential market for the northern peripheral locations, allowing for a continuing demand. However, climate change is not taken into account in such forecasts.

Adaptation within different geographical, organisational or personal aspects can also be seen as anticipatory or reactive (Carter and Kankaanpää 2003). However, the possible adaptation and mitigation strategies (Figure 7.2) are not independent of but rather interdependent with socioeconomic processes (Lundmark *et al.* 2008). Anticipatory planned adaptation is needed among both private entrepreneurs and public sector bodies (Sievänen *et al.* 2005). There is widespread debate surrounding the need for and urgency in political action regarding restrictions on mobility and air transport, which would affect the tourism industry in a profound way (Gössling and Hall 2006; Gössling et al. 2010). However, restrictions could be both good and bad for the areas in the north. Enterprises that can survive with a domestic market will be promoted when more distant destinations are substituted, under the assumption that demand is constant but perhaps changing direction.

		ANTICIPATORY	REACTIVE
Natural systems			*Impact* • Warmer climate • Increased precipitation • Increased frequency and intensity of extreme weather events • Impact on flora and fauna
Tourism system	**Demand**	• Changes in preference and behaviour patterns	• Changes in preference and behaviour patterns
	Supply	• Insurance • Geographical risk spreading • Management • Diversification of business • Innovation	• Changes in business structure • Diversification
	Public	• Environmental protection measures (mitigation) • Laws, rules and regulations • Civil emergency planning • Cooperation between levels • Political stability	• Laws, rules and regulations (transport and emission restrictions) • Civil emergency planning

Figure 7.2 Summary of adaptation to and mitigation of climate change in the tourism system

Geographically adaptation takes place from the micro level to the global level. Publicly, climate change is planned for by general means of adaptation; privately, in businesses or within organizations, different strategies might be implemented to adapt. How this adaptation is carried out for different actors in the tourism production system varies at different levels and for different actors. Entrepreneurs might choose to insure their business to a higher extent, spread their risks geographically or diversify and innovate new products to become less vulnerable to climate change (Lundmark *et al.* 2008) (Figure 7.2). People might also have different adaptation strategies as individuals than as entrepreneurs. Since tourism is international it is sensitive to changes that interrupt the equilibrium between destinations. Destinations dependent on natural resources in order to compete for tourists are mostly affected by such changes, whereas destinations with a majority of tourists coming for business reasons or for culture and history are not so vulnerable (Bigano *et al.* 2006).

The impact and vulnerability of the tourism sector depends on the flexibility of the enterprise. In part this flexibility lies within a structural framework. One might argue that there is a hierarchical flexibility to climate change within the tourism production system: the tourist is most flexible and thus if the destination does not meet the preferences the tourist will go somewhere else. The travel organisers are less flexible, although they are able to change their supply given a season or two. The local tourism entrepreneurs are the least flexible because they are dependent on the local environment and climate. There are also some general obstacles for business development in tourism in the north. In part this is related to the business structure, in which small-scale businesses dominate. More than half of the enterprises have at most only one person employed full time and one-sixth do not have any employees (Nutek 2007). Fierce competition and laws and regulations are the most important hindrances for growth according to business owners. Therefore, it is the small-scale locally owned place and resource embedded nature-based tourism businesses that are potentially most vulnerable to climate change (Saarinen and Tervo 2006).

Adaptation strategies with reference to ski resorts and businesses (Bürki *et al.* 2003; Moen and Fredman 2007) are ones related to:

- What individual businesses can do, including engaging in artificial snowmaking, developing at higher altitudes and cooperating with and expanding into other areas with snow.
- What the public can do in terms of government subsidies for education, retraining and development.
- Development of alternatives to skiing with diversification into activities not connected to snow and all-year tourism.

The alternative strategy is one of business-as-usual or to cancel ski tourism altogether.

Conclusions

Outdoor recreation and nature-based tourism are inextricably linked to the northern parts of Scandinavia. The vast areas of forest and abundant free space are increasingly in demand from the national and international public. This is good news for the tourist entrepreneurs in the region. However, the entrepreneurs' opportunities, possibilities and constraints for development and change largely lie in circumstances over which the entrepreneurs have no control, such as the climate, its variations and changes. Rapid climate change is predicted in high-latitude areas (see chapter 2) and studies show that tourists and thus nature-based tourism is sensitive to changes in climate and subsequent impacts. Research shows that there are many ways in which entrepreneurs can adapt to climate change. Flexibility, knowledge and adequate information and support from local, regional and national governments are vital for successful adaptation on the entrepreneurial level. Because adaptation strategies and vulnerabilities depend on the general socioeconomic structures of a society, uncertainties for understanding future adaptation and vulnerabilities largely lie in understanding the dynamics linking tourism systems to a broader socioeconomic framework. Although the vulnerability to climate change impact from the business perspective is high, climate change is seen by both stakeholders and researchers as a minor problem compared with other external factors for entrepreneurs in tourism (Sievänen *et al.* 2005; Saarinen and Tervo 2006; Scott *et al.* 2007a, 2007b). This is because, so far, adaptive capacity is high for the areas considered here. However, there are large uncertainties regarding the future, and there are five main issues that cause a high degree of uncertainty for tourism studies and climate change in northern Scandinavia.

Firstly, all predictions concerning climate change have uncertainties that make the ecological impact difficult to foresee, especially on a regional scale. Having established that the natural environment forms the basic supply and attractiveness for an area and the economic base of an enterprise offering nature-based activities, this knowledge is vital for local predictions within tourism supply. From a longer-term perspective adaptive capacity depends on how seriously the entrepreneurs take the information on climate change. Investments in infrastructure could be costly if not all the circumstances are taken into account.

Secondly, there are large uncertainties about how demand will change in the future. The preferences held by tourists may change as a result of changing climate conditions. Missing in all studies so far encountered is a discussion about the changed preferences as part of the changes occurring at the place of origin of the tourists. How will the effects of a decreasing amount of snow in the south of Scandinavia and Europe affect the demand on ski resorts in the north? This is especially important because the current demand is largely domestic.

Thirdly, adaptation strategies of an economic activity, such as nature-based tourism, depend on how well society at large is doing. Therefore, the level of general wealth and disposable income is important for the relative vulnerability of tourism businesses. The result of vulnerability analysis seen from a regional perspective may be completely different from analysis made from an enterprise level. Climate change might possibly also have other and unforeseen effects on an elderly population since preferences, economic circumstances and health issues change with stages in the life course. However, demographic changes have not been a part of studies concerning trends and future demand for tourism services and destinations, other than in predictions of number of people (Hamilton *et al.* 2005). In terms of an ageing population this should be important for future tourism scenarios with or without climate change in focus (Lundgren 2005).

Fourthly, tourism in general is important for the number of visitors and consumption of nature-based tourism products. The main reason for visiting an area might be to do something else, but the tourist ends up doing something nature based. If the reason for travel is not explicitly to enjoy nature or to engage in nature-based activities, then the impact, vulnerability and adaptive capacity are harder to estimate.

Fifthly, research on vulnerability and adaptation to climate change from a supply side of the tourism system has primarily focused on winter tourism. This bias could be an indication that the most vulnerable activities are related to the winter season. However, it could also be attributed to the simple reason of snow cover being the first obvious and the most visual effect of climate change. Effects of climate change depend on the time perspective used in research and even although snow cover is currently changing it does not mean that it will be the most important change in a longer perspective. Therefore, future studies in tourism, climate change and entrepreneurship must include determining which tourism activities, actors, regions and tourism systems are most vulnerable to climate change and variability and what time frame is important.

Whether or not the future brings cool trips or hot deals in northern Scandinavia there are possibilities for nature-based tourism in the future. Considering a time perspective which allows for generational changes within the business as well as within the tourists suggests that although some of the tourism flows and entrepreneurship depend on traditions, it is also possible to develop new alternatives to make nature-based tourism a viable business alternative in the north.

References

Aall, C. and Höyer, G.K. (2005) 'Tourism and climate change adaptation: the Norwegian case', in C.M. Hall and J. Higham (eds) *Tourism, Recreation and Climate Change*, Clevedon: Channel View Publications.

Arctic Climate Impacts Assessment (ACIA) (2005) *Arctic Climate Impact Assessment*. Cambridge University Press

Berrittella, M., Bigano, A., Roson, R. and Tol, R. (2006) 'A general equilibrium analysis of climate change impacts on tourism', *Tourism Management,* 27: 913–24.

Bigano, A., Hamilton, J., Maddison, D. and Tol, R. (2006) 'Predicting tourism flows under climate change', *Climatic Change*, 79: 175–80.

Bürki, R. (2000) 'Klimaänderung und Anpassungsprozesse im Tourismus – dargestellt am Beispiel Wintertourismus', Dissertation, Universität Zurich, Zurich.

Bürki, R., Elsasser, H. and Abegg, B. (2003) Climate Change – Impacts on the Tourism Industry in Mountain Areas, 1st International Conference on Climate Change and

Tourism, Djerba, 9–11 April 2003. Online. Available HTTP: http://www.world-tourism.org/sustainable/climate/pres/rolf-buerki.pdf (accessed 30 October 2007).

Carter, T. and Kankaanpää, S. (2003) *A Preliminary Examination of Adaptation to Climate Change in Finland*, Suomen ympäristö 640, Finnish Environment Institute. Online. Available HTTP: http://www.ymparisto.fi/download.asp?contentid=5115&lan=fi (accessed 10 February 2006).

Dewar, K. (2005) 'Everyone talks about the weather...' in C.M. Hall (ed.) *Tourism, recreation and climate change*, Clevedon: Channel View Publications.

Fredman, P., Boman, M., Lundmark, L. and Mattsson, L. (2008) *Friluftslivets ekonomiska värden – en översikt*. Report Svenskt friluftsliv. Östersund: Mid-Sweden University,

Gómez Martín, B. (2005) 'Weather, climate and tourism', *Annals of Tourism Research*, 32: 571–91

Gössling, S. and Hall, C.M. (2006) 'Uncertainties in predicting tourism flows under scenarios of climate change', *Climatic Change*, 79: 163–73.

Gössling, S., Hall, C.M., Peeters, P. and Scott, D. (2010) 'The future of tourism: a climate change mitigation perspective', *Tourism Recreation Research*, 35(2), in press.

Hall, C.M. (2008) 'Tourism and climate change: knowledge gaps and issues', *Tourism Recreation Research*, 33: 339–50.

— (2009) 'Changement climatique, authenticité et marketing des régions nordiques : conséquences sur le tourisme finlandais et la « plus grande marque au monde » ou « Les changements climatiques finiront-ils par tuer le père Noël? »', *Téoros*, 28(1): 69–79

Hall, C.M., Müller, D. and Saarinen, J. (2009) *Nordic Tourism*, Clevedon: Channelview Press.

Hamilton, J.M. (2003) *Climate and the Destination Choice of German Tourists*. Working Paper FNU-15, Research Unit for Sustainability and Global Change, Centre for Marine and Climate Research, University of Hamburg. Online. Available HTTP http://www.feem.it/NR/rdonlyres/D81D6072-FC01–482E-BEF3–5FD10A94 E733/1051/2104.pdf (accessed 31 October 2007).

Hamilton, J., Maddison, D. and Tol, R. (2005) 'Climate change and international tourism: a simulation study', *Global Environmental Change*, 15: 253–66.

Intergovernmental Panel of Climate Change (IPCC) Third Assessment Report (2001) *Climate Change 2001: Impacts, Adaptation and Vulnerability, contribution of Working Group II to the Third Assessment Report of the Intergovernmental Panel of Climate Change*. Online. Available HTTP: http://www.grida.no/climate/ipcc_tar/wg2/index.htm (accessed 31 October 2007).

Intergovernmental Panel of Climate Change (IPCC) (2007) 'Summary for Policymakers,' in S. Solomon, D. Qin, M. Manning, Z. Chen, M. Marquis, K.B. Averyt, M.Tignor and H.L. Miller (eds.) *Climate Change 2007: The Physical Science Basis. Contribution of Working Group I to the Fourth Assessment Report of the Intergovernmental Panel on Climate Change*. Cambridge: Cambridge University Press.

Kelly, P.M. and Adger, W.N. (2000) 'Theory and practice in assessing vulnerability to climate change and facilitating adaptation', *Climatic Change* 47: 325–52.

Keup-Thiel, E., Blome, T., Goettel, H., Hagemann, S., Podzunand R., and Jacob, D. (2005) '*Regional climate change simulations: what can we expect?*', BALANCE mid-term assessment meeting, 5th project meeting February 17–18, 2005 at the Scott Polar Research Institute, University of Cambridge, U. K. Online. Available HTTP: http://balance1.uni-muenster.de/ (accessed 31 October 2007).

Lordkipanidze, M., Brezet, H. and Backman, M. (2005) 'The entrepreneurship factor in sustainable tourism development', *Journal of Cleaner Production*, 13: 787–98.

Lundgren, A. (2005) *Microsimulation and Tourism Forecasts*, Gerum report series (Licentiate thesis), Umeå: Department of Social and Economic Geography, Umeå University.

Lundmark L. (2005) 'Economic restructuring into tourism: the case of the Swedish mountain range', *Scandinavian Journal of Hospitality and Tourism*, 5(1): 23–45.

Lundmark, L., Pashkevich, A., Jansson, B. and Wiberg, U. (2008) 'Effects of climate change and variability on forest communities in the European North', *Climatic Change*, 87: 235–49

Maddison, D. (2001) 'In search of warmer climates? The impact of climate change on flows of British tourists', *Climatic Change*, 49: 193–208.

McMullen, C.P. and Jabbour, J. (2009) *Climate Change Science Compendium 2009*, Nairobi: United Nations Environment Programme, EarthPrint.

Ministry of the Environment (2001) *Sweden's third national communication on climate change*, DS 2001:71, Ministry of the Environment, Sweden.

Moen J. and Fredman P. (2007) 'Effects of climate change on alpine skiing in Sweden', *Journal of Sustainable Tourism*, 15: 418–37.

Notzke, C. (1999) 'Indigenous tourism development in the Arctic', *Annals of Tourism Research*, 26(1): 55–76.

Nutek, Årsbok (2007) Online. Available HTTP: http://www.nutek.se/content/1/c4/52/24/SLV%20Arsbok%202007%20low.pdf (accessed 19 November 2007).

O'Brien, K.L., Sygna, L. and Haugen, J.E. (2004) 'Vulnerable or resilient? A multiscale assessment of climate impacts and vulnerability in Norway', *Climatic Change*, 64: 193–225.

Richardson, R. and Loomis, J. (2004) 'Adaptive recreation planning and climate change. A contingent visitation approach', *Ecological Economics*, 50: 83–99.

Rinne, P. and Saastamoinen, O. (2005) 'Local economic role of nature-based tourism in Kuhmo Municipality, Eastern Finland', *Scandinavian Journal of Hospitality and Tourism*, 5(2): 89–101.

Saarinen, J. and Tervo, K. (2006) 'Perceptions and adaptation strategies of the tourism industry to climate change: the case of Finnish nature-based tourism entrepreneurs', *International Journal of Innovation and Sustainable Development* 1: 214–28.

Scott, D., Jones, B. and Konopek, J. (2007a) 'Implications of climate and environmental change for nature-based tourism in the Canadian Rocky Mountains: a case study of Watertons Lakes National Park', *Tourism Management*, 28: 570–79.

Scott, D., McBoyle, G. and Minogue, A. (2007b) 'Climate change and Quebec's ski industry', *Global Environmental Change*, 17: 181–90.

Sievänen, T. (2007) *Nature-based Tourism, Outdoor Recreation and Climate Change*, Online. Available HTTP: http://www.metla.fi/metinfo/monikaytto/lvvi/esitelmat/2007/klimatforandringar-tourism-friluftsliv.pdf (accessed 17 February 2009).

Sievänen, T., Tervo, K., Neuvonen, M., Pouta, E., Saarinen, J. and Peltonen, A. (2005) Nature-based tourism, outdoor recreation and adaptation to climate change. FINADAPT working paper 11, *Finnish Environment Institute Mimeographs* 341.

Sykes, M. and Prentice, I. (1999) *Modelling the effect of climate change on Swedish forests*, Swedish Environmental Protection Agency, Report 5029.

Viner, D. and Agnew, M. (1999) Climate Change and Its Impacts on Tourism, Report Prepared for WWF-UK Climatic Research Unit, University of East Anglia. Online. Available HTTP: http://www.wwf.org.uk/filelibrary/pdf/tourism_and_cc_full.pdf (accessed 30 October 2007).

Zillinger, M. (2007) *Guided tourism – the role of guidebooks in German tourist behaviour in Sweden*, ETOUR scientific book series 2007:18.

8 Sustainability and Emerging Awareness of a Changing Climate

The tourism industry's knowledge and perceptions of the future of nature-based winter tourism in Finland

Jarkko Saarinen and Kaarina Tervo

Introduction

The issue of climate has always been important in tourism but recently its role has emerged as one of the most urgent issues in tourism research, development and policy. With links to sustainability, regional and product development it perhaps represents the most timely theme in tourism studies today (see Bramwell and Lane 2008). Most tourism activities are directly dependent on climate and weather (Abegg 1996), and thus the global process of climate change will most probably have an impact on all kinds of tourism by changing, among others, travel and tourist destination patterns, tourist decision-making, product development and public perceptions concerning travelling (Lise and Tol 2002; Gössling and Hall 2006). However, some forms, activities and regions of tourism are more sensitive to changes in climate than others. In particular nature-based tourism and winter (snow-based) tourism, which are the focus of this chapter, are seen to be vulnerable because the activities are produced in natural or semi-natural environments where natural conditions and their quality play an important role.

Based on the interrelationships between tourism and climate change, Dubois and Ceron (2006: 400) have outlined three types of issues in tourism raised by climate change: (1) the effects of climate change on the environmental resources of tourism, including seasons and regions (this dimension calls for adaptation strategies in the industry); (2) the contribution of tourism to global climate change, especially through transportation (this relation implies needs for mitigation); and (3) the effects with respect to mitigation policies on GHG and carbon taxes, for example (this topic is still largely ignored in tourism and climate change research but it will probably be the one with the greatest impact in the short term).

The adaptation and mitigation needs with policy implementation are the crucial dimensions in tourism and climate change discussions and research. However, Patterson *et al.* (2006) call for a more sophisticated model to approach the relation between tourism and climate change. Instead of seeing the relation as a two-way street, they suggest moving beyond the reciprocal model towards a multiple states and changes model in the tourism system in order to lead tourism towards sustainability. By doing so 'the "vicious circle"…relating to tourism, its impacts, and climate change, can be broken down analytically and revised as the "virtuous circle" needed to support the transition towards sustainable tourism' (Patterson *et al.* 2006: 340). Thus, they aim to direct the tourism and climate change discussions closer to the context of sustainability in tourism. Sustainability is an obvious framework for such discussions but is not very often used in tourism and climate change studies. A reason for this may be the problematic nature of sustainability in tourism. Although tourism is already a part of the global economy and represents an indicator of global scale processes the focus of sustainability has been mainly on destinations and tourism practices and impacts in those areas, grasping the most visible manifestations of the impacts, but only a fragment of the total (see Gössling 2000; Saarinen 2006). Therefore, in the context of global scale processes such as climate change the present conceptual framework of sustainable tourism has perhaps been seen too narrow and limited (Hall 2010).

However, despite the interpretational problems of the conceptualisation of sustainable tourism in the past it is also important to look beyond the present impacts at the destinations in order to promote tourism development that is truly sustainable (Gössling and Hall 2006). As indicated by Bramwell and Lane (2008: 1), the new emphasis on sustainable tourism is – or should be – more global in scale (see also Holden 2003; Saarinen 2006). This 'new sustainable tourism' with a more ethical, integrative and holistic approach is not an easy one to implement in practice, but as indicated by Patterson *et al.* (2006) also other larger scales than the individual, site or local destination level should be recognised in tourism and climate change models, and possible successful implementations and practices of sustainable tourism should be placed in the wider spatial and time contexts of tourism and in local social, economic and ecological systems. Naturally the broader the scale of concerns involved the more abstract and intangible the actions and perceptions become from those looking on from a microscale.

What is common in the reciprocal and multiscale models of tourism and climate change is the key role of knowledge and perceptions concerning the impacts, adaptations and mitigations. Knowledge and perceptions emerge differently in various scales and depending on the actors involved. For example, the national and international policy processes create structures guiding and limiting certain type of tourism consumption but tourists are the ones who make the final travel decision based on their resources, and also tourism entrepreneurs have an important role as providers, marketers and developers for tourism activities and destinations (see Becken 2004; Hall 2006). The industry creates needs for (potential) tourists by commodifying the (changing) environment for tourists to consume. Although limited in scale, the entrepreneurs' level of knowledge, attitudes and nature of perceptions concerning climate change and its impacts on the business are important to recognise when planning adaptation strategies and the future of the industry in different scales of the tourism–climate change nexus.

In this chapter, the climate change-related knowledge – specifically the attitudes and perceptions – of tourism entrepreneurs is under discussion. Following the findings of Saarinen and Tervo (2006) on the importance of the media and tourism entrepreneurs' observations on climate as sources of climate change-related information, and the findings of Tervo and Saarinen (2009) on changing attitudes towards climate change, this chapter studies the potential effect of the media and past climate conditions on the entrepreneurs' conceptions of climate change and its effects on the tourism industry. The specific focus is nature-based winter tourism in Finland and its future prospects. Broadly speaking nature-based winter tourism refers here to various forms of tourism that are based mainly on the attractiveness and possibilities of the natural environment in the winter season and touristic activities situated and performed in such an environment (see Hall *et al.* 2009). In respect to climate change the nature-based tourism activities in winter are perhaps the most vulnerable forms (and in the most vulnerable season) of tourism in Finland and northern Europe in general. Although the future of nature-based winter tourism will depend on many interrelated processes and actors the knowledge in the industry (i.e. people working in and directly involved with the tourism business) is in a crucial position in defining the future activities, possibilities and policies of tourism development. This is relevant also in relation to sustainable tourism when evaluating the present and future priorities and practices of the industry.

Adaptation and sustainability

Adaptation strategies

All tourism activities and actors will be influenced by global climate change. However, the impacts of the change and the needed adaptation or mitigation procedures are difficult to define and establish because of the complexity of the tourism–climate change nexus and the involvement of not only direct but also indirect effects. These factors create a complex system of changes, costs and benefits, varying in time and space, i.e. the effects are spatially differentiated and evolve differently during the processes and factual or perceived outcomes of changing climate. Thus, the impacts of climate change and also perceptions concerning their effects on the industry most probably differ between regions and also between different scales and actors (Agnew and Viner 2001; Patterson *et al.* 2006; Hall and Lew 2009).

It is impossible to evaluate which scales and actors should be addressed first in order to turn the tourism–climate change nexus towards sustainable tourism development. To begin with, the main actors in tourism include the customers, i.e. tourists who are the ones to make the final travel decision under the changing conditions and policy frames. On the other hand, tourism entrepreneurs have an important role as providers, marketers and developers for tourism activities and destinations (Becken 2004; Hall 2006) because the industry also creates needs for (potential) tourists by commodifying the distant places and environments for tourists to consume. As a result of this commodification winter tourism in Nordic counties, for example, is not based only on traditional forms of cross-country and downhill skiing, but increasingly on a wide range of snow-related activities such as snowmobiling, reindeer- and dog-sledding, arctic trekking, snow and ice castle activities and Christmas and New Year outdoor programmes. All these current forms of so-called new tourism and experience economy are based on snowy and cold winter landscapes and images referring to such conditions (Hall *et al*. 2009).

The complex system of costs and benefits in the tourism–climate change nexus calls for diversified strategies and tactics in the adaptation process of regional tourism industry. Bürki *et al*. (2005) have outlined four main strategies and attitudes towards climate change among tourism stakeholders using ski tourism as a representative of the (nature-based) winter tourism in mountainous regions:

1   Maintaining ski tourism
2   Searching for alternatives to ski tourism
3   Depending on subsidies
4   Being fatal

Even although Bürki *et al*. (2005) focus on ski tourism, the strategies can be applied to other forms of winter tourism in general, with certain exceptions. The first strategy involves methods such as artificial snowmaking, development of higher terrain for activities, advanced ski slope design and increasing collaboration as related sets of tactics. Searching for alternatives to ski tourism represents a proactive attitude with development of non-snow-related activities and all-year tourism products. This diversifies the site and destination scale tourism supply. In contrast to that fatalism and subsidies as adaptation strategies refer to reactive and passive attitudes towards the change. Fatalism in particular aims to capitalise on the existing conditions while they last without serious attempts to see the challenge and alternative development paths.

One of the main problems for the tourism industry and its ability and will to define a specific adaptation strategy and search for alternative techniques is the slow pace of change and the nature of the industry. Tourism businesses are generally small and medium-size units that often cannot look beyond the next few years or in some cases even beyond the following season(s) (Patterson *et al*. 2006). Therefore, many entrepreneurs and actors in the industry aim to wait until knowledge about the change and its effects increases and becomes more precise. According to Dubois and Ceron (2006), these kinds of attitudes refer to short-term responses that are based on the assumption that it is financially more efficient 'to wait and see' than to adopt a precautionary attitude with related measures or to use and develop techniques to cope with the changing environment. In addition, the small and medium-size character of the industry is sometimes perceived beneficial by enabling the business units to change their production orientation and practices faster compared with larger companies with heavy infrastructures and other investments (see Saarinen and Tervo 2006).

Adaptation and sustainability

In addition to the slow pace of changing climate the different time horizons between the tourism industry and sustainable development are problematic. As an ideology sustainable development refers to a process that meets the needs of the present generations without endangering the ability of the future ones to meet their own needs (United Nations World Commission on Environment and Development [WCED] 1987). On the basis of this definition sustainability rests on three integrated elements: the ecological, sociocultural and economic, including three underlying fundamental principles called futurity, equity and holism (Redcliffe and Woodgate 1997). Futurity refers to the needs of future generations, which underlines a long-term perspective for evaluating the impacts of human activities and socioeconomic development. The demand for equity states that different generations should have fair and equal opportunities. The equity should apply to everybody and not only at present but also in future (intergenerational and intragenerational equity). The last principle of holism implies that development should be considered within broad (global, political, social, economic, ecological) contexts and perspectives.

These principles are relatively challenging for tourism as a site- and destination-based economic activity. Like global climate change the idea of sustainability calls for long-term and multiscale strategies but tourism mainly works with local (i.e. destination-scale) impacts and processes. These impacts may be the most visible ones but they cover only a portion of the needs for adaptation strategies in the context of sustainable tourism. For example, the increasing facilities for artificial snowmaking benefit the industry and enhance its ability to cope with reduced or delayed snow cover in winter tourism destinations in changing climate and weather conditions. However, they have also increased the energy and water consumption levels in operations contributing to the impacts of tourism on climate change, which conflicts with the idea of sustainable development in tourism. As indicated by Dubois and Ceron (2006), developing off-ski activities, such as cultural tourism, nature tourism and hiking/walking facilities, in winter tourism destinations may be economically more effective in the future than investing in artificial snowmaking. However, in the time horizon of the industry this may be arguable and contested, but not in the context of sustainable tourism calling for longer, and geographically and socially wider perspectives in development (Saarinen 2006).

Changes in nature-based winter tourism

Nature-based winter tourism in northern Finland

In Finland, and especially in the northern parts of the country, the natural environment represents the main attraction for both international and domestic tourists. Tourism and tourists provide more employment opportunities in Finnish Lapland, for example, than any other field of the economy that makes direct or indirect use of natural resources. In 2006 the estimated direct employment effect of tourism was over 4,100 full-time jobs in Lapland (Lapin liitto 2007). Among the nature-based winter tourism activities, cross-country and downhill skiing are still the most important form of winter tourism activities that directly use northern nature (Saarinen 2003). These activities are mainly based on the domestic market, which explains the relatively high volumes but moderate growth rates. However, the international demand has also grown in downhill skiing (Figure 8.1), but the share of international demand has been especially significant in nature-based tourism safari services (including mainly snowmobile, dog and reindeer safaris), which has led to considerable growth rates in Finnish Lapland (Figure 8.2) (chapter 1).

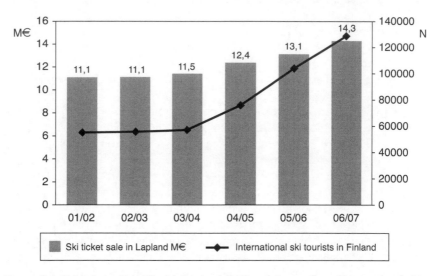

Figure 8.1 Ski ticket sale in Finnish Lapland (M€) and the number of international ski tourists in Finland from winter 2001–02 to winter 2006–07

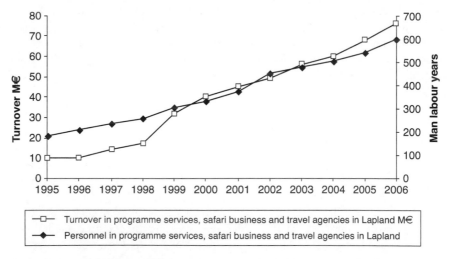

Figure 8.2 Growth of programme services and related sectors in Lapland since 1995

Changing climate and nature-based winter tourism

The future of nature-based tourism under a changing climate depends on many interrelated issues, such as the intensity of the change, the forms and seasonal aspects of tourism activities and the policy-making processes (see Hall and Higham 2005), which are spatially differentiated, also inside Finland. In Saarinen and Tervo's (2006) study conducted in the spring and early summer of 2005, the entrepreneurs in eastern Finland noted that their region had already lost customers to northern Finland, mainly not because of changing conditions but because of perceptions among tourists and tour operators. Thus, the negative impacts of climate change have been socially spatialised to cover not only southern but also eastern parts of Finland, with tourists and tour operators having a perception that regions relatively close to the snow-deficient southern parts of the country also suffer from lack of snow, no matter how factually different the climatic conditions in these areas actually are.

In Finland climate change in general will probably change seasonality by shortening the winter season and lengthening either summer or the so-called shoulder seasons, or both. Thus, this will enhance the summer season, while the winter season may be facing difficulties in the future (Marttila *et al*. 2005). The most significant changes in the climatic conditions in Finland are expected to take place during the winters (see Jylhä *et al*. 2004; Jylhä *et al*. 2008). Wintertime (December–February in Jylhä *et al*. 2004) warming (1.2–5°C) until 2040 is predicted to be much higher than summertime (June–August in Jylhä *et al*. 2004) warming (0.6–1.6°C). The implications of warming winters include a decrease in the number of frost days and an increase in the number of days when temperatures cross the zero point, both of which will worsen the conditions for providing winter tourism activities. On the other hand, the short-range effects of precipitation changes may increase the amount of snow in Northern and Central Finland, which may, in the near future, give Northern Finland competitive advantage at the expense of winter tourism regions located in more southern regions (e.g. Central Europe and Southern Finland). Nevertheless, by the end of the 21st century, the number of days with snow will decrease by 40 to 60 days.

Naturally, some forms of tourism are more weather-sensitive and more dependent on natural conditions, especially when it comes to temperature and amount of snow, but also the timing of the peak seasons may cause differences between activities (Saarinen and Tervo 2006; Tervo 2008). Besides these, policy-makers and the reactions of both tourists and tourism entrepreneurs will have an influence on the form and scope of nature-based tourism in the coming years (see Patterson *et al*. 2006). However, the relatively new policy document *Finnish Tourism Strategy 2020* (Suomen matkailustrategia…2006), outlined by the different governmental ministries and bodies involved with the national scale tourism policy, does not recognise the issue of climate change as a factor to be considered.

The Finnish tourism industry's views on climate change

Methods and data

This case study analyses the findings of two studies that were conducted after winter seasons 2004–05 (see Saarinen and Tervo 2006) and 2006–07 (see Tervo 2008; Tervo and Saarinen 2009) among nature-based tourism entrepreneurs in Finland and discusses potential factors affecting the findings of the studies. As the differences between the results of the two studies have been discussed in more detail by Tervo and Saarinen (2009), the focus of this study is mainly on the potential factors behind the observed changes in attitudes towards climate change.

Besides the data from the two studies, climate data are used to assess the congruence between climatic perceptions and actual climatic conditions. Climate data include temperature and precipitation data from three climate stations (Lahti, Rovaniemi, Muonio) located in the vicinity of three winter tourism destinations in Finland (Messilä, Rovaniemi, Ylläs) (Figure 8.3). The main focus in climate data analysis is, because of the dependency of tourism on sufficient snow cover, on the timing and length of the season of permanent snow cover. Newspaper data (the occurrence and nature of climate change related news in *Helsingin Sanomat [HS]*)

Figure 8.3: The location of climate stations of Lahti, Rovaniemi and Muonio, which are close to the major winter tourism destinations of Messilä, Rovaniemi and Ylläs

are used to examine the role of the media in the formation process of climate change knowledge. *HS* was chosen as the representative of the media as it is the most widely read and is considered the national newspaper; other newspapers in Finland often reflect the news published in it. Numerical data are gathered from the *HS* internet archives and other data from *HS* newspaper from years 2005 and 2007. The interviews in the study reported by Saarinen and Tervo (2006) were undertaken in spring 2005, whereas the survey reported by Tervo (2008) and Tervo and Saarinen (2010) took place in summer 2007. Both the climate data and newspaper data are analysed with a focus on the time periods preceding these two studies.

Tourism entrepreneurs' attitudes towards changing climate

The findings of Saarinen and Tervo (2006) indicate that in 2005 the nature-based tourism entrepreneurs in Finland had general knowledge about the issue of climate change, but there was a lack of precise information about its effects on the region's tourism sector and doubt about whether the phenomenon actually exists. Half of the 19 respondents thought that climate was changing while one-third was reluctant to commit itself on the matter. Therefore, tourism entrepreneurs were sceptical about the effects climate change might have on their business, and the assumed change was seen only as a minor threat by respondents, if a threat at all, particularly relative to other factors (e.g. competing forms of land use) that might have an effect on the industry and its future prospects.

According to Saarinen and Tervo (2006), the general media were considered the most important source for climate change information for all tourism entrepreneurs that participated in the study. More than 75% of the entrepreneurs interviewed by Saarinen and Tervo (2006) did, nevertheless, question the reliability of information transmitted by the media. Making personal observations was another important way to either gain climate change information or to critically evaluate the information provided by the media. In Saarinen's and Tervo's study, half of the entrepreneurs reported having observed climatic phenomena that supported their perception on climate change. Only a few entrepreneurs sought information on climate change from scientific publications or other academic sources.

The other study, conducted 2 years after the one mentioned above, reported changed attitudes among winter tourism entrepreneurs operating in Finland (Tervo 2008; Saarinen and Tervo 2009). In 2007, the majority of respondents stated that they believe in human-induced climate change (Table 8.1). The role of the tourism industry was not seen in such a central position in global climate change; still half of the respondents felt that tourism entrepreneurs themselves could influence the intensity of climate change in the future. Climate change was nevertheless considered a more important factor for the future of enterprises than competition for space and resources with the other forms of land use such us forestry and leisure habitation, for example.

The attitudes and perceptions towards climate change and its existence were common for all entrepreneurs regardless of the region in which they operated (no statistically significant differences between subregions of Finland). The entrepreneurs had also noticed the effect of European Alpine snow deficiency on Finland's tourism potential. Entrepreneurs agreed with snowless winters in the Alps having brought more tourists to Northern Finland, but the level of agreement varied between regions. Entrepreneurs operating in Northern Finland felt this to be true more strongly (80% agreed or strongly agreed with this) while the entrepreneurs operating elsewhere in Finland were not so convinced (57–67 % agreed).

Almost two-thirds of the entrepreneurs had observed shortening of winters and delays in the arrival of lasting snow during the time they had been operating (Table 8.2). Furthermore, half of the respondents considered that the amount of

Table 8.1: Attitudes towards climate change related issues among tourism entrepreneurs (%) (Source Tervo and Saarinen 2009)

	Climate is not changing	Climate change is not caused by human actions	Tourism operators cannot influence the speed of the change	Other land-use more severe threat than climate change	Snow uncertainty in the Alps has increased winter tourists in N. Finland
Agree/ strongly agree	5	11	38	30	73*
Neither agree nor disagree	17	6	10	15	20*
Disagree/ strongly disagree	78	83	51	55	7*
	N=166	N=166	N=165	N=165	N=166

*p < 0,05

Table 8.2: The frequency (%) of perceived changes in winter conditions in different regions according to tourism entrepreneurs (Tervo and Saarinen 2009)

	All a	Southern Finland	Western Finland	Eastern Finland	Northern Finland (Rovaniemi)
Shorter winters than before *	65	74	68	79	55 (75)
Less snow than earlier **	48	65	47	70	36 (69)
Snow arrives later	71	70	63	73	73 (100)
Snow melts earlier **	50	65	26	70	45 (44)
	(N=172)	(N=23)	(N=21)	(N=33)	(N=91)

a = all entrepreneurs includes also enterprises operating in whole Finland (n=4)

* p < 0,05; ** p < 0,01 (Kruskal-Wallis)

snow had decreased and that snowmelt occurs earlier. The perceptions on changes in climatic conditions were dependent on the region in which entrepreneurs operated. In Northern Finland, the experiences of the entrepreneurs operating in Rovaniemi differed slightly from the great majority.

Based on the perceptions of the climate change, the future of winter tourism in Finland was considered negative. Half of the entrepreneurs believed that the future of their main activity would be negative so that the activities would have to be cut down (at least partially). This attitude was shared by 14% of the respondents, who did not believe that operations in the future would be possible. One-fifth had faith in their future and every tenth entrepreneur believed that climate change would not affect their current products. These attitudes did, however, depend on the region in which the enterprise operates. Entrepreneurs in Northern Finland had more optimistic perceptions about their future than entrepreneurs elsewhere in Finland.

Role of the media and climate history in growing knowledge and changing perceptions

The occurrence of articles referring to climate change remained steady until 2006 (Figure 8.4). In 2005, preceding the interviews reported by Saarinen and Tervo (2006), climate change was mentioned in *HS* 67 times (January–April). Important issues that took place during the spring 2005 included the publication of Finland's *National Strategy for Adaptation to Climate Change* (January) and the Kyoto Protocol, which came into force in February. These issues received attention in the media, but news questioning the existence of change was also present.

2006 was the year when climate change and its problematic nature were recognised globally and awareness of its causes and impacts grew considerably (*HS* 2 January 2007). In 2006, the number of news items with a reference to climate change almost doubled from 2005 (from 255 to 421), but the peak number of news with a reference to climate change was reached in 2007, with 1,159 pieces of news about climate change. Climate change *per se* was not the main focus of all the newspaper articles but the term was, nevertheless, mentioned and it provided the context for other matters discussed.

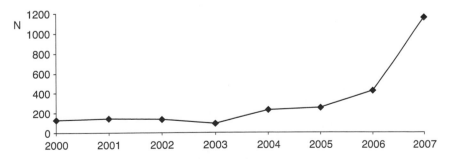

Figure 8.4 Number of newspaper articles mentioning climate change in *HS* in 2000–07

According to the archives, there were 525 pieces of news with reference to climate change in spring 2007 (January–May), before the 2007 survey to tourism entrepreneurs was sent out. The actual number of news articles focusing mainly on climate change and climatic conditions was 366. During the time that was allowed for the entrepreneurs to answer and return the questionnaire, climate change was mentioned in the newspaper almost daily. Important news preceding the second survey in June 2007 included the publications of the Stern review (October 2006) and the IPCC's fourth assessment report on climate change (February 2007), which both highly increased the visibility of climate change in the media. Al Gore's film *An Inconvenient Truth* was released earlier in 2006, but the discussion over it continued briskly also in 2007 when the IPCC and Gore became Nobel Peace Prize laureates.

According to climate statistics, December 2006 was the warmest ever measured in Finland. The arrival day of permanent snow (according to Finland's Meteorological Institute, permanent snow cover refers to the longest continuous period of the winter with a minimum of 1-cm-deep snow) has varied greatly between the years throughout Finland (Figure 8.5), even although the trend has been towards later arrival of permanent snow, especially in Rovaniemi. Compared with winter 2006–07, winter 2004–05 was not exceptional, even although in Rovaniemi it was the second winter in a row when permanent snow arrived relatively late. Winter 2006–07 can, in this light, be considered extreme in Lahti and Rovaniemi as permanent snow arrived later than ever during the study period. In Muonio, the situation was different as snow arrived much earlier than the previous winter. The variability in the melting date of snow has been less and also the trends indicate smaller changes (Figure 8.6).

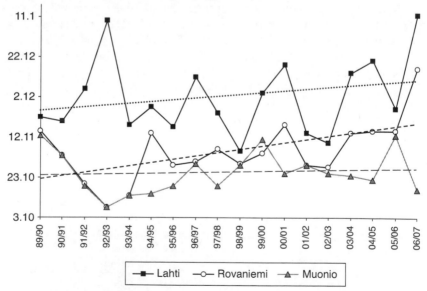

Figure 8.5 The arrival date of permanent snow cover in Lahti, Rovaniemi and Muonio, with a dashed line showing the trend from winter 1989–90 to winter 2006–07

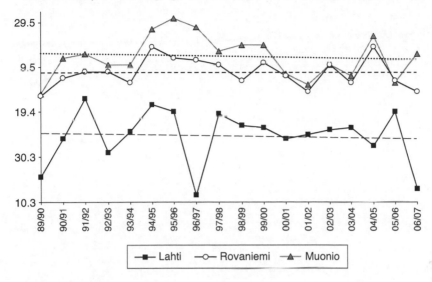

Figure 8.6 The melting date of the permanent snow cover in Lahti, Rovaniemi and Muonio

Along with other climate parameters, the mean snow depth and the number of days with snow also vary between winters (Figures 8.7 and 8.8). The trend lines for the 18-year study period show minor changes in the amount of snow. The snow conditions in Lahti and Rovaniemi varied between the two winters preceding the studies. Winter 2006–07 can be considered exceptional in Rovaniemi and Lahti as the mean snow depth in winter 2006–07 was the smallest during the study period

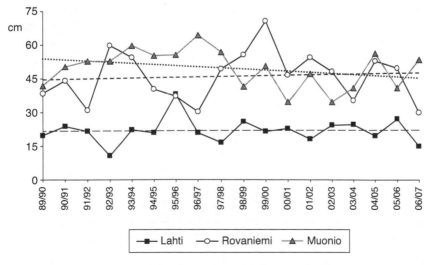

Figure 8.7 The mean snow depth between winters 1989–90 and 2006–07 in Lahti, Rovaniemi and Muonio

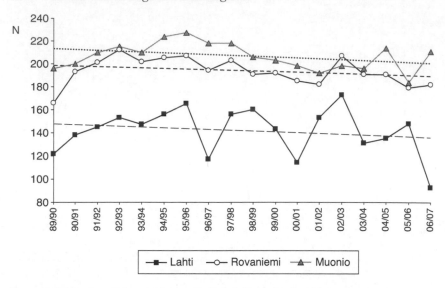

Figure 8.8 Number of days with snow in Lahti, Rovaniemi and Muonio

Discussion

Climate change will have an impact on all kinds of tourism, but nature-based tourism activities in particular will face significant changes in the near future. Tourism entrepreneurs in Finland seem to be aware of human-induced climate change and share similar opinions about it; basically, climate change is considered a threat that has mainly negative effects on the future of nature-based winter tourism. The comparison between the two studies conducted in 2005 (Saarinen and Tervo 2006) and 2007 (Tervo 2008; Tervo and Saarinen 2009) indicates that the attitudes and knowledge of Finnish tourism entrepreneurs on climate change have changed in recent years. However, the earlier study was based on the interview approach, with a relatively small number of enterprises ($n = 19$) covered and does not support direct comparison with the more recent survey data. On the other hand, there have been two relatively warm and snow-deficient winters in 2005–06 and 2006–07, which may have conveyed the issue to the people involved in the industry. Indeed, the entrepreneurs participating in both studies have changed their perceptions on climate change and its impacts and seriousness. Some of the respondents also stated having recently been forced to shut down their businesses temporarily because of the warm weather during the winter seasons.

In addition, the increased awareness may be a result of growing public interest and debate on global climate change and its local impacts, and there has been increasing media coverage in Finland dealing with the issue. It has been difficult to avoid climate change debate in the media (especially during spring and summer 2007) as news mentioning the phenomenon has been visible almost daily. In future, the awareness and attitudes towards climate change may continue to change, at least partly, because of the great amount of attention that global change will receive, in both the Finnish and the international media. The nature of the information about climate change will most probably change according to the viewpoints of the scientific community. It has been only lately that the focus has transferred from impacts and adaptation towards mitigation measures and their impacts on society and diverse industries.

Since most of the entrepreneurs have noticed some changes in the winter conditions during the existence of their enterprise, personal experiences may also have affected the attitudes. If the respondents have noticed that winters are considerably shorter and that in particular the arrival of permanent snow has been delayed significantly, climate change becomes more concrete. This may explain the worries stated by entrepreneurs in the Rovaniemi region, where the major part of tourism revenue is based on the Christmas season (see also Hall 2008). A shortening season and, especially, the late arrival of permanent snow have already increased the pressures on entrepreneurs. The start of the Christmas season has to be delayed or extra efforts with additional costs need to be taken in accordance with the arrival of the snow, which shortens the season considerably as tourists' interest in Christmas tourism and visits to Santa Claus and Santa Park decreases considerably after Christmas.

As a result of the emphasised increasing knowledge, climate change is now considered a more important issue for tourism enterprises than competing land uses, which received much attention in the previous study (Saarinen and Tervo 2006). There is also less doubt about the existence of the climate change phenomenon and its causes. Only every twentieth entrepreneur believes that climate is not changing and one-tenth of the respondents do not agree with human-induced climate change. Increasing knowledge of the change does not, nevertheless, necessarily add to the perceived adaptive capacity of nature-based tourism. The entrepreneurs have negative views towards their future prospects in the warming climate. However, some tourism destinations in northern Finland have already seen to be gaining at the expense of other tourism regions such as the Alps and southern and eastern Finland. There is no coherent evidence about the perceived shift of tourist flows towards the north, but this kind of assumption and experience of tourism entrepreneurs may have put more weight on the perceptions that support the existence of climate change.

The other key aspect in the reciprocal model concerning the tourism–climate change nexus is mitigation. Although that was not in the central focus of this paper it seems that mitigation aspects are less familiar issues for the entrepreneurs. This calls for more information and also research; over one-third of the respondents were practically unaware of their possibilities to participate in mitigation of change. The issue of missing mitigation knowledge refers to the tourism industry's challenges in respect to sustainability, and there are also other processes potentially conflicting with the basic idea of sustainability in tourism development. Although climate change may provide a competitive advantage during the next 20–30 years for nature-based winter tourism in northern Finland (compared with southern and central Finland and central Europe), the reliability of snow in the north will also be threatened in future. This calls for the development of adaptation technologies that may not be environmentally unproblematic; for example artificial snowmaking uses electricity and also creates water quality problems after the winter season (see Molles and Gosz 1980; Rixen *et al*. 2003; Wemple *et al*. 2007).

Based on the existing destination development plans and strategies the number of tourists is aimed to double in Finnish Lapland by 2020 (see Lapin matkailus-trategia...2007). The growth is estimated to be based on increasing international tourist flows, e.g. in Levi the goal is to increase the portion of international tourism to 50%. Thus, the investment plans for 2008–09 were over one billion euro in Finnish Lapland; the Levi resort alone covers approximately 450 million euro, with the goal to increase the present 20,000-bed capacity to 36,000 bed places by 2020. Based on the existing development and investment plans it seems as if no threats or limits to growth for tourism exist in northern Finland.

According to the national and regional tourism strategies, the strengths of tourism in the north (referring to the attractiveness of the natural environment, including snow-based safari products and other activities) are perceived to be relatively the same in the future as they are currently (Suomen matkailustrate-gia...2006; Lapin matkailustrategia...2007). However, for many of the present nature-based winter tourism products the 'best before' date is also approaching and the present major strengths may be valid only for a certain, relatively short, period of time. The industry perceives a 20- to 30-year period, or rather the future after that period, as too distant for any serious consideration and planning. In addition the next two to three decades are assumed to be successful because of the estimated competitive advantage. However, the development of present 'products of success' based on direct or indirect use of snow, ice and related images took more than 20 years to achieve. Therefore, rather than aiming to solve the future (and thus present) challenges mainly by building more capacity it is important to keep the long-term development perspective and needs in mind and call for new activities and adaptation measures today. The present attitude focusing mainly on capacity development indicates a fatal attitude towards the processes of climate change; there is no serious consideration yet of what happens after the estimated period of competitive advantage of tourism in northern Finland. In addition, the indirect effects of climate change have not been discussed and are unknown, an issue that may challenge the estimated competitive advantage in the near future.

Acknowledgements

This paper has been produced as a part of Thule Institute's (University of Oulu) research programme 'Northern land use and land cover' and funded by the Academy of Finland under the auspices of the FiDiPro-programme 'Human-environment relations in the north: resource development, climate change and resilience' and the European Social Fund (KeMMI-project).

References

Abegg B. (1996) *Klimaänderung und Tourismus. Klimafolgenforschung am Beispiel des Wintertourismus in den Schweizer Alpen*, Zürich: Hochschulverlag AG an der ETH.

Agnew M.D. and Viner, D. (2001) 'Potential impacts of climate change on international tourism', *Tourism and Hospitality Research*, 3: 37–60.

Becken, S. (2004) 'How tourists and tourism experts perceive climate change and carbon-offsetting schemes', *Journal of Sustainable Tourism*, 12(4), 332–45.

Bramwell, B. and Lane, B. (2008) 'Editorial: Priorities in sustainable tourism research', *Journal of Sustainable Tourism*, 16: 1–4.

Bürki, R., Elsasser, H., Abegg, B. and Koenig, U. (2005) 'Climate change and tourism in the Swiss Alps', in C.M. Hall and J. Higham (eds) *Tourism, Recreation and Climate Change*, Clevedon: Channel View Publications.

Dubois G. and Ceron J-P. (2006) 'Tourism and climate change: proposals for a research agenda', *Journal of Sustainable Tourism*, 14: 399–415.

Gössling, S. (2000) 'Sustainable tourism development in developing countries: some aspects of energy use', *Journal of Sustainable Tourism*, 8: 410–25.

Gössling S and Hall, C.M. (2006) 'An introduction to tourism and global environmental change', in Gössling S. and Hall, C.M. (eds) *Tourism and Global Environmental Change. Ecological Social, Economic and Political Interrelationships*, London: Routledge.

Hall C.M. (2006) 'New Zealand tourism entrepreneur attitudes and behaviours with respect to climate change adaptation and mitigation', *International Journal of Innovation and Sustainable Development*, 1: 229–37.

— (2008) 'Santa Claus, place branding and competition', *Fennia: International Journal of Geography*, 186(1): 59–67.

— (2010) 'Changing paradigms and global change: from sustainable to steady-state tourism', *Tourism Recreation Research*, 35(2): in press.

Hall C.M. and Higham, J. (eds) (2005) *Tourism, Recreation and Climate Change*, Clevedon: Channel View Publications.

Hall, C.M. and Lew, A. (2009) *Understanding and Managing Tourism Impacts: An Integrated Approach*. London: Routledge.

Hall, C.M., Muller, D. and Saarinen, J. (2009) *Nordic Tourism: Cases and Issues*, Clevedon: Channel View Publications.

Holden, A. (2003) 'In need of new environmental ethics for tourism', *Annals of Tourism Research* 30: 94–108.

Jylhä, K., Fronzek, S., Tuomenvirta, H., Carter, T.R and Ruosteenoja, K. (2008) 'Changes in frost, snow and Baltic sea ice by the end of the twenty-first century based on climate model projections for Europe', *Climatic Change*, 86: 441–62.

Jylhä, K., Tuomenvirta, K. and Ruosteenoja, K. (2004) 'Climate change projections for Finland during the 21st Century', *Boreal Environment Research*, 9: 127–52.

Lapin Matkailutilastollinen vuosikirja 2007. Lapin liitto. http://www.lapinliitto.fi/julkaisut/matkailutilastollinen%20vuosikirja%202007.pdf (accessed 20 January 2009).

Lapin matkailustrategia 2007–10 (2007) Lapin liitto. Online. Available HTTP: http://www.lapinliitto.fi/paatoksenteko/lh221007/liite8.pdf (accessed 10 October 2008).

Lise W. and Tol, R.S.J. (2002) 'Impact of climate on tourism demand', *Climatic Change*, 55: 429–49.

Marttila, V., Granholm, H., Laanikari, J., Yrjölä, T., Aalto, A., Heikinheimo, P., Honkatukia, J., Järvinen, H., Liski, J., Merivirta, R. and Paunio, M. (2005)

'Ilmastonmuutoksen kansallinen sopeutumisstrategia', Maa-ja metsätalousministeriön julkaisuja 1/2005.

Molles, M. and Gosz, J. (1980) 'Effects of a ski area on the water quality and invertebrates of a mountain stream', *Water, Air, and Soil Pollution,* 14: 187–205.

Patterson, T., Bastianoni, S. and Simpson, M. (2006) 'Tourism and climate change: two-way street, or vicious/virtuous circle?', *Journal of Sustainable Tourism,* 14: 339–48.

Redcliffe, M. and Woodgate, G. (1997) 'Sustainability and social construction', in M. Redcliffe and G. Woodgate (eds) *The International Handbook of Environmental Sociology,* Cheltenham: Edward Elgar.

Rixen, C., Stoeckli, V. and Ammann, W. (2003) 'Does artificial snow production affect soil and vegetation of ski pistes? A review', *Perspectives on Plant Ecology, Evolution and Systematics,* 5: 219–30.

Saarinen, J (2003) 'The regional economics of tourism in Northern Finland: the socio-economic implications of recent tourism development and future possibilities for regional development', *Scandinavian Journal of Hospitality and Tourism,* 3: 91–113.

— (2006) 'Traditions of sustainability in tourism studies', *Annals of Tourism Research,* 33, 1121–40.

Saarinen J. and Tervo, K. (2006) 'Perceptions and adaptation strategies of the tourism industry to climate change: the case of Finnish nature-based tourism entrepreneurs', *International Journal of Innovation and Sustainable Development,* 1: 214–28.

Suomen matkailustrategia vuoteen 2020 & toimenpideohjelma vuosille 2007–13 (2006) KTM Julkaisuja 21/2006. Helsinki: KTM.

Tervo, K. (2008) 'The operational and regional vulnerability of winter tourism to climate variability and change: the case of the nature-based tourism entrepreneurs in Finland', *Scandinavian Journal of Hospitality and Tourism,* 8: 317–32.

Tervo, K. and Saarinen, J. (2010)(in press) 'Climate change and adaptation strategies of the tourism industry in Northern Europe', in P. Maher, E. Stewart and M. Lück (eds) *Polar Tourism: Human, Environmental and Governance Dimensions,* Wallingford: CABI Publishing.

United Nations World Commission on Environment and Development (WCED) (1987) *Our Common Future.* Oxford: Oxford University Press.

Wemple, B., Shanley, J., Denner, J., Ross, D. and Mills, K. (2007) 'Hydrology and water quality in two mountain basins of the northeastern US: assessing baseline conditions and effects of ski area development', *Hydrological Processes,* 21: 1639–50.

9 Constraints and Opportunities in the Development of Diamond Tourism in Yellowknife, Northwest Territories

Jamie L. Noakes and Margaret E. Johnston

Introduction

In the Northwest Territories (NWT), a jurisdiction that is part of Canada's sub-Arctic and Arctic region, tourism exists as an important element of the economic landscape. The leading economic driver is mining, founded upon rich deposits of gold, tungsten and, more recently, diamonds. The next largest driver is petroleum production, followed by tourism in third place. Tourism has had a long history in NWT and cannot be overlooked as a component of the present economy and as a hope for the future. Yet, the NWT economy has seen considerable change over the last decade as a result of global economic and political events. For tourism, these events included the 9/11 terrorist attacks, the Canadian outbreak of bovine spongiform encephalopathy (mad cow disease), and the severe acute respiratory syndrome (SARS) crisis. The NWT tourism industry was negatively affected by these events because of its strong dependence on international travelers, particularly Japanese and American visitors, segments that were sensitive to the personal security implications of these global events (Government of the Northwest Territories [GNWT] 2003).

In contrast, the mining industry has been experiencing growth, largely because of a considerable increase in global mineral prices during the last decade. This has encouraged resource exploration activities and sustainable production. The coincident discovery of diamond deposits and the development of three major diamond mines in NWT have added to the boom that is being experienced primarily in the government centre and transportation hub of its capital city, Yellowknife. The interplay of changes in both mining and tourism has resulted in one unexpected outcome: the possibility of diamond tourism at a time when diversification in the tourism sector is needed.

This paper is based on a study that attempts to understand the development of diamond tourism by examining how stakeholders in Yellowknife view the opportunities and constraints associated with this tourism subsector. This chapter describes the context of the emergence of diamond tourism, outlines fieldwork results, and explores the relationships between the tourism impacts of diamond mining and economic development in Yellowknife, NWT.

Nature and diamonds: tourism in NWT

The history of tourism in NWT dates back to the exploration of Canada's Arctic regions in the 16th century and the trading era in the 19th century (see Marsh 1987; GNWT 2007a, b; Noakes and Johnston 2008); however, visitor numbers are not available for this earlier travel, which incorporated fur trading, mapping, and mineral exploration. Tourism in NWT was founded on exploration, wildlife, hunting and fishing (GNWT 2007a, b; NWT Tourism 2007; Tukto Lodge 2007). As a result, the tourism industry has been active for more than 50 years in NWT; initially it was comprised of fishing lodges, hunting outfitters, airlines and a few hotels (GNWT 2007a). A significant development occurred in the tourism industry in the late 1950s when tourism operators came together to create an industry association that would represent their needs (GNWT 2007a). Over the next 40 years this initiative grew and in 1996 NWT Tourism was established. NWT Tourism had a unique dual role of representing the tourism industry as the industry association, as well as assuming the role of a tourism marketing agency. It has grown to include eight full-time employees and has an annual budget of CAN$3 million (GNWT 2007a).

Visitor numbers were recorded as 600 visitors in 1959 and 47,600 visitors in 1992 (Hall and Johnston 1995). These statistics predate the territorial divide in 1999 and, therefore, are representative of NWT and Nunavut tourism before division (Noakes and Johnston 2008). Statistics since 1999 for either territory reflect this division. Figure 9.1 provides visitor numbers for the period of 2000–07 and includes a breakdown of business and pleasure travellers. All these numbers are estimates based on exit surveys that are not completed annually. The two most recent exit surveys were completed in 2002 and 2006. Exit survey numbers are based on data collection between 15 May and 15 September of the particular survey year, with extrapolation to the remainder of the year. In the 2006–07 tourist year it was estimated that 60% of visitors travelled for leisure and 40% travelled for business (GNWT 2007a) (see also chapter 1).

For leisure travellers it was estimated that 19% were aurora viewers, 23% were visiting family and friends, 14% were fishing, 4% were hunting, 6% were taking part in outdoor adventure, and 35% were involved in general touring. For the 2006–07 tourist year, the estimated 62,045 non-resident travellers who visited NWT contributed an estimated CAN$110.2 million to the NWT economy (GNWT 2007c, 2007a).

The 2006 GNWT exit survey shows that 35,956 non-resident travellers visited NWT between 15 May 2006 and 15 September 2006 (GNWT 2007c). Of these visitors, 62% were male and the average age was 50 years old. Further, 66% had at least a college diploma and the annual household income was CAN$90,000 (GNWT 2007c). In addition, 23% of visitors were retired and 31% were professional or held managerial occupations. The primary tourist activities undertaken while in NWT were sightseeing (62%), photography (60%), shopping (50%) and wildlife viewing (49%).

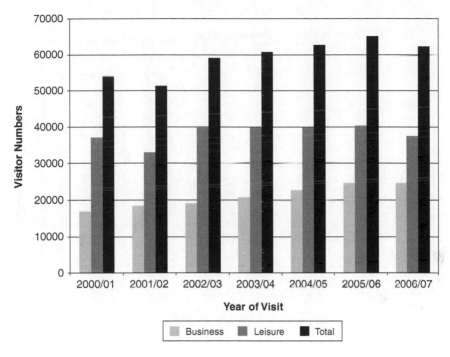

Figure 9.1 North Western Territories visitation (Olmstead 2007)

An interesting sector to highlight is the aurora viewing sector, which, by the late 1990s, had become an important segment for the tourism industry in NWT. Figure 9.2 illustrates a steady growth from 1989 to a sharp decline in 2001–02 following the 11 September (9/11) 2001 terrorist attacks and subsequent effects on international travel. As a result these events affected the Japanese tourist markets, which were important to the aurora tourism subsector. These numbers are estimates and are based on a variety of sources, including information provided by operators, and a variety of industry-specific studies. Although the numbers might not be entirely dependable, there is a sense that there has been some recovery following the 2001 decline, but not enough to bring the subsector back to its peak. Industry concern over the numbers resulted in a government-funded review of the entire aurora industry from a supply-side and competition standpoint (Western Management Consultants 2007). A variety of endogenous and exogenous factors were found to be affecting the rejuvenation of the aurora industry. Some of these factors included lack of marketing support for the destination, tour operator conflicts, lack of direct flights from Japan to Yellowknife, destination issues and increased global competition (Western Management Consultants 2007). The report identified several options to help revive aurora tourism; one of these was the linking of aurora tourism with the developing diamond tourism subsector, a possibility originally noted in a previous consulting report (The North Group 2004).

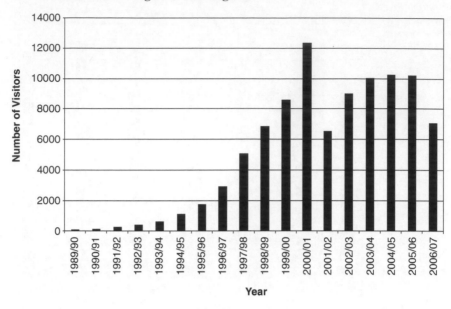

Figuure 9.2 North Western Territories visitors (Marsh 2007)

The idea of diamond tourism in NWT has developed over the last few years as government officials and tourism entrepreneurs have begun to see its potential. Diamond tourism exists in other locations (e.g. Kimberly, South Africa; Amsterdam, The Netherlands; Argyle, Australia) and is based on a combination of mine tours, cutting and polishing factory tours and diamond display exhibits (The North Group 2004). In the context of Yellowknife, diamond tourism is proposed as an educational experience that follows the diamond production process from start to finish (The North Group 2004). According to The North Group (2004), participating in diamond tourism will not be the primary reason for a visit to Yellowknife and NWT, but rather such experiences will complement visits related to the existing subsectors such as hunting and fishing, business travel and aurora tourism. Visitors are therefore expected to engage in diamond tourism as a secondary attraction.

In contrast to some other locations where diamond tourism exists, the vision for diamond tourism in NWT does not include a visit to a diamond mine. This arises because of security constraints related to working mines and because of geographical distance from the major centres. Instead, a diamond tourist in NWT will be able to experience aspects of the mining process through interpretive displays at the visitor centre and museums, and will be able to see cutting and polishing demonstrations at the Northern Frontier Visitor Centre. The opportunity exists to charter a plane for sightseeing over the mine sites; however, as a relatively expensive experience, this will be limited to a small number of tourists. A key component of this vision is the expectation that visitors will purchase a Canadian certified diamond from one of the jewellery stores in Yellowknife (The North Group 2004).

It has been estimated that diamond tourism will contribute just over one million dollars to the NWT gross domestic product (GDP) by 2010 and create over 130 new jobs (The North Group 2004). Even although NWT had CAN\$4,103 million in GDP in 2006 (GNWT 2008), the potential for additional economic revenues through this source continues to be of interest to the municipal and territorial governments, and appears especially promising given the recent declines in the aurora tourism subsector. Yet it is important to determine whether this figure is realistic and whether diamond tourism has had any impact thus far in contributing to GDP and job creations.

Framework and methods

This research has been conceptualised as examining a rural and northern economic development effort that falls into the broad realm of the social economy. Ideas and concepts in the social economy provide a perspective for understanding some of the processes taking place in the development of diamond tourism. The social economy has been described in many ways around the world, but a number of features are consistent. The social economy is situated between the private sector and government and includes organisations and activities such as cooperatives, non-profit-making organisations, credit unions and the voluntary sector (Quarter 1992). These sectors include enterprises that 'are run like businesses, producing goods and services for the market economy, but manage their operations and redirect their surpluses in pursuit of social and environmental goals' (Government of Canada 2007). Further, 'the social economy refers to enterprises and organisations which use the tools and some of the methods of business, on a not-for-profit basis, to provide social, cultural, and economic and health services to communities that need them' (Canadian Social Economy Suite 2006). Social economy organisations pursue goals related to social, environmental and economic aspirations that are not primarily oriented to the creation of profit (see Evans 2006; Painter 2006; Restakis 2006).

A social economy approach is useful in this situation given the prominent role of non-profit organisations in diamond tourism development. In general, the tourism industry tends to have a dependency on non-profit organisations for community and industry training, management for local and regional marketing efforts, assistance with the creation and maintenance of attractions, and for providing community-level support to visitors. Such organisations work to achieve particular goals that enable tourism product development and organised marketing efforts to proceed.

Seven non-profit organisations operating in Yellowknife contribute to the development of tourism initiatives and subtourism sectors (see Table 9.1). In some cases, the core functions and mandates of these groups also incorporate economic and social goals, which are key components of non-profit groups within the social economy.

Table 9.1 Organizations involved in diamond tourism development in Yellowknife

Organization	Function	Mandate	Funding	Board & Staff
Northern Frontier Visitor Association (NFVA)	Assists in tourism development. Works closely with all levels of government. Member-based.	To promote and maintain tourism in the North Slave Region.	Membership, advertising, donations, government	Paid staff, volunteer board
NWT Tourism	Markets destination and functions as tourism industry association. Member-based.	To market tourism in the NWT to a global market.	Government, advertising, memberships	Paid staff, volunteer board
NWT Mining Heritage Society	Preserves and promotes mining heritage in the Northwest Territories.	To establish a mining heritage centre at Giant mine site.	Membership, fundraising, government, donations	Volunteer staff, volunteer board
Prince of Wales Heritage Centre	Houses the territorial museum, the NWT Archives, and heritage programs.	To preserve the heritage and culture of the Inuit, Inuvialuit, Dene, Metis, and non-aboriginal peoples of the NWT.	Government, fundraising, donations, on-site gift shop	Paid staff, volunteer board
NWT Chamber of Mines	Represents the interests and concerns of the mining industry in the Northwest Territories and Nunavut.	To promote the industry and the North to Northerners, Canadians, and the world.	Membership, fundraising	Paid staff, volunteer staff, volunteer board
Diamond Tourism Working group – Product Development	Coordinates the diamond display through the NFVA.	To encourage and plan product development for diamond tourism.	Government, private investment	Ad hoc, volunteer committee
Diamond Tourism Working group – Marketing	Coordinates various marketing initiatives for diamond tourism.	To encourage & plan marketing initiatives for diamond tourism	Government, private investment	Ad hoc, volunteer committee

Source: Primary data; NWT Mining Heritage Society (2008); Prince of Wales Heritage Centre (2008); Northern Frontier Visitor Association (2008); Noakes, Johnston and Koster (2008)

This study included representatives of these non-profit organisations; other participants in the study included representatives of diamond mining companies, local retailers, and tour operators. It is all of these people who are the focus of this study as their beliefs about constraints and opportunities are the foundation for the current and future evolution of diamond tourism. This study used a qualitative approach, with focus groups and interviews as the primary method of data collection. During the summer and early autumn of 2007, four focus groups and 18 interviews were held in Yellowknife. There were a total of 20 participants, 12 of whom participated in focus groups. Following the focus groups, eight people participated in follow-up interviews and then another eight participants were interviewed as they had been unable to participate in focus groups. Two participants were interviewed twice because of their depth and knowledge of the tourism industry. All but two interviews were conducted in person in Yellowknife. The remaining two interviews were conducted via telephone because of difficulties coordinating schedules during fieldwork in Yellowknife.

Findings: constrains and opportunities

This section describes views of the participants in focus groups and interviews, and provides additional information from relevant documents. There is an emphasis on describing the themes arising from the participants' views, which were collected until saturation was achieved. First, results are organised into two broad groupings of constraints and opportunities, and then into points related to physical, social and political aspects. Two final categories bring together the comments on development and diversification.

Constraints

The first category of constraints discussed is physical and includes both the geographical and environmental constraints, as well as those related to infrastructure and attractions. The regional geography of diamond mining plays a significant role in terms of physical constraints in the development of diamond tourism. Study participants noted that physical distance stands as a major constraint to offering guided tours of the mines. All mines are located 200 to 300 km from Yellowknife, making it a time-consuming journey by land (between 15 and 20 hours) or an expensive one by charter aircraft (Diavik 2008; Ekati 2008). Two participants noted that, although workers at the mines are regularly transported by air, there is no guarantee tourists would be able to participate in this schedule, nor would it necessarily be flexible enough to accommodate tourists. The mines are accessible during the winter via ice roads, but eight participants noted that there are no service stations along the road and that harsh winter conditions, along with primarily industrial traffic, make safety a major concern for road travel. These issues, along with security constraints, hinder tourists from reaching the mines.

Another physical constraint noted is related to security concerns of management at the cutting and polishing facilities and the diamond mines related to allowing tourists to observe their sites. Several participants mentioned that the mine administration is extremely vigilant about security related to the behaviour of employees at the mines and mining companies have taken considerable steps to ensure the security of their facilities and product. As one participant noted, the mines were not established to accommodate tours and it appears to be too risky for the companies to open their doors to the general public in the form of tourism, at this time. These same concerns were present in relation to the cutting and polishing facilities located in Yellowknife. The lack of a focal point attraction was particularly of concern to participants because it was seen as a major competitive disadvantage when compared with other diamond mining destinations. The inability to tour mines and related facilities was viewed as requiring extra compensation in other components of the diamond tourism experience.

The lack of access into the mines and cutting and polishing facilities is linked to additional constraints in the lack of infrastructure and cost of developing infrastructure. Almost all stakeholders viewed the deficiency of concrete diamond tourism activities as a hindrance to the success of diamond tourism. All were aware of the impending construction of a diamond exhibit at the Northern Frontier Visitors Association (NFVA), opened to the public in June 2008. This CAN$750,000 project incorporates displays of diamonds, a cutting and polishing wheel for demonstrations, information on the mining process and a giant kimberlite model (Aldrichpears Associates 2007). Several stakeholders suggested that it would be beneficial and strategic to upgrade a cutting and polishing facility as the next logical product development initiative. Stakeholders agreed that development initiatives of physical products are crucial to the overall success of diamond tourism and, in essence, the overall tourism industry and supply package in Yellowknife.

Another constraint associated with infrastructure development is the flight scheduling and insufficient capacity of Yellowknife Airport. Stakeholders stressed that there was a lack of direct flights linking Yellowknife to large urban centres such as Vancouver and Toronto, and beyond to centres that would connect the city to the majority of international travellers to NWT in Japan and the USA. Stakeholders noted there was a need for airport improvements in order to accommodate larger long-haul aircrafts, as well as an upgrade to airport equipment used in servicing aircrafts.

Another attraction-related physical constraint noted by stakeholders was the lack of visual displays and tourism theming around the city. Many stakeholders expressed the need to display mining equipment (preferably related to gold and diamond mining), signs, billboards and other items that would show the rich history of gold mining and the potential for a prosperous diamond mining future.

Many stakeholders described a need for incorporating diamonds with art work and educating artists on how to work with diamonds. Stakeholders believed that this is an untapped market that would allow the community to benefit greatly with some attention from the tourism industry. In addition to the constraint of diamonds and artwork, it was pointed out that currently no local jewellery manufacturers in Yellowknife could set diamonds in jewellery pieces on a large scale. This was viewed as creating limitations to jewellery retail stores, which are otherwise a vital component of the diamond tourism experience.

The current state of the aurora tourism sector was a topic widely discussed by stakeholders. The decline in aurora numbers after 2001 engendered questions about the strength of the subsector. This decline was seen as a constraint to diamond tourism because the aurora subsector had been targeted for linked marketing strategies. Further, the aurora decline caused concern among study participants because other subsectors also had encountered problems that called into question the state of the overall tourism supply package.

The second category includes the social constraints related to diamond tourism development and includes interpersonal as well as structural issues. During interviews and focus groups, a number of participants indicated that they were angered by and frustrated with other stakeholders because of the failure of initiatives in the past. These conflicts between individuals and groups were seen as constraints to moving forward in developing future diamond tourism initiatives. Another social constraint noted is the lack of trained individuals who are available for employment in the subsector. More than 15 participants pointed out that this extends beyond diamond tourism to the tourism industry as a whole, which is experiencing a human capital deficit related to the existence of high-paying jobs in the resource sector. Many participants expressed the belief that the tourism industry generally is finding it difficult to attract skilled tourism workers to the north primarily because tourism businesses are unable to pay competitive wages. At the time of this fieldwork, Yellowknife's economy was still growing because of stable oil, gas and diamond mining operations. Participants noted that this issue had even affected training opportunities and that Aurora College in Yellowknife did not offer its diamond cutting and polishing program for 2007 because of limited enrolment. Stakeholders viewed this as a constraint, hindering the development of diamond tourism in the community. As a result, the Northern Frontier Visitor Centre was unable to find and fund someone to demonstrate cutting and polishing on the wheel at the new diamond display, thereby limiting the fulfilment of the intentions for the display in diamond tourists' experiences.

Another social constraint also related to the larger community was that stake-holders believed that the community was unaware of the benefits of tourism and had limited insight as to how diamond tourism could contribute to community development. Study participants noted that these issues relate to the lack of community vision in Yellowknife. Stakeholders suggested that a possible way to eliminate this constraint would be to educate the community about the positive aspects of tourism development and the overall benefits of tourism to the economy.

The third theme is political constraints and these concern administration as well as government priorities. Participants noted several constraints that lie within this category. The first was disorganisation within the government in its work on diamond tourism initiatives and marketing. This was noted particularly for departments within the territorial government. Three participants mentioned that NWT diamond product development and marketing had been far more organised when a dedicated diamond division existed. This was a division within Industry,

Tourism and Investment of the territorial government that had a responsibility to market and promote diamonds and diamond tourism through various initiatives such as the 'Rare in Nature' campaign and the Canadian Diamond Certification Program (see also GNWT, Diamond Division 2006). The division was closed because of government budget cuts and its responsibilities were allocated to other departments. According to these three participants, the departments each took on the new responsibilities and proceeded to complete various marketing tasks without consulting the other departments. This led to numerous, and ineffective, attempts to market diamond tourism through departments that did not specialise in this sector.

Another political constraint noted by participants was limited cooperation and involvement among levels of government. Participants believed that there was a general consensus that diamond tourism should be promoted, but thought that the initiative sat differently on the priority lists for all levels of government. Many participants mentioned that this creates difficulty for government departments trying to cooperate on diamond tourism initiatives in terms of funding and budgeting. Related to this, participants noted a lack of support, funding and recognition toward the diamond tourism vision on the part of both the government and regional tourism destination marketing organisation. Stakeholders agreed that the marketing organisation was underfunded compared with other Canadian marketing organisations; nonetheless they believed that with increased attention, a better effort could be achieved. Over half of the participants extended this lack of support to the mine management, arguing that with some level of attention and support from this group, diamond tourism initiatives would benefit.

The issues of support, funding and recognition are linked to the final constraint identified by stakeholders: a lack of suitable research on diamond tourism as a subsector and the tourism industry overall. Participants stressed the need for regular and consistent exit surveys, noting that only two exit surveys had been completed since the territorial divide. Participants were concerned that tourism development decisions were based on estimations that could be debated and provided no true picture for the industry of trends and changes.

Opportunities

The second grouping of themes covers the opportunities for diamond tourism as viewed by participant stakeholders. These points are organised into three categories: physical, social and political. In regard to physical aspects, nearly all participants stated that opportunities exist in the areas related to infrastructure and attractions. They noted that temporary museum exhibits, a visitor centre in Yellowknife operated by one of the mining companies, and the new diamond display at the Northern Frontier Visitor Centre contributed to the advancement of facilities. Many stakeholders suggested that a video presentation could be created to accompany the new diamond display, suggesting that an IMAX movie or 360° cinema would allow tourists to have some experience of the mine sites they are unable to visit. Several stakeholders also discussed the idea of upgrading one of the cutting and polishing facilities so that tourists were able to view diamonds being cut and polished on site. In addition to these ideas, some participants stated that it would be beneficial to have a dedicated diamond interpretive centre, a facility that would house education, cutting and polishing activities and a variety of jewellery stores. This centre would function as the primary destination for diamond-seeking tourists. Although this idea was suggested by four participants, its implementation would require considerable thought, coordination, planning and funding.

Another physical opportunity described by participants was packaged tours incorporating diamond displays and exhibits, visitor centres, the Aurora College, jewellery stores, restaurants and other attractions around Yellowknife. Many stakeholders suggested that packaged tours would increase stakeholder cooperation and partnerships, as well as allow visitors to experience everything that Yellowknife has to offer. Stakeholders stated that incorporating Aurora College into packaged tours might help expand its programmes through international awareness. Stakeholders proposed that the college programme offer diamond-setting courses for artists and gemology courses. Many participants also connected artwork into the packages and indicated that art incorporating diamonds could be linked into attractions in order to provide mutual benefit for the providers. Another link identified by participants was the opportunity to connect package tours with mining heritage more generally.

In terms of social opportunities, perhaps the most important element noted by participants is employment, reiterating the forecast by The North Group (2004) of the creation of new jobs through diamond tourism. Several participants thought that these jobs would be dispersed among government positions, tour operators, hospitality, and cutting and polishing facilities. Another social opportunity that many participants touched on is greater economic cooperation. Eight participants stated that, should diamond tourism become established, there is a natural marketing opportunity between the aurora and diamond subsectors on which many businesses might be able to capitalise. There is also an opportunity for cooperation between the tourism and mining industry. Already participants were seeing this emerge. Seven participants noted that three diamond mining companies contributed financially to the diamond display at the visitor centre; in return they were given a voice in suggesting the types of displays they would like to see presented at the centre. These partnerships could benefit both sides by allowing the mining industry to showcase its community involvement and environmental efforts to a global market and by increasing resources for the tourism industry to help with diamond tourism development and promotion initiatives.

The final set of social opportunities includes a series of points that are centred around tourism development and diversification. Stakeholders stated that tourism development and diversification would help communities with economic stability following diamond mine closures because tourism is a renewable resource. Stakeholders also saw diamond tourism as an opportunity for the community to learn about the benefits of tourism diversification and development more generally.

The last category is political opportunities. Four participants stated that the municipal government had become involved in diamond tourism because it sees an opportunity for economic diversification through strengthening the current tourism package (see City of Yellowknife 2007). This interest acknowledges the boom and bust history of Yellowknife related to fluctuating natural resource prices. Diversifying the economy to include a broader tourism industry was seen as an option for securing a stronger future for the residents of Yellowknife. Four participants noted that the territorial government also has a vested interest in tourism because of the opportunity for economic diversification. Although participants did not mention the federal government's interest in this, it is apparent that economic diversification in the north in order to increase stability in the northern economy is an issue (Government of Canada 2007b). Some stakeholders considered diamond tourism a good subsector for strengthening the current tourism package because it could have more appeal to female travellers, an area currently limited in the traditional hunting and fishing subsectors.

Aside from economic diversification and development opportunities, stakeholders strongly believed that diamond tourism should be part of the tourism strategy to encourage appropriate levels of commitment, support, funding and marketing from all levels of government. As well, stakeholders discussed the opportunities related to diamond tourism and global marketing possibilities given the attention that diamonds as a prestigious product attract from international markets.

Discussion

A number of overarching themes arose time and again in the focus groups and interviews, notably economic diversification and development of diamond tourism, and the role of government and industry in these initiatives. These themes are relevant both for consideration of the place of diamond tourism in the larger tourism industry and for understanding the role of social economy organisations in tourism development. This section discusses these two themes with reference to both areas.

The social economy framework helps provide an understanding of the constraints and opportunities seen by participants, in that many of the findings relate to cooperation, partnerships, responsibilities and communication among stakeholders. In essence, the findings direct us towards the need for people to work together not for the individual or company profit, but rather to improve the situation of tourism in a general sense. Despite the constraints relating to the lack of community awareness and interest generally in tourism, economic diversification via tourism development could provide additional economic stability that may be needed during economic downturn (Noakes *et al.* 2008). The development of the diamond tourism subsector could play a role as a component in a diversification plan that would strengthen the overall industry and contribute more generally to diversification goals in the broader economy. The boom and bust nature of resource-dependent economies means that economic development and planning must include an emphasis on diversification.

Numerous comments that refer to the role of government agencies on the constraints and opportunities on diamond tourism provide a sense of the importance of government in supporting development initiatives. In part, support includes funding for the social economy. This is the scenario for diamond tourism development where the non-profit organisations were granted government funding to pursue development objectives for the subsector. As well another key role of government is to facilitate various aspects of tourism development through programmes that help community groups and entrepreneurs meet their objectives. It was in this organisational structure and effectiveness that participants saw a deficiency in Yellowknife.

Diamond tourism was viewed as an important opportunity in diversification because it would strengthen several aspects of the tourism industry. One of these related to drawing in more female travellers to counter some of the dependence on hunting, fishing and outdoor adventure on male travellers (GNWT 2007d). Another related to the possibility that the new subsector could complement and help support the deteriorating aurora sector. Many participants viewed diamond tourism as the ticket to the recovery of the aurora industry. Beyond these aspects, however, additional strengthening for the tourism industry was identified in relation to infrastructure and promotional activities that would enhance the tourism experience for all visitors through displays, exhibits, interpretation, themes and provision of information. This is where participants saw possible links to the wider community that would provide broader benefits by connecting diamond tourism attractions to diamond fabrication facilities such as cutting and polishing sites, training facilities such as Aurora College, and to retail stores. Such links have the potential to develop the economy further through creating work opportunities and to help sustain the social economy by support educational facilities. Further, connections to the mining industry itself, through funding for diamond tourism initiatives and development support, are part of the broader benefits with positive outcomes for the community, the tourism industry and even for the mining industry.

Conclusions

This paper has examined the conditions surrounding the development of diamond tourism in NWT and perceptions related to constraints and opportunities for its development held by those who are influencing the subsector. Constraints and opportunities were described through three categories: physical, social and political. As an economic development and diversification effort, nurturing of diamond tourism is being undertaken by all three levels of government and by the tourism industry, with some contributions from the mining industry. It is also being supported by organisations in the social economy that are working on a not-for-profit basis either to support the tourism industry generally or in particular to help advance the emergence of this new subsector.

Members of these latter groups, the diamond tourism working groups, should pay special attention to the constraints identified in this study, while using the opportunities as a foundation for progress. Although some of the constraints might not be able to be resolved, many of them can be managed through concerted efforts of all stakeholders. Likewise not all of the opportunities will be realised, but it will require some focused efforts to take advantage of those that are most possible. It seems apparent that the two working groups, whose mandates are to support diamond tourism, should be prepared to take the lead in influencing its direction, perhaps influencing through strategic planning that will take stakeholders beyond the vision that now exists and the preliminary product development and marketing efforts and gear stakeholders towards achievable goals that reflect the current conditions and likely changes in the near future.

References

Aldrichpears Associates (2007) Design Development, available at the Northern Frontier Visitors Centre, Yellowknife, NWT.

Canadian Social Economy Suite (2006) *Understanding the Social Economy: The Diversity of the Canadian Experience*, Canadian Social Economy Hub, British Columbia, Victoria. Online. Available HTTP: http://www.socialeconomyhub.ca/ (accessed 6 November 2007).

City of Yellowknife, Department of Economic Development (2007) *Report on Economic Development*, Northwest Territories: Yellowknife. Online. Available HTTP: http://www.yellowknife.ca/City_Hall/Departments/Economic_Development.html (accessed 10 November 2007).

Diavik Diamond Mine (2008) Fact Sheet. Online. Available HTTP: http://www.diavik.ca/QF.htm (accessed 9 July 2008).

Ekati (2008) 'About Ekati'. Online. Available HTTP: http://bhpbilliton.com/bb/ourBusinesses/diamondsSpecialtyProducts/ekatiDiamondMine/aboutEkati.jsp (accessed 9 July 2008).

Evans, M. (2006) 'The social economy and the shadowy side of the life course', *Horizons*, 8: 48–53.

Government of Canada (Western Economic Diversification Canada) (2007a) Definition of Social Economy, Online. Available HTTP: http://www.wd.gc.ca/ (accessed 3March 2007).

Government of Canada (Indian and Northern Affairs Canada) (2007b) Ontario, Ottawa, Online. Available HTTP: http://www.ainc-inac.gc.ca/sd/index_e.html (accessed 7 November 2007).

Government of the Northwest Territories, Industry, Tourism and Investment (GNWT) (2003) *The impacts of September 11 on Travel in the Northwest Territories*, Yellowknife: Northwest Territories, Online. Available HTTP: http://www.iti.gov.nt.ca/publications/2007/TourismParks/Travel_Impacts_of_September_11_on_the_NWT.pdf (accessed 21 September 2007).

— (2007a) Tourism Development Handbook for the Northwest Territories, Yellowknife, NWT.

— (2007b) A Brief History of Travel in Canada's Northwest Territories, Northwest Territories, Yellowknife. Online. Available HTTP: http://www.iti.gov.nt.ca/parks/education/p_t/travel_history.htm (accessed 10 November 2007).

— (2007c) Northwest Territories: 2006 Visitor Exit Survey – Summary Report. Online.

Available HTTP: http://www.iti.gov.nt.ca/publications/2007/ Tourism parks/2006% 20 Exit%20Survey%20-%20Summary.pdf (accessed 02 August 2008).
— (2007d) Northwest Territories: 2006 Visitor Exit Survey – Outdoor Adventure. Online. Available HTTP: http://www.iti.gov.nt.ca/publications/2007/ tourismparks/2006%20 Exit%20Survey%20-%20Outdoor%20Adventure.pdf (accessed 02 August 2008).
— (2008) Statistics Quarterly, Yellowknife: Bureau of Statistics, Northwest Territories.
Hall, C.M and Johnston, M.E. (1995) 'Introduction: Pole to pole: tourism issues, impacts and the search for a management regime in polar regions', in C.M. Hall and M.E. Johnston (eds) *Polar Tourism: Tourism in the Arctic and Antarctic Regions*, Chichester: John Wiley & Sons.
Marsh, J.S. (1987) 'Tourism and conservation: case studies in the Canadian north', in J.G. Nelson, R. Needham and L. Norton (eds) *Arctic Heritage: Proceedings of a Symposium*, Ottawa: Association of Canadian Universities for Northern Studies.
Marsh, S. (2007) email information 28 March 2007, undisclosed email Coordinator, Research and Planning Tourism and Parks.
Noakes, J. and Johnston, M.E. (2008) 'A diamond in the rough: views on the constraints and opportunities of diamond tourism in Yellowknife, NWT', in Conference Proceedings, Tourism and Global Change in Polar Regions, Oulu, Finland.
Noakes, J., Johnston, M.E. and Koster, R. (2008) 'Economic diversification and tourism in Yellowknife, NWT', in *Conference Proceedings*, The Association for Nonprofit and Social Economy Research (ANSER), Vancouver, British Columbia.
NWT Tourism (2007) 'Historic Sites' Northwest Territories, Yellowknife. Online. Available HTTP: http://www.explorenwt.com/adventures/historic-sites/index.asp (accessed 10 November 2007).
Northern Frontier Visitor Association (NFVA) (2008) Contact Us. Online. Available HTTP: http://www.northernfrontier.com/02_Contact/contact.html (accessed 12 August 2008).
NWT Mining Heritage Society (2008) A Vision. Online. Available HTTP: http://www. pwnhc.ca/nwtminingcentre/ (accessed 20 July 2008).
Olmstead, D. (2007) email information, 11 November, undisclosed email Executive Director of Northern Frontier Visitor Association
Painter, A. (2006) 'The social economy in Canada – concepts, data and measurement' *Horizons* 8: 30–34.
Prince of Wales Northern Heritage Centre (2008) Site map. Online. Available HTTP: http://pwnhc.learnnet.nt.ca/admin/intro.htm (accessed 20 July 2008).
Quarter, J. (1992) *Canada's Social Economy: Co-operatives, Non-profits and Other Community Enterprises,* Toronto: J. Lorimer.
Restakis, J. (2006) Defining the Social Economy – The BC Context, BC Social Economy Roundtable, British Columbia Co-operative Association.
The North Group (2004) A Perfect Setting: Diamond Tourism in the Northwest Territories, available at the Northern Frontier Visitor Association, Yellowknife, NWT.
Tukto Lodge (2007) A History of Great Fishing. Online. Available HTTP: http://www. arcticfishing.com/history-tukto-lodge.php (accessed 10 November, 2007).
Western Management Consultants (2007) Northwest Territories Tourism: Competitive Analysis: Aurora Viewing Tourism, report available at the Northern Frontier Visitors Association, Yellowknife, NWT.

10   Cultural Heritage Tourism in Antarctica and Svalbard

Patterns, impacts and policies

Ricardo Roura

Introduction

For several centuries the polar regions have been the focus of activities of people originating from outside these regions, including explorers, whalers, seal hunters, and scientists. Their activities have left many material remains in the polar landscape such as supply depots, huts and shelters, industrial remains, research stations, and crosses, graves and other memorials. These and similar cultural remains are significant, among other reasons, because they tell the history of polar exploration and exploitation of the polar regions. Following on those earlier activities, contemporary polar tourism represents a new phase in the 'exploration' and exploitation of the polar regions. Many significant historic sites in Antarctica and Svalbard have now become tourist 'destinations', where tourism landings are a seasonal feature (e.g. Hughes 1994; Hughes and Davis 1995; Geitz 2004; Roura 2009).

This chapter compares and contrasts organised cruise tourism at protected historic sites in Antarctica and Svalbard (before 1925 the archipelago was known as Spitsbergen; it is now usually referred to by its Norwegian name of Svalbard.) (Figure 10.1.). The purpose is to identify the patterns and impacts of organised tourism at historic sites in the context of existing tourism policies for each region. In this context a historic site (any location that demonstrates past human activity, exemplified by the presence of artefacts, ecofacts, features, structures, or other material remains (Kipfer 2007) is distinguished from a landing site (places where people set foot ashore). A landing site may or may not also be a historic site, and vice versa. A further distinction exists between sites of past human activity depending on whether or not they are legally protected. The protected sites and remains of past activities can be regarded, in a legal sense, as part of the region's cultural heritage. Heritage, however, may be more broadly defined (e.g. Ashworth and Graham 2005; Lowenthal 2005).

Cultural heritage tourism in Antarctica and Svalbard consists primarily of organised visits, mostly by ship, to historic sites. Visits focus on the places, material remains, and associated historic events. The following research questions are addressed in this chapter: What are the patterns of tourism at historic sites, both regionally and locally? How do visitors behave at historic sites, and what are

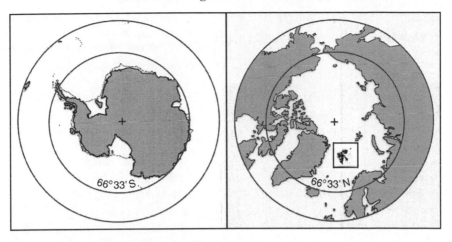

Figure 10.1 Antarctica and Svalbard (Spitsbergen)

the traces of their behaviour? And how effective is the protection of historic sites in the context of existing tourism policies?

Overview: contrasting Antarctica and Svalbard

Background

The Dutch pilot Willem Barentsz is generally acknowledged to have discovered the High Arctic archipelago of Spitsbergen in 1596. The earliest sighting of Antarctica might have been in 1599 by the Dutchman Dirk Gerritsz Pomp (Ligtendag 2002), but others suggest 1820 as a likely date (Headland 1989). At any event, neither of these regions had indigenous populations, and human presence on the land began in the 17th century in Spitsbergen and in the early 19th century in Antarctica. Following their discovery both regions have experienced broadly analogous historic developments, including exploration, natural resources exploitation, science, tourism, and the establishment of comprehensive environmental protection regimes. However, the timing and tempo of developments were different in each case, and a range of events in Spitsbergen's history (hunting and trapping, large-scale industrial developments, and warfare during World War II) have no or a limited Antarctic equivalent.

Both Antarctica and Spitsbergen have been regarded as *terra nullius* and originated territorial ambitions. Resulting tensions were in both instances resolved through international treaties (e.g. Mathisen 1954; Beck 1986; Triggs 1987; Ulfstein 1995). Svalbard is subject to the 1920 *Treaty Concerning the Archipelago of Spitsbergen*, which comprises all the islands situated between 74° and 81° N and 10° and 35° E, and grants the 'full and absolute' sovereignty of Spitsbergen to Norway (Article 1) while maintaining equal rights for all contracting parties, subject to Norwegian laws. These include rights to hunt, fish, or engage in all maritime, industrial, mining and commercial operations (Article 3). Norway's *Svalbard Act* of 17 June 1925 establishes that Svalbard is part of Norway. A Norwegian-appointed Governor of Svalbard is responsible for ensuring compliance with the provisions of the Treaty and current Norwegian legislation (Ulfstein 1995; Norway 2004).

The Antarctic Treaty Area, which includes the Antarctic continent, islands, and seas south of 60°S of latitude, is governed by the 1959 *Antarctic Treaty* and related instruments, notably the 1991 *Protocol of Environmental Protection to the Antarctic Treaty* (the Protocol). This set of instruments comprises what is known as the Antarctic Treaty System. Seven states claim parts of Antarctica and two others reserve the right to place future claims. There are overlapping claims over the Antarctic Peninsula area as well as one unclaimed sector. Article IV of the *Antarctic Treaty* 'freezes' the status quo regarding territorial claims. The Antarctic Treaty Consultative Meeting (ATCM), which currently meets annually, makes decisions about the governance of the region (e.g. Beck 1986; Triggs 1987; Bastmeijer and Roura 2004).

Cultural heritage

Cultural heritage protection is a subset of environmental protection laws in both regions. Many more cultural heritage remains have been inventoried and listed as protected in Svalbard than in Antarctica. Cultural heritage in Svalbard has a broader range of types and functions than in Antarctica (Figure 10.2 a–d).

The Protocol and other Antarctic Treaty instruments protect the Antarctic cultural heritage, which is represented by designated Historic Sites and Monuments (HSMs). Any party may propose a site or monument of recognised historic value for listing as an HSM. The proposal for listing may be approved by a measure adopted at an ATCM (Protocol Annex V, Article 8(2)). By ATCM XXXII (2009) there were 79 listed sites and monuments numbered 1–84 (some have been delisted or subsumed into other HSMs). Of these, approximately 70% are the sites and remains of past Antarctic activities and about 30% are memorials and monuments. The list of HSMs is subject to periodic review and updates, but it is neither comprehensive nor representative of different periods or themes of Antarctic history. HSM designation gives an international status to elements that have primarily a national value (Roura 2008).

Listed HSMs shall not be damaged, removed or destroyed. Historic remains predating 1958 whose existence or present location is not known also have a degree of protection (ATCM Resolution 5, 2001). HSMs may be designated as protected areas. Past activity remains that are not otherwise protected are subject to removal under Protocol requirements (Annex III, Article 1(5)) to clean up past and present waste disposal sites on land and abandoned worksites. Existing provisions pertaining to the designation and management of historic sites have now been consolidated into a set of guidelines (ATCM Resolution A, 2009).

Unlike in the Antarctic (and indeed, mainland Norway) from a Norwegian legal perspective the natural and cultural heritage of Svalbard are considered together

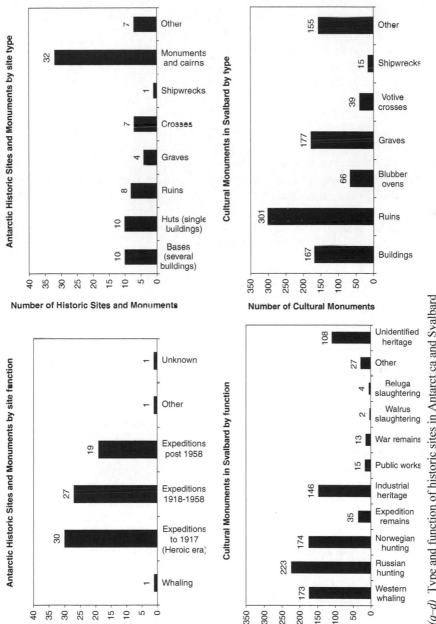

Figure 10.2 (a–d) Type and function of historic sites in Antarctica and Svalbard

as part of the environment (*miljø*) (P.K. Reymert, personal communication, 22 September 2006). The Treaty Concerning the Archipelago of Spitsbergen allows Norway to set measures to ensure the preservation of fauna and flora (Article 2). In Norway this has been interpreted as a requirement to protect the archipelago's environment. Norway's 2001 *Svalbard Environmental Protection Act* protects Svalbard's cultural monuments (*kulturminner*) and states that Svalbard's cultural heritage shall be protected 'as an element of a coherent system of environmental management' (section 38). Approximately 920 cultural monuments in Svalbard have been identified to date, covering all periods of the archipelago's history (see also Marstrander 1999). The law protects structures, sites, and movable historical objects predating 1946, as well as more recent cultural remains that are of particular historic or cultural value and that are protected by a decision of Norway's Directorate of Cultural Heritage. Cultural features such as human graves and certain animal slaughtering sites are also protected irrespective of their age. Camping, lighting a fire or leaving other traces is prohibited within 100 m from a cultural monument (Det Kongelige Miljøverndepartement 2001). Over 50 sites containing cultural monuments have been identified as having high priority for protection (Governor of Svalbard 2000).

Organised tourism and tourism policies

Antarctica and Svalbard present fairly different conditions for cruise tourism, which is the main form of tourist access to historic sites. The landmass of Antarctica (14×10^6 km^2) is much larger in surface area than Svalbard (61,022 km^2). Less than 1% of Antarctica is ice free, compared with approximately 40% in Svalbard (Statistics Norway 2005). With the exception of the Antarctic Peninsula, the Antarctic coastline is located 3,000 km or more from the closest continent. Svalbard is about 1,000 km from Norway. Svalbard has a comparatively mild climate for its latitude as a result of the influence of the Gulf Stream. Unlike Antarctica, Svalbard is accessible by air year-round and tourism is promoted for both summer and winter. The regions' flora and fauna are substantially different and the ecology of species such as penguins, polar bears and walruses influences tourism patterns. In basic characteristics such as access, density of landing sites, and contemporary cruise tourism patterns, Svalbard bears a closer resemblance to the northwest Antarctic Peninsula than to the rest of Antarctica.

The first tourism cruise to Spitsbergen was organised in 1871 (Conway 1906). Tourism began to increase following the opening of an airport in Svalbard in 1975, and then with the Norwegian government designation of tourism as one of three priority areas for Svalbard in 1990 along with mining and education and science (Viken and Jørgensen 1998; Norway 2004; Kolltveit 2006). In Antarctica the first organised cruise was in 1958, and although it continued for the next three decades it did not begin to increase substantially until the 1990s (e.g. Bastmeijer and Roura 2004) (see also chapter 1). Cruise tourism is largely characterised by 'expedition cruising', in which vessels are comparatively small and thus able to land people ashore despite a lack of infrastructure (Geitz 2004: 7). Periodic landings are complemented by excursions on inflatable boats and by cruises to scenic areas, and by on-board lectures. Some cruises visit either region as part of more extended itineraries including adjacent regions such as mainland Norway or South America. In Svalbard there are also day cruises and other forms of local tourism. The cruise tourism season usually extends from November to March in Antarctica and from June to September in Svalbard.

Cruise tourism in these regions is currently characterised by growth (an increase in ships, tour operators, and tourists); diversification (an increasingly broad range of transport modalities and activities on offer), and geographic expansion (an increase in the number of sites used for tourism) (e.g. Bastmeijer and Roura 2004; Geitz 2004) (see also chapter 1). In 2006 more than 28,000 tourists arrived in Svalbard in overseas cruise ships, and more than 12,000 tourists boarded 'expedition' cruises and day cruises (Governor of Svalbard 2006). More than 35,000 ship-borne tourists visited Antarctica in the summer of 2006–07, of whom more than 28,000 landed ashore (IAATO 2008).

Tour operators in Antarctica and Svalbard are organised in industry associations, respectively the International Association of Antarctic Tour Operators (IAATO) and the Association of Arctic Expedition Cruise Operators (AECO). Among other functions, these associations agree on self-regulation measures. More than 70% of AECO members are also IAATO members and operate in both regions. Some guides work regularly in both regions, and some tourists visit both.

Antarctic Treaty Consultative Parties generally have accepted that tourism will continue to operate in the region, and that it needs to be managed to preserve the intrinsic values of Antarctica (New Zealand and Australia 2006: 4). However, how tourism is or should be managed is the subject of intense debate, the detail of which is beyond the scope of this chapter. Antarctic tourism is primarily ruled by generic regulation applicable to all Antarctic activities, by specific regulation on insurance and contingency planning and landing requirements (ATCM Measures 4 (2004) and 15 (2009) are the only tourism instruments that will be legally binding once they become effective), and by non-legally binding guidelines emanating from the ATCM and from the tourism industry. There is generic guidance for visitation to historic sites (ATCM Recommendation XVIII-1) and site-specific guidelines for some frequently visited sites. Voluntary site-specific guidelines have been developed for 25 of the most visited sites in Antarctica, including seven designated HSMs. Visits to some 'heroic age' huts require a permit. Overall, Antarctic tourism must meet certain conditions but it is not subject to restrictions (Bastmeijer and Roura 2004). However, recent shipping accidents involving cruise vessels may result in the future adoption of more restrictive tourism regulation. For instance, the recently adopted Measure 15 (2009) seeks to prevent landings from vessels carrying more than 500 passengers.

Tourism is one of the activities prioritised to support Norwegian presence in Svalbard but it should take place in the context of environmental protection (Vistad *et al.* 2008). The Norwegian government policy against tourism in

Spitsbergen changed officially in 1990. Tourism is managed by state regulation, which enforces a restrictive preservation policy, complemented by industry self-regulation (Viken and Jørgensen 1998; Norway 2004). The Regulations relating to tourism and other travel in Svalbard, issued by Royal Decree of 18 October 1991, cover matters such as insurance, accountability and notification for trips organised in Svalbard. The Governor has the authority to alter or prohibit trips. Some natural or historic sites have permanent or seasonal restricted access (e.g. Geitz 2004). However, one of the goals for Svalbard's cultural heritage is protecting and sustaining it 'for the enjoyment of present and future generations' (Governor of Svalbard 2000: 8). Tourism is therefore acceptable under current cultural heritage policy.

In 2009 the Governor of Svalbard recommended that a general ban on traffic be introduced at or near several cultural heritage sites that are automatically protected by law. The objective of the proposal is to preserve several relatively unaffected and significant cultural heritage sites from wear and tear and other negative effects caused by traffic (Governor of Svalbard 2009). This proposal was under discussion at the time of writing.

Elements of visitation: methods

An integrated approach was used to assess the behavioural elements and material traces elements of visitation at historic sites (Rathje 2001). These provided a mutually complementary perspective of tourism use of historic sites. Direct observations and site surveys of different kinds constituted the main research methods. Tourism statistics (Governor of Svalbard 2006; IAATO 2008) were analysed to assess landing patterns. Semi-structured interviews with key informants complemented other research methods.

Cultural heritage tourism in Antarctica and Svalbard is largely ship-based; and tourists are regularly taken ashore to visit places of interest. Observers can be part of a tourism contingent and follow its itinerary (which may be a form of participant observation). Alternatively observers can be based at a landing site and observe landings as they take place. Both approaches were used for this study. In Antarctica direct observations were conducted on opportunistic bases during stays at Deception Island (2002), King George Island (2006) and Ross Island (2008). In Spitsbergen observations were conducted on day cruises in the Ice Fjord (2006), on a week-long cruise to northwest Spitsbergen (2007) and during stays at Ny-Ålesund and Ny-London in Kings Bay (2007). Observations were made of both group and individual behaviour. Observations were conducted from an *etic* perspective, that is, tourist behaviour was described regardless of the apparent motivations or perspectives of the individuals (Pearce 2005). Observations followed an *ad libitum* sampling pattern, i.e. whatever was visible and seemed relevant at the time was recorded (Martin and Bateson 1993). The traces of behaviour and activity visible on the terrain were surveyed (Schiffer 1987; Bernard 2002). The focus here was not on the structure of behaviour itself (as identified in direct observations) but on the consequences of that behaviour.

Results and discussion

Tourism patterns and cultural heritage

Cruise tourism in Antarctica and Svalbard relies on the long-term seasonal use of certain sites that have been established as destinations. Historic sites are attractive destinations because they have material remains (there is something to show) and a history (there is a story to tell) (Roura 2009). Key historic sites are regularly included in mainstream tourist itineraries both in Antarctica and Svalbard, adding to sites that are visited for their natural or scenic values or for other reasons. Tourism landings at historic sites therefore reflect general tourism patterns. Cultural heritage is also the subject of more specialised tourism.

Antarctic tourism visits are concentrated at fewer than 35 sites (IAATO 2008). An examination of Antarctic tourism statistics shows that tourists have visited approximately 200 sites in the Antarctic Peninsula region since 1989, including 20 research stations. About 50 of these sites have received 100 or more visitors in any one season. In contrast, about the same number of sites have been visited only once. At least about 100 sites have been visited elsewhere in Antarctica, mostly in the Ross Sea area. Tourists have visited almost 300 sites in Svalbard over the years (Geitz 2004: 10–11). Between 100 and 200 landing sites are currently visited each season in both regions (Figure 10.3). Visitor landings currently exceed 80,000 for Svalbard and 170,000 for Antarctica (Figure 10.4).

Key historic sites are among the most visited sites in both regions (Figure 10.5 a–c). The most visited historic sites are situated in the northwest Antarctic Peninsula and the Ross Sea area of Antarctica (Figure 10.6) and in northwest Spitsbergen (Figure 10.7). In 2006–07 nearly 50,000 visitor landings took place at 15 significant historic sites in Antarctica (about 20% of all landings). Some

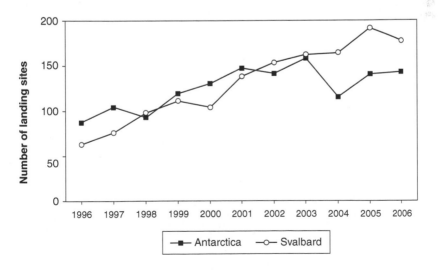

Figure 10.3 Number of landing sites in Antarctica and Svalbard

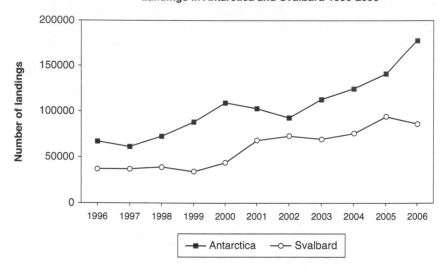

Figure 10.4 Visitor landings in Antarctica and Svalbard. Visitors include tourists, staff, and crew.

historic sites have become what can be regarded, by Antarctic standards, as mass tourism destinations. These sites receive upward of 10,000 visitors annually and include Port Lockroy in Goudier Island and Whalers Bay in Deception Island. In 2006 more than 25,000 visitors landed at 30 high-priority historic sites in Svalbard (more than 30% of all landings). These figures exclude sites that contain a range of attractions in addition to historic sites, such as some Antarctic research stations and Svalbard settlements.

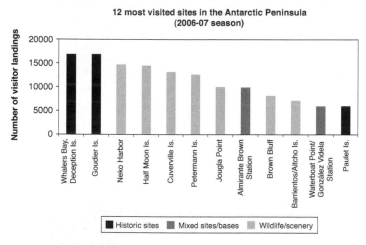

Figure 10.5 (a) The 12 most visited sites in the Antarctic Peninsular; in continental Antarctica excluding the Antarctic Peninsula; and in Svalbard, classified according to main attractions

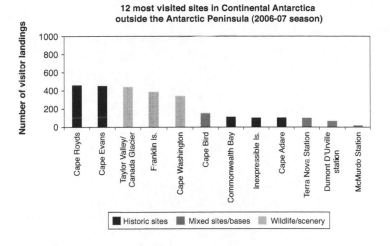

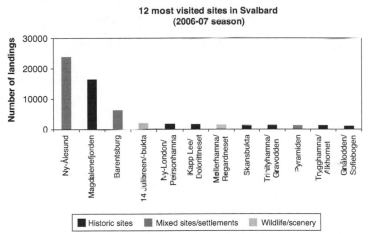

Figure 10.5 (b–c) The 12 most visited sites in the Antarctic Peninsular; in continental Antarctica excluding the Antarctic Peninsula; and in Svalbard, classified according to main attractions

Each landing is choreographed differently depending on site characteristics, site-specific regulations, and logistic or other factors. Generally tourists visit the most significant (or prominent) features of a historic site, where guides may deliver a lecture or interpret the site. At a landing groups may remain together, disperse, or combine both behaviours. Although these aspects are not developed here, it is apparent that the dominant nationality of a tourist group and the ability of the tour guides and tourists to communicate with each other influence visitation and behavioural patterns. Free roaming is allowed in some Antarctic sites, but is generally not allowed in Svalbard because of polar bear risk. For instance, all tourists who land at Ny-Ålesund are allowed to walk around the settlement's 1.5-km 'nature, research and cultural heritage' trail. However, only the passengers

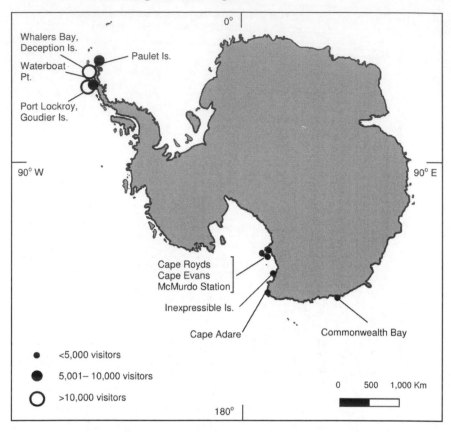

Figure 10.6 Most visited cultural heritage sites in Antarctica, 2006–07 Austral summer

of ships carrying ca. 50–100 passengers are taken to visit the airship mooring mast of the 1926 'Amundsen-Ellesworth-Nobile Transpolar Flight' (Amundsen's mast), which is only 300 m from Ny-Ålesund but requires the presence of polar bear guards (Figure 10.8 a, b).

Site-specific knowledge influences visitation patterns. The more visitors know about a site and its history, the more thorough and extended the visits can be. For instance, a group of tourists visiting Ny-Ålesund looked briefly at Amundsen's mast (which one guide described as 'one of the ten, or perhaps five, most significant sites in the Arctic') and instead visited the small cemetery nearby. This group's guides reported not to know much about the mooring mast's history (personal observation, 29 June 2007). Most tourist groups visiting Whalers Bay in Deception Island spend 2 or more hours visiting whaling and other remains spread around the bay. Eight tourists travelling in a commercial yacht visited only conspicuous parts of the site and returned to their vessel 75 minutes later. The yacht's skipper was ashore supervising the visit but did not lead the tourists through the site (personal observation, 15 February 2002).

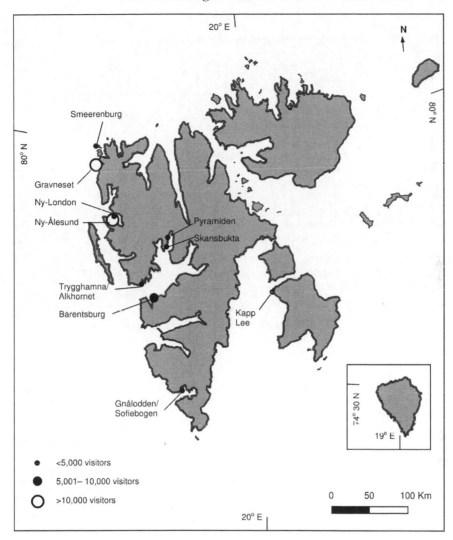

Figure 10.7 Most visited cultural heritage sites in Svalbard, 2006 Boreal summer

Antarctic tourism statistics (IAATO 2008) suggest an increase in activities at or near historic sites that are unrelated to the sites' historic values. These include kayaking, scuba diving, and hiking at landing sites such as Cape Royds in Ross Island and Snow Hill Island, which have significant remains of the 'heroic age' of exploration. At least one marathon took place at Whalers Bay in Deception Island, in which participants run among whaling remains (Racing the Planet [no date]). A comparable Svalbard example is the holding of beach buffets and parties next to the XVI whalers' graveyard at Gravneset in the Magdalenafjord.

Figure 10.8 (a, b) A group of tourists approaches the airship mooring mast at Ny-Ålesund (top) while another group watches it from the distance (bottom).

Tourism impacts and cultural heritage

Tourism behaviour

Observations of tourist visits to historic sites enabled development of a basic behavioural repertoire. Basic visitor behaviour includes moving around the sites (walking, standing); gazing upon historic features and surrounding flora, fauna, and landscapes; gathering and receiving information (reading, listening, asking); and documenting the visit, whether by taking something away (e.g. photographs) or leaving something behind (e.g. a signature in a visitors' book) (Figure 10.9). These behavioural events often take place simultaneously, e.g. people moving objects in order to take photographs (e.g. Hughes 1994). Naturally, these are not the only possible forms of visitor behaviour at a historic site, but they are the broad patterns of usual behaviour. There might be unacceptable (or illegal) forms of basic behaviour, e.g. looting an artefact may be regarded as a way of documenting the visit.

For individual tourists impact-causing behaviour may result from a single action or a concatenation of actions exposing cultural remains to physical contact and possible damage. For instance, behaviour observed at Amundsen's mast included people standing, leaning or sitting on parts of the mast to take photographs, gain a higher viewing point, rest, and tie their bootlaces. The airship mooring mast may not be particularly vulnerable to these forms of behaviour, but other cultural remains might be.

Group behaviour that may generate impacts may include spreading out or crowding over or around sensitive areas. For instance, in Smeerenburg, a 17th century whaling station, visitors must stay away from the remains of the furnaces, which are built of sand cemented with whale blubber (Figure 10.10). However, the whole area is an archaeological site (Figure 10.11). Even if visitors stay away from such fragile features, they tend to stand in the area immediately around the furnaces, which may contain vulnerable surface or subsurface remains.

Figure 10.9 Basic tourist behavioural repertoire at a historic site

Figure 10.10 A lecture around a blubber oven at Smeerenburg, Svalbard

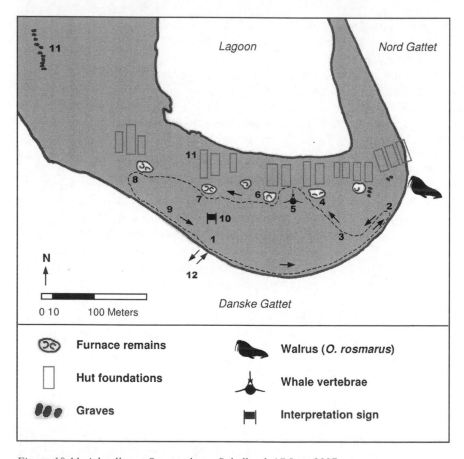

Figure 10.11 A landing at Smeerenburg, Svbalbard, 17 June 2007

Visitation to a historic site does not necessarily imply full immersion in history. Tourists may focus on a site's historic features, but also on the views from the site, and on plants, wildlife, scenery, or people. For instance, tourists leaned on Amundsen's mast to photograph saxifrage flowers inside the mast's structure, which protected the plants from trampling, or stood on the mast footings to have a picture taken (Figures 10–12 a, b). Some tourists looked away as lectures on the history of the mast were delivered (Roura 2009). The highlights of a visit to Smeerenburg were the natural events unfolding during the visit, rather than the site's historic features (Figure 10.11). The visitors' focus on something other than historic features when visiting a historic site is not inherently problematic, but it may lead to inadvertent damage to those features.

Figure 10.12 Tourist behaviour at Amundsen's Mast, Ny-Ålesund: leaning on the mooring mast (left); standing on the mast's footing (note broken edge)

Tour guides are primarily responsible for enforcing regulations and supervising tourists. During observations some guides delivered enthusiastic lectures on historic events, others lectured mechanically, and others simply answered questions when asked. Some guides informed tourists about the rules that applied to a site before a visit, and others let the tourists know as some behaviour seen as reproachable was happening or immediately after. Some guides reminded tourists not to touch or stand on cultural remains, keep a certain distance, or not to walk in some areas, but other guides did not seem to issue any instructions while on site. Most guides took photographs during landings, and for a small minority this constituted a distraction from guiding. In turn, most tourists broadly followed the instructions given to them, but some tourists did not, whether inadvertently or otherwise.

Tourism behaviour traces and impacts

Based on Schiffer (1987), polar tourism can be regarded as a cultural process of historic site (trans)formation (Roura 2009). From a management perspective, an activity-output-exposure-impact framework, usually applied to the natural environment (COMNAP 2005), is useful to differentiate conceptually the activity itself from its consequences. Each activity at a historic site has specific outputs to which cultural remains may or may not be exposed. Exposure to a particular output may or may not result in an impact. Thus a footfall may leave a footprint on the ground but not in itself cause an impact on historical values. However, a footfall on an artefact may break it. In addition, the cumulative effect of successive footprints may damage the subsurface archaeological archive and contribute to overall site degradation (e.g. Hofman and Jatko 2000; Hacquebord 2004).

Direct visitation impacts may include trampling damage, the dismantling of sites, and the removal of artefacts (Table 10.1). However, it can be difficult to differentiate unambiguously actual traces of tourism behaviour from those caused by other contemporary or historic cultural processes, by nature, or by a combination of processes. In some instances it may only be possible to attribute an impact to visitation by direct observation. Nevertheless, it is possible to overlay observed patterns of visitation with behaviour traces and identify locations within a historic site where activity traces can reasonably be attributed to recurring tourism landings. These can be defined as contemporary 'tourist activity areas' partly overlaying the area where earlier activities took place.

The most obvious evidence of visitation identified in this study was trampling disturbance on the ground and vegetation cover at some frequently visited sites, including path development and erosion on or around prominent features at Whalers Bay in Deception Island and some 'heroic era' remains at Ross Island. In Svalbard trampling disturbance was observed at parts of the 17th century whaling station in Smeerenburg; around Amundsen's mast (Figure 10.13); and on and around some historic remains in the mining settlement at Ny-London (Figure 10.14). Smaller scale behaviour traces included footprints on top of a 17th/18th century mass grave; a broken glass artefact damaged during handling; urine stains

Table 10.1: Examples of known impacts on historic and past activity sites in Antarctica and Svalbard from tourism and other visitors

Impact	Type of remains and location	Reference
Erosion of footpaths	Several popular landing sites in the Antarctic Peninsula, including Penguin Island, Barrientos (Aitcho) Island, and Hannah Point. Sites are visited primarily for their natural attractions but contain artefacts/ecofacts from whaling times.	United Kingdom (2006a)
Erosion of footpaths, trampled vegetation	Material remains from World War II at Signehamna, Svalbard	Geitz 2004
Wear and tear - ground erosion around prominent features	Airship mooring mast at Ny-Ålesund, Svalbard	Roura 2009.
Wear and tear	Whaling graveyard dating from the early 17th to the late 18th century, Gravneset, Magdalenafjord, Svalbard	Viken and Jorgensen 1998; Geitz 2004
Recent graffiti on buildings, oil tanks	Early- to mid-XX century whaling and scientific base remains at Whalers Bay, Deception Island, Antarctica.	Argentina, Chile, Norway, Spain, the United Kingdom and the United States (2006)
Damage to outer patina of historic hay bales	Shackleton's Nimrod Hut, Cape Royds, Ross Island, Antarctica	Hughes and Davis (1995)
Removal of artifacts - Souveniring (by National Program expedition members)	Wilkes Station, Antarctica, an abandoned IGY station protected by Australian domestic law	Hughes and Davis (1995)
Removal of artifacts - Souveniring (ca. 1950s)	'Heroic era' huts in the Ross Sea region, Antarctica.	Harrowfield, D.L. (2005)
Removal of artifacts - 'Almost certain' souveniring (ca. 1960s-1970s)	Sealers' refuges in Byers Peninsula, Livingston Island, Antarctica	Lewis Smith and Simpson (1987)
Unspecified acts of vandalism.	Nordenskjöld Hut, Snow Hill Island, Antarctica	Argentina and Sweden (2007)
Dismantling of site - Bricks removed from historic tramping hut ruins, used to write the word "OPEN" on the ground	Russetuft in Trygghamna, Svalbard	Governor of Svalbard (1999)
Dismantling of site - Logs, boards from historic hut ruins used as firewood; stones from historic site used to hold tents	Laegerneset, Belsund; Beautnest, Barenstsoya, Svalbard	Governor of Svalbard (1999); Per Kyrre Reymert, Cultural Heritage Adviser, Sysselmannen på Svalbard, personal communication 22-Sep-06, Longyearbyen
Dismantling of site - Wood from historic site used to line a thermal spring in volcanic beach	Whalers Bay, Deception Island, Antarctica	http://mikehorn.com/index.php/site/page/dairy_archive_october_2008
Damage to inactive station - Breaking into locked buildings. Doors left open resulted in significant wind and snow damage to buildings	Leningradskaya, a Russian scientific station unoccupied since the early 1990s, Antarctica. While not currently protected as a historic site, the base is a 'time capsule' of Soviet times.	Russian Federation (2008)

at a historic cross; and the occasional presence of lost or discarded items. To the extent that it was possible to differentiate the effects of visitation from those caused by other processes, these could be characterised as minor but fairly widespread over historic sites, as well as more significant but localised effects, e.g. in a single artefact.

Figure 10.13 Effect of trampling at Amundsen's mast

Figure 10.14 Effect of trampling at historic earthworks in Ny-London

Table 10.2: Examples of changes to historic sites in Antarctica and Svalbard resulting from the management of tourism and other visitors

Changes	Location	Source
Building of observation hut and fence around graveyard	Graveneset, Svalbard	Geitz (2004)
Use of a historic hut as a manned "living museum", which includes post office and souvenir shop	British Base A at Port Lockroy, Goudier Island, Antarctica	United Kingdom (2006b)
Additions to historic hut ruins (remains of an upturned boat) include placing a monolith with a plaque and metal structure with an interpretation sign; digging around the hut's foundation so that its outline became more visible; and erecting a fence around remains	Waterboat Point hut, which is adjacent to Chilean station Gabriel González Videla, Danco Coast, Antarctica	Chile (2008).
Stains caused on historic huts by interpretation plaques	(Unspecified) 'Heroic era' huts in the Ross Sea region, Antarctica.	Hughes and Davis 1995
Planned private salvage of a historic aircraft forced authorities to remove it from site. (While not strictly a tourism-related impact, this is a dramatic example of the actions taken to manage private activities in Antarctica)	Mid-XX century scientific base remains at Whalers Bay, Deception Island, Antarctica.	United Kingdom (2004)
Reconstruction, fencing of historic stone hut	Nordenskjöld hut at Hope Bay, Antarctica, which is adjacent to Argentina's Esperanza Base.	Described as "…a recreation of an original Swedish stone hut…" (emphasis added) in United States Department of State (2006: 29).

An additional effect of tourism is the transformation of the original site function (e.g. industry, exploration) and its replacement by a new function (tourism). This transformation may entail not only changes to the site through wear and tear, for example, but also through the installation of infrastructure to manage (or attract) tourism (Table 10.2). In some instances historic site adaptation to tourism uses, which may involve intrusive restoration and the establishment of tourism management structures, may be regarded as an indirect tourism impact on historic values.

Conclusions

The patterns of organised cruise tourism in Svalbard and Antarctica are broadly similar in terms of modus operandi, scale and characteristics of landing sites. Key historic sites are among the most visited sites in both regions. However, more visitors land at fewer historic sites in Antarctica than in Svalbard. Consequently, current tourism pressure on popular Antarctic historic sites (in terms of the number of visitors) is greater than on equivalent sites in Svalbard. Historic sites in both regions may be affected by wear and tear resulting from normal behaviour, or by acts of misbehaviour.

During this study, tourist behaviour that could cause an impact in vulnerable historic sites (but not necessarily did cause one*)* was noted in most visits. Visitation traces were evident at most landing sites that contained historic remains, underscoring the role of tourism as an agent of site transformation. However, 'impact' is a management term that implies a value judgement. Opinions will vary widely as to what traces of visitation constitute an impact, because of varying perceptions on their scale, duration, intensity and overall significance. However, some behaviour traces may detract from the condition or integrity of a historic site or its components, and should be regarded as impacts.

The potential of tourism to cause a significant impact on historic remains depends on spatial and functional patterns of site use and on tourist behaviour. Minimising the exposure of cultural remains to visitors depends on separate mechanisms to manage tourism and manage historic sites themselves. Under current policies tourism is likely to continue to increase in both regions, with an ensuing increase in visitation pressures at key historic sites. Tourism in Svalbard is promoted as a key economic activity, and regulated by Norwegian authorities, which aim to make the archipelago one of the best-managed wilderness areas in the world. In contrast, there is no Antarctic Treaty-wide policy on tourism at present, although XXXII ATCM (2009) approved Resolution K (2009) 'General Principles of Antarctic Tourism', which may be the basis of a future Antarctic tourism policy. So far the preferred approach has been to manage tourism using existing generic legally binding instruments, such as the Protocol, complemented with specific non-binding guidelines. Following the rapid growth of tourism and several accidents involving cruise vessels Antarctic tourism may in the future be subject to additional legally binding regulation. However, Antarctic decision-making on tourism issues has so far been slower than the pace of tourism developments.

The cultural heritage protection regime in Svalbard is inclusive (all cultural remains predating 1946 are automatically legally protected, plus some more recent remains), whereas in Antarctica it is exclusive (with some exceptions, only designated HSMs are protected). In addition, the regime of governance is national for Svalbard and international for the Antarctic region as a whole. Norwegian authorities manage all cultural remains in Svalbard regardless of their origin. This brings greater consistency and integration with regards to the management of both tourism and historic sites. It also brings the advantages of an administrative, monitoring and enforcement structure associated with an acting government authority. However, this approach takes the direct control of non-Norwegian historic sites away from the country where that heritage originated, resulting in potential issues of site access, ownership and management approaches. Instead, individual historic sites in Antarctica are usually managed by the party or parties that originated the sites and promoted their designation as HSMs. Consequently, the degree to which Antarctic historic sites are managed actively, and to which tourism at those sites is restricted or promoted, varies considerably from site to site. Overall, there seems to be greater consistency in the management of historic sites in Svalbard than in Antarctica, even although many key Antarctic historic sites are effectively managed.

Historic sites are sometimes time capsules of past times and lives, but are not in themselves static. Historic site transformation takes place in the context of broad changes across the polar regions, in which tourism is both a cause and a consequence of change. Notwithstanding the legal and practical framework in place to manage both tourism and historic sites in Antarctica and Svalbard, and the diverse circumstances of each region and each site, the potential exists for the cultural remains of these remote regions to be degraded, destroyed or removed from context as a result of tourism – and with them the history they tell.

Acknowledgements

I thank Prof. Dr Louwrens Hacquebord and Dr Maarten Loonen (University of Groningen and Netherlands Arctic Station), Dr Kees Bastmeijer (University of Tilburg), Dr Alan Hemmings (University of Canterbury), and Per Kyrre Reymert (Government of Svalbard) for discussions on issues relevant to this article, without implicating them in my interpretations. Fieldwork in Svalbard was funded by the Groningen Institute of Archaeology, University of Groningen. Opportunistic fieldwork in Antarctica was enabled by the Antarctic and Southern Ocean Coalition and Gateway Antarctica. Finally, I thank Dr Dag Avango, Dr Peter Capelotti, Janet Dalziell and Dr Jessica O'Reilly for helpful criticism of an earlier draft.

References

Argentina, Chile, Norway, Spain, the United Kingdom and the United States (2006) *Deception Island Antarctic Specially Managed Area (ASMA) Management Group.* Information Paper 19, Edinburgh: XXIX ATCM.

Argentina and Sweden (2007) *Directrices para la visita del turismo a Cerro Nevado.* Working Paper 40, New Delhi: XXX ATCM.

Ashworth, G.J. and Graham, B. (2005) *Senses of Place: Senses of Time*, Aldershot: Ashgate.

Bastmeijer, K. and Roura, R. (2004) 'Regulating Antarctic tourism and the precautionary principle', *The American Journal of International Law,* 98: 763–81.

Beck, P.J. (1986) *The International Politics of Antarctica*, London: Croom Helm.

Bernard H.R. (2002) *Research Methods in Anthropology. Qualitative and Quantitative Approaches,* Oxford: Altamira Press.

Chile (2008) *Recuperación del Sitio Histórico N° 56 Base Aérea Antártica "Pdte. Gabriel González Videla"*, Information Paper 12, Kiev: XXXI ATCM.

Council of Managers of National Antarctic Programs (COMNAP) (2005) *ATCM Guidelines for Environmental Impact Assessment in Antarctica,* Hobart: COMNAP. Online. Available HTTP: http://www.comnap.aq/publications/guidelines (accessed 1 September 2008).

Conway, W.M. (1906) *No Man's Land: A History of Spitsbergen from Its Discovery in 1596 to the Beginning of the Scientific Exploration of the Country*, Cambridge: Cambridge University Press.

Det Kongelige Miljøverndepartement (2001) *Svalbardmiljøloven. Lov 15 juni 2001 nr om miljøvern på Svalbard*, Oslo: Det Kongelige Miljøverndepartement.

Geitz, M. (ed.) (2004) *Cruise Tourism on Svalbard – A risky business?* Oslo: WWF International Arctic Programme. Online. Available HTTP: http://assets.panda.org/downloads/wwfcruisetourismonsvalbard2004_v5p3.pdf (accessed 1 September 2008).

Governor of Svalbard (2000) 'Kulturminneplan for Svalbard 2000–2010', *Sysselmannens rapportserie* 2/2000, Longyearbyen: Governor of Svalbard.

— (2006) *Reiselivsstatistikk for Svalbard 2006*, Longyearbyen: Governor of Svalbard.

— (2009): *Proposal for Amendments to Protection Regulations*. Online. Longyearbyn: Governor of Svalbard. Available HTTP: http://www.sysselmannen.no/hoved.aspx?m = 44365&amid = 2487842 (accessed 4 April 2009).

Hacquebord, L. (2004) 'Dutch cultural heritage in the Arctic', S. Barr and P. Chaplin (ed.) *Cultural Heritage in the Arctic and Antarctic Regions, ICOMOS Monuments and Sites* VIII. Oslo: International Polar Heritage Committee.

Harrowfield, D.L. (2005) 'Archaeology on ice. A review of historical archaeology in Antarctica,' *New Zealand Journal of Archaeology*, 26: 5–28.

Headland, R.K. (1989) *Chronological List of Antarctic Expeditions and Related Historical Events*, Cambridge: Cambridge University Press.

Hofman, R. and Jatko, J. (2000) *Assessment of the possible cumulative environmental impacts of commercial ship-based tourism in the Antarctic Peninsula area*, Proceedings of a Workshop held in La Jolla, California, June 2000. Washington DC: National Science Foundation.

Hughes, J. (1994) 'Antarctic historic sites: the tourism implications', *Annals of Tourism Research*, 21: 281–94.

Hughes, J. and Davis, B. (1995) 'The management of tourism at historic sites and monuments', in C.M. Hall and M.E. Johnston (eds) *Polar Tourism: Tourism in the Arctic and Antarctic Regions*, Chichester: John Wiley.

International Association of Antarctica Tour Operators (IAATO) (2008) *Tourism statistics.* Providence, USA: IAATO. Online. Available HTTP: http://www.iaato.org/stats/ (accessed 1 September 2008).

Kipfer, B.A. (2007) *The Archeologist's Fieldwork Companion*, Oxford: Blackwell Publishing.

Kolltveit, B. (2006) 'Deckchair explorers: the origin and development of organised tourist voyages to north and south polar regions', *International Journal of Maritime History* 18: 351–69.

Lewis Smith, R.I. and Simpson, H.W. (1987) 'Early nineteenth century sealers' refuges on Livingston Island, South Shetland Islands,' *British Antarctic Survey Bulletin*, 74: 49–72.

Ligtendag, W. (2002) 'Dirck Gerritsz Pomp en Antarctica', in K.W.J.M.Bossaers and P. Broon (eds) *Dirck Gerritsz Pomp alias Dirck China*, Enhuizen: Vereniging Oud Enkhuizen.

Lowenthal, D. (2005) 'Natural and cultural heritage', *International Journal of Heritage Studies,* 11: 81–92,

Marstrander, L. (1999) 'Svalbard cultural heritage management', in U. Wråkberg (ed.) *The Centennial of S.A. Andrée's North Pole Expedition,* Stockholm: Royal Swedish Academy of Sciences, Centre for History of Science.

Martin, P. and Bateson, P. (1993) *Measuring Behaviour. An Introductory Guide, 2nd ed.* Cambridge: Cambridge University Press.

Mathisen, T. (1954) *Svalbard in International Politics 1871–1925: The solution of a unique international problem.* Norsk Polarinstitutt Skrifter 101. Oslo: Brøggers Forslag

New Zealand and Australia (2006) *Regulation of Land-Based Infrastructure to Support Tourism in Antarctica.* Working Paper 045 rev.1, Edinburgh: XXIX ATCM.

Norway (2004) *Polar Tourism: Experience gained and lessons learned from Svalbard,* ATME Paper 24 presented at the Antarctic Treaty Meeting of Experts in Antarctic tourism, Tromsø-Trondheim, March 2004.

Pearce, P.L. (2005) *Tourist Behaviour: Themes and Conceptual Schemes,* Clevedon: Channel View.

Racing the Planet (no date) The Last Desert Antarctica. Online. Available HTTP: http://www.4deserts.com/thelastdesert/# (accessed September 2008).

Rathje, W. (2001) 'Integrated archaeology. A garbage paradigm', in V. Buchli and G. Lucas (eds) *Archaeologies of the Contemporary Past,* London: Routledge.

Roura, R. (2008) 'Antarctic scientific bases: Cultural heritage and environmental perspectives 1983–2008', in S. Barr and P. Chaplin (eds) *Historical Polar Bases: Preservation and Management,* ICOMOS Monuments and Sites Series No. XVII, Oslo: International Polar Heritage Committee.

— (2009) 'The polar cultural heritage as a tourism attraction: a case study of the airship mooring mast at Ny-Ålesund, Svalbard,' *Téoros,* 28(1): 29–38.

Russian Federation (2008) *Proposals for Regulating the Adventure Tourism and Non-Governmental Activity in The Antarctic,* Working Paper 50, Kiev: XXXI ATCM

Schiffer, M.B. (1987) *Formation Processes of the Archaeological Record.* Salt Lake City, University of Utah Press.

Statistics Norway (2005) Svalbard Statistics 2005, Cultural heritage in Svalbard, by type and function. Online. Available HTTP: http://www.ssb.no/english/subjects/00/00/20/nos_svalbard_en/nos_d330_en/tab/017.html (accessed 10 September 2009).

Triggs, G.D. (ed.) (1987) *The Antarctic Legal Regime: Law, Environment and Resources.* Cambridge: Cambridge University Press.

Ulfstein, G. (1995) *The Svalbard Treaty. From Terra Nullius to Norwegian Sovereignty,* Oslo: Scandinavian University Press.

United Kingdom (2004) *Area Protection and Management. Historic Site No. 71 – Whalers Bay, Deception Island. Salvage of the de Havilland Single Otter from Whalers Bay, Deception Island by the British Antarctic Survey.* Working Paper 45. Cape Town: XXVII ATCM.

— (2006a) *Report of the CEP Intersessional Contact Group on Site Guidelines for Visitors to Antarctica,* Working Paper 1, Edinburgh: XXIX ATCM

— (2006b) *Site Guidelines for Goudier Island, Port Lockroy,* Working Paper 40, Edinburgh: XXIX ATCM.

United States Department of State (2006) *Report of Inspections under Article VII of the Antarctic Treaty and Article 1 of the Protocol on Environmental Protection, November 12-December 1, 2006.* Washington: United States Department of State.

Veal, A.J. (2006) *Research Methods for Leisure and Tourism,* 3rd ed. Harlow: Pearson Education Limited.

Viken, A. and Jørgensen, F. (1998) 'Tourism on Svalbard', *Polar Record,* 34(189), 123–28.

Vistad, I.O., Eide, N.E., Hagen, D., Erikstad, L. and Landa, A. (2008) 'Miljøeffecter av ferdsel og turisme i Arktis. En litteratur-og forstudie med vekt på Svalbard', *NINA Report* 316. Lillehammer/Trondheim: Norsk institutt for naturforskning.

11 Narratives of History, Environment and Global Change

Expeditioner-tourists in Antarctica

Mark Nuttall

Introduction

Tourist numbers in Antarctica have risen dramatically over the last decade, from 9,604 in 1997–98 to an estimated 34,000 in the 2008–09 Austral summer tourist season (see chapter 1). The majority of these visitors do not make shore landings and their experience of Antarctica is usually only a glimpse of the continent or a few sub-Antarctic islands as part of a South American/South Atlantic cruise (the total figure for tourist visits also includes people who fly over Antarctica on flight-seeing tours). With the exception of the few ships sailing to the Ross Sea area, most tourists who do make landings from marine vessels are concentrated at specific accessible and historic sites, including visits to Antarctic research stations, in ice-free coastal areas of the Antarctic Peninsula region. Many of them make the trip to these far southerly latitudes aboard 'expedition-style' cruise ships, sailing from Punta Arenas in Chile or from Ushuaia in Argentina, taking 2 or 3 days to reach the Antarctic Peninsula across the Drake Passage, compared with a 10-day voyage across the Southern Ocean from New Zealand or Australia to reach the Ross Sea region. Some of these are small to medium-size chartered vessels, often ice-strengthened Russian research craft, and carry anywhere from 30 to 200 passengers, while others are much larger cruise ships with several hundred people on board.

Pioneered by Lars-Erik Lindblad's ecotourism approach in the 1960s, one characteristic of such trips to Antarctica has been the cultivation of an 'expedition' atmosphere, in which tourists are regarded and treated as expeditioners, people who are not merely sightseers but intrepid travellers venturing into pristine icy waters and the unexplored continent beyond. They are accompanied by a team of expedition leaders, guides, and lecturing staff, whose jobs are to brief passengers about the wildlife they see, and to provide informative lectures to help them understand the geology, ecology, history of exploration, contemporary geopolitics, and the global environmental issues impacting the continent. This lends expedition-style cruises to Antarctica some further legitimacy and authority, with their claims of voyaging to the ends of the earth with expert knowledge not only to explore, but to experience first hand the impacts of global processes. It is on one of these vessels, MS *Explorer*, that I worked as a lecturer and field guide during the 2006–07 cruise ship season. My role aboard *Explorer* was that of historian, but this chapter is an attempt at anthropological reflection on my experiences. I came away from Antarctica interested in the narratives about, and presentations and interpretations of, Antarctic landscapes of both the travel company and the expedition team on board the ship, as they conveyed them to the tourists. I also considered the anticipations, expectations, perspectives and narratives of the tourists themselves.

The guides are 'acknowledged authorities', 'renowned experts', 'seasoned polar travellers', and, if one is lucky, 'Antarctic veterans' themselves who have overwintered while being employed by a national Antarctic scientific programme. These categories of Antarctic experts are just one of several social types that serve to structure social relations and hierarchies on board the vessel, making these ships, like all cruise ships, examples of globalization at sea (Wood 2006). However, while it is commonly remarked that the destination for most cruise ship passengers is the cruise ship itself, and the contemporary large cruise ship is 'a uniquely deterritorialised destination in a number of senses' (Wood 2006: 4), a voyage to Antarctica on an 'expedition' promises more than an encounter with the ship's bar and sauna. The ship is not distanced from the sea; by being on an expedition tourists are made to feel that they are on a scientific study tour and will return home having discovered something about the impact of human activity on this fragile planet. In their encounter with Antarctica, they may also learn something about themselves. Landings are made at selected sites, to which passengers are ferried from the ship in inflatable craft. Once there, they are accompanied by knowledgeable guides, and Antarctica ceases to be a travel destination but presents itself – or rather is presented – as a place of narrative and personal encounter with wildlife and the traces of exploration. Antarctica, as tourists come to see it, is a place of adventure and a wilderness, yet one under global threat.

Antarctica and adventure tourism

In his introduction to the edited volume *Tarzan was an Eco-tourist*, Robert Gordon (2006: 1) says that 'we live in a post-explorer world where it is widely considered that the feats of the great adventurers are remnants of history and that the Earth's mysteries, mysterious places and peoples have long "been discovered". Yet adventure enjoys ubiquitous status in public culture and late capitalism.' This is clearly the case when one considers the growth and interest in adventure tourism, with wild places representing locations that offer opportunities for escape, excitement, and the pursuit of risk as both leisure and pleasure (Rojek and Urry 1997; Beedie and Hudson 2003). Antarctica may have been discovered, and most of its remote valleys and mountain ranges mapped, but as the website for the Norwegian company Hurtigruten promises in advertising its cruises to Antarctica, 'To take a voyage past Cape Horn, across the Drake Passage to the peninsula is to join what is still an exclusive group of intrepid travelers inspired by the legacy of Antarctic exploration.' Antarctica is described as a land of superlatives, a place where 'the ghosts of Scott, Amundsen and Apsley Cherry-Garrard remain.' Many companies play on the increased awareness of global environmental issues supposedly expressed by passengers as one of the main reasons for travelling to Antarctica, but they also emphasise the continent as a place of extreme hardship and difficulty for those who have ventured there to explore and discover.

In his 1911 essay 'The Adventurer', George Simmel wrote that adventures are experiences or episodes that occur outside the humdrum of everyday life. Adventurers, argued Simmel, are a pronounced social type who have removed themselves from ordinary temporality and causality. Adventure is a reaction to everyday life and experience which is entangled in conflicting webs of causal entailment, adventures have definite beginnings and ends and their protagonists seem to act according to a unique mixture of fate and chance. One of the defining features of adventure is, then, this 'extraterritoriality with respect to the continuity of life', the separation between normal life and adventure (Simmel 1965 [1911]: 246).

Antarctica figures prominently in the emergence of adventure tourism but, as Beedie and Hudson (2003: 627) argue, 'the most significant factor in the development of adventure tourism is the extent to which one really engages in adventure.' Adventure involves danger and risk and is associated with uncertainty of outcome (Swarbrooke *et al.* 2003). Even in the comfort of a cruise ship, a trip to Antarctica is billed as something that still feels like an expedition, a trip that remains a rare privilege, but 'there exists something of a paradox whereby the more detailed, planned, and logistically smooth the itinerary becomes the more removed the experience is from the notion of adventure' (Beedie and Hudson 2003: 627). But this is exactly how adventure tourism is marketed, so that tourists know where they are going and when they will return. Trips on *Explorer* were no exception, with the day's itinerary and places to be visited (including the approximate time of arrival and time to be spent ashore pinned on the ship's notice board every morning). Passengers would gather around the notice board before breakfast to discuss the day's route; following breakfast there would be a briefing in the ship's lounge about the places to be visited. Even if the first landing of the day was to be cold, wet, and uncomfortable, and possibly involve a little strenuous walking to reach the penguin colonies, everyone would be reassured that they would be back on board ship in time for lunch.

This aspect of marketing, but also of the careful cultivation of each trip to Antarctica as an adventure, was brought home to me when, on my first trip as a staff member, I awoke around 6 am during the first morning of our journey from Ushuaia. We were somewhere south of Cape Horn in the Drake Passage. Rolling in swells of 7 m it was almost impossible to get out of my bunk, and I lay there in a state of rising nausea wondering how I could best make it to the lecture theatre that morning to give my first lecture, which was to be about Antarctica and the geographical imagination. As the ship rolled in the grey seas, then suddenly decided to pitch instead, the expedition leader came on the cabin intercom and announced to all passengers our position, our course, and that the first morning's programme of lectures and briefing sessions would be delayed until the weather was calmer. 'Some of you may find this a little uncomfortable,' he remarked, 'but remember, we are on an expedition and if it was easy to get to Antarctica then everyone would be going there.'

With this, he simultaneously underscored the idea that we were indeed on an expedition, that this was a difficult place to get to, and impressed upon everyone that they were somehow different from other cruise ship passengers. Adventurers are, as Simmel would say, people who have removed themselves from ordinary temporality and causality, and the crossing of the notoriously rough Drake Passage is itself emblematic of the difficult and uncomfortable nature of reaching Antarctica. Adventure, according to Swarbrooke *et al.* (2003: 14), is, in this sense, a state of mind, in which people are 'voluntarily putting themselves in a position where they believe they are taking a step into the unknown, where they will face challenges, and where they will discover or gain something valuable from the experience.' Finally, when the seas had calmed sufficiently for us to give our first talks, I began my series of lectures as the ship's historian with an account of Antarctica's representation as *Terra Australis Incognita* and ranged far and wide from the *antarktos* imaginings of the ancient Greeks to the voyages of Drake and Cook. When I quoted from Drake's journals how he described sailing into the stormy waters that now bear his name (it was 'an intolerable tempest', he remarked) there were murmurs of recognition from the audience. This was something that people could relate to. And in a sense, I was grateful that the rough seas had provided a backdrop to my talks about a place that I tried to illustrate had lain beyond the world's geographical imagination for centuries. Crossing Drake Passage, and particularly crossing the Antarctic Convergence, like crossing any imaginary line on a map (such as the Arctic and Antarctic circles), was for many on board a rite of passage, marking the separation between normal life and adventure, Simmel's 'extraterritoriality with respect to the continuity of life.' Of course, having crossed Drake Passage, there was only one way back and throughout each voyage people reminded themselves and one another that they had to experience that intolerable tempest once more. There was a sense of anxious anticipation and anticipatory nausea.

The experience of disoriented and the feeling of difference

This speaks to another aspect of adventure that goes beyond feelings of excitement, risk and danger: that of the experience of disorientation. In this sense, being tossed around on a rough sea and being terribly seasick is a bodily feeling of losing one's place. One can be totally lost and disorientated in a white-out on the polar icecap, or lost in fog or a mountain landscape, but the feeling that comes from disorientation when confined to your bunk in your cabin on a ship and from seasickness marks a failed orientation of one's self. Seasickness is a violent, gut-wrenching experience, a feeling of losing one's place. In his description of seasickness as disorientation, Jacques Rolland uses the metaphor of sinking:

> We have seasickness because we are at sea, that is, off the coast, of which we have lost sight. That is, again, because the earth has gone, the same earth into

which, ordinarily we sink our feet in order for this position or stance to exist. Seasickness arrives once the loss of the earth is given.

(Rolland 2003: 17).

The crossing of Drake Passage in a vessel affectionately known as 'the little red ship' was something to be endured, rather than enjoyed by many. As Levinas wrote in *On Escape*, 'To be nauseous is to want to be elsewhere, but have no place to go.' But once back in port at the end of each trip, *Explorer* would tie up at the harbour alongside other cruise ships that would dwarf it in size. Passengers would comment on how little the passengers on these larger vessels would feel the swell and the force of the sea in Drake Passage: "I imagine they would just glide over it, as if it was a mill pond, no matter how rough", said one man, while another remarked, 'I bet they had a good sleep getting to Antarctica. It's just a huge floating hotel!'

There were certain feelings of pride in being real travellers who had experienced Drake's 'intolerable tempest.' To experience travel that is uncomfortable, risky and potentially dangerous is to give people the legitimate right to place themselves appropriately within the hierarchy of travellers. Many tourists seem curiously embarrassed at each other's presence when they encounter one another, but as many of us are at some point or other tourists we take comfort in ascribing to ourselves identities as different kinds of tourists, and if others ascribe that status to us to, the better it is; many of us may prefer to be recognised as being a traveller, but to be an adventurer sounds even better.

In making distinctions between luxury cruise ships and the small expedition cruise ship, both the tour company and the passengers themselves constructed a pair of mutually defining extremes, ordinary cruise tourists and expeditioner-tourists, two categories of traveller that perhaps correspond with what literary scholar Syed Islam distinguishes as sedentary travellers and nomadic travellers in his book *The Ethics of Travel* (1996). Sedentary travellers are not necessarily inactive, but with their focus on reaching a predetermined destination they do not notice the ground that is covered. As Islam says, regardless of how fast they travel and how many miles they cover, they remain on a rigid line which keeps them grounded in the enclosure of their home. They simply move from locale to locale rather than noticing or feeling a movement across a textured terrain. Nomadic travellers, on the other hand, follow a 'supple' rather than a 'rigid' line, and experience movement as a continuous and shifting process, a vivid and bumpy ride across boundaries and cultures. Islam argues that nomadic travellers have an openness to encounters with difference and undergo a process of becoming.

It is too simplistic to generalise about all tourists to Antarctica in this way, as both larger cruise ships and smaller vessels like *Explorer* would contain a diversity of different passengers who would fit easily into each notional category. But it is important to point out that these are perceived differences. They are referred to by the tourists on board and are called upon as people position themselves as Antarctic travellers. There are two examples of how this happened on the trips I experienced.

Firstly, the tour company marked itself off as different from other companies that offer similar cruises. Its marketing and advertising are very much in keeping with a general observation that the destination for most cruise ship passengers is the cruise ship itself, not the ports they call at. The tour company and expedition staff both aim to continue and honour a tradition of expedition travel to remote and relatively inaccessible regions, acting as a conduit between their passengers and the natural world. Moreover, by being on an 'expedition', passengers are made to feel less like tourists and more like adventurers traveling in the spirit of early explorers and latter-day scientists and naturalists. Emphasis is placed on environmental ethics, respect for landscape, environment and wildlife, an awareness of the exploration and history of the continent, and a desire to empower passengers to make similar contributions at their local level once they return home, as well as acting as ambassadors and stewards for Antarctica. In this way, the company continues to carve out a market niche to attract a specific clientele in a growing industry marketing a place that is visited by ever-increasing numbers of people.

Secondly, the Antarctic expeditioner-tourists on board (at least as I encountered them) were themselves influenced by popular and literary accounts of Antarctica and the polar regions more generally. Many had prepared for the trip by reading widely on Antarctic exploration and adventure. Most I spoke to thought of themselves as travelling to what they imagined and understood as a place beyond the usual tourist destinations, a place at the end of the earth. Antarctica is marketed as 'the last continent', where people are promised unforgettable encounters with wildlife and environment, with penguins, whales, seals, and cathedral-sized icebergs. As nomadic travellers, those on board relished the nameless spaces in between ports of call, they anticipated delays and detours, and the prospect of unforeseen encounters. Although I imagine most would have preferred not to have been in a situation where the order was given to abandon ship (as happened to *Explorer* in November 2007), to be challenged and to negotiate those challenges are essential to the experience.

It is one of the curious aspects of travelling that, perhaps because places one visits have been visited by someone you talk to, or someone they know, that the place itself becomes of less interest. So in this way, as most cruise ships must cross Drake Passage to reach the Antarctic Peninsula, the crossing is something that everyone visiting Antarctica seems to have experienced. However, if it is a vivid and bumpy ride, causing people to collapse into their bunks with bouts of extreme seasickness, then that is a way of marking off one experience of Drake Passage as worse than another. In fact, the bumpier the ride and the more uncomfortable the experience, the better.

Narratives of history and global change

Central to the narratives of both the expedition team and the passengers was an emphasis on both the historical and modern difficulty of travelling to and in Antarctica, reinforced on ship and during shore landings by the retelling of stories, tales and histories of the heroic age of exploration, which lend themselves variously to cultural myth-making about starvation, privation, the race to the South Pole, and death on the ice. In this way, adventure is a form of narrative as well as an experience removed from ordinary temporality, into which listeners can always seek to transpose themselves in imaginative ways. As the ship's historian, I presented lectures on Antarctic discovery and exploration, but also pointed out places of significance in the landscape as we cruised. Onshore, when we visited historic sites, such as old whaling stations and expedition huts, I talked about the expeditions and the people who were there. Some of the favourite kinds of stories people liked to listen to were about ships crushed in the ice and the ordeal to return home (such as Shackleton's famous *Endurance* expedition of 1914–16), of unanticipated overwintering (such as the *Belgica* expedition led by Adrien de Gerlache at the end of the 1890s), or of solitude and survival on the vast expanses of the continent (such as the experiences of Douglas Mawson and Richard Byrd). Whether the anthropologist Vilhjalmur Stefansson was correct in writing that 'adventure is a sign of incompetence,' tourists nonetheless seem to want to hear of hardship, masochism, discomfort, failure and death on the ice.

To travel in Antarctica, no matter how fleetingly, to lecture about its human history, and to tell stories about it, is to evoke and attribute symbolic meaning to the spirit of great Antarctic explorers such as Scott, Shackleton, Nordenskjöld and Amundsen. It is a conventional script, with recognisable names, and people came expecting to hear me read from it. The occasional improvisation from this script was tolerated, but not necessarily what people were expecting. During one lecture, I spoke at length on John Cleves Symmes Jr and his theory of concentric spheres and polar voids. I talked about how, in the early 19th century, Symmes declared that the Earth was hollow and open at both poles, and about how this had influenced Edgar Allan Poe's novel *The Narrative of Arthur Gordon Pym of Nantucket*, and Jules Verne's *Journey to the Centre of the Earth*. However, following my lecture, several people approached me throughout the day and asked when I was going to talk about Scott, Amundsen and the race to the South Pole. 'All this about the Greeks and holes in the earth is very interesting,' one woman remarked to me, 'but I'm looking forward to hearing your argument for why Scott didn't make it back from the South Pole.' Added to this conventional script is talk about Antarctica within the global discourse of an environment at risk, again with conventional narratives reinforcing the scientific consensus about climate change. Tourists may be made to feel that their activities and very presence in Antarctica involve an element of risk, but they are made to feel that they are travelling in an environment that is itself at risk. The experience, wonder and realisation of being in a place that is under threat of disappearing, as the ice sheet melts and yet another ice shelf collapses, added a sense of nervous edginess to things. As one woman from the United Kingdom told me, 'We came here just in time. If we'd left it any longer there may be no ice to see.'

Tourists are taught to read Antarctica as a multilayered landscape, infused with the histories of ecological impact (by sealers and whalers), of imperial hopes and ambitions, as a harsh environment to be endured and tested by, and as a continent for science and environmental protection. Furthermore, the theme of environmental change, and the representation of Antarctica as a fragile environment and region at risk from an ever-widening ozone hole and climate change, are emphasised to deepen the experience and heighten the encounter between tourist and landscape. This encounter is not only meaningful because of the meanings of these stories, narrative and themes, but also because of the sheer act of reciting them and by being in a place where tourists can imagine themselves seeing the ice disappearing, and of feeling that they are sailing through a place undergoing a cataclysmic meltdown as a result of global change.

Adventures as a tourist have beginnings and ends. The experience of adventure is temporary, necessitating the construction of its precarious nature. The narratives of history, of the discoverers, explorers and adventurers, have a certain immediacy that resonates with tourists to Antarctica, but one fundamental difference is that the tourists have an idea when their own particular journey will come to an end. The pursuit of adventure is an enduring social form, but a momentary experience in terms of the realisation of self for Antarctic tourists. But what does it mean to feel that you, as a tourist, are having an adventure? The tourists I spoke to on board the ship believed they were getting away from it all and were off on adventures of a lifetime. They were getting away to a far-flung destination, a place that has long existed on the edge of experience and imagination. Yet Antarctica, like the Arctic, has moved to the centre of discourses of global environmental change, and onboard lectures often frame their subject matter with sharp-edged attention to the vulnerability of the polar regions.

Grasping at experience

In her essay on adventure in the work of Virginia Woolf, Maria DiBattista (2009: 141) writes,

> An adventure encompasses more than an experience marked by risk and latent either with death or transfiguration. Adventure is not experienced or even recognizable *as* an adventure unless and until the mind acknowledges the possibility of extinction or exaltation that the adventure fortuitously but fatefully presents. There is no adventure but thinking makes it so.

In adventure tourism, however, and perhaps more so in Antarctica, this sense of adventure is tempered somewhat. Chance, risk-taking and adventure in Antarctic tourism are organised affairs. The ship is a specially, yet tightly organised social space and adventure, or the idea of it, is controlled. Markwell (2001), drawing on his work in Borneo, argues that tourist–nature interactions are constructed and mediated by the tourist industry. Antarctic tourism seems exemplary of this, and many tourists told me that when they made actual landings they felt a certain irony in travelling to experience such a remote place, yet were there with one hundred other people at the same time, walking a clearly defined and managed path. Of his experience of being directed by the guides (myself included) around penguin nesting sites, one English tourist told me he felt 'like he was being herded' and described us as 'sheepdogs waiting to nip at the heels of any poor soul who happened to wander away from the flock.' Another, overhearing this, agreed:

> The guides follow you, watch you, tell you to stand at a safe distance from the penguins and elephant seals. They tell you to keep to a specific line, they monitor you and communicate with one another by radio. This is a surveillance operation! And it's rushed. They usher you back in the Zodiacs and check your number tags once you are back on the ship.

Some tried to get around this and break away from the group once they were ashore, ignoring the rules and wandering off by themselves. It was a form of escape, something that Levinas (2003) recognised as 'the need to get out of one's self.' I was interested in the ways they told me how they tried to immerse themselves in the moment, to seek to experience the landscape through their feet and through the senses, to take a moment to walk around, and to sit, or feeling the need to be radical in order to turn mere experience into adventure, as Simmel argued, or to escape the rigid nature of the cruise that prevents 'the possibility of pure communion with the place' (Leane 2005: 7). In the *Phenomenology of Perception* Merleau-Ponty (2002) discusses the distinction between 'straight' and 'oblique', relating it to the distinction between 'distance' and 'proximity'. These categories are only meaningful in relation to phenomenal or orientated space, and his discussion is about the things we can grasp, the things we attempt to hold on to. For some tourists I spoke to at length, their attempts to grasp at understanding and experiencing Antarctica were articulated with words that conveyed 'distance' and a realisation that they may never have the opportunity again. 'It's a far place'; 'You really feel you're at the ends of the earth'; 'This is a once in a lifetime experience for me…it's too far to come, what a journey!'

The tourist experience as an embodied one may suggest a more direct encounter, but as Markwell (2001) notes the body too can act as a site of mediation within the context of tourism. As I spoke with people, this intensely personal relationship with nature that some were seeking became, in the end, an experience of frustration. Antarctica is perceived as being remote and beyond the horizon, yet it is reachable. The irony for the tourist, though, is that at the same time as one is there, gazing at the landscape, walking on it, one has to leave and move on, go back to the ship and its tightly controlled social space. For many tourists, Antarctica becomes an oblique place and is experienced as a remote, essentially unknowable place that slips away into an unreachable distance.

Antarctic tourism and the explorer narrative

Whereas exploration and science have been regarded as heroic endeavours and quests for discovery, tourism is seen as a resource activity. In this way it is constructed and represented as intrusive; indeed, textbooks on Antarctica tend to deal with tourism within sections and chapters on environmental impacts and human impacts on the environment. Research on tourism and tourists in Antarctica tends, on the whole, to focus on impacts to the environment, the disturbance of penguin colonies and other wildlife breeding sites, how to manage them and how to manage tourism as an industry, and how to lessen the impact of tourists on the environment. And so, quantitative surveys and studies concern themselves with determining the numbers of tourists to Antarctica, where they come from, what they do once they are there, and the reasons for travelling. Much of this literature inevitably focuses on the images tourists have of the continent, and the feelings they have once they are there. Much of this research sees the growth of tourism as 'alarming' and the tourist as 'intrusive'.

Such concerns over the environmental impacts of tourism have been raised since the dramatic rescue of 154 passengers and crew from the *Explorer,* which took in water and began to list after hitting a large chunk of ice in November 2007. The ship eventually sank. The tourism boom, say critics, threatens the Antarctic environment and puts tourists' lives at risk. The sinking of *Explorer* is grist to the mill for those who fear mass tourism brings the danger of catastrophic accidents and environmental damage. For example, the response of the Antarctic and Southern Ocean Coalition (ASOC) was that the sinking of the *Explorer* could be considered a best-case scenario and pointed to the potential threat from tour operators running larger cruise ships with greater numbers of people. All of this concern continues to focus attention on appropriate management regimes.

Ironically, the sinking of *Explorer* may reinforce the feeling of the intrepid nature of Antarctic travel. Those who highlight the risks and the dangers are speaking precisely about some of the very things that attract tourists to Antarctica in the first place, and which gives them a heightened sense of being intrepid, adding to their own feelings of venturing to a place that is still risky to go to. From this perspective, Antarctic tourism may be growing ('booming even'), but it is still not like going to Tenerife or Disneyland. Tourist companies are business operations; will they also take advantage of exploiting this desire to come to Antarctica before it is too late? The adventure is one of the imagination, yet grounded in real and perceived risk. Again, one of the ironies of the *Explorer* incident is that it was on the last section of a cruise called the 'Spirit of Shackleton'. One can only wonder whether the drama of this *Explorer* trip will enter the annals of Antarctic adventure folklore; after all, the vessel was the first to really pioneer this kind of travel to the continent, and the first to sink there. It now has its own narrative to contribute to the grand narrative of Antarctica.

References

Beedie, P. and Hudson, S. (2003) 'Emergence of mountain-based adventure tourism', *Annals of Tourism Research*, 30: 625–43.

DiBattista, M. (2009) *Imagining Virginia Woolf: An Experiment in Critical Biography*, Princeton: Princeton University Press.

Gordon, R. (2006) 'Introduction,' in L.A. Vivanco and R. Gordon (eds) *Tarzan was an Eco-Tourist... and other Tales in the Anthropology of Adventure*, Oxford: Berghahn.

Islam, S.M. (1996) *The Ethics of Travel: From Marco Polo to Kafka*. Manchester: Manchester University Press.

Leane, E. (2005) 'Antarctic travel writing and the problematics of the pristine: two Australian novelists' narratives of tourist voyages to Antarctica', in L. Lester and C. Ellis (eds) *Imaging Nature: Media, Environment and Tourism*. Proceedings of Conference held on 27–29 June 2004 at Cradle Mountain, Tasmania, Australia.

Levinas, E. (2003) *On Escape*, Palo Alto: Stanford University Press.

Markwell, K. (2001) '"Borneo, Nature's Paradise": constructions and representations of nature within nature-based tourism', in P. Teo, T. C. Chang and K. C. Ho (eds) *Interconnected Worlds: Tourism in Southeast Asia*, New York: Pergamon.

Merleau-Ponty, M. (2002) *The Phenomenology of Perception*, London: Routledge

Rojek, C. and Urry, J. (1997) *Touring Cultures*, London: Routledge

Rolland, J. (2003) 'Introduction' in E. Levinas *On Escape*, Palo Alto: Stanford University Press.

Simmel. G. (1965) 'The adventurer', in K. Wolff (ed.) *Georg Simmel: Essays on Sociology, Philosophy and Aesthetics*. New York: The Free Press.

Swarbrooke, J., Beard, C., Leckie, S. and Pomfret, G. (2003) *Adventure Tourism: the New Frontier*, Oxford: Butterworth-Heineman.

Wood, R.E. (2006) 'Neoliberal globalization: the cruise ship industry as a paradigmatic case', paper presented at the Annual Meeting of the American Sociological Association, Montreal Convention Center, Montreal, August 2006.

12 'Awesome size...magnitude of the place...the incredible beauty...'

Visitors' on-site experiences in the Ross Sea region of Antarctica

Patrick T. Maher

Introduction

Tourism in remote locations is in many instances seen as a valuable commodity. Both as an economic benefit, and also because of the expectation that as a result of their on-site experience visitors may return as advocates for that remote setting (see Maher 2007a; Maher and Stewart 2007). Tour operator Rodney Russ (as quoted by Janes 2003: D3) notes important learning occurs with this experience on-site; tour operators 'show [Antarctica] to people who go on to be advocates for protecting Antarctica'. Since the early 1990s Antarctic tourism has grown significantly and it is now projected that over 35,000 visitors will land in each of the next two seasons (IAATO 2008; chapter 1). With such numbers, there is growing concern for the type of on-site experience to be had, particularly in heavy traffic areas of the Antarctic Peninsula.

This chapter shares information from the author's doctoral work (Maher 2007b), examining the notion of the on-site experience for visitors in the Ross Sea region (RSR) as one portion of a wider study of the overall spectrum of experience. The RSR is a region of the Antarctic that sees fewer visitors than the Peninsula (see IAATO 2008; Maher 2007 b, c), serving as an excellent contained population of visitors to study, with far fewer access points and operations.

Methods and context

Many researchers have suggested that the Antarctic visitor experience needs to be better examined (e.g., see Davis 1995; Mason and Legg 1999; Tracey 2001; Hemmings & Roura 2003). Previous studies of the leisure and tourism experience have argued that the experience should not be considered as one-dimensional, but is in fact a multiphase entity, specifically, that experience 'on-site' interacts with many pre-visit (anticipation) and post-visit (recollection) factors.

Several authors have presented a five-phase model (Arnould and Price 1993; Clawson and Knetsch 1966; Fridgen 1984). Bauer (2001) presents a three-phase model in an Antarctic context, incorporating travel to and from the site with the on-site phase. Three phases would also be congruent with the experience work of Beedie and Hudson (2003). A three-part methodology was thus used by the author to examine the full cycle of experience: (1) anticipation of the visit (see Maher *et al*. 2006), (2) on-site during the visit (this chapter), and (3) upon return home after the visit (see Maher 2007c, 2009).

Those included in the research were commercial tourists, as well as media representatives, artists and writers, distinguished government and industry leaders, and those visiting through educational programmes. Four organisations (two ship-based tour operators, one national Antarctic programme, and one tertiary education provider) assisted with their visitors' voluntarily participation and with a number of data-gathering methods during the 2002–03 season. In the 2003–04 season supplemental data were also collected, which included a famil-iarisation trip to New Zealand's Scott Base and subsequent participant observation, and informal interviews held there.

Methods used to collect the data for this chapter included personal narratives or journals while on the trip (regardless of trip length: 4–28 days). As no previous Antarctic studies have provided this type of in-depth information there are no data upon which to base comparison in discussion. This type of qualitative data provides individuals' personal stories and so is very much unique to the context from which it was collected. Quotes in this section are presented in a method similar to the work of Bricker (1998), Potter (1993), and Raffan (1992), insomuch as a complete story is woven together from various responses. This style allows the respondents to tell their story, with only occasional input from the author.

However, it is important to attribute responses throughout this chapter in order to differentiate between visitor groups and thus differentiate between the unique programmes that may influence their responses. Respondents 1–25 travelled under the auspices of Antarctica New Zealand (ANZ). Although students in the Graduate Certificate in Antarctic Studies (GCAS) also travelled through ANZ, their experiences on-site will be separated as they are a distinct, uniform group (respondents 26–45). Heritage Expeditions (HE) respondents are those numbered anywhere from 46 to 328. The Quark Expeditions (QE) journals from the 2002–03 season (250 in total distributed to the company) also fall in this range, but there was no response from this visitor group. All QE responses from the 2003–04 season were numbered beginning at one again. Thus QE respondents are clearly identified with the letter 'Q' prior to their respondent identification number.

Generic itineraries for the various organisations are shown in Table 12.1 so that the differences and similarities can be understood by the reader. Visitors with QE also travelled in the 2003–04 season, whereas the others travelled the previous season (2002–03). This distinction is important, as each Antarctic season is generally unique in terms of many factors that may impact the visitor: factors such as weather, political climate/access, and physical access. Between 2002–03 and 2003–04 there were no major differences in these factors.

For ease of understanding, the following narratives examine the on-site experience through the journals of all respondents within each particular visitor group. This separation of groups serves to provide room for comparison, but also for the fact that between the land-based and ship-based visitors there are huge differences in their access to sites, length of time in the region, and many other factors, all of which make full combination of the narratives relatively impossible.

Table 12.1: Typical itineraries for Ross Sea region visitors.

Ship-based visits

These tours are typical of those aboard either IIE or QK vessels.

Typically 25-30 days for a Ross Sea voyage.

Day 1: Generally begin in one of the following gateway cities: Lyttleton, Bluff, or Hobart. If Bluff is the gateway, usually overnight is spent in Invercargill with transfer to the ship in Bluff in the morning. Lyttleton is similar, with accommodation either in Christchurch or Auckland the night prior.

Day 2: Depart for the Sub Antarctic.
If leaving from Hobart, the voyage generally stops at Macquarie Island, then the RSR, then the Auckland Islands (Enderby Island) and Campbell Island on return. This is generally the case if the voyage is Hobart to Hobart or Hobart to Bluff or Lyttleton. If the voyage is in reverse, then the island visits are generally reversed too, regardless of whether the voyage is Bluff-Bluff, Lyttleton-Lyttleton, or Bluff/Lyttleton-Hobart. Occasionally visits are made at the Snares or the Balleny Islands if conditions and itinerary match. Due to regulations these visits are just cruises around the islands in zodiac/naiad rubber inflatable boats.

Days 3-8: Spent exploring the Sub-Antarctic Islands

Day 8-10: spent crossing the remainder of the Southern Ocean. Crossing the Antarctic convergence, Antarctic Circle and coming into contact with first icebergs and pack ice. During these first 10 days much time has been spent aboard the ship with preparatory safety information, landing information, educational lectures, social events, and limited landing at Sub-Antarctic sites. Once in the RSR, much more time is spent on landings, and follow-up lectures take place on the return crossing of the Southern Ocean.

Days 10-22: During these 12 days, every attempt is made to conduct as many landings as possible, given weather conditions and other logistical matters of visiting some sites on the way into the region and others on the return outwards. Landings are still conducted using zodiac, rubber inflatable craft, or when/if possible using helicopters. Possible landing sites include:

- Cape Adare – site of Borchgrevink's hut and a large Adélie penguin rookery
- Cape Hallett – former site of a US-NZ station
- Terra Nova Bay – site of Italy's Mario Zuchelli Station
- Drygalski Ice tongue
- Franklin Island
- The Ross Ice Shelf and its various large numbered icebergs (i.e. B15)
- The Dry Valleys – Only accessible by helicopter, this region is ice-free, desert-like and eroded by strong wind.
- Ross Island – views of Mt. Erebus, sometimes helicopter sightseeing flights.
- Cape Bird – Large Adélie penguin rookery
- Shackleton's Hut at Cape Royds
- Scott's Hut at Cape Evans
- McMurdo Sound – the furthest south you can go on any ship in Antarctica
- McMurdo Station – the US research station, Antarctica's largest
- Scott Base – the NZ scientific base
- Scott's Discovery Hut at Hut Point
- Possession Islands

Days 23-27: Depending on the route, these four days are spent re-crossing the Southern ocean, with stops at the remaining Sub-Antarctic Islands not visited on the initial crossing.

Day 28-29: Arrive in and depart at the scheduled gateway city.

Land-based visits

GCAS

The GCAS programme typically begins in early November in Christchurch. During the time in Christchurch, students are engaged in a variety of lectures, tours of Antarctic-related facilities, and an initial field camp at Cass, near Arthur's Pass National Park in New Zealand's Southern Alps.

The field portion of the course is typically 16 days in duration. The field portion will be examined with the itinerary of all Antarctica New Zealand programmes to follow. Approximately a week after the field portion of the course has ended students are back in New Zealand and lectures reconvene. Lectures end approximately a month later, and are then followed up by final project work, submission and presentations.

Antarctica New Zealand

The length of Antarctica New Zealand visitor programmes vary greatly. Generally familiarisation trips are the shortest; perhaps less than one week in length, where as the secondary school programme lasts up to two weeks and the media or other educational programmes are individually tailored to the project, so may last eight days, two weeks or even longer.

- Regardless of length, the first day begins early with a few hours at the USAP passenger terminal, followed by a flight 6-8 hours in length, assuming it isn't 'boomeranged', turned back by the weather at the runway in Antarctica.
- Once on the ice there is transport from whichever runway the plane arrives at (depends on the timing of visit within the season), followed by a regular procedure of briefings, introductions and tours for new arrivals at Scott Base. This if all followed by approximately 2 days of Antarctic Field Training (AFT), inclusive of survival training, rescue techniques, etc.
- For short-term visitors, all of AFT may not be necessary, and familiarisation for these visitors may commence with tours of McMurdo Station, Discovery Hut, and the general Scott Base vicinity. For those who visit early in the season, there will likely be the opportunity to visit Cape Royds and/or Cape Evans by Hagglund (a tracked, tank-like vehicle). If it's later in the season these visits are only possible with helicopter access, unlikely except for the most distinguished visitors.
- After AFT, each programme is very dependent on its application. A geology focused educator may join a science party in the Dry Valleys, media, artists or general educators may visit a number of science parties and visit a wide-spread of the labs and facilities in the vicinity, and an educator with military interests may spend more time with the NZAF staff around base.
- For the GCAS students they now spend up to 12 days camped at Windless Bight, taking part in a variety of scientific, writing, and other projects. As the GCAS programme usually operates over the Christmas/New Years period, this holiday is often a big part of several days. Walks on the sea ice, cross-country skiing, using the Scott Base ski lift, and visiting IMAX crevasse are a few unique opportunities available to Antarctica New Zealand's land-based visitors.
- At the end of any ANZ-related visit, visitors generally come into Scott Base at least one day prior to the scheduled departure in order to deal with their equipment,

paperwork and de-brief with various Scott Base personnel. Flights back to Christchurch are usually in the late-afternoon or evening, and so 'bag drag', packing, and buying souvenirs can usually take place the morning of departure. All of these final preparations are often extended or changed at little notice if the morning flight from Christchurch is turned around.

Itineraries adapted from: Antarctica New Zealand (2000); Curtin (2004); Gill (1996); Headland (1993); Henzell (2003a-d); Heritage Expeditions (no date); Lindblad and Fuller, (1983); Orsman (1998); Quark Expeditions (2004); Thomas (1994); Webster (2001); Zehnders (1990); as well as information from respondents, and the author's personal experience and observations (see Maher 2007b).

Results

ANZ

For those visiting through ANZ, the on-site experience began with a flight; not an average commercial flight, however, as it was with the United States or New Zealand Air Force:

> The 5½ hours of flight went quiet slowly…then finally we were told to prepare for landing. That was the longest 'approach' I've ever endured and with no windows, it was the biggest tease, as we had no idea when we'd actually touch down…it finally happened and before long we were out of the aircraft and onto the continent itself. Yeehaah!!! The hour drive from Pegasus landing field to Scott Base went by in the flash of an eye and then the next few hours of orientation were a whirlwind of information.
>
> (Respondent 1)

First impressions seemed to focus around how impressive the sight was, or how different it seemed:

> My first impression of Antarctica – wonder, awe. So much beauty and so clear – a magic day. Unbelievable…The thing that struck me was the silence and beauty – the stillness, plus I kept expecting it to get dark!
>
> (Respondent 9)

> Antarctica…its vastness, the first experience of troop-plane transport… Stepping out of the Hercules onto the ice runway was unforgettable. One could spend the rest of my life trying to reproduce that feeling…I had an immediate feeling of elation and delight.
>
> (Respondent 11)

But this amazement, is also somewhat tinted, by the feeling of rush:

> Early morning start. 5-hour plane trip. Landed on sea ice runway – didn't have much time to get bearings before being whisked to Scott Base…

Immediately given lecture about base housekeeping – feeling very tired, headachy and assaulted by faces and rules...

(Respondent 7)

After the initial landing, and a period of catching one's bearings, the majority of ANZ visitors undertake Antarctic field training:

Then it was off to the icefall for some cramponing and ice axe techniques. 'Twas marvellous to be wandering around up there amongst the seracs and crevasses!...There are definitely some people in our group that are like babes in the wood in this environment and need help with basics like tying their mukluks up! I hope they're not 'unsupported' in the field...

(Respondent 1)

In general there are just tremendous feelings of gratitude:

Gratitude for the opportunity to be here – all other flights seem to be cancelled @ present due to deteriorating weather...Staring into the great white vastness, it's easy to get a bit of a feel for how it must have seemed for those early explorers – only they didn't have a cosy base to return to at the end of their walk.

(Respondent 1)

But reality does set in:

Antarctica is an amazing place, so peaceful not a sound at night, and the crunch of feet when you walk. Heard the shelf ice crack, makes you remember where you are. It can be easy to think of it as a big ski field otherwise. This is real...Need to get more out of base to get the real feel of the place – can't wait to see animal life.

(Respondent 10)

And this new sense of reality can still be awkward without all the social comforts of home:

First few days see one bombarded with new routines/regulations/expecta-tions – nervous of doing the wrong thing; have to learn a whole new set of ways of operating.

(Respondent 8)

As the huts are a very tangible symbol of the RSR (see Figure 12.1), they invoke themselves into respondents' experience and narratives almost immediately:

In the afternoon I had my first visit to Discovery Hut...It was the most amazing feeling – like stepping back in time. The smells of seal blubber, the

Figure 12.1 Tourists at Discovery Hut (McMurdo Station and US Antarctic Program icebreakers in the background)

cold and dark. Trousers still hung up, blubber stoves with evidence of soot everywhere. A unique experience for me – it gave me some understanding of the hardships Scott, Shackleton and the Ross Sea party went through especially once the wind came up!

(Respondent 9)

However, each new day there is a new 'best' experience ever:

The highlight of my trip so far though was this evening when we went skiing! What a buzz that was! Although it was overcast and the light was a bit flat,

the experience was truly awesome and I felt extremely privileged to be there. There were 2 people in the group who had never skied before so to see them skiing for the first time in Antarctica was also a big buzz! The ride home on the skidoo was almost as exhilarating but skiing would have to be up in the top 10 things I've ever done in my life!

(Respondent 1)

And days later:

I'm sure I've said it already 10 times in this journal, but this was the best day here yet!…summit attempt of Mt. Falconer!

(Respondent 1)

The social side of Antarctica is also not lost on respondents. Respondent 8 pays particular attention to this facet of the experience:

> Really a reinforcement of earlier idea rather than a new notion – the way the community/society is based – so many procedures and routines to know and follow (all very important and for safety). Undoubtedly they become very familiar, but at the beginning there seems to be so much to get to know.
>
> (Respondent 8)

> I've become very aware of the need for people to have places to retreat to and personal space – a great irony that in a continent with so much space that 'space' is at a premium.
>
> (Respondent 8)

But again, the reality of the situation fades in:

> I can't believe how 'at home' I feel here. For all its so-called hostility I'm completely happy and relaxed and enjoying every moment. Oh how sad I will be to leave – and how hard I'll work to get back!
>
> (Respondent 1)

And then the emotions of the final day:

> A bit tired and emotional. The whole experience, which has been very short, seems surreal.
>
> (Respondent 8)

GCAS Students

As with other visitors travelling through ANZ, GCAS students dealt with flights to get to the ice. Their thoughts reflect a range of emotions:

> It has been a huge day. It is now after 10.30 pm, and I was up at 5 am this morning. We left Christchurch in a NZ Air Force Hercules at 9 am this morning, and got to McMurdo Sound around 4.30 pm. It was a horrible flight, stinking hot, with no way to escape the heat and congestion of so many passengers. I couldn't sleep or read, so spent most of the time sitting and looking at my watch, hoping the time would go quicker. It felt so good when we passed the point where you turn back if the weather is bad, and we started to see mountains and breaking up sea ice out of the port holes.
>
> (Respondent 35)

But in a sense, had the mystique worn off already for some?

…My most emotional time was when I picked up my clothing 2 days before departure.

(Respondent 28)

Socially, the GCAS group arrived as a much more cohesive unit. They knew each other, they had had many weeks of preparation together, but group dynamics still appear to fluctuate:

It's funny that different people grate different people in different ways, i.e. one person may piss off another, but be fine to a different person. I guess we're all different…Life is an effort in Antarctica, Some people are lazy and inconsiderate, some people just don't think sometimes, it's amazing how people can cope under extreme conditions.

(Respondent 28)

The focus on people is not always directed at those actually on-site. There is a sense of people at home, which lasts throughout the experience, and also a thought for those outside the group:

I felt a bit sad to be leaving but looking forward to my comfortable bed and partner!

(Respondent 28)

Again, as with ANZ visitors, there appears to be a sense of awe surrounding the historic huts:

Privilege to be here – how lucky we are, how much gear we have compared to the early explorers. How the early explorers all passed by here, and the hardships they suffered. The contrast between their equipment/communications and ours…a real treat to be able to see them. To stand where past heroes lived and overwintered.

(Respondent 44)

In general, the on-site experience in the RSR invoked a lot of interesting thoughts, and because of the nature of the GCAS course they cover many subjects from the views, the activities, the place and more:

Today we were supposed to go to our field camp. The day began as last night was, very windy (40 knots) and snowing. Temp. still about −4°C. I was quite disappointed in many ways that we could not go to camp, as I was looking forward to getting there and building things from snow. I was also happy because Scott Base is beginning to be quite fun. It would be a life that would be very easy to get used to, and very difficult to leave. Everyone here is very friendly, which is great.

(Respondent 35)

Figure 12.2 A Hagglund waiting on the Hut Point peninsula

Once all the seals had been read (i.e. their tags) we headed back across the sea ice, this time in crampons, and collapsed in the Hagglunds [see Figure 12.2]. Back at camp the weather was mild and I spent the whole evening 6–12 pm outside talking to people, hanging out in the camp kitchen and enjoying our camp concert which began with a *Blackadder* play, some juggling and then a return to childhood games like trains and stations, tying ourselves into knots, action songs and the limbo. It was probably my best day on the ice so far. The right combination of work and play.

(Respondent 33)

At the end of it all, the beginnings of a reflection process shape an overview of what the experience consisted of:

…Antarctica strikes me as not much different than anywhere we live. It's up to you to get out and experience it. Life is pretty limited (due to safety) and seems quite easy in terms of people cleaning up after you and cooking for you. The people at Mactown seem to forget the outside world is there at all. We're not so bad I hope. I like the way time spends itself here, and you never get as tired as would if you were at a place that gets dark and has dirty air. I like the way it's all screwy.

(Respondent 26)

On reflection, I can honestly say that my 17 days there have been perhaps the most enjoyable of my life. I loved the aspect of Scott Base the most. I had such a great time socially there – both in the pub in the evenings, but also just spending quality time with small groups of people. I enjoyed the camping, but didn't love it. I was really happy to get back to 'civilisation' as such. I loved getting to know people/staff at Scott Base, I also loved the freedom we had there with our free time. I think if the experience has changed me in any way it has given me a more 'just do it' attitude especially in regards to the outdoors. I can see myself getting into my tramping, surfing etc heaps more.

(Respondent 33)

HE

As the first of two sections on the typical, commercial tourist, one will notice a few differences between these sections and those directly preceding. Both HE and QE offer an experience which is at least 24 days in length. This extended length of the trip, on the surface, simply generated more data, but also meant that there was a different transition from New Zealand (or Australia) to the RSR. The longer multiday journey at sea is simply not comparable with the multihour journey by plane. Respondents generally do not know each other, apart from perhaps a spouse or close friend, and so may be similar to visitors with ANZ. Thoughts from the voyage through the sub-Antarctic islands have been included in the results to emphasise the voyage to and from the ultimate destination.

   Getting started, regardless of whether in Bluff or Hobart, begins with fresh ideas, and an influx of information: information to frontload the trip and cover vital ideas such as safety:

Awoke to howling, whistling wind – a sign of things to come!...After breakfast received a message from the Expedition Leader, telling us that our ship just returned from the previous trip. They could not go to McMurdo Sound. Unusual ice conditions caused by the Delaware-sized iceberg, which calved off the Ross Ice Shelf a year or so ago, prevented the pack ice from drifting north and melting. The berg turned sideways and blocked the exit of the pack ice. There were also gale-force winds. The ship tried for 3 days to find an open channel but could not. Rather, it nearly got stuck in the ice and the safety of the ship was threatened. They only got to 74 degrees south.

(Respondent 46)

After leaving the safety of harbour, the first impressions in either direction tend to be of the rough days at sea:

Another rock and roll night, so there were still a fair number who did not make breakfast, or any of the other meals for that matter. Our meals are simple and not too much which is just as well considering the ship's movement. Evidently a crew member admitted to one of the passengers that the degree of rolling we are experiencing is common to all trips. The 'expedition leader's' optimism must be an effort to cheer us up.

(Respondent 61)

The sub-Antarctic islands provide dimensions for an experience similar to that found off the Antarctic Peninsula. New Zealand and Australia's sub-Antarctic islands are home to a wealth of wildlife (penguins and albatross in particular) not seen further south in the RSR, but seen throughout the Falkland and South Shetland Islands. These islands also provide welcome respite from the rough seas; a break in the storm so to speak:

> There were a lot of happy, smiling faces at dinner and everyone appeared to be buzzing as much as I after their particular experiences of the day. I'm sure most of us would have loved to spend another night and day there especially when the rumour went round that we were heading for Force 8 conditions to the south.
>
> (Respondent 52)

The sentiment of education and the need for learning runs throughout respondents' journals, as does attention to each detail. Many produce quite impressive lists of birds seen, vegetation, and history. Respondent 318 also gave excellent GPS positions for each day of the trip: Day 7 – 6/02/03Noon Position 64°10'S, 170°13'E, Distance 287.

Onwards from the sub-Antarctic islands and the experience reverted back to the rough and tumble nature of the Southern Ocean:

> Crashing into a southerly has slowed the vessel down. The [Antarctic] Circle-crossing party on lower deck (Naiads deck) and the shopping spree in the lecture room (also lower deck 1 level) both postponed. Yesterday was like a mill pond and would have been fine for these events, but today is a very different story.
>
> (Respondent 318)

Whilst difficult to 'stomach' sometimes, this period of travel through the Southern Ocean allowed for reflection; simply time to think:

> The main objective for my visit is to visit the historic sites at Ross Island. When you read the accounts of the explorers nearly 100 years ago it is impossible to visualise how they got onto the ice barrier, apart from surviving in the Antarctic.
>
> (Respondent 322)

Once properly in the RSR sights and sounds abound and any sense of dread from the voyage quickly disperses:

> This could be described as a spectacular day – clear skies – mountains of 12,000' [feet] so many miles away were crisply visible. Cracking through the ice which was so white with contrast of dark blue flat sea was a unique experience. Large chunks of pavlovas floating around the boat and huge

white 'container' flat topped icebergs which had broken off the ends of glaciers made a magnificent scene. Still sunny at 11.00 pm…4 sightings of whales – Minke.

(Respondent 314)

However, there are times when reality sets in, and one realises that the weather, the political situation, and the social structure of the journey do not always match:

By supper time we had just about got to the point furthest South that we had got to yesterday. This could be easily seen on the electronic chart and course plotter which John had learned to operate. On the way we saw several animals much as we had the day before. The weather remained glorious…the ship stopped and over the PA it was announced that we were giving up, permanently, our quest to find a way further South…Losing all hope of reaching Ross Island, the ice shelf and the Ross expedition huts was a very great disappointment to everyone on board. There were some quite bitter comments made by those whose major interest was the historical huts of Scott and Shackleton.

(Respondent 61)

Despite its isolation, people in the RSR do appear to play an important role in respondents' experiences; people both on the HE vessel and off. The nationalities of passengers serve as an illustration for the official IAATO (2008) numbers:

Meeting all the passengers – 42 of them – hard to remember names, but we are all wearing name tags, which helps…I did an assessment and found we had 1 Canadian, 9 Americans, 2 Australians, 1 Netherlander, 16 New Zealanders, 2 Scottish, 9 English and 2 half and half – they were originally from NZ, but had lived in England for 25 years or so…

(Respondent 318)

We have quite a few nationalities aboard – British, one Canadian, many New Zealanders, Australians and just a few Americans. It is interesting talking with others and seeing differences and similarities.

(Respondent 328)

The following quotes examine how those with HE experienced the huts and were left feeling (see Figure 12.3):

We walked up some hills and then down onto snow and rocks until, in a bowl-shaped little valley stood Shackleton's "hut". It was awesome!….and that is an understatement. Left as it was 95 years ago. Only the roof had been replaced and secured with crossed cables to protect it from the fierce winds.

Figure 12.3 A box of supplies at Scott's Discovery Hut

In this very dry climate, nothing deteriorates. Outside was the stable and some dog houses, as well as many, many crates which were still holding canned foods. All around the hut were cans and jars containing foods, some of which had rusted open and we could see dried beans and peas in them.

(Respondent 46)

Having absorbed the atmosphere of the hut's location and surrounds, I duly cleaned my boots and entered it, and like everyone else from the ship was totally blown away by the treasure trove inside. I reckon you could spend all day in there and still find new things to marvel at. We are just **so** lucky to have the chance to see these wondrous places.

(Respondent 52)

The hut really looks as if the residents have gone off for an expedition and will be back shortly. Many of the supplies could be bought today at home and the suppliers are still in business...Again entering Scott's Hut gives you a strong emotional feeling. Looking at photographs is no substitute and in the future any reading will be now much more vivid.

(Respondent 322)

With the huts, the scenery, and the wildlife experienced the return trip back to

New Zealand and Australia begins. Already there is an air of reflection about what has happened:

> It was very sad to say goodbye to Antarctica. So many dreams and hopes smashed by the weather. Most of us will not be back here again. The pristine-ness of the area is overwhelming. Interesting to note that none of the research stations will give any help to a private enterprise, only in emergency.
>
> (Respondent 62)

Despite warnings of the 'rocking and rolling' set to come, there is hope in leaving this beautiful region:

> Was an amazing day really with the ice, wind change and performance of the seals. Full of admiration for the captain and staff getting out of the pack ice. I think the danger was limited, but the storm was bad! Very poor visibility… The phases of weather here are very interesting and challenging. Can only have the highest regard for early explorers in their small boats. Must have been great seamen.
>
> (Respondent 53)

> We left Antarctica without setting foot on the continent – ice conditions were too severe – perhaps 2 large icebergs C19 and B15, restricted ice flows, perhaps a lack of storms to disperse ice – visiting various huts was interesting, but not my main reason for the journey – I wanted to get to the continent and have a look so feel disappointed that I spent a lot of time and money and did not have that experience of being truly in Antarctica. Having said that it has been a memorable experience overall as a visit to an alien and at times vaguely scary place and I certainly am now aware that the conditions control man, not the other way around. The selection of photos are trying to convey the different moods of my Antarctic experience.
>
> (Respondent 54)

Leaving the protection of the pack ice, the same ride as coming to the RSR begins again:

> Spent much of the rest of the day reading in the lounge and having hot drinks. The sea is not rough, but the swells are huge and we ROLL. Saw black-browed albatrosses, white-chin (giant) petrel, and sooty shearwater. Had glass of wine and dinner and then returned to lounge for cup of tea. Still rolling!…I hate rolling!!
>
> (Respondent 53)

To end the voyage, back in civilisation, there are many thoughts that have already surfaced:

It was a fantastic experience to see so many new things and the group seems to have mixed well without any jarring personalities...In a nutshell, having had time to consider – the utter unreliability of the weather, and the power of water in its different forms are the most impressive aspect of Antarctica – and puts attempts at human control in contempt!

(Respondent 49)

The trip has been the fulfilment of a long and dearly held dream. I chose this trip because I wanted the complete experience and adventure of crossing the Southern Ocean, despite being concerned about whether I'd be seasick or not. I also hoped to reach Scott Base, where a number of my friends had worked. The reality was all I had hoped for and much much more. It was packed with excitement, beauty and wonderful wildlife experiences...Overall, the disappointment of not making Scott Base was more than outweighed by all the bonus experienced caused by the unusually heavy ice year. It was a fantastic trip, packed with memorable moments – the trip of a lifetime and probably a life-changing event for me.

(Respondent 52)

It has been a wonderful 4 weeks. Experiences that are not captured on film and will be hard to describe. However, on this trip we nearly all feel nature has cheated us of our main goal, that being of course, the trip down to McMurdo Sound. Because of this, something is definitely missing of our total experience.

(Respondent 62)

QE

Similar in length to the on-site experiences had by HE passengers, the primary differences between the two groups of commercial tourists is really two aspects: logistics and season. Logistically QE has more ability to access sites. Having the icebreaker *Kapitan Khlebnikov*, QE is sometimes able to push further south than the ice-strengthened *Akademik Shokalskiy* can. QE also uses helicopters (see Figure 12.4), and so can access inland sites such as the Dry Valleys, and can reach huts easier when the ice surrounding Ross Island is a problem, and can provide opportunities such as flight-seeing over Mount Erebus. The non-logistical difference between the two groups is that QE's passengers reporting in this research were from the 2003–04 season and thus weather and ice conditions were not exactly the same as those encountered the previous season by HE.

Once in the RSR, which is where most QE passengers began their journals, initial thoughts abound on a number of topics:

Compared to the peninsula which is more varied and photogenic...Unique is not the right word, one of a kind, spectacular scenery.

(Respondent Q59)

Figure 12.4 A helicopter from the *Kapitan Khlebnikov* picking up tourists at Scott Base

The vastness, emptiness of a huge continent. It was a shocking thought to realise that we were touching on only a very, tiny part of the continent…the huge influence it has on the world's weather; watching the icebreaker work its way through the pack ice and fast ice and pondering on the similarities between the different slabs of ice, riding over or chopping under other slabs – replicating in miniature the tectonic forces at work in shaping planet earth.

(Respondent Q61)

The vastness of Antarctica was to me a new concept. To read this over and over is one thing, but to experience it is another. When it takes 6 days to get to a place – that's a long way away.

(Respondent Q91)

Amongst QE respondents thoughts of amazement seem to prevail and there is less chronological consistency or transitions mentioned. Again, a trip to the RSR does not seem complete without mention of the people involved. QE passengers tended to mention the quality of staff/lecturers more so than other groups:

What we got to do was amazing – but more so because we had 7 straight days of sun and mostly little wind! Our staff was so incredibly competent that we made all our scheduled landings and extras. Capable ship, Capable crew. Major emphasis on 'taking care of the environment' – treading lightly, not disturbing animals, respect critical areas. We visited all 4 huts, 2 stations, Dry Valleys, ice tongues, etc.

(Respondent Q127)

First off the ship and crew were fabulous. The vessel we travelled in was perfect for the place and type of trip we were on. The people generally shared a similar view of the environment, the educational sessions and the overall impression I received was that many of them are well travelled.

(Respondent Q128)

As with all other groups, the huts provide a myriad of reflections, but respondents also have questions for the future:

I was impressed to visit all of the pioneer explorers' huts and to feel their very palpable presence amongst their hastily discarded stores and other gear. I was also appalled at the conservation problems, which they present, if other travellers are to be able to enjoy them. The huts and their surroundings must inevitably deteriorate, however careful visitors may be. Accepting that, it would seem ideal if they could be re-created elsewhere, perhaps at the Antarctic Museum in Christchurch, as they now exist. To excessively repair and renovate them in the original locations would seem to risk creating an Antarctic Disneyland.

(Respondent Q32)

My most unique and emotional feeling was to visit the huts to see how close famous men lived and how different history would have been if they had the beautiful weather we experienced.

(Respondent Q96)

At the end of it all, QE's respondents seemed to reflect just as others had:

I was an emotional see-saw the whole time, swinging from despair and fury at Man in general and some individuals in particular, to elation I could hardly bear at the beauty I was experiencing. And I'm known as a down-to-earth, sensible person. I who never cry (not even when a child though life was grim enough) wept at having to return. I wanted never to leave. The only other times I've experienced place so intensely were in the Himalaya and on the St. Elias ice field in the Southern Yukon. And, or course, in my 'heartland' of the Main Range, Kosciusko National Park where I lived for many a year.

(Respondent Q44)

The visit as a whole has been a totally rewarding experience, which I feel privileged to have experienced. I am more knowledgeable and more committed to Antarctica's preservation and responsible management for future generations.

(Respondent Q63)

Conclusions

Overall, given the lack of comparative studies, and the nature of qualitative, exploratory research, conclusions made regarding on-site results are focused specifically to this study in the time frame it was undertaken: November 2002–March 2004. The mood of visitors seems to be very positive, similar to that found in anticipation results (see Maher *et al.* 2006). From the journals, there are some differences between visitor groups' responses, but some generalisations can also be made.

There was a sense of impressiveness, and amazement at some point in every respondent's journal. For ANZ visitors this appeared to happen right at arrival, despite the rush to get through all the processes and mandatory events such as Antarctic field training. GCAS visitors had mixed emotions upon arrival, but had the cohesive group to draw strength from. HE visitors had lots of information to take in at first (safety briefings, etc.), and then they had a 'rock and roll' through the Southern Ocean. This fear towards the difficulty of travel then disperses once in the RSR proper, and turns to amazement like all the other visitors. QE visitors do not mention the trip south, which can be attributed to the slightly different methods used to access journal data from them. More so than the other groups, QE and GCAS groups mention people in their journals.

Every group seems mystified by the huts, and that combined with the simple amazement are the two primary aspects upon which all the groups come together. GCAS students had a much wider variety of experiences in the field, in the bases and such, but miss out on the wildlife as experienced by QE and HE visitors. ANZ visitors spend more time in base, and so seem to have a greater appreciation for the dynamics of politics and base staff interaction. Neither ANZ nor GCAS visitors have the same sense of transition to and from the RSR (based on flying south), but even the QE visitors do not mention it much.

Linking with the research literature, it seems that RSR visitors have had an extraordinary and deeply meaningful experience, consistent with the work of Arnould and Price (1993) and Beedie and Hudson (2003). Both of these studies reported that respondents took this new awareness and appreciation for a particular place as a result of focused interaction with it and created a new reality, perhaps increasing a sense of advocacy as a result. How this on-site experience in the RSR specifically translates post-voyage can be seen in Maher (2007b, 2007c, 2009).

Acknowledgements

This chapter presents work from my doctoral studies and thus I must also thank my supervisory team at Lincoln University, New Zealand: Associate Professor Alison J. McIntosh (now at the University of Waikato) and Dr Gary D. Steel. Financial, in-kind and logistical support of my research was provided by: the Commonwealth Scholarship Programme; the Environment, Society & Design Division at Lincoln University; New Zealand Post; Antarctica New Zealand; McEwings Mountain Sports; and Macpac Wilderness Equipment. However, most importantly, thank you to visitors, and the organisations and operators who supported their travels: Antarctica New Zealand, Graduate Certificate in Antarctic Studies at the University of Canterbury, Heritage Expeditions and Quark Expeditions.

References

Antarctica New Zealand (2000) *Proceedings of the Antarctic Tourism Workshop, Christchurch, 23 June 2000*. Christchurch: Antarctica New Zealand.

Arnould, E.J. and Price, L.L. (1993) 'River magic: extraordinary experience and the extended service encounter', *Journal of Consumer Research,* 20(1): 24–45.

Bauer, T.G. (2001) *Tourism in the Antarctic: opportunities, constraints and future prospects*. New York: The Haworth Hospitality Press.

Beedie, P. and Hudson, S. (2003) 'Emergence of mountain-based adventure tourism', *Annals of Tourism Research,* 30(3): 625–43.

Bricker, K.S. (1998) Place and preference: a study of whitewater recreationists on the South Fork of the American River, unpublished Doctor of Philosophy thesis, Pennsylvania State University.

Clawson, M. and Knetsch, J.L. (1966) *Economics of Outdoor Recreation*. Baltimore: Johns Hopkins University Press.

Curtin, R. (2004) 'The world's best kept secret', *Antarctic*, 22(1): 12, 13.

Davis, P. (1995) Wilderness visitor management and Antarctic tourism, unpublished Doctor of Philosophy thesis, Scott Polar Research Institute, University of Cambridge.

Fridgen, J.D. (1984) 'Environmental psychology and tourism', *Annals of Tourism Research*, 11(1): 19–39.

Gill, J.F. (1996) 'Crashing through the frozen Antarctic on a Russian icebreaker', *New York Times*.

Headland, R.K. (1993) *Voyage of the Russian icebreaker Kapitan Khlebnikov – Fremantle (Australia) to Antarctica to Bluff (New Zealand); 1992–93 Austral Summer*. Unpublished document for Quark Expeditions.

Hemmings, A.D. and Roura, R. (2003) 'A square peg in a round hole: fitting impact assessment under the Antarctic Environmental Protocol to Antarctic tourism', *Impact Assessment and Project Appraisal*, 21(1): 13–24.

Henzell, J. (2003a) 'Antarctica is truly summit special', *The Press,* 18 December: A6.

— (2003b) 'Learning a cold, hard lesson in Antarctica', *The Press,* 22 December: A6.

— (2003c) 'Cracker of a Christmas on the Ice', *The Press,* 26 December: A10.

— (2003d) 'A cool reception for visitors', *The Press,* 30 December: A6.

Heritage Expeditions (no date) *Expedition Cruises*. [Catalogue]. Christchurch: Heritage Expeditions.

International Association of Antarctica Tour Operators (IAATO) (2008) *Tourism Statistics*. Online. Available HTTP: www.iaato.org /tourism_stats.html (accessed 30 May 2008).

Janes, A. (2003) 'Antarctic tourism walks a tightrope', *New Zealand Sunday Star Times,* July 20: D3.

Lindblad, L-E. and Fuller, J.G. (1983) *Passport to Anywhere: The Story of Lars-Eric Lindblad*. New York: Times Books.

Maher, P.T. (2007a) 'Arctic tourism: a complex system of visitors, communities, and environments', *Polar Geography*, 30(1–2): 1–5.

— (2007b) Footsteps on the ice: visitor experiences in the Ross Sea region, Antarctica, unpublished Doctor of Philosophy thesis, Lincoln University.

— (2007c) 'Advocating for Antarctic wilderness: short-term visits and human values', in A. Watson, J. Sproull, and L. Dean (Comps) *Science and Stewardship to Protect and Sustain Wilderness Values*: Eighth World Wilderness Congress Symposium; September 30–October 6 2005, Anchorage. Proceedings RMRS-P-49. Fort Collins, CO: USDA, Forest Service, Rocky Mountain Research Station.

— (2009) 'Ambassadors for the experience: perspectives from the Ross Sea Region', in P.T. Maher, E.J. Stewart and M. Lück (eds) *Polar Tourism: Human, Environmental and Governance Dimensions*, Elmsford: Cognizant Communications.

Maher, P.T., McIntosh, A.J. and Steel, G.D. (2006) 'Examining dimensions of anticipation: inputs for experience prior to visiting the Ross Sea region, Antarctica', *Tourism in Marine Environments*, 2(2): 51–63.

Maher, P.T. and Stewart, E.J. (2007) 'Polar tourism: research directions for current realities and future possibilities', *Tourism in Marine Environments*, 4(2–3): 65–68.

Mason, P.A. and Legg, S.J. (1999) 'Antarctic tourism: activities, impacts, management issues, and a proposed research agenda', *Pacific Tourism Review*, 3(1): 71–84.

Orsman, C. (1998) 'Eight days in Antarctica', in T. Shaw (ed.) *A Passion for Travel: New Zealand Writers and Their Adventures Overseas*, Auckland: Tandem Press.

Potter, T.G. (1993) A journey through wilderness weekend experiences, unpublished Doctor of Philosophy dissertation, University of Alberta.

Quark Expeditions (2004) *Quark Expeditions-Antarctica: Ultimate Antarctica*. Online. Available: HTTP: http://www.quarkexpeditions.com/antarctica/prog_ua04.shtml (accessed 20 January 2004).

Raffan, J. (1992) Frontier, homeland and sacred place: a collaborative investigation into cross-cultural perceptions of place in the Thelon Game Sanctuary, Northwest Territories, unpublished Doctor of Philosophy – Geography dissertation, Queen's University.

Thomas, T. (1994) 'Ecotourism in Antarctica: the role of the naturalist guide in presenting places of natural interest', *Journal of Sustainable Tourism*, 2(4): 204–9.

Tracey, P.J. (2001) Managing Antarctic tourism, unpublished Doctor of Philosophy thesis, Institute of Antarctic and Southern Ocean Studies, University of Tasmania.

Webster, K. (2001) 'A collective vision', *Art News New Zealand*, 21(1): 36, 37.

Zehnders, W. (1990) 'Tourism in Antarctica', *Aurora – ANARE Club Journal*, 10(1): 22–25.

13 Images of Antarctica and Ushuaia (Argentina) as a Gateway Port

Antarctic visitors and their expectations

Marisol Vereda

Introduction

Antarctic sea-borne tourism has shown substantial increase in recent years as shown by the different types of product offers (themes and activities) that appear in trip programmes, the various ships that make the voyages, and an increase in the total number of passengers transported to the Antarctic Peninsula and Ross Sea (including large cruise ships whose passengers did not land) (see chapter 1). Most of the Antarctic cruise companies take Ushuaia in Argentina as the base port for Antarctic maritime tourism operations because of its infrastructure (port and airport) and convenient location (1,000 km from the Antarctic Peninsula); the latter plays an important role in the schedule of the companies that operate in Antarctica throughout the season, since it allows them to cross the Mar de Hoces or Drake Passage in less time, enabling addition of another voyage by the end of the season. It is estimated that in recent years approximately 90% of the cruise passengers to Antarctica passed through the port of Ushuaia (Instituto Fueguino de Turismo [INFUETUR] 2006).

Antarctica as a destination

Even although Antarctica is a continent that covers approximately 14,000,000 km², most cruise ship itineraries concentrate on the Antarctic Peninsula because of its proximity to South America and also for the variety and abundance of natural and historical resources situated along the coast and by the islands. Nevertheless, some trips also visit the Ross Sea, for which Australian and New Zealand ports serve as gateways (Hall 2000; IAATO 2007).

Antarctica is generally described as an exceptional setting for tourists that awakens emotions generated by the experiences that take place in a pristine remote area (chapter 12). The superlative way in which it is usually characterised, i.e the coldest, driest, windiest, iciest, highest, remotest, place on Earth, has imprinted a very specific image that reinforces the idea of the wild (see chapter 12). This strong image stands for the values assigned to the place, grants it symbolism, giving it the attribute of unique and of the last place on earth where humans may reach (see chapter 1). As Bigné and Sánchez (2001) point out, the tourist image of a destination refers to the global perception or the mental representation a person has about a place. San Martín Gutiérrez (2005) adds that these impressions and attributes about the place can be tangible, abstract, common and unique. The tourist image of a destination can be built through cognitive and affective components. The cognitive image refers to all those attributes which are vastly known and socially accepted for the place; the affective one is directly related to the feelings deposited by a tourist on the destination, the way the person gives value to the objects (Yüksel and Akgül 2007; Bigné and Sánchez 2001).

Expectations of Antarctic visitors

The formation of visitor expectations is founded on the grounds of a flow of information from different origins. Yüksel and Akgül (2007) note that destination authorities use brochures as a means of enhancing awareness of their areas as well as seeking to generate a desire to purchase their destination. However, this possibility does not apply to Antarctica because it is a continent ruled by the Antarctic Treaty System, under which tourism is not promoted by any destination marketing organisation, and is instead marketed by commercial private industry. Furthermore, there is neither a native nor a permanent community in Antarctica who may be particularly interested in the development of tourism (the only settlements are strictly related to stations devoted to science where people live temporarily). Consequently, the main sources for this information may come through travel brochures, documentary films, motion pictures, fiction books, travel book guides, explorers' narratives, lectures, photographs, and activities generated by environmental and scientific organisations. In 2007–08, the promotional efforts of the International Polar Year may have had an important influence. In this way the potential traveller receives different kinds of information that encourage the beginning of an assessment process about the place, shaping a mental construct of Antarctica as a destination. Expectations determine performance perceptions of products and services as well as perceptions of experiences. These expectations about the future experience are, therefore, built on the basis of the perceived image or mental representation of the destination (San Martín Gutiérrez 2005).

The case study

Data gathering for this study took place in several stages. Firstly, surveys were made to Antarctic visitors in order to know their expectations of the Antarctic trip. The form was distributed as soon as the passengers arrived in Ushuaia, before embarkation. Then, on their way back from the Antarctic voyage another form was given to those same passengers asking them how their expectations of Antarctica had been fulfilled. Consequently, a total of 282 surveys, forming 141 pairs, were obtained. Secondly, another set of surveys (the third) was given to Antarctic visitors while they were in Ushuaia in order to know their opinion about Ushuaia as a complementary destination to Antarctica. In this case a total of 213 forms were obtained. Finally, 30 itineraries in brochures and travel book guides about Antarctica were analysed to see how Antarctica is presented to tourists and in what way Ushuaia is characterised.

Expectations of Antarctic visitors

Data were collected through the before-the-trip form. The sample consisted mainly of Americans, British and Australians (31%, 18% and 14 % respectively), followed by Dutch and Spanish (9% and 7 %) and other nationalities (Canadian, German, Japanese, Argentine, Swedish, Swiss, French) represented 19%, and 2% did not specify. Passengers travelled on board small and medium-sized cruise ships, and in all cases they experienced landings in Antarctica.

An open-ended question was asked: 'What are your expectations towards your Antarctic trip?' in order to let the visitors express themselves freely, without

Table 13.1: Expectations of Antarctic visitors: cognitive components

Cognitive Components	
Attribute	%
Scenery (included the items below and the general mention of 'scenery')	82
– Ice	9
– Icebergs	19
– Glaciers	9
– Mountains	2
Wildlife (included the items below and the general mention of 'wildlife')	91
– Penguins	32
– Whales	23
– Others (birds and seals)	16
Location (included the items below and the general mention of 'location')	27
– Seventh Continent	6
– Remotness/Isolation	6
– Antarctic Circle	4
– Stepping on Continent	4
Harsh environment (included the items below and the general mention of 'hostile conditions')	23
– Cold weather	13
– Difficult sea cross	6
History	
– Early explorers	5
– Shackleton	4
Activities	
– Adventure	4
– Trekking	5
– Camping	2
– Kayaking	1
– Cross-country skiing	1
– Taking photographs	5
Services on board	1
– Knowledgeable staff	4

Table 13.2: Expectations of Antarctic visitors: affective components

Affective Components	
Attribute	*%*
Mystique	12
Quietness	4
Few people encounter	6
Experience	
– As privilege distinction	6
– Once in a lifetime	5
– Unique	26
Sharing with others	7
Gaining awareness (included the items below and the general mention to the 'desire of learning')	14
– Climate change	3
– Ecology	4
– Ongoing research	2

limiting the flow of images that could emerge. Passengers included more than one expectation, so responses could be grouped first in two main areas as regards cognitive and affective components and, in turn, into different categories (see Tables 13.1 and 13.2).

Level of satisfaction after the voyage

To know how those expectations were fulfilled, a second form was distributed among the same people on their way back from Antarctica. In this case, they were asked: 'How were your expectations towards Antarctica fulfilled?' Since a large number of people expressed that their expectations had been 'surpassed' or 'far exceeded', three levels were taken into account: surpassed, satisfied and not satisfied. Figure 13.1 indicates the high degree of satisfaction.

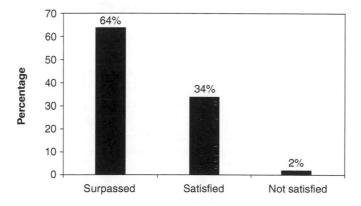

Figure 13.1 Level of satisfaction

As San Martín Gutiérrez (2005) points out, satisfaction can be defined as a cognitive-affective judgement that derives from the visitor's experience in relation to the product or service; it is the individual's response to a process in which the experience is compared with the expectations. In this respect, he also affirms that the visitor will trust more in the experiences rather than in his or her cognitive judgements, because this may imply an excessive mental effort. Following San Martín Gutiérrez (2005), it can be suggested that in the particular case of Antarctic visitors, the previous expectations of the trip as well as the emotions derived from the experience can explain the high degree of satisfaction that resulted from the surveys.

In respect to the 'not satisfied' expectations, the three responses belonged to passengers on board different ships. In one of the cases it was explained that having seen few orcas and whales was disappointing and, besides, the trip was too expensive. This particular person had the following expectations: 'I'd like to see whales and penguins, to be in an entirely natural setting, not created by humans. To experience sights, smells and sounds which are nowhere in the world'. The other two persons referred to the number of people seen in Antarctica; the first one wrote: 'I thought there would be fewer ships with tourists around the area. Besides, I expected fewer people on the ship and when we were on land the group was too big'. Thus, the respondent had very high expectations while travelling on a medium-sized ship. He also referred to quietness and to the desire of finding a great place. The last one said that he 'had wished to be on a smaller ship (this person was also on board a medium-sized cruise ship) capable of getting closer to land and doing more landings'; his expectations were related to seeing abundant wildlife and a beautiful landscape.

Despite the high level of satisfaction responses, some visitors included remarks about some disappointment. To begin with, four people claimed that they had expected to be with fewer people, summarised in phrases like this: '—for full enjoyment you have to go away from the group or else you are still among people'. Other notes of disappointment were stated in these categories: (1) wildlife: had seen few sea mammals (three responses) and had expected to encounter the emperor penguin (two responses); (2) activities: would have liked to do more trekking/hiking/camping out in Antarctica (three responses); (3) location: would like to have spent more time in the continent (one response); (4) weather: expected some blue skies (one response); (5) service on board: food could be improved (two responses). Nonetheless, all these people (16 responses) indicated that their expectations had been satisfied regardless of the remarks mentioned above.

From the surveys obtained in this phase of the study, several characteristics that arose from the experience were assigned to the cognitive components that had been identified during the expectation formation process:

Scenery: 52% mentioned scenery when referring to the way their expectations were fulfilled. Glaciers, ice and icebergs were the main elements in the descriptions, followed by mountains. The key words that appear as most relevant to giving meaning to the Antarctic landscape were: 'really impressive', 'beautiful and unique', 'amazing', 'great', 'beauty', 'pristine', 'stunning', 'sheer beauty', 'fantastic', 'spectacular', 'magnificent', 'majestic', 'magic', 'awe-inspiring', 'unforgettable', 'wonderful'.

Wildlife: 53% referred to wildlife as an important contributor to the satisfaction of expectations. Of that total most travellers centred their attention on the abundance and richness of wildlife, particularly related to penguins. In some cases proximity to penguins and, to a lesser extent, variety of wildlife, were also highlighted. In the expectation form many people had pointed out the possibility of seeing wildlife in its natural habitat.

Location: 20% mentioned that this item also plays an important part in the Antarctic experience. The idea of 'world's end' and the sense of remoteness are attributes particularly assigned to Antarctica as it is considered the most difficult place to reach; other words such as 'isolation' reinforce this idea. The Antarctic Circle operates as a material point for conveying meaning for being further south, whereas the seventh continent also evokes the last place on Earth to visit, especially for more experienced travellers.

History: Few people (6%) mentioned history as a remarkable part of their experience. In these cases it was highlighted that visiting the huts of early explorers as well as experiencing a hostile environment put the hardships of the members of expeditions into perspective. Particularly, explorers' vicissitudes, especially those of the 'heroic era' are clearly visualized as symbols that incite discovery, that seduce through the challenge that their quest represents or that intimidate because of the challenge for survival that the place seems to have (see González Bernáldez 1981).

Activities: Apart from one case ('I camped on Forged Island—I will indeed always remember—'), no other comment was given on the satisfaction form, except for those expressing disappointment, as has already been described.

Services on board: 17% mentioned this topic and gave positive answers, in particular towards the members of staff and the planning of the voyage. However, six persons referred to the high price of the voyage.

In regard to the other components, the affective ones, many opinions were expressed. This dimension had probably predisposed visitors to be more open to experiencing Antarctica through the emotion of what the 'pristine' image stands for. This dimension is also highly reinforced through the writings of explorers, generating a most sensitive image by which to judge Antarctica (see chapter 11). For example, before his journey Edward Wilson wrote:

> I am going—they accept me in spite of everything if I will go at my own risks. I don't care in the least if I live or die–all is right and I am going; it will be the making of me...

...and then, while in Antarctica:

> The sunlight at midnight in the pack is perfectly wonderful. One looks out upon endless fields of broken ice, all violet and purple in the low shadows, and all gold and orange and rose-red on the broken edges which catch the

light, while the sky is emerald green and salmon pink, and these two beautiful tints are reflected in the pools of absolutely still water which here and there lie between the ice floes. Now and again one hears a penguin cry out in the stillness—only intensified by the wonderful stillness and beauty of the whole fairy-like scene—

(Wilson and Elder 2000: 87).

Different expressions gave value to the natural environment, connected to its aesthetic qualities. Most likely, this outcome may be related to being far away from everyday industrialised urban spaces, facing completely opposite circumstances. Some testimonies allow us to visualise the emotions that touched visitors:

I wouldn't be surprised if it had a profound impact on my life in the future.
Nothing can prepare someone for spectacular Antarctica.
The place was awesome in the true sense of the word.
Antarctica can't be explained to one who hasn't been there. Pictures only offer a taste of the adventure.
It was indeed a trip I will always remember.
I saw more than expected, the impressions are truly memorable.
I will always speak about the serenity and the magic of Antarctica.
I cannot say enough about the trip as a life enriching experience, opposed to merely a holiday.

Further responses with regard to affective components are presented below:

Gaining awareness: 20% mentioned the learning experience that they had had. This makes us think of the important role that environmental education has for the Antarctic visitor. In this respect people indicated that the experience made them change their minds about some aspects of conservation and also encouraged their will to raise others' awareness about Antarctica. Besides, many people agreed that lectures had largely contributed to their personal enrichment and understanding about environmental issues. In this case through direct experience and specific knowledge obtained, a deeper state of mind about the meaning of the Antarctic environment had been gained.

Mystique: 11% mentioned in different words a certain spirituality that had made them think of abstract matters such as religion: 'I was awed by the beauty and serenity of Antarctica. It reminded me of the wonder of all of Lord's creation'.

Quietness: Only 6% explicitly referred to having been in a 'quiet place' or in a 'peaceful environment'.

Uniqueness: 11% expressed the idea of Antarctica as a singular place. In most cases it was described as 'untouched', reinforcing the idea of being a continent of its own, that is to say, without too much influence from human beings. Some phrases were: '—this continent is in a class of its own', 'I was thrilled by the view of untouched (almost) nature', 'And it's *so* different from anywhere else', 'More unique than I could have imagined'.

Few people encountered: Only one answer referred to this item. In contrast with their own entity as tourists, 4% of the answers stated that they feared Antarctica would become more visited by tourists. Probably people had been moved by the threat that tourism in Antarctica may become massive, thus losing its feature of 'unique', risking the values that make it appear as the 'last place on Earth', untouched and preserved.

Experience: It appears in many answers; 16% expressed that they had had a positive experience; half of this total mentioned a 'once in a lifetime experience'.

Sharing with others: Three people referred to the nice atmosphere on board and sharing with 'such nice fellow travellers'.

According to the testimonies of visitors, emotion is an irreplaceable component of the Antarctic experience that had not been anticipated in their expectations, except for the ones involving mystique. Some passengers also commented that despite having been to different places in the world where the landscape shares some of the features of Antarctica (such as mountains and glaciers), the feelings and sensations that they experienced in this trip were unique and without comparison.

Taking the above into account, it is important to emphasise some remarks in the results. Firstly, the references to the cost of the Antarctic journey observed in the surveys. Secondly, the idea of visiting Antarctica as a privilege that can create an inequality among travellers, discriminating those who can access the continent from those who cannot. Thirdly, the rise of activities such as hiking, trekking and camping, mentioned in both surveys (before and after the trip). Finally, the disappointment shown at being aware that other ships were in the area and also the desire that tourism figures should not increase. These arguments are highlighted because they did not appear in previous surveys analysed (e.g. Bauer 2001; Vereda 2004; chapter 12). Most likely, the changes that are appearing in the industry (more and larger ships and an increasing number of passengers, more diverse offerings that include several activities, and more sophisticated onboard services in order to be different from other tour operators) may be understood as a warning of a change with regard to the Antarctic voyage.

Ushuaia as a gateway to Antarctica and its potential as a complementary destination

To know the opinion of Antarctic visitors of Ushuaia and its relationship with Antarctica, data were gathered through a survey that was carried out during the 2006–07 season. In many cases the surveyed passengers were the same ones as in the previous surveys taken. A total of 213 forms were completed, covering the following nationalities: American, British, Australian and Canadian (26%, 20%, 17% and 8%, respectively), followed by Dutch, Spanish, South African and New Zealander (6%, 5%, 2% and 2%, respectively) and other nationalities (German, Austrian, Swedish, Argentine, Japanese) (14%). In respect to the age, percentages were distributed as follows: 15–24 years (7%), 25–44 years (31%), 45–64 years (38%), 65 years or more (16%), while 8% did not specify.

Two questions referred specifically to Ushuaia in its relationship with Antarctica: 'How important do you think Ushuaia is as a gateway to Antarctica?'

and 'How much do you think Ushuaia fits in the Antarctic trip programmes?' In the first case, all passengers assigned either a 'very important' or 'important' response (77% and 19%, respectively, whereas the other 4% referred to 'of little importance'). In the second case, 52% thought that it fitted 'very much', 36% 'much', 3% answered 'little' and another 4% 'very little' (5% did not specify).

Three questions specifically related to Ushuaia. The first one asked about the passengers' stay, the second inquired into their interest in staying more time in Ushuaia if they could and, in that case, what kind of places they would like to visit and what activities they would like to do. For the first item, 13% of the surveyed passengers had been in Ushuaia the minimum time required to be able to board the ship (between 4 and 10 hours), most had stayed for one night (47%), some had been for 2 nights (12%), some for 3 nights (7%), others for more time (15%), and 6% did not specify. Of visitors, 93% stated that they would have liked to stay more time in Ushuaia to visit the attractions of Tierra del Fuego, and only 4% expressed that they would not, whereas the other 3% did not answer. Passengers were also asked to complete a grid with several activities and places that they would like to visit if they could stay more time (Figure 13.2).

The main interests of visitors are related to wildlife observation, trekking, visiting protected areas and cruising opportunities provided by the Beagle Channel (Figure 13.2). These preferences are very similar to the expectations with regard to the voyage to Antarctica. Activities such as trekking and hiking also seem to occupy an important place. The results clearly suggest that there is potential for Ushuaia to develop a role as a destination beyond its current gateway function (Vereda 2008).

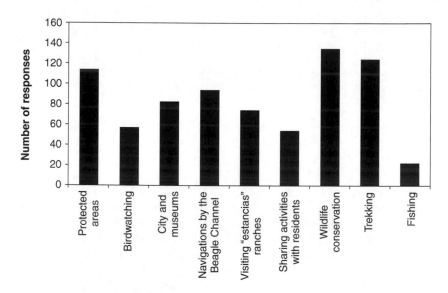

Figure 13.2 Activity preferences of Antarctic visitors for Ushuaia/Tierra del Fuego

Tourist itineraries

Thirty itineraries from different brochures from the 2006–07 season were analysed (even although there are many tour operators, the selected brochures were issued by the companies that operate most of the ships that organise landings); travel book guides were also reviewed. The names of the different voyages primarily referred to the principal areas they proposed to visit in the Antarctic Peninsula and surrounds. Titles included: 'Crossing the Circle: Southern Expedition'; 'Across the Circle', 'Antarctic to the Polar Circle', 'Antarctic Circle Quest', 'Antarctic Deep South', 'Antarctic Circle Crossing'. Activities could also be identified as specialised programmes: 'Antarctic Adventure: Actively Exploring the Peninsula', 'Climbers and Photographers', 'Across the Circle for Climbers and Divers'. Thematic itineraries also highlighted the symbolism of Antarctica as a place for exploration and quest: 'Epic Antarctica', 'Explorers' Routes', 'Shackleton Odyssey', 'In the Boss' Tracks' (chapter 11).

The main components that were mentioned in all the brochures coincide with those analysed before in the expectation and satisfaction phase, especially in relation to the cognitive components. With respect to wildlife, a detailed enumeration of species (penguins, other birds, whales and seals) appeared in almost all the brochures. The scenery was described as 'breathtaking', 'stunning', 'dramatic', 'spectacular' and, in all cases, ice and icebergs were highlighted. Early explorers were mentioned in half of the itineraries, Shackleton being the most used, and then Nordenskjöld and Larsen (when visiting Cerro Nevado, Snow Hill, and the Weddell Sea). Reference was also found to Cook, Weddell and Byrd.

In all these itineraries Ushuaia was the gateway from which the companies operate and it appeared as the embarking and disembarking port. Only in six of the itineraries was there a specific mention of Ushuaia as a destination, Tierra del Fuego National Park was highlighted along with some aspects of its wildlife. In these brochures Ushuaia was also characterised as the world's southernmost city and its landscapes were also referenced. Only one photograph of the city was included. There was one case that took into account a possibility for passengers to add a 'pre or post cruise' in Ushuaia.

Ushuaia appeared among the gateways to Antarctica in two guidebooks with a brief description of its location, history and city attractions. In this respect, it is clearly stated that Ushuaia is seen only as the most convenient port to operate to Antarctica, but apparently it has not yet been perceived as a possible destination that may complement the Antarctic trip.

Conclusions

Antarctica represents a destination that may allow visitors to live deep experiences associated with wilderness, remoteness and solitude. In this respect, the images generated may stand for an irreplaceable component of the tourist experience. When analysing expectations about the Antarctic voyage, it can be seen that emotion plays an important role in the satisfaction level achieved. Attributes related to different aspects of Antarctica as a destination reinforced the idea of 'the wild', 'world's end', 'extreme', and 'unique' (see chapters 11 and 12). However, it is important to point out that some experiences in Antarctica turned out to be disappointing as a result of the encounter with other ships and the number of visitors in the area. This feeling of 'crowd' together with the increase in tourism in the Peninsula seem to indicate potential changes in the level of satisfaction with the experience.

Ushuaia appears as one of the most convenient gateways for Antarctic maritime tourism, but it is not currently considered as a destination that may complement the voyage to the Antarctic. In this respect, surveys assigned a high and positive value to it as a potential complementary relationship. However, it could be possible to create an image of Ushuaia related to Antarctica through the development of specific excursions for Antarctic visitors while they stay in Ushuaia before or after their voyage. These tours should deal with themes closely connected with tangible symbols of the Antarctic heritage, since many ties exist between these two places.

References

Bauer, T. (2001) *Tourism in the Antarctic: Opportunities, Constraints, and Future Prospects*, New York: The Haworth Press.

Bigné, E. and Sánchez, M. (2001) 'Evaluación de la imagen de destinos turísticos: una aplicación metodológica en la Comunidad Valenciana', *Revista Europea de Dirección y Economía de la Empresa*, 3: 189–200.

González Bernáldez, F. (1981) *Ecología y Paisaje*, Madrid: Ediciones Blume.

Hall, C.M. (2000) 'The tourist and economic significance of Antarctic travel in Australian and New Zealand Antarctic gateway cities', *Tourism and Hospitality Research: The Surrey Quarterly Review*, 2(2): 157–69.

Instituto Fueguino de Turismo (INFUETUR) (2006) 'Ushuaia Puerta de entrada a la Antártida. Informe sobre el tránsito antártico a través de Ushuaia. Temporada 2006–7', Unpublished, Tourism Board of Tierra del Fuego.

International Association of Antarctica Tour Operators (IAATO) (2007) 'Overview of Antarctic Tourism 2006/2007 Antarctic Season, Information Paper 121', *XXX Antarctic Treaty Consultative Meeting*. Online. Available HTTP: ‹http://www.iaato.org/info.html› (accessed 1 August 2008).

San Martín Gutiérrez, H. (2005) 'Estudio de la imagen del destino turístico y el proceso global de satisfacción: adopción de un enfoque integrador'. Online. Available HTTP: ‹http://www.tesisenxarxa.net/TDX/TDR{_}UC/TESIS/AVAILABLE/TDR-1011106-122314//HSMtesis.pdf › (accessed 1 August 2008).

Vereda, M. (2004) El desarrollo de Ushuaia como puerta de entrada del turismo antártico. Tendencias y competitividad, unpublished thesis, Universidad Internacional de Andalucía.

— (2008) 'Ushuaia – Tierra del Fuego y Antártida: un inventario de recursos susceptibles de uso turístico desde la idea de complementariedad de destinos' *Estudios y Perspectivas en Turismo*, 3/4:199–225.

Wilson, D. and Elder, D. (2000) *Cheltenham in Antarctica. The life of Edward Wilson*, Cheltenham: Reardon Publishing.

Yüksel, A. and Akgül, O. (2007) 'Postcards as effective image makers: an idle agent in destination marketing', *Tourism Management*, 28: 714–25.

14 Business as (un)Usual

Integrated scenario analysis of tourism in Antarctica

Machiel Lamers, Bas Amelung and Jan. H. Stel

Introduction

In 1775, after an unsuccessful 3-year search for the Antarctic continent, Captain James Cook concluded: 'I can be bold to say, that no man will venture farther south than I have done, and that the land which may lie to the south will never be explored' (cited in Landis 2001: 24–25). Being an explorer from the pre-industrial age, James Cook could not have known that the technological and economic developments that followed in the next 225 years would prove his prediction to be wrong. Future forecasts are always informed about what we know about the present and coloured by the position and opinion of the predictor. Predicting the future is difficult for any continent, including Antarctica, particularly because this most remote and isolated continent on the planet has always been relatively untouched by human developments.

The last two decades have seen a rapid development of tourism in Antarctica, with increasing visitor numbers, from a few hundred to almost 45,000 (IAATO 2008), and a diversifying supply of transport modes and activities (see Figure 14.1) (see also chapter 1). It has been argued that in recent years operational strategies in Antarctic tourism have been increasingly dominated by economies of scale, in addition to the traditional niche tourism products (Lamers *et al.* 2008). Antarctica is a special tourism destination for a number of reasons, i.e. the extreme climatic and weather conditions, the short 4- to 5-month season, the unique ecosystems and wildlife populations, the lack of an indigenous population, the limited human (infra)structures and activities, and the successful tailor-made international governance system. These characteristics are often considered intrinsically connected to the Antarctic continent, unchangeable, and independent from external globalisation processes. However, whether these Antarctic conditions remain untouched remains to be seen and cannot be guaranteed.

In view of these developments, many stakeholders and academic authors are becoming concerned about Antarctic tourism. Recent policy discussions at Antarctic Treaty Consultative Meetings (ATCMs) reflect these concerns and focus on the need for additional legal instruments and measures, such as site-specific guidelines and shipping standards, to mitigate some of the negative effects of tourism. A range of authors (e.g. Bastmeijer and Roura 2004; Molenaar

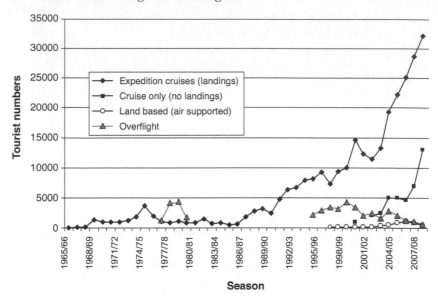

Figure 14.1 Tourists visiting Antarctica in different industry segments 1965–2008

2005; Amelung and Lamers 2006; ASOC 2006) argue that, in addition to these rather reactive measures, a more proactive long-term tourism policy is needed, based on a strategic vision on Antarctic tourism. Recently, the tourism industry and a number of Antarctic Treaty Parties have taken up this idea of a strategic tourism policy vision (Antarctic Treaty System [ATS] 2008; Scully and IAATO 2008; United Kingdom 2008). The development of consistent and plausible scenarios for tourism in Antarctica could play an important role in this policy process.

The future of Antarctic tourism has been systematically studied only a few times before (Bauer 1994, 2001; Snyder 1997). Only once has this led to the drafting of a diverse set of scenarios (Snyder 1997), without receiving much attention from policy-makers and the tourism industry. In many articles, conference presentations and workshop reports on Antarctic tourism, loose snapshots of future visions are given. These visions are usually focused on single issues, such as the growing numbers of tourists or visitor sites, the increasing ship sizes, the creation of land-based tourism facilities and infrastructures, and forms of government-supported tourism (Kershaw 1998; Landau 2000). Many of these visions fail to reach beyond the parameters of the current situation: the 'business-as-usual' of the expedition cruise industry. In many of these visions a moral judgement is included, reflecting stakeholder interests or personal opinion. Different recent development pathways, or single future issues, have never been jointly considered in a consistent way.

The aim of the research presented in this chapter is to develop and analyse Antarctic tourism scenarios based on a combination of future storylines that were developed in a participatory way during three stakeholder workshops and a range of global scenarios. Integrated scenarios combine insights at various levels of scale, from a range of sources, to arrive at a more complete analysis of the future of a system than can be achieved by singular disciplinary approaches or individual opinions. Integrated scenario analysis can provide a valuable tool in the development of a broadly supported long-term Antarctic tourism policy. Cook's error demonstrates the necessity of creating a diversity of future visions that go beyond the 'business-as-usual' of tourism in an unusual part of the world.

The next section introduces the concept of integrated scenario analysis and elaborates on the methodological considerations involved in developing them. We then present the results of our study: four Antarctic tourism scenarios. The chapter then goes on to discuss the validity of the results as well as the relevance and implications for Antarctic tourism policy.

Theoretical and methodological considerations

Integrated scenario analysis

Integrated scenario analysis is a well-established tool to explore the implications of a large range of possible developments (Ringland 1998; Greeuw *et al.* 2000). Scenarios can be defined as 'coherent descriptions of alternative hypothetical futures that reflect different perspectives on past, present and future developments, which can serve as a basis for action' (van Notten *et al.* 2003). The creation of a diverse set of plausible scenarios discovers the uncertainties that are inherent in future studies, so that these can be addressed. In addition, the use of scenarios allows the effectiveness of policy measures and other plans to be 'tested' under a variety of circumstances. Scenarios can be developed as a desktop exercise, but if time and money allow it is often recommendable to develop them in a participatory way to benefit from the knowledge, know-how, creativity and perspectives of a broad range of stakeholders, as well as to stimulate social learning between different stakeholders.

Scenarios are used in a variety of ways and for a range of purposes. Van Notten (2005) classifies scenarios according to the project goal, the process design and the scenario content. In relation to the goal of the scenarios, a distinction is made between exploratory and pre-policy scenarios. Whereas exploratory scenarios are aimed at such ends as learning and investigating the interaction of societal processes, pre-policy scenarios have a strong normative aspect, in that they examine alternative paths to the future that vary according to their desirability. The design of the scenario development process can range from intuitive to analytical. Intuitive designs strongly depend on qualitative insights, whereas analytical approaches regard scenario development as a quantitative modeling exercise. The third dimension of scenarios refers to the level of complexity of their content. Whereas simple scenarios may be limited to extrapolations of isolated trends, complex scenarios take a web of interrelated causes and effects into account. Exploring the many facets of tourism development, capturing different perspectives and opinions, and social learning are key components of the current research project. Therefore, the scenarios developed in this project can be characterised as exploratory, intuitive and complex (Amelung and Lamers 2006).

Typically, scenario processes consist of a number of steps, including:

- The identification of factors, actors and sectors important to the issue at hand;
- The elicitation of a wide range of possible landmark events in the future by using brainstorming techniques;
- The combination of trends, landmark events and possible actor behaviour into 'snippets' or strings of events (storylines) that emphasise the relationships between a limited number of factors;
- The elaboration and recombination of these storylines into full-blown scenarios;
- Discussion of the set of scenarios with the stakeholders, resulting in a set of modified scenarios; and
- Exploration of the opportunities and challenges that these scenarios pose to stakeholders, and identification of strategies to take advantage of them, adapt or mitigate them.

Data collection

The material upon which the analysis of this chapter is based has been elicited during three future workshops and a literature review. Expert knowledge and judgement of the current and future development of Antarctic tourism and its implications were yielded from three stakeholder workshops, including tour operators and expedition staff, policy-makers, NGO representatives, managers of science operations and Antarctic researchers, held in the Netherlands and New Zealand (see Table 14.1 for an overview). A report providing details on the methodology, process and outcomes was prepared for each workshop. Draft workshop reports were sent back to the participants for revisions and consent before finalisation. In case of workshop results reference will be made to the reports, which can be obtained from the authors (Haase and Lamers 2006; Lamers and Amelung 2006; Lamers and Amelung 2007).

Besides the factors and insights gained from stakeholders a literature survey was conducted consisting of articles published in academic journals and books, Antarctic tourism policy documents tabled at the ATCMs, reports of other relevant workshops and meetings, and a number of global scenario studies.

Internal and contextual development factors

Participatory scenario development has taken place in small groups to stimulate the active participation by all stakeholders in the creative process of storyline development and scenario analysis. The groups were generally given great freedom in these tasks, to maximise social learning and to increase the chance of obtaining new and unexpected insights. The factor analysis resulted in the

Table 14.1: Overview of workshops

Date	Country	Objectives of the workshops	Participants
Sept. 29 2005	The Netherlands	Identify important development factors Brainstorm of possible future events Develop future storylines in small groups	17
April 6 2006	New Zealand	Identify important development factors Discuss draft future scenarios, assess feasibility and desirability in small groups Identify policy, industry and NGO responses Address future challenges and concerns	21
Sept. 23 2006	The Netherlands	Discuss draft future scenarios, assess feasibility and desirability in small groups Explore implications for policy, identify policy solutions Address future challenges and concerns	12

conceptualisation of the Antarctic tourism opportunity spectrum (see Figure 14.2) (Lamers *et al.* 2008). The model provides an integrated view on the factors that determine the opportunities for Antarctic tourism development, i.e. accessibility, other resource users, existence of tourist infrastructures, facilities and attractions, operational factors, acceptability of impacts, and regulation and management. By experimenting with different levels and combinations of these internal factors storylines were drafted and revised at consecutive workshops (see (Haase and Lamers 2006; Lamers and Amelung 2006; Lamers and Amelung 2007).

Looking only at factors internal to the Antarctic tourism system was not considered enough. Figure 14.1 indicates that contextual factors, such as global developments, influence the internal factor opportunities for future tourism development in Antarctica. To enlarge our understanding of these global drivers and constraints a number of global scenario studies were consulted. However, a consistent set of global tourism development scenarios is non-existent, with the exception of the 20-year projection of the UNWTO (2001). Therefore, different sets of more general global scenarios were identified suitable for our purpose. Three criteria were used to select global scenarios: the scenarios need to be state of the art and recent; the scenarios need to provide a description of global developments, and the scenarios need to be relevant to our theme. Based on these criteria two sets of scenarios were selected: the Global Environmental Outlook 4 (GEO4) scenarios of UNEP (2007) and the Millennium Ecosystem Assessment (MEA) scenarios (Carpenter *et al.* 2005). The MEA presents four consistent global scenarios focused on the implications for ecosystems, and ecosystem services, around the globe. GEO4 presents four global scenarios in which different interests are dominant, i.e. markets, policy, environment and sustainability.

In the MEA, tourism- and recreation-related issues are mainly used to illustrate possible implications for local ecosystems; none of these illustrations includes implications for Antarctic or polar ecosystems. The GEO4 scenarios contain a section describing the polar regions in which implications for the ATS, climate changes, fisheries and wildlife are detailed. Limited attention is given to tourism

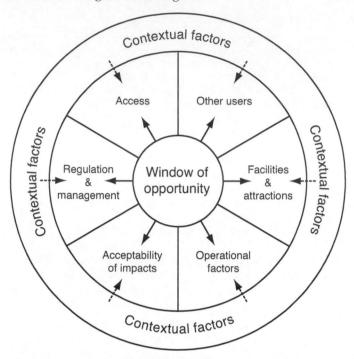

Figure 14.2 Overview of factors influencing future Antarctic tourism development
opportunities

and Antarctica, but both scenario studies can provide important contextual input. Following Huynen (2008), who performed an integrated scenario analysis for globalisation and health, the global scenarios were clustered into four main scenario themes (ST) (Huynen 2008). An overview of the main characteristics, differences and similarities is given in Table 14.2

The factor model of Figure 14.1 functioned as a conceptual framework for an assessment, whereby the role of the main tourism development factors was analysed in a matrix under influence of the clustered global scenario directions. The storylines developed and revised by Antarctic tourism stakeholders during the workshops were coupled with the matrix, leading to Antarctic tourism scenarios. The focus of our analysis is to look at a time horizon of 25 years, so up to 2030, despite the fact that both the MEA and GEO4 scenarios extend this horizon. The results are presented in the following section.

Scenarios

Coupling the main development factors from the Antarctic Tourism Opportunity Spectrum with the global ST results in a matrix in which the relations are indicated on a five-point scale (from very negative relation (–), to neutral (+/-), to very positive relation (++)) (Table 14.3).

Table 14.2: Global scenarios generally clustered by theme (adapted from Huynen (2008))

Scenario theme	Variation in scenario outcome	Scenarios
1. Globalisation with a market focus	Low mitigation capacity of economic and technological development; social and environmental problems largely remain or increase.	–Markets First (MF-GEO4)
	High mitigation capacity of economic and technological development; social and environmental problems largely decrease.	–Global Orchestration (GO-MEA)
2. Globalisation with a sustainability focus	Rapid progress towards sustainability; wider-ranging societal transformation.	–Sustainability First (SF-GEO4)
	Slow progress towards sustainability; -policy-driven approach with mixed results -green technologies but neglect of social issues.	–Policy First (PF-GEO4) –TechnoGarden (TG-MEA)
3. Fragmentation with a market focus	Threats of global terrorism, growing income disparity, global migration, forces wealthy nations to take protective measures and secure national resources.	–Security First (SF-GEO4) –Order from Strength (OS-MEA)
4. Fragmentation with a sustainability focus	Human societies will focus more on learning about survival and adaptation to major socio-ecological changes on the local level.	Adapting Mosaic (AM-MEA)

Table 14.3 Scenario matrix defining some of the main differences between the scenarios

FACTOR CATEGORY	ST 1.	ST 2.	ST 3.	ST 4.
1) Accessibility factors	++	+	–	+/–
–Availability of expedition cruise ships	+	+	–	+/–
–Availability of large cruise liners	++	+	++	—
–Availability of infrastructure for air links	++	–	+	+/–
–Occurrence of information/media attention	++	+	–	—
–Ability of tourists to cover travel costs	++	+	–	+/–
2) Relations with other users	++	+	–	+
–Occurrence of logistical cooperation	+	+/–	—	++
–Compatibility of tourism with other users	+/–	++	—	+
3). Presence of key attractions	++	–	+	–
–Availability of interesting sites/wildlife	–	+	—	++
–Occurrence of adventure activities	+	+	+/–	++
4) Presence of on-site facilities	++	–	+	+/–
–Availability of accommodation	++	–	+	+/–
–Occurence of on-site managing facilities	+	—	+/–	+
4) Operational factors	+/–	++	—	+
–High number and diversity of operations	++	+	–	+
–Availability of quality staff and crew	–	+	—	++
5) Level of impact	++	–	++	—
–Occurrence of environmental impact	++	–	+	+/–
–Occurrence of human risk/SAR incapability	++	–	+	+/–
–Erosion of intrinsic value	++	–	++	+/–
6) Presence of regulation	—	++	—	–
–Comprehensiveness of ATS regulation	–	++	—	+/–
–Level of self-regulation among operators	+/–	++	—	++

The storyline material from the workshops was used to analyse and flesh up this conceptual frame into full-blown scenarios. The next paragraphs present the results of this analysis.

Four Antarctic Futures

The sky is the limit: globalisation with a market focus

This scenario is based on the following storylines: 'SOS Antarctica' (Lamers and Amelung 2006), 'Increasing interest/high risk and incidents' (Haase and Lamers 2006) and 'The sky is the limit' (Lamers and Amelung 2007). In the Global Orchestration (GO-MEA) and Markets First (MF-GEO) scenarios, the focus is largely global, with commercial interests prevailing over other issues. In the GO-MEA scenario the tourism industry is mentioned both as a victim of ecosystem degradation resulting from activities of other industries, and as one of the culprits, especially in coastal regions. Industrialised lifestyles are promoted through travel and tourism and air travel becomes highly affordable for middle-income citizens around the world. Technological innovation, economic growth and urbanisation are high in these scenarios. Invasive species and infectious diseases are increasing and impacting global tourism mobility. The GO-MEA and the MF-GEO differ in their elaboration of the role of global political cooperation and the scenario outcome.

Conditions described in this scenario group provide excellent prospects for global tourism developments, including Antarctic tourism. Access will greatly improve as a result of growing global affluence, improved information and communication technology, affordable long-haul travel, improved infrastructure and transport technology. New tourist-generating markets will be developed, including South America, China, India and Russia. Market forces will open up the Antarctic for fisheries, mineral exploitation, and an increasing diversity of tourism ventures. A number of National Antarctic programmes privatise their infrastructures, making it easier for tour operators to acquire access to accommodation and air strips. Larger-scale operations, such as cruise liners and large expedition ships, will eventually prevail over smaller-scale expedition cruise vessels as these prove less economic to build and to operate in the Antarctic Peninsula. Land-based tourists will be catered for in a series of ecolodges, based on the best environmental standards, and transported to and from the South American continent by aircraft and ferries. On King George Island a passenger-handling facility will be developed to organise the transfers. A wide range of adventurous and experiential tourist products is developed alongside. As well as cooperative corporate players, increasing numbers of private actors will be active, beyond effective legal control, such as yachts and adventurers. Niche tourism operators will venture deeper into the Antarctic wilderness, and the opportunities for land-based tourism will increase because of the presence of new commercial resource users and available polar technology. Intrinsic Antarctic wilderness values will further erode as a consequence as the Antarctic is increasingly seen as a resource for humans. The current self-regulatory system will be overwhelmed and different industry segments will establish their own cooperative associations to guarantee safety and minimise environmental degradation. The changing scale and structure of the industry increase the risks of incidents and resulting impacts. Cumulative impacts are increasingly detectible on landing sites and nearby facilities because of larger-scale operations. On the other hand, search-and-rescue capabilities within the Peninsula will also develop. Climatic changes continue to affect the Antarctic Peninsula, resulting in biodiversity loss and invasive species. Nevertheless, the acceptability of impact will be higher as a result of other industries with enormous impacts. The growing and diverging interests of different stakeholder groups create increasing difficulties for the ATS to come up with restrictive and binding measures to regulate tourism. Global commercial interest will gradually increase the number of members of the ATS; however, the tourism debate is pushed to the background. It is estimated that by 2030 approximately 250,000 tourists will visit Antarctica.

Business as (un)usual: globalisation with a sustainability focus

This scenario is based on: 'Polar Profit' (Lamers and Amelung 2006), 'Increasing interest/low risk and incidents' (Haase and Lamers 2006), 'High environmental awareness/low risk and incidents' (Haase and Lamers 2006) and 'Business as Unusual' (Lamers and Amelung 2007). Three scenarios have been categorised under this theme: Policy First (PF-GEO), Sustainability First (SF-GEO) and TechnoGarden (TG-MEA). In these scenarios a globalisation trend is combined with a strong role of government to safeguard social and environmental issues, based on more equitable values and in some cases supported by new institutions. Global companies that preempt sustainability policies are seen as role models, including tourism companies. With the help of global NGOs and governments, tourism initiatives are taken worldwide for the conservation of ecosystems and wildlife. Urban environments are reorganised to create more green spaces. Technological innovations will facilitate global travel and communication for civil society, global companies and organisations. A global climate policy is adopted that strongly mitigates GHG and slows down the warming trends in the polar regions.

Both global tourism and the Antarctic environment will most likely continue to bloom under this scenario. The media attention for climate change and polar science will continue to keep the Antarctic on the radar screen of many consumers in the world. Economic growth in most Antarctic tourist-generating markets will continue steadily. Tourist numbers will continue to grow as the global consumer becomes aware of Antarctic tourism products, but activities will be more constrained and carefully controlled. Oil prices and the global climate change policy will contribute significantly to the travel costs of tourists travelling to the south and mitigate some of the demand for Antarctic travel. Consumers are not put off by these rising costs and are willing to pay for an Antarctic experience. The ATS recognises the unique Antarctic wilderness values and makes wilderness preservation its most prominent objective, whereby large parts of the continent will be preserved, large-scale commercial activities and commercial land-based infrastructures strongly regulated. The modus operandi of the tourism industry will remain largely ship based, with cooperation being an important value. The fleet of current expedition cruise ships will be replaced by purpose-built polar vessels with high eco-efficient performance. The tourist industry will continue to diversify into different ship-based and small-scale land-based products. Cruise-only itinerary products will develop alongside expedition cruising. Impacts of tourism remain low as a result of proactive management guidelines and effective emergency response. Pressure on industry self-regulation is mounting but through supporting policies of the ATS it remains an important vehicle for control in the field. Part of the revenues generated by tour companies will be contributed to a fund managed by the ATS for monitoring and conservation of the Antarctic. The result is that Antarctic tourists are increasingly seen as ambassadors for Antarctic conservation. The role of ATS policy increases with active monitoring programmes and strategic policies, enforced by a combination of the tourist industry and observers. It is estimated that by 2030 around 150,000 tourists visit Antarctica.

Cold hostage: fragmentation with a market focus

This scenario is based on: 'Negotiation' (Lamers and Amelung 2006), and elements of 'High environmental awareness, low risk and incidents' (Haase and Lamers 2006), 'Go large, go small, or go home' (Lamers and Amelung 2007). In the SF-GEO and Order from Strength (OS-MEA) scenarios the world becomes compartmentalised resulting from an inward and nationalistic focus in response to threats of global terrorism, migration from developing countries, and resource protection. The liberal democratic nation is considered the best protection against these threats and wealthy nations are securing their natural resources and citizens from outside influences by closing the borders. National security measures in the rich countries will not be beneficial for the global tourism industry, because of reduced mobility and degradation of natural attractions because of lack of funds. A new world order arises of three blocs: the Americas; Europe and Africa; and Asia.

In the first decade tourist numbers and diversity of activities will further increase. Smaller expedition cruise operators are being bought out by large global cruise companies. Eventually these smaller vessels disappear from the scene and are being replaced by larger and more luxurious cruise vessels. A growing number of these large cruise companies start operating outside the self-regulating framework of the industry association. This leads to increased risks for environmental impact and safety. During the second decade access to Antarctica will decline as a result of rising fuel costs and national protection measures by some of the claimant gateway states. Antarctic Treaty Parties start grappling with the enormous resources that are stored in the Antarctic, including oil and fresh water. A number of large multinationals, including a few tourism companies, manage to secure access by negotiating with the respective governments. This has major implications for the ATS that eventually collapses under the rivalry between claimant states, and between claimant and non-claimant states. This whole development will lead to a major media campaign of ENGOs. Fishing and mineral exploitation takes off, leading to permanent infrastructures and residence of workers. Tourism companies will be given certain sectors of the Peninsula region where they can undertake their activities without disturbance from the other resource users. Other resource uses will prevail over tourism activities. However, elite groups from the rich northern countries will most likely continue to be interested by Antarctic niche tourism products, such as small-scale land-based activities or expedition cruising. Permanent residence in the Antarctic becomes a status symbol for some of the world's wealthiest people. As a result of the presence of more exploitative industries the acceptability of impacts will increase.

Special interest tourism: fragmentation with a sustainability focus

This scenario is based on: 'Special interest tourism' (Lamers and Amelung 2007). In the Adapting Mosaic (AM-MEA) scenario human societies will focus more and more on learning about human survival and adaptation to major socioecological changes on the local level. On the one hand, trade barriers will increase, but information and communication barriers, on the other hand, will disappear as a result of innovations in information technology. The role of civil society grows and the emergence of partnerships between NGOs and industry, and NGOs and governments.

In this scenario, Antarctic issues, including tourism, will continue in their current state without much influence from global drivers. No major investments are made in tourism infrastructure and logistics. The main operational modus remains a combination of small-scale ship- and land-based activities. Media attention for Antarctica will most likely fade, and for some countries Antarctic science will most likely cease to exist, as nations are too self-absorbed or focused on regional cooperation. For the science programmes that stay cooperation with tour operators is essential to secure affordable and effective logistics. Smaller-scale Antarctic tourism niche products, both ship- and land-based, will increase the prices significantly and they will be affordable only for rich and purist travellers. As no major international regulatory efforts are made, self-regulation will be the key, with a continued important role for an industry association in managing tourism and other non-governmental activities.

Stakeholder responses and policy implications

During the future workshops, underlying this scenario analysis, it was stressed that the history of Antarctic tourism cannot be seen as a linear trend but is characterised by unpredictable feedback effects, events and incidents. Nobody could foresee the availability of ice-strengthened vessels for the tourism market after the collapse of the Soviet Union driving the development of tourism in the 1990s.

Several times tour operators and policy-makers have been confronted with accidents, causing impacts for science programmes or Antarctic ecosystems, such as the sinking of the *Bahia Paraiso* in 1989 and the recent sinking of the MS *Explorer,* leading to discussion about the future. It makes stakeholders realise how open the future of tourism in this continent is. Nobody knows what might happen if a large cruise liner sank in the Antarctic, or if it is possible to stop a large international hotel chain from building a hotel in the Antarctic. We will probably never be able to fully understand the scale of consequences of these dystopias and discontinuities.

However, the scenarios do point our attention to a number of important issues. Many stakeholders voice their concern for particular potential developments or events. A prominent feature in most scenarios is the increase in tourist arrivals, albeit the growth rates will likely vary substantially. Regardless of the uncertainties involved, increasing growth in tourist numbers seems to be almost inevitable. This may have implications that go beyond the tourist industry, as tourism growth has been linked to increasing environmental pressure and catastrophic impacts. Second, growth does not necessarily mean more of the same, as the scenarios show. The nature or form of tourism activities and tourism logistics in Antarctica might shift substantially: from medium-sized expedition vessels to large cruise liners and from ship-based to land-based tourism, serviced by air links. During the workshops suggestions were typically made to make the storylines more extreme in the form and scale of Antarctic tourism. The scenarios emphasise that Antarctic tourism is not a closed regional system, but a global industry influenced by many global developments, such as economic growth in traditional and new demand regions, terrorism and climate change. International water and energy shortages, as well as biological invasions and the spread of disease, might have a great influence on the destiny of Antarctic tourism development. The supply side of tourism is also highly influenced by external factors, such as corporate take-overs, marketing, energy prices, and media attention. Some of the scenarios allude to the inherent tensions in the structure of the tourist industry by featuring 'rogue entrepreneurs' who upset the self-regulatory system or work outside ATS regulations. Strict self-regulation measures increase the incentives for tour operators to withdraw from IAATO or to refrain from joining in the first place. The scenarios address the challenge of self-regulation to maximise compliance, yet minimise the risk of defection.

The scenarios suggest that a more active involvement by the ATS is warranted, starting with the development of a strategic vision on tourism in Antarctica. Scenario development can support this process, by exploring salient uncertainties and incorporating a broad range of stakeholders and perspectives. Scenarios provide a framework for discussing the implications of a wide range of plausible future developments and the effectiveness of different responses to address them. The 'what-if' exercises that are made possible by scenarios do not decrease the fundamental uncertainties in any way, but they allow policy-makers and stakeholders to explore and prepare for a wide range of eventualities. Scenario development is an iterative process, going back and forth between the identification of relevant factors, the development of limited strings of events, and the recombination of these storylines into full-blown consistent scenarios. Taking into account our short-sightedness regarding the future and analysing previous future studies it becomes clear that if we want to build a proactive policy for Antarctic tourism, based on accurate information, future assessments should be part of this policy, repeated every 5 to 10 years.

Coupling the storylines developed and assessed during three future workshops with the main characteristics of global scenarios highlights a number of interesting points. To start, most storylines and other visions presented in the literature of future Antarctic tourism seem to fit best in the two ST characterised by globalisation. This suggests that most stakeholders in our project assume that global developments will be driven by globalisation, and that the future pathways of fragmentation are not seriously considered. Also, there is a notable difference between the future visions expressed in the literature and the storylines developed during participatory future workshops. During workshops in which a mixture of stakeholder groups participate future visions tend to frame the issue on the collective level instead of on the level of a particular stakeholder group. Logically, disregarding the individual interests there is a high level of agreement on the level of the collective interest. For the development of longer-term Antarctic tourism policy organising sufficient meetings where relevant stakeholder groups are able to exchange ideas on these collective interests seems to be a key issue.

Many important issues in the development of Antarctic tourism can potentially be anticipated using scenarios, but we have to acknowledge that simultaneously many factors remain uncertain and unexplained. Many of the global scenarios, particularly the GEO4 scenarios, were designed to address trends in issues of poverty, and inequalities of resource access. In many of these scenarios human societies are facing major problems whereby tourism, and especially tourism to destinations like Antarctica, would be the last thing on their mind. Antarctic tourism, so far, is really an issue of the richest people in the world and can hardly be discussed in the frame of these issues. On the other hand we could argue that there will probably always be groups of rich people doing whatever rich people do, like going to remote exotic destinations. Whether other groups in the world will also be able to visit Antarctica in the future remains uncertain. It can also be questioned whether the development of tourism in the Antarctic is based on the same principles as anywhere else in the world, and can be effectively studied using global scenarios.

Scenarios remain stereotypical depictions, whereas many of the issues could be playing at the same time, for example trends of globalisation and fragmentation could be occurring at the same time depending on your perspective. This study could have benefited enormously from a consistent and plausible set of global tourism scenarios, but this is currently missing from the literature. We feel that developing and analysing global tourism scenarios would be worthwhile and is certainly a research recommendation coming from this study.

Conclusions

Tourism has grown and diversified substantially over the past 2 decades. Realising that a certain level of coordination would be beneficial for the tourist industry as a whole, the Antarctic tour operators founded IAATO, which subsequently developed a system of self-regulation. This arrangement has produced satisfactory results so far, but it may come under increased stress in the future as a result of tensions among IAATO partners or the emergence of issues that simply cannot be solved by a sectoral organisation such as IAATO.

We believe the global scenarios analysed in the previous section have proven valuable in the context of Antarctic tourism for analysing important issues, uncertainties, and risks that might become more prominent in the future, such as the development of land-based tourism infrastructures and air travel, the appearance of rogue operators, and the robustness of self-regulation. In addition, it becomes clear that in terms of potential tourist demand the limits have not been reached, both in the traditional and in potentially new Antarctic tourist markets, resulting from growing affluence (in all scenarios), growing world populations, ageing (in all scenarios), and technological innovations. Further, the scenarios point at a number of global developments that might lead to new commercial and industrial interests, and opportunities or deadlocks for its current activities, including energy shortages, water shortages, and global terrorism. GEO4 scenarios even suggest that global drivers could eventually collapse the ATS.

Finally, the ATS is currently exploring ways to address many of the risks and changes presented in this chapter in the form of a strategic vision for Antarctic tourism. Policy-makers and other stakeholders have to realise that change is under way. Scenarios can be used to develop a strategic vision and take a proactive approach by setting policies and limits that will safeguard intrinsic Antarctic values and ecosystems for future generations.

References

Amelung, B. and M. Lamers (2006) 'Scenario development for Antarctic tourism: exploring the uncertainties,' *Polarforschung,* 2–3: 133–39.

Antarctic Treaty System (ATS) (2008) Final Report of the XXXI ATCM Kyiv, Ukraine.

Antarctic and Southern Ocean Coalition (ASOC) (2006) IP120 Strategic Issues Posed by Commercial Tourism in the Antarctic Treaty Area. Antarctic Treaty Consultative Meeting XXIX, Edinburgh, United Kingdom.

Bastmeijer, C. and Roura, R. (2004) 'Regulating Antarctic tourism and the precautionary principle', *The American Journal of International Law,* 98: 763 – 781.

Bauer, T. (1994) 'The future of commercial tourism in Antarctica', *Annals of Tourism Research,* 21: 410–13.

Bauer, T. G. (2001) *Tourism in the Antarctic: Opportunities, Constraints, and Future Prospects,* New York: The Haworth Hospitality Press.

Carpenter, S., Pingali, P., Bennett, E.M. and Zurek, M.B. (eds) (2005) *Ecosystems and Human Well-being: Scenarios,* Vol. 2, Millennium Ecosystem Assessment, Washington DC: Island Press.

Greeuw, S., Van Asselt, M. Grosskurth, J., Storms, C., Rijkens-Klomp, N., Rothman, D.S. and Rotmans, J. (2000) Cloudy crystal balls: an assessment of recent European and global scenario studies and models, European Environment Agency Environmental Issues Series 17, Luxembourg: Office for Official Publications of the European Communities.

Haase, D. and Lamers, M. (2006) *The Future Governance of Antarctic Tourism*. Workshop Report Maastricht/Christchurch: ICIS/Gateway Antarctica.

Headland, R. (1994) 'Historical development of Antarctic tourism', *Annals of Tourism Research*, 21: 269–80.

Headland, R.K. (2009) *A Chronology of Antarctic Exploration. A Synopsis of Events and Activities from the Earliest Times until the International Polar Years, 2007-09*. London: Bernard Quaritch.

Huynen, M. (2008) *Future Health in a Globalising World*. Maastricht: Universitaire Pers.

International Association of Antarctica Tour Operators (IAATO) (2005). IAATO Overview of Antarctic Tourism 2004/05 Antarctic Season. Antarctic Treaty Consultancy Meeting XXVIII, Stockholm, Sweden.

— (2006) IAATO Overview of Antarctic Tourism 2005–6 Antarctic Season. Antarctic Treaty Consultative Meeting XXIX 2006, Edinburgh – United Kingdom.

— (2007) IP121 IAATO Overview of Antarctic Tourism 2006–7 Antarctic Season. XXX Antarctic Treaty Consultative Meeting, New Delhi.

— (2008) IP85 IAATO Overview of Antarctic Tourism 2007–8 Antarctic Season and Preliminary Estimates for 2008–9 Antarctic Season. Antarctic Treaty Consultative Meeting, Kyiv, Ukraine.

Kershaw, A. (1998) Destination Last Wilderness. Antarctica 2010: A Notebook. Proceedings of the Antarctic Futures Workshop 28–30 April 1998. Christchurch: Antarctica New Zealand.

Lamers, M. and Amelung, B. (2006) The Future of Tourism in Antarctica. Workshop Report Maastricht University, ICIS.

— (2007) *Tourism in Antarctica: Scenarios for 2030*. Maastricht, International Centre for Integrated assessment and Sustainable development.

Lamers, M., Haase, D. and Amelung, B. (2008) 'Facing the elements: analysing trends in Antarctic Tourism', *Tourism Review*, 63(1): 15–27.

Landau, D. (2000) Tourism Scenarios. Proceedings of the Antarctic Tourism Workshop. Christchurch, Antarctica New Zealand.

Landis, M. J. (2001) *Antarctica: Exploring the Extreme*, Chicago: Review Press Inc.

Molenaar, E. J. (2005) 'Sea-borne tourism in Antarctica: avenues for further intergovernmental regulation', *International Journal for Marine and Coastal Law,* 20: 247–95.

Ringland, G. (1998) *Scenario Planning*, Chichester: John Wiley & Sons.

Scully, T. and IAATO (2008) IP19 Chairman's Report from the Miami Meeting (March 17–19, 2008) on Antarctic Tourism. Antarctic Treaty Consultative Meeting, Kyiv, Ukraine.

Snyder, J. (1997) *Alternative Future for Tourism to Antarctica – and a Preliminary Assessment of their Resource Management Implications*, Littleton: Strategic Studies, Inc.

United Nations Environment Programme (UNEP) (2007) *Global Environmental Outlook 4*, London: Earthscan.

United Kingdom (2008) Developing a Strategic Vision of Antarctic Tourism for the next Decade. Antarctic Treaty Consultative Meeting, Kyiv, Ukraine.

Van Notten, P. (2005) *Writing on the Wall: Scenario Development in Times of Discontinuity*, Boca Raton: Dissertation.com.

van Notten, P., Rotmans, J., van Asselt, M. and Rothman, D. (2003) 'An updated scenario typology', *Futures,* 35: 423–43.

World Tourism Organization (UNWTO) (2001) *Tourism 2020 Vision: Global Forecasts and Profiles of Market Segments*, Vol. 7, Madrid: World Tourism Organisation.

15 Tourism, Conservation and Visitor Management in the Sub-Antarctic Islands

C. Michael Hall and Sandra Wilson

Introduction

Consisting of 22 major islands and island groups, the sub-Antarctic islands number some 800 individual islands and have an area double that of the Hawaiian island group (Clark and Dingwall 1985). All are oceanic, far from continental land masses and each other, with climates strongly influenced by the Southern Ocean, which surrounds them. Although the sub-Antarctic islands are relatively species poor, they provide breeding and moulting grounds for large numbers of marine mammals and avifauna and have a high degree of endemism because of their geographical and ecological isolation (Chown et al. 1998, 2001). The location of the islands means that they are often romanticised for their isolation and naturalness. For example, Higham (1991: 58) writes of them as being among the last 'bastions of nature in a world beset by massive and rapid change through human activity'.

The isolation of the sub-Antarctic islands means that they are ideally suited as refuge for threatened plants and animals; however, as the island biota is often specialised, it is consequently highly vulnerable to external disturbance, especially human-induced impacts such as tourism visitation (Frenot et al. 2005; chapter 2). Over a quarter of a century ago Clark and Dingwall (1985: 4) described the situation facing the islands:

> Experience reveals that the natural environments of these southern oceanic islands are readily disturbed and destroyed but virtually impossible to rehabilitate or replace...managers have an awesome responsibility to secure island protected areas against the deleterious influences of man. In recent years the expansion of commercial interests in fishing, mineral exploration and tourism, and increased scientific activity, are inexorably eroding the isolation of the southern islands and pose problems for their effective management as protected areas
>
> (Clark and Dingwall 1985: 4).

Although not so well recognised as tourism on the Antarctic continent, sub-Antarctic visitation has also been increasing since the late 1980s (Hall 1993; Hall and

McArthur 1993; Hall and Wouters 1994; Wouters and Hall 1995a, 1995b; Ingham and Summers 2002; Glass, and Ryan 2003; Molenaar 2005; Landau 2007; Tracey 2007; Lamers *et al.* 2008; chapter 1 [this volume]). Visitors to the sub-Antarctic islands appear generally propelled by the same motivations as visitors to the Antarctic: the wilderness and isolation of the sub-Antarctic islands, their wildlife, and the brief, but highly exploitative, human history (chapter 12). However, sub-Antarctic tourism has additional components that do not occur in Antarctic tourism management. The major difference between Antarctica and the sub-Antarctic islands is the pattern of jurisdiction. Whereas Antarctica is administered under the Antarctic Treaty System, the sub-Antarctic islands are administered by individual nations. Some of the islands in the sub-Antarctic also have a permanent or semi-permanent human population aside from research staff, for example, on the Falklands, Tristan da Cunha and South Georgia (Table 15.1), whose inhabitants also participate in recreational and local tourism activities.

Although, the sub-Antarctic islands are sovereign territories, the management strategies brought to bear in visitor management are still relevant to the Antarctic situation and to the broader issues of tourism management in polar regions. It has been suggested that the tourism management and conservation strategies that have been developed for the sub-Antarctic may have application in other polar areas (Davis 1999). This chapter examines the nature of sub-Antarctic tourism, its impacts, and management. The chapter is divided into four main sections. First, it defines which islands constitute the sub-Antarctic. Second, it identifies the institutional arrangements for conservation on the islands, with particular reference to international heritage agreements. Third, it discusses tourism and visitation in the sub-Antarctic islands, including an overview of the tourism policies and management strategies that have been put in place to control visitation in the various sub-Antarctic territories. Finally, the chapter concludes with a discussion of the sub-Antarctic tourism management regime and its future prospects and issues.

Definition and characteristics

The sub-Antarctic islands lie close to the Antarctic Convergence in the Southern Ocean, an important oceanographic boundary where cold water from the ocean to the south meets warmer water from the north (Selkirk *et al.* 1990). The northern boundary of the sub-Antarctic region is known as the Subtropical Convergence, where the surface waters of the Southern Ocean meet the warmer subtropical waters of the Pacific, Indian, and South Atlantic Oceans. The southern boundary is known as the Antarctic Convergence. Various systems of classifying these southern islands have been used, based on latitudinal, climatic or vegetational criteria. The classification of the island areas discussed in this chapter are derived from Clark and Dingwall (1985), who used the term Insulantarctica from the work of Udvardy (1975) on Antarctic biogeography, comprising the sub-Antarctic, maritime Antarctic and cool temperate islands (Table 15.1):

Table 15.1: Sub-Antarctic island characteristics

Island Group	Sovereignty	Permanent Population / Occupants	Total Area km²	Year Round Snow-Free Area km²	Maximum Elevation m	Latitude °South	Biogeographical Classification
South Georgia	UK (British Overseas territory)	20–35 (111)[b]	3755	1500	2934	54	Sub-Antarctic
South Sandwich	UK (British Overseas Territory)	0[c]	618	85	1370	56–59	Maritime Antarctic
Tristan da Cunha	UK (part of the British overseas territory of Saint Helena, Ascension and Tristan da Cunha)	270[a] Gcugh Island has a meteorological station	111	111	2060	37	Cool Temperate
Gough Island	UK (part of the British overseas territory of Saint Helena, Ascension and Tristan da Cunha)	8 (South African weather station)[c]	65	–	910	40	Cool Temperate
Falkland Islands	UK (British Overseas Territory)	3,200[a]	13000	–	705	51–52	Cool Temperate
Bouvetoya	Norway	0[c]	50	4	780	54	Maritime Antarctic
Prince Edward & Marion	South Africa	14 (51)[a]	335	335	1230	46	Sub-Antarctic
Iles Amsterdam	France	25 (40)[a]	55	–	911	37	Cool Temperate
Iles Saint-Paul	France	0	7	–	272	38	Cool Temperate
Iles Crozet	France	30 (50)[a]	233	233	934	46	Sub-Antarctic
Iles Kerguelen	France	70 (125)[b]	3626	2900	1960	49	Sub-Antarctic
Heard &MacDonald	Australia	0[c]	380+	70	2745	53	Sub-Antarctic
Macquarie	Australia (Tasmania)	25 (60)[a]	118	118	433	54	Sub-Antarctic
Antipodes Islands	New Zealand	0[c]	22	22	402	49	Cool Temperate
Auckland Islands	New Zealand	0[c]	625	525	660	50	Cool Temperate
Bounty Islands	New Zealand	0[c]	1.35	1.35	73	47	Cool Temperate
Campbell Islands	New Zealand	0[c]	113.3	113.3	560	52	Cool Temperate
The Snares	New Zealand	0[c]	3.5	3.5	130	48	Cool Temperate

Notes: a) approximate permanent population; b) approximate maximum number year round, total approximate number of annual occupants including non-tourist visitors in brackets (in part adapted from Chown et al. 1998; de Villiers et al. 2005); c) no accurate figures available for average approximate number of annual occupants including non-tourist visitors.

- *Cool temperate,* the northern limit of which is approximately the Subtropical Convergence and the southern limit of which is the north of the Antarctic Convergence;
- *Sub-Antarctic islands* in the vicinity of the Antarctic Convergence; and
- *Maritime Antarctic islands* which are appreciably south of the Antarctic Convergence, but outside the Antarctic Treaty Area (see Figure 1.1).

This chapter uses the term sub-Antarctic to embrace all these island groups. However, although the concept of grouping the world's southern islands is useful for defining ecologically based conservation regions and political relations in the Southern Ocean, it is extremely broad with respect to the wide-ranging climate, oceanographic, biological and institutional factors that characterise these islands. However, this characterisation facilitates the analysis and discussion of management, in particular for tourism, of the islands in the Southern Ocean (Hall 1992a, 1993; Hall and Wouters 1994; Wouters and Hall 1995a, 1995b; Tracey, 2007).

The sub-Antarctic islands are regarded as generally including Iles Crozet, Macquarie Island, Marion Island and Prince Edward Island to the north of the Antarctic Convergence; Heard Island, MacDonald Island and South Georgia to the south; and Iles Kerguelen, which straddles it. These islands experience cool, wet, windy conditions, with considerable variation in daylight hours between summer and winter. North of the islands above the sub-Antarctic lie the cool temperate islands: Antipodes, Auckland, Bounty, Campbell and Snares Islands in the New Zealand region; the Falkland Islands; Gough, Inaccessible, Nightingale and Tristan da Cunha Islands in the Southern Atlantic Ocean; and Iles Amsterdam and Iles St Paul in the southern Indian Ocean. The South Sandwich Islands and Bouvetøya are regarded as maritime Antarctic islands (Walton 1985; Selkirk *et al.* 1990).

The islands range widely in their latitudinal extent, from the Tristan da Cunha group at latitude 37°S and north of the Subtropical Convergence, to the South Shetland Islands, at latitude 62°S and enclosed by pack-ice for much of the year. The Southern Ocean has a strong influence on their ecosystems. The remoteness of the islands, the often limited areas available for establishment and the cold summers have all tended to limit biodiversity in both the flora and fauna (Walton 1985). Consequently, the islands have extremely important conservation values, particularly as refuges for rare and threatened species. However, the islands are also vulnerable to loss through disturbance and are difficult to restore (Molloy and Dingwall 1990; Frenot *et al.* 2005; de Villiers *et al.* 2006).

The conservation significance of the Sub-Antarctic Islands

Maintenance of the island ecosystems in their natural state is of great importance to global conservation and science as they provide significant benchmarks with which to examine the effects of global environmental change and because of their wider role as habitat for Southern Ocean biota. However, there are considerable difficulties in managing them to preserve their uniqueness (Selkirk *et al.* 1990;

Glass and Ryan 2003; de Villiers 2006). Their isolation was their best protection for many millennia; however, that remoteness and wildlife are making them increasingly attractive for nature-based and adventure tourism, as well as becoming part of Antarctic maritime tourism itineraries, with limited air access also available to the Falklands. Commercial tourism is also allowed in all island groups except the Prince Edward Islands and some of the islands of the five New Zealand groups, with the potential that environmental impacts are mitigated by various restrictions, including the limitation of visitor access to certain zones and in some cases, to certain islands in a group (Department of Conservation 1998; de Villiers *et al.* 2005; Tracey 2007). However, even in those islands where commercial tourism is restricted there are opportunities for visits from private yachts as part of leisure trips (Wouters and Hall 1995a, b). Table 15.2 provides an overview of some of the institutional aspects of conservation management in the islands.

Many of the sub-Antarctic islands have already suffered considerably from human exploitation as a result of marine wildlife harvesting in the 19th and early 20th centuries. Regimes to reduce this impact have been put in place, but whereas in the Antarctic implementation of such a regime is difficult because of its unique transnational structure, it is paradoxically complex in the sub-Antarctic *because* of the number of sovereign nations and lack of a single enforcement agency (Wouters and Hall 1995a). However, international cooperation in the region has proven to be of great conservation value. For example, the joint Scientific Committee on Antarctic Research (SCAR)/IUCN workshop on the biological basis for conservation of sub-Antarctic islands encouraged national authorities to develop and implement conservation policies and plans, devised specifically for each island or island group, that consider more fully the control of the human impact on the natural ecosystem, including the use of national authority observers on commercial tours (Walton 1985). To a great extent, as this chapter demonstrates, this has been achieved. Significantly, the workshop recommended that national authorities be encouraged to consider which areas might be proposed for international designation as World Heritage Sites or Biosphere Reserves, measures that have also been substantially adopted.

As Table 15.2 indicates, the islands not only have protected status under international law but also have achieved a considerable profile under international heritage agreements, a factor which may also be significant for their longer-term attractiveness as tourist destinations (Hall 1992b; Hall and Piggin 2002). As of October 2010 there were four World Heritage Sites in the sub-Antarctic islands: Gough and Inaccessible Islands, Heard and MacDonald Islands, Macquarie Island and the New Zealand sub-Antarctic islands (Antipodes Islands, Auckland Islands, Bounty Islands, Campbell Islands, The Snares). Prince Edward and Marion Islands are on South Africa's list of indicative World Heritage Sites (Table 15.3 provides details of the sites). Macquarie Island is also a Biosphere Reserve under the United Nations Educational, Scientific and Cultural Organization (UNESCO) Man and the Biosphere (MAB) programme established in 1977, the same year that the island was listed. Biosphere reserves are protected areas that are designed to show a balanced relationship between human use and nature conservation as

Table 15.2: Sub-Antarctic island institutional arrangements for conservation management

Island Group	National conservation measures	World Heritage Site	Biosphere Reserve	RAMSAR Sites	Marine Reserves	Environmental Impact Assessment required for major developments
South Georgia	Protected area	No	No	No	Yes	Yes
South Sandwich	Protected area	No	No	No	Yes	Yes
Tristan da Cunha	Gough and Inaccessible islands have nature reserve status	Gough and Inaccessible Islands listed	No	Yes, Gough and Inaccessible Island	Yes	No, approval of Tristan da Cunha government required
Falkland Islands	There are a number of nature reserves on the islands	No	No	Yes (Bertha's Beach, Sea Lion Island)	Yes, some marine reserves	EIAs are required for some projects otherwise applications are dealt with by the Environmental Planning Department
Bouvetoya	Nature reserve	No	No	No	Yes	Yes
Prince Edward & Marion	Special nature reserves	Tentative List for South Africa	No	No	Yes	Yes
Iles Amsterdam	Nature reserve	No	No	Yes	Yes	Yes
Iles Saint-Paul	Nature reserve	No	No	Yes	Yes	Yes
Iles Crozet	Nature reserve	No	No	Yes	Yes	Yes
Iles Kerguelen	Nature reserve	No	No	Yes	Yes	Yes
Heard &MacDonald	Commonwealth reserve	Yes	No	No	Yed	Yes
Macquarie	Nature reserve (Tasmanian jurisdiction)	Yes	Yes	No	Yes	Yes
Antipodes Islands	Nature reserve	Yes	No	No	Yes	Yes
Auckland Islands	Nature reserve	Yes	No	No	Yes	Yes
Bounty Islands	Nature reserve	Yes	No	No	Yes	Yes
Campbell Islands	Nature reserve	Yes	No	No	Yes	Yes
The Snares	Nature reserve	Yes	No	No	Yes	Yes

Source: Hall 1992c; Wouters and Hall 1995a; de Villiers et al. 2005; RAMSAR Secretariat 2009; World Heritage Centre 2009; WWF 2009

Table 15.3: Sub-Antarctic island World Heritage sites

Site	Country	Date of inscription	Location of Property	Area	Criteria	Key dimensions of nomination
Gough and Inaccessible islands	Tristan da Cunha Island group, St Helena Dependency	1995; extension 2004	S40 19 29.0 W9 55 43.0	Property: 7 900.0 ha Buffer zone: 390 000.0 ha	vii, x	• one of the least-disrupted island and marine ecosystems in the cool temperate zone • one of the world's largest colonies of sea birds • high degree of bird, plant and invertebrate endemism
Prince Edward & Marion	South Africa. For administrative purposes, the Prince Edward Islands are regarded as part of the Cape Town Magisterial District of the Western Cape Province	Tentative List for South Africa. Nomination submitted 8/7/2009	—		vii, viii, ix, x	• a volcanically active subantarctic island • one of the most important and well-conserved examples of sub-Antarctic islands • harbors a significant percentage of the world population of breeding seabirds - in the case of some species up to 30% and even 40% of the world population • some of the least disturbed sub-Antarctic floral communities • high endemism
Heard & MacDonald	Australia, Territory of Heard Island and McDonald Islands	1997	S53 6 0 E73 33 0	38 600.0 ha	viii, ix	• a volcanically active subantarctic island • ongoing geomorphic processes and glacial dynamics • high conservation because of pristine ecosystem, absence of alien plants and animals
Macquarie Island	Australia, State of Tasmania	1997	S54 35 41 E158 53 44	12 785.0 ha	vii, viii	• only place on earth where rocks from the earth's mantle (6 km below the ocean floor) are being actively exposed above sea-level. • unique exposures include excellent examples of pillow basalts and other extrusive rocks
New Zealand Sub-Antarctic Islands (Antipodes Islands, Auckland Islands, Bounty Islands, Campbell Islands, The Snares)	New Zealand	1998	S50 45 0 E166 6 16	76 458.0 ha	ix, x	• high level of productivity, biodiversity, wildlife population densities and endemism among birds, plants and invertebrates. They are particularly notable for the large number and diversity of pelagic seabirds and penguins that nest there. There are 126 bird species in total, including 40 seabirds of which five breed nowhere else in the world.

Notes re criteria:

XII. to contain superlative natural phenomena or areas of exceptional natural beauty and aesthetic importance;

XIII. to be outstanding examples representing major stages of earth's history, including the record of life, significant on-going geological processes in the development of landforms, or significant geomorphic or physiographic features;

IX. to be outstanding examples representing significant on-going ecological and biological processes in the evolution and development of terrestrial, fresh water, coastal and marine ecosystems and communities of plants and animals;

X. to contain the most important and significant natural habitats for in-situ conservation of biological diversity, including those containing threatened species of outstanding universal value from the point of view of science or conservation.

Source: Derived from World Heritage Centre 2009

Table 15.4: Sub-Antarctic island Ramsar wetland sites

Site	Country	Date of inscription	Location of Property	Area
Gough Island	Tristan da Cunha Island group, St Helena Dependency (UK overseas territory)	20/11/2008	40°19'S 009°56'W	229 811 ha
Inaccessible Island	Tristan da Cunha Island group, St Helena Dependency (UK overseas territory)	20/11/2008	37°18'S 012°41'W	126 524
Bertha's Beach	Falkland Islands, UK overseas territory	24/09/2001	51°55'S 058°25'W	4 000 ha
Sea Lion Island	Falkland Island, UK overseas territory	24/09/01	52°25'S 059°05'W	1 000 ha
Réserve Naturelle Nationale des Terres Australes Françaises (includes Crozet, Kerguelen, Amsterdam and Saint-Paul)	France, overseas territory, Terres Australes et Antarctiques Françaises	15/09/2008	43°07'S 063°51'E This centre coordinate is purely notional	2 270 000 ha

Source: Derived from Ramsar Secretariat 2009

part of sustainable development. Macquarie is the only sub-Antarctic island that is part of the programme (UNESCO MAB Secretariat 2009). In addition there are five wetland sites listed under the Ramsar Convention (Table 15.4), of which the French Réserve Naturelle Nationale des Terres Australes Françaises includes the islands of Crozet, Kerguelen, Amsterdam and Saint-Paul.

Issues and trends in Sub-Antarctic tourism

Tourist visitation to the sub-Antarctic has historically been less frequent than that to the Antarctic and is mainly limited to private expeditions and commercial cruises (Hall and Wouters 1994). However, the growth of Antarctic cruise tourism has had a significant spillover to the sub-Antarctic islands. This can be explained via several mechanisms:

1   Stopover at sub-Antarctic islands on the way to or from Antarctica as both a way of providing an additional attraction for tourists but, in some cases, also providing a means of ensuring landing ashore at some stage in a trip. This may be especially important at the beginning and end of the Austral summer for Ross Sea tourism but may even be applicable to the Antarctic Peninsula as well.
2   The amount of cruise ship tourism in the Antarctic Peninsula is now so great that sub-Antarctic islands provide a means to increase capacity by extending the cruise area covered in space and time. Hall and Wouters (1994) observed that even in the early 1990s the relative tourist overcrowding of the Antarctic Peninsula was leading some operators to search for other remote destinations that can convey an Antarctic experience for visitors without other tourists being seen.
3   The growth in cruises that circumnavigate the Antarctic also provides opportunities for island visitation, whereas the growth in the number of cruise ships has also created stopover opportunities for cruises heading to and from the main Antarctic Peninsula cruise season. This particularly creates opportunities for Tristan da Cunha.

In addition, the sub-Antarctic islands are also attractions in their own right, knowledge of which has arguably increased as a result of the number of natural history documentaries featuring the islands that are shown on television.

Cruise ships are reasonably frequent visitors to the Falklands, South Georgia, South Sandwich, and Macquarie Islands as well as the southern islands of New Zealand. Nevertheless, tourism at Prince Edward and Marion Islands has historically not been encouraged by the South African Government, nor at the Iles Kerguelen by the French, possibly because of the islands' military facilities (Hall 1987; Hall and McArthur 1993). More recently tourism at the Prince Edward and Marion Islands is being restricted because of the scientific importance of the islands (Davies *et al.* 2007; Cooper *et al.* 2009).

A contributing factor to visitor growth is also the increase in private leisure yacht travel in the Southern Ocean. The exact numbers and destinations of these tourists are difficult to determine, because, similar to yacht visits in Antarctica, sub-Antarctic yacht-based visitors are able to visit a wide range of localities without necessarily being observed. Nevertheless, yacht-based cruises have grown substantially. For example, in the 1970s only one or two yachts were operating in the Southern Ocean; this figure had grown to six in the early 1980s, and to over 20 by the start of the 1990s (Poncet and Poncet 1991). In 2007–08 18 different yachts made a total of 22 visits to South Georgia alone. About a third of these were on charter to small tour groups or supporting expeditions or government-related projects (Government of South Georgia and South Sandwich Islands [GSGSSI] 2008c). According to Poncet and Poncet (1991: 6), 'the proliferation of private yachts in the Southern Ocean has added a new and largely unwelcome element to the tourist problem. The activities of these yachts seem at the moment, to be beyond any general control'. With the exception of the Falklands, airborne tourism does not exist in the sub-Antarctic islands. Although overflights would be possible, the use of planes would not be commercially viable as the islands are at great distances from each other, however, some Antarctic cruise ships carry helicopters that are used for aerial sightseeing and landing passengers at more remote locations. Table 15.5 provides an overview of tourism activity in the sub-Antarctic islands

Although conservation is a key goal in the management of all the island authorities, those island groups with a permanent population clearly have different objectives with respect to tourism than those islands which do not have such local economic demands. Therefore, the Falkland Islands and Tristan da Cunha have been greatly encouraging of tourism as a means of diversifying and increasing the economic base.

The strategic development of the tourism industry in the Falklands and the marketing of the Islands' tourism product is the responsibility of the Falkland Islands Tourist Board (FITB). The FITB have developed a *National Tourism Strategy 2008–2012*, which has the vision that 'the Falkland Islands will have a worldwide reputation for its unrivalled wildlife and natural environment, as well as the friendly hospitality and quality experience. Customer satisfaction and repeat visitation will be high, and tourism will provide a sustainable and substantial economic return to the Islands' (FITB 2008: 3). Between 2000–01 and 2006–07 the Falkland Islands experienced a 6% per annum growth in flight arrivals and a 15% growth in cruise ship passenger arrivals. The estimated value of the sector was just below £4.25 million in 2008 with an estimated average visitor spend of £74.51 (FITB 2008). This comprises almost 5% of the islands' GDP. Five main objectives have been identified for the 2008–12 period:

1   *Substantial growth in land-based tourism.* To grow land-based tourism in excess of global and regional trends, through increasing arrival numbers, length of stay and average spend in a sustainable manner (including a target annual increase in overnight visitors and their average daily spend of 5%).
2   *Exceed regional (Antarctica and South America) cruise ship growth.* To ensure that the Falkland Islands are able to accommodate in all aspects any

Table 15.5: Sub-Antarctic tourism key characteristics

Island Group	Visits by permit only	Tourist visits	Estimated number of tourists per annum	Limit on no. of visitors per season	No. of vessels per day	No. of passengers per ship	Visitor group size	Time ashore	No. of visitors ashore at one time	Overnight visits	Camping	Adventure sports
South Georgia	Yes	Yes	Approx. 8 000	No limit	Limit, 1–3 site dependent	>500 not permitted	<20 guided	Limited at one site	≤65–≤300 site dependent	Allowed in some areas	Allowed	Allowed, Permit required
South Sandwich	Yes	Yes	Approx. 250	No limit	Restricted by permit	>500 not permitted	<20 guided	Restricted by permit	Restricted by permit	Restricted by permit	Restricted by permit	Restricted by permit
Tristan da Cunha	Yes	Yes	Approx. 2 000	No limit	No limit	No limit	Not specified	Not specified	Restricted by infrastructure and lodging	Allowed	Possible	Possible
Gough	Yes	Yes	Approx. 100	No limit	Limit, one	No limit	Restricted by permit	Restricted by permit	Restricted by permit	Restricted by permit	Restricted by permit	Not allowed
Inaccessible Islands	Yes	Yes	Approx. 200	No limit	Limit, one	No limit	≤8 guided	Restricted by permit	Restricted by permit	Restricted by permit	Restricted by permit	Not allowed
Falkland Islands	No	Yes	>70 000 (Approx 95% by cruise ship)	No limit	No limit	No limit	No limit	No limit	No set limit. Amount restricted by infrastructure and lodging	Allowed	Possible	Allowed
Bouvetøya	Yes	Rare (few landings)	–	No limit	No limit	Not specified	Restricted by permit	Restricted by permit	Restricted by permit	Restricted by permit	Restricted by permit	Not allowed
Prince Edward & Marion	Yes	Rare (few landings)	–	Restricted by permit	No limit	Restricted by permit	Restricted by permit	Restricted by permit	Restricted by permit	Restricted by permit	Restricted by permit	Not allowed
Iles Amsterdam	Yes	Yes	Approx. 60	No limit	No limit	No limit	No limit	Limited	Allowed in one hut near base	Not allowed	Not allowed	Not allowed
Iles Saint-Paul	Yes	Yes	Approx. 60	No limit	No limit	No limit	Recom. ≤15 guided	Limited	No limit	Not allowed	Not allowed	Not allowed
Iles Crozet	Yes	Yes	Approx. 60	No limit	No limit	No limit	Recom. ≤15 guided	Limited	No limit	Not possible	Not allowed	Not allowed
Iles Kerguelen	Yes	Yes	Approx. 60	No limit	No limit	No limit	Recom. ≤15 guided	Limited	No limit	Allowed in 3–4 huts	Not allowed	Not allowed
Heard	Yes	Yes	<100	No limit	No limit	No limit	≤15 guided	Limited	≤30–≤60 site dependent	Permit required	Permit required	Permit required
MacDonald	Yes	Rare (no landings)	–	Restricted by permit	No limit	Restricted by permit	Restricted by permit	Restricted by permit	Restricted by permit	Restricted by permit	Restricted by permit	Restricted by permit
Macquarie	Yes	Yes	<750	<750	Limit, one	>200 not permitted	≤15 guided	Limited	No limit	Not allowed	Not allowed	Not allowed
Antipodes Islands	Yes	Yes (no landings)	<150	No limit	Limit, one	No limit	Limited	Restricted by permit	Restricted by permit	Restricted by permit	Not allowed	Not allowed
Auckland Islands	Yes	Yes	<600	<600	Limit, one	No limit	≤20 guided	Limited	≤50–≤150 site dependent	Not allowed	Not allowed	Not allowed
Bounty Islands	Yes	Yes (no landings)	<150	No limit	Limit, one	No limit	Limited	Restricted by permit	Restricted by permit	Restricted by permit	Not allowed	Not allowed
Campbell Islands	Yes	Yes	<600	<600	Limit, one	No limit	≤20 guided	Limited	≤50–≤150 site dependent	Not allowed	Not allowed	Not allowed
The Snares	Yes	Yes (no landings)	<150	No limit	Limit, one	No limit	Limited	Restricted by permit	Restricted by permit	Restricted by permit	Not allowed	Not allowed

Source: Hall 1992a; Wouters and Hall 1995a, 1995b; Chown et al. 1998; Department of Conservation 1998, 2006, 2008; Poncet 2003; Australian Antarctic Division 2005a, 2005b; de Villiers et al. 2005; Tasmanian Parks and Wildlife Service 2005, 2006; West 2005; Pasteur and Walton 2006; Poncet and Crosbie 2006; Tracey 2007; Falkland Islands Tourist Board 2008; Government of South Georgia and the South Sandwich Islands 2008a, 2008b, 2008c, 2009a, 2009b, 2009c; Tristan da Cunha Government and the Tristan da Cunha Association 2009; World Heritage Centre 2009

growth within the cruise ship sector, therefore maximising all potential economic benefit.

3   *Increase average, per head, passenger revenue from all cruise ships*. Through product development, marketing, training, relationship building and infra-structure developments, increase revenue from passengers off yachts and cruise vessels.

4   *Create, develop, invest in and maintain a sustainable world-class tourism offering*. Develop the tourism product in the Falkland Islands to meet and exceed the expectations of visitors, trade and the community whilst conserving and enhancing the environment on which tourism depends.

5   *Increase awareness and build a positive perception of the Falkland Islands as a tourism destination*. Across all key markets and sectors, develop a strong and positive consumer knowledge and interest in the Falkland Islands as a tourist destination through brand and marketing efforts (FITB 2008).

However, there are a number of constraints to the Falklands achieving their economic goals, particularly with respect to infrastructure and achieving greater air accessibility, especially via the development of new routes. Another important economic dimension of tourism to the Islands is that it helps to reinforce United Kingdom sovereignty.

Although governed separately to the Falklands, fishing, tourism and other activities in South Georgia and the South Sandwich Islands also directly and indirectly contribute to the Falklands economy. South Georgia aims to encourage sustainable tourism with revenues contributing to the environmental management of the islands. In the Austral 2008–09 summer season South Georgia received a total of 70 cruise ship and 25 yachts visits carrying 7,800 passengers. This represents a 120% increase in passenger numbers over the last 5 years. However, following the full implementation of the revised South Georgia visitor management policy which restricts ships to those carrying 500 passengers or fewer (GSGSSI 2009a), this trend is not expected to continue, with some operators also indicating that they did not intend to return in 2009–10 (McKee 2009; GSGSSI 2009b). Ship visitation is primarily focused on South Georgia but the South Sandwich Islands do receive a significant amount of commercial and private visitation as part of cruise itineraries. As with the Falklands, tourism activity also helps to reinforce UK sovereignty over the two island groups against Argentinian claims.

Tristan da Cunha is a British overseas territory which is part of Saint Helena, Ascension and Tristan da Cunha (previously known as St Helena and Dependencies until September 2009, when a new constitution came into force giving the three islands equal status within the territory). Tristan da Cunha consists of the inhabited main island of Tristan da Cunha, and the Nightingale Islands, Inaccessible Island and Gough Island which are all nature reserves. Inaccessible Island and the Nightingale Islands are located 35 km southwest of the main island, while Gough Island is located 395 km south-southeast. Gough and Inaccessible Islands are World Heritage Sites, with Gough also housing a meteorological station leased by South Africa. The South African link is important as the lease arrangement provides for ship visits to the main island as part of the annual supply of the Station. The supply ship also takes paying passengers, which gives visitors an opportunity to stay on Tristan, which has a small range of accommodation available, including home stays. The greatest difficulty in developing tourism for Tristan da Cunha is the accessibility of the island as although cruise ship tourism is gradually increasing in significance, sea and weather conditions and schedule demands at times deny passengers the opportunity to visit the main island.

In contrast to the Falkland Islands and Tristan da Cunha, and to an extent South Georgia and the South Sandwich Islands, the remaining sub-Antarctic islands have a more restrictive approach towards visitation. For example, the Conservation Management Strategy for the New Zealand sub-Antarctic islands provides for a high degree of control over human activities and advocates a precautionary approach to granting visitor permits (Department of Conservation [DOC] 1998; West 2005). For the purposes of management the islands have been categorised into minimum impact and refuge islands based on their ecosystem condition and vulnerability to disturbance (DOC 1998). The distinction between these two categories relates primarily to the presence, either current or in the recent past (refuge islands), or absence (minimum impact islands) of introduced mammals and the effects that these introduced species have had on the fauna and flora of each island. Most of the islands have been classified as minimum impact and with entry strongly limited. The refuge islands are Auckland, Enderby and Masked Islands in the Auckland Island group plus Campbell and Folly in the Campbell Island group (West 2005). Tourist numbers are limited to a maximum of 600 per annum at large sites and 150 per annum at small sites and access is limited to a few locations on just three islands (Campbell, Enderby and Auckland Islands) (West 2005). Any visitor to the islands requires a permit and they must follow the 'minimal impact code' for visitors (DOC 2008). The 'minimal impact code' requires that all visits be accompanied by a government representative, includes details of areas that can be visited and that visitors fulfil biodiversity-related requirements such as quarantine.

Historically, the New Zealand sub-Antarctic island management plans (Wouters and Hall 1995a, b) have greatly influenced the management of Macquarie Island by the Tasmanian Department of Parks, Wildlife and Heritage, which has tended to adopt similar costing and management strategies, and guidelines for tourism operations (Hall 1993; Hall and Wouters 1994). Similarly, Australia's visitor management and conservation experiences have influenced New Zealand sub-Antarctic management strategies.

Australia's Macquarie Island has one of the longest histories of any of the sub-Antarctic islands as a tourist destination. A series of New Zealand Government expeditions to the Auckland Islands, Campbell Island and Macquarie Island from 1887 to 1927 is the earliest evidence of the carriage of tourists to Macquarie Island (Headland 1994). Headland (1994) states these expeditions were made at least annually, with some of the passengers described as tourists. Early tourism continued up to the mid-1950s, with a number of tourists travelling aboard ships on voyages to Antarctica for a variety of purposes, including the relief of scientific staff, the provision of supplies, castaway searches and the provision of mail services.

Initially protected as a sanctuary under the Tasmanian *Animals and Birds Protection Act* 1928, Macquarie Island was proclaimed a wildlife sanctuary in 1933. Macquarie Island became a Conservation Area in 1971, and in 1972 it became a State Reserve. The Tasmanian National Parks and Wildlife Service (TPWS) declared Macquarie Island a Nature Reserve in 1978, giving it status equivalent to a national park, and renamed it Macquarie Island Nature Reserve. In 1977, UNESCO accepted the island as a biosphere reserve in the MAB programme (Davis and Drake 1983; Selkirk *et al.* 1990). A biosphere reserve is an area set aside so that human impact on the environment as compared with unaltered ecosystem can be monitored. It differs from a national park in that it is a representative example of a particular terrain and species, whereas a national park is intended to conserve unique or spectacular sites and species (Davis 1983; Bonner and Lewis Smith 1985; Rounsevell and Copson 1985).

Like many sub-Antarctic islands Macquarie Island has a significant history of human activity. It was discovered by a sealing brig in 1810 and exploitation of the island's marine mammals and penguins for oil continued until 1919. The first shore stations of sealers and whalers constitute some of the earliest industrial sites in Australia. Scientific research commenced in 1820 with the first Australian station established during 1911–14 by Douglas Mawson. In 1948 the Australian Government established a research and meteorological station, which has been in continuous operation since (TPWS 2006). The island was not declared a restricted area, i.e. requiring visitors to acquire permits, until 1979.

Macquarie Island is subject to both State and Commonwealth legislation. The State Government of Tasmania, through the TPWS, is responsible for the management of Macquarie Island and the surrounding waters out to 3 nautical miles. The Commonwealth Government is responsible for the management of the area from 3 nautical miles to the Exclusive Economic Zone around Australia (Environment Australia 2001). Because of this situation legislation providing for the conservation of Macquarie Island includes both the Commonwealth (Australian Federal Government) *Environment Protection and Biodiversity Conservation Act 1999* and the Tasmanian *Nature Conservation Act 2002* and *National Parks and Reserves Management Act 2002*, which replaced the State's *National Parks and Wildlife Act 1970*. An objective of the *Environment Protection and Biodiversity Conservation Act 1999* is to provide for the protection of the environment, in particular those aspects of the environment that are matters of national environmental significance. In Tasmania reserves are declared under the *Nature Conservation Act 2002*, which sets out the values and purposes of each reserve class and are managed under the *National Parks and Reserves Management Act 2002* according to the management objectives for each class of reserve.

In 2006 the TPWS (2006) released a detailed Management Plan for the Macquarie Islands, replacing the previous 2001 plan. Because of the different jurisdictions the Commonwealth Government prepared a separate management plan for the marine park (Environment Australia 2001). The TPWS (2006: iv) notes that 'the reserve is of great public interest and educational value. Although tourism and recreation are not objectives of management for Tasmanian nature reserves, controlled tourism for educational purposes is the only form of tourism permitted in this reserve'. For this purpose three tourism management areas (TMAs) have been zoned within the reserve for the purposes of viewing wildlife, geological and historical sites. Facilities to minimise impact and disturbance include boardwalks, viewing platforms, and interpretation panels. Visits to the TMAs may be undertaken only in accordance with the Tourism Guidelines (TPWS 2005) and in the presence of guides approved by the Director. The specific objectives of TMAs are to:

- provide appropriate areas of interest for educational tourism access to foster and promote awareness, understanding and appreciation of the World Heritage Area, biosphere reserve, National Estate and nature reserve values of the reserve;
- minimise risk of accidental introduction of alien species; and
- provide access for visitor groups only to areas where safety risks and wildlife disturbance can be minimised as far as possible, while still meeting the previous two objectives (TPWS 2006: 86).

In 2003, the criteria used to select educational tourism operators included the following:

1 benefits to the state of Tasmania (e.g. employing Tasmanians or resupplying in Tasmania);
2 benefits to the management and protection of Macquarie Island Nature Reserve (e.g. assistance with programs, or with transport of equipment and personnel);
3 minimisation of environmental impacts both offshore and on land, based on the environmental impact statement submitted with the application;
4 adherence to strict safety guidelines, including a degree of self-reliance in such matters;
5 clear communication to the company's clients, crew and staff of appropriate messages about the natural and cultural values of the island, including the role that visitors play in protecting those values;
6 forms of tourist operator accreditation and relevant qualifications held by the company and its regular staff members;
7 flexibility of operating timetables (for instance if weather or Australian Antarctic Division [AAD] shipping changes caused delays); and
8 past performance in this or related operations.

Australia's other sub-Antarctic island territories, the Heard Island and McDonald Islands (HIMI), are solely under Commonwealth government authority. The Territory, including the marine reserve, has been managed as an IUCN category 1a strict nature reserve since 1996, in accordance with the provisions of the Heard

Island Wilderness Reserve Management Plan made under the Territory's *Environment Protection and Management Ordinance* (AAD 2005a). In October 2002, the Territory and parts of the surrounding marine area were declared a Commonwealth Reserve under the *Environment Protection and Biodiversity Conservation Act 1999*. The islands are administered by the AAD in accordance with a stringent management plan. As well as a management plan (AAD 2005a) there is also an Environmental Code of Conduct for Visitors to Heard Island (AAD 2005b), providing general guidelines to help prevent or minimise visitor impacts.

Because of their isolation the islands have been little visited. Since the first landing on Heard Island in 1855, there have been only approximately 240 shore-based visits to the island and only two known landings on McDonald Island. A small number of private yachts and commercial tourist vessels have visited Heard Island, although few successful landings have been made because of poor weather. Other private expeditions include brief visits by ham radio enthusiasts, private scientific groups and mountaineering parties (AAD 2005a). Nevertheless, the AAD (2005a: 128) recognised that the 'wildlife, vegetation, cultural heritage, spectacular landscape and remoteness of HIMI are major attractions for private recreational and tourist visits'. This, combined with the growth of Antarctic tourism, is recognised as possibly leading to increased recreational and tourism activities concentrated on Heard Island.

As part of the management plan a Visitor Access Zone has been identified on Heard Island consisting of three areas. According to the AAD (2005a: 30):

> These areas provide for appropriate management of low-impact, short-term, land-based visitor activities in the Reserve, and allow for a balance between conservation goals and the desire to maximise the experience and enjoyment of visitors in the brief time they are likely be ashore. As weather conditions usually differ dramatically around the island and tourist ships are usually on tight itineraries, the wide distribution of the three Visitor Access Zone areas improves the chances of visitors being able to get ashore.
>
> The areas within the Visitor Access Zone provide relatively safe landing sites, albeit not in all conditions, and access to a range of attractions within approximately one hour's walk of these landing sites. Attractions within, or visible in close proximity to, these low-lying areas include heritage sites, extensively vegetated areas, wildlife colonies and a range of spectacular landscape features. Only low-impact access, such as beach landings by vessels or helicopter landings at designated points, and low-impact activities (such as walking, photography and wildlife observation) will be allowed in the Visitor Access Zone.

Visits to the reserve require permits and the significant conditions placed on visitors will restrict the development of commercial operations. However, the identification of specific access zones does highlight the willingness of the AAD to accommodate potential demand while continuing to conserve the islands'

Table 15.6: Summary of potential visitor impacts

Terrestrial Environment	Marine environment
– localised damage to vegetation, soil structure and invertebrate/ burrowing bird habitat through trampling, aircraft landings and lighting of fires	– introduction and spread of marine alien species via vessels, small craft and other equipment used in the water
– localised and/or wider disturbance of marine mammals and seabirds, including breeding, by persons on foot or by the use of vessels or aircraft	– vessel collision with marine mammals and seabirds
– introduction and spread of terrestrial and freshwater alien species via footwear, clothing, equipment, foodstuffs, human waste, vessels and aircraft, including possible introduction of disease.	– disturbance of marine mammals from vessel noise
– loss or degradation of cultural and natural heritage items through damage, disturbance or souveniring	– ingestion or entanglement in floating debris by marine mammals and seabirds
– damage to coastal and near-shore habitats, ecosystems and species from marine pollution	– oil and chemical spills

Source: Hall 1992a, 2010; Wouters and Hall 1995a, 1995b; Chown et al. 1998; Department of Conservation 1998; Pfeiffer and Peter 2004; Australian Antarctic Division 2005a; Frenot et al. 2005; Pasteur and Walton 2006.

biodiversity and geomorphology. The HIMI model may therefore potentially influence French, Norwegian and South African sub-Antarctic island management given that the management strategy recognises that 'Both the World Heritage Convention and the Australian World Heritage management principles..., call for the presentation of the World Heritage values of the Reserve to the community. It is generally accepted that such presentation should not be to the detriment of the values of the property' (AAD 2005a: 49).

Tourism impacts

Large-scale sub-Antarctic tourism is a relatively recent phenomenon. The most serious concern surrounding tourism in these islands is the potential adverse impacts tourism may have on the physical environment, especially via the introduction of alien and invasive species (AAD 2005a; chapter 2). These impacts can be divided between those arising from the development of land-based infrastructure, such as accommodation facilities, toilets, airports, roads and jetties and associated buildings and structures, and those from visitation (Hall 1992). Given that with the exception of the Falklands and Tristan da Cunha there is currently little dedicated land-based infrastructure for tourism in the sub-Antarctic islands the main focus is on visitor activities. (A summary of these potential impacts is provided in Table 15.6.) A number of the sub-Antarctic islands have already suffered marked human impact through the exploitation of whale, seal, and fisheries resources for most of the past 300 years (Clark and Dingwall 1985; White 1994). However, the islands of the Southern Ocean have generally not been permanently inhabited or had a permanent human presence since industrial times and exploitation periods have been short. Several southern island groups have not been modified by humans at all. The sub-Antarctic islands contain some of the world's least human-impacted biotas, and their relative isolation has been their greatest conservation asset, but it is these same harsh conditions that are now attracting visitors in increasing numbers. The relative fragility of these islands means that even minute changes brought about by human impacts, such as tourist activity, may have long-term impacts on ecosystem stability (Hall 1993).

The types of impact by visitors on and around islands include inadequate waste disposal, litter, vegetation trampling, disturbance to wildlife, and the potential threats of fire and the introduction of invasive plant and animal pests and disease (Pfeiffer and Peter 2004; AAD 2005a; Frenot *et al.* 2005). But, as in the case of Antarctic tourism, environmental impacts on the islands depend on the nature of the activity. Overflights generally provide minimal disturbance of the environment, although low overflights of wildlife colonies may panic the birds or marine animals. For example, in June 1990, around 7,000 King penguins stampeded, piled up on top of each other and died from suffocation when an Australian Air Force Hercules circumnavigated Macquarie Island at an altitude of 250 m (Swithinbank 1993), resulting in the development of policies with respect to overflights in the reserve plan (TPWS 2006). The impacts of ship-based tourism are more controversial. Cruise travel occurs in the Austral summer, coinciding with the peak breeding periods of many species, and may disturb breeding sites (Frenot *et al.* 2005; chapter 2). Ships can also pollute over a large area through oil spill and indiscriminate disposal of waste and sewage, affect wildlife, as well as be a vector for invasive marine species (de Villiers *et al.* 2005; chapter 2). For example, in 2007–08 a serious birdstrike was reported in Stromness Bay, South Georgia. According to McKee (2009: 6), 'In excess of 280 birds (prions and diving petrels) struck the vessel, of which there were at least 17 mortalities…In this instance, the reasons for the bird strike were very clearly a combination of excessive lighting and poor visibility. This incident could and should have been prevented'.

Given the specialisation of island biota, the islands are highly vulnerable to external disturbance and environmental change, especially human-induced impacts (Chown 2003; de Villiers *et al.* 2005; Frenot *et al.* 2005). The extinction of species is particularly common on islands when new competitors or physical conditions are introduced. One of the greatest threats to island biota is therefore the introduction, accidental or deliberate, of alien plants and animals, in particular through seed dispersal or the transfer of mammals such as rats and mice. Therefore, many of the management plans for the sub-Antarctic islands place a great deal of attention on biosecurity and quarantine procedures (e.g. DOC 1998; AAD 2005a; TPWS 2006). Careless behaviour by tourists would certainly increase this threat, and excessive disturbance of plants and animals by tourist visits, as has occurred in areas of the Falkland Islands, must be avoided. In order to encourage appropriate behaviour codes of conduct have been developed for both operators and visitors (e.g. AAD 2005b; TPWS 2005; DOC 2008; Falkland Islands Government Environmental Planning Department 2008).

Impacts of tourism in the sub-Antarctic are mainly associated with the physical environment, but there is also concern over the conservation of cultural heritage. A number of early European sites associated with farming, sealing, and whaling exist on the islands, and some early exploration bases are of substantial historical significance (Hall 1993; Hughes 1994; TPWS 2006). The cultural history is part of the attraction of the islands to tourists, and is used by tour operators as a major visitor drawcard. However, the isolation of the islands means that it is difficult for authorities to regulate access to cultural and natural heritage sites and even though the majority of commercial operators are careful about their activities, there is little control, if any, over the activities of visitors on private yachts.

The future of the Sub-Antarctic Island tourism management regime

As noted above, there are two main approaches to the management of tourism in the sub-Antarctic islands. Those islands with a permanent population have a strong economic interest in encouraging tourism. In some cases this may complement policy measures to reinforce sovereignty. The remainder tend to have a more restrictive approach to tourist visitation, although where there is a strong connection to an Antarctic gateway location such as in Australia and New Zealand (Hall 2000) a moderate degree of tourism visitation is permissible. For example, in the case of Macquarie Island the first criterion used to select educational tourism operators is benefits to Tasmania (see above) (TPWS 2006). In all situations national and regional jurisdictional legislation and regulation attempts to restrict the introduction of alien species, prohibit the harvesting of any living resources except under special licence, and protect indigenous flora and fauna and landscapes from interference and disturbance. Since the early 1990s more comprehensive approaches to conservation on the islands have been developed but their enforcement in some cases is difficult because of the lack of a permanent presence. Increasing tourist interest in the islands may require more vigorous prosecution of regulations if they are to be of any use. The proliferation of private yachts in the Southern Ocean in particular has added a new element to the management equation. The activities of these yachts seem, at the moment, to be beyond any general control, regulation and enforcement unless there is a more substantial increase in management resources than at present. A major weakness in visitor regulation and codes of conduct is the assumption that these have been consulted by private yachts as well as commercial operators, although even in the case of the latter, regulations may not be met. In the case of South Georgia, McKee (2009: 2) reported to the IAATO meeting:

> It has been brought to the attention of GSGSSI that in recent seasons, in an effort to avoid dense populations of fur seals at the designated Stromness landing site, some expedition staff have been landing passengers closer to the former station than permitted (inside marker cordons of the safety exclusion limit). This is not an acceptable practice and this development is concerning for a number of reasons. Not only is the safety of passengers and staff being potentially compromised, but the [Expedition Leaders] involved have taken it upon themselves to ignore very clear Government instructions.

and went on to note

> Despite repeated requests, it is still apparent that not every vessel operator is ensuring that the information, which accompanies permits, reaches all of their Expedition Leaders [EL] before they embark their vessels. This includes important additional information, beyond that contained in the current Information for Visitors to South Georgia booklet, which all EL's and staff should refer to well in advance of their arrival
>
> (McKee 2009: 5).

The issue of meeting guidelines is clearly one not only of practical conservation importance but also an area of potential future research.

The challenge to island managers is to maximise the benefits from recreation and minimise the detrimental impacts. As in the case of many current Antarctic tourist operators, sub-Antarctic commercial operators and private recreation entrepreneurs may also become conservation advocates. For example, educational goals are an important element in allowing visitation to Heard and Macquarie

Islands (e.g. TPWS 2006). Nevertheless, while short-term evaluations of educational tourism are often part of the management plans of sub-Antarctic islands and a justification for such tourism (Powell *et al.* 2008), there is little long-term research in the extent to which travel to such high-value conservation sites does lead to permanent changes in behaviours and attitudes.

Management must be based on adequate knowledge if it is to be truly effective. Ecological studies and long-term monitoring are required, in particular interaction of human activities with the sub-Antarctic ecosystems. Activities must be regulated to avoid unnecessary disturbance to wildlife and the environment. This requires active and extensive research. Information flow can be improved when national authorities, operating agencies and scientists promote free and full exchange of all information and data, especially on those aspects that concern conservation and environmental protection of these unique islands, including social science based research on tourism and visitation.

The management of tourism in the islands of the Southern Ocean poses special challenges. Twenty-five years ago Clark and Dingwall (1985: 179) argued that 'with adequate precautions and international cooperation in regulating tourist operations, tourism should be compatible with scientific and conservation objectives in protected areas on islands of the Southern Ocean'. To a significant extent these hopes have been realised. Indeed, the fees paid by tourists have in theory contributed substantially to the environmental management of the islands. However, the isolation of the islands can no longer be regarded as adequate protection for the islands. Tourism has become a reality in the management of the island ecosystems. Somewhat optimistically, O'Connor and Simmons (1990, p.192) argue that 'In itself, the image of the last islands of nature in a spoiled world promotes a nature tourism use.' However, evidence from other polar regions suggests that wise and careful use is not always the outcome of nature-based tourism visitation.

Perhaps most significantly, the sub-Antarctic islands are not isolated independent units either in tourism or ecological terms. Marine mammals and seabirds migrate over large distances between the islands and numerous animal and plant species are endemic to island groups or to the whole Southern Ocean region. Many cruise ships and tourists visit a number of sub-Antarctic islands during a single voyage, as well as visiting Antarctica. Management of tourism to Antarctica and the sub-Antarctic islands should thus be considered an entity. Despite the variations of sovereignty, Antarctic and sub-Antarctic tourism are invariably linked.

References

Australian Antarctic Division (AAD) (2005a) *Heard Island and McDonald Islands Marine Reserve: Management Plan*. Kingston, Hobart: Australian Antarctic Division.
— (2005b) *Environmental Code of Conduct for Visitors to Heard Island*. Kingston, Hobart: Australian Antarctic Division.
Bonner, W.N, and Lewis Smith, R.I. (eds.) (1985) *Conservation Areas in the Antarctic,*

International Council of Scientific Unions, SCAR, Scott Polar Research Institute, Cambridge

Cessford, G.R. and Dingwall, P.R. (1994) 'Tourism on New Zealand's Sub-Antarctic islands', *Annals of Tourism Research*, 21(2): 318–32.

Chown, S.L. (2003) *The Probability of Introduction of Non–indigenous Species to Heard and McDonald Islands: Taxa, Risks and Mitigation*. Kingston: Australian Antarctic Division, Department of the Environment and Heritage.

Chown, S.L., Gremmen, N.J.M. and Gaston, K.J. (1998) 'Ecological biogeography of Southern Ocean Islands: species-area relationships, human impacts, and conservation', *American Naturalist*, 152: 562–75.

Chown, S.L., Rodrigues, A.S.L., Gremmen, N.J.M. and Gaston, K.J. (2001) 'World Heritage status and conservation of Southern Ocean islands', *Conservation Biology*, 15: 550–57.

Clark, M.R. and Dingwall, P.R. (1985) *Conservation of Islands in the Southern Ocean*, Cambridge: International Union for Conservation of Nature and Natural Resources, Cambridge University Press.

Cooper, J, Bester, M.N., Chown, S.L., Crawford, R.J.M., Daly, R., Heyns, E., Lamont, T., Ryan, P.G. and Shaw, J.D. (2009) 'Biological survey of the Prince Edward Islands, December 2008', *South African Journal of Science*, 105(July/August): 317–20.

Davies, S.J., Chown, S.L. and Joubert, L.S. (2007) 'Renewed management system and provisions for South Africa's sub-Antarctic islands', *Papers and Proceedings of the Royal Society of Tasmania*, 141(1): 115–20.

Davis, B.W. (1983) 'Australia's Biosphere Reserves: the role of Macquarie Island', *Australian Ranger Bulletin*, 2(3): 93.

Davis, P.B. (1999) 'Beyond guidelines: a model for Antarctic tourism', *Annals of Tourism Research*, 26(3): 516–33.

Davis, B. W. and Drake, G. A. (1983) Australia's Biosphere Reserves: Conserving Ecological Diversity, Australian National Commission for UNESCO, Canberra: AGPS.

Department of Conservation (DOC) (1998) *Conservation Management Strategy, Subantarctic Islands*. Southland Conservancy Conservation Management Planning Series 10. Invercargill: Department of Conservation.

— (2006) *Marine Protection for the New Zealand Subantarctic Islands*. Wellington: Department of Conservation.

— (2008) *Subantarctic Islands Minimum Impact Code*. Invercargill: Southland Conservancy, Department of Conservation.

Environment Australia (2001) *Macquarie Island Marine Park Management Plan*, Canberra: Environment Australia.

Falkland Islands Government Environmental Planning Department (2008) The Falkland Islands Countryside Code, Online. Available HTTP: http://www.epd.gov.fk/?page_id = 167 (accessed 1 October 2009).

Falkland Islands Tourist Board (FITB) (2008) *Falkland Islands Draft National Tourism Strategy 2012*, Draft version 1.3 June. Stanley: Falkland Islands Tourist Board.

Frenot, Y., Chown, S.L., Whinam, J., Selkirk, P.M., Convey, P., Skotnicki, M. & Bergstrom, D.M. (2005) 'Biological invasions in the Antarctic: extent, impacts and implications', *Biological Reviews*, 80: 45–72.

Glass, J.P. and Ryan, P.G. (2003) 'Conservation challenges in small communities: conservation management in the Tristan islands', in M. Pienkowski (ed.) *A Sense of Direction: A Conference on Conservation in UK Overseas Territories and Other Small Island*

Communities. UK Overseas Territories Conservation Forum, Online. Available HTTP: www.ukotcf.org (accessed 1 October 2009).

Government of South Georgia and the South Sandwich Islands (GSGSSI) (2008a) Information for Visitors to South Georgia. Online. Available HTTP: http://sgisland.gs/index.php/(v)Information_for_Visitors_to_South_Georgia?useskin = vis (accessed 11 January 2009).

— (2008b) Important Laws in South Georgia. Online. Available HTTP: http://www.sgisland.gs/index.php/%28g%29Important_Laws_in_South_Georgia?useskin=ov (accessed 11 January 2009).

— (2008c) 'Overview Of the 2007/8 tourist season', *South Georgia Newsletter*, July 2008. Online. Available HTTP: http://www.sgisland.gs/index.php/%28h%29South_Georgia_Newsletter%2C_July_2008 (accessed 11 January 2009).

— (2009a). Tourism Management Policy. March. Online. Available HTTP: http://www.sgisland.gs/index.php/(g)Tourism_Management_Policy?useskin=gov (accessed 1 October 2009).

— (2009b) 'More cruises, less passengers', *South Georgia Newsletter*, July 2009. Online. Available HTTP: http://www.sgisland.gs/index.php/%28h%29South_Georgia_Newsletter%2C_July_2009 (accessed 1 October 2009).

— (2008c) 'Expected visitor numbers dip during the recession', *South Georgia Newsletter*, August 2009. Online. Available HTTP: http://www.sgisland.gs/index.php/%28h%29South_Georgia_Newsletter%2C_Aug_2009 (accessed 1 October 2009).

Hall, C.M. (1987) 'Tantamount to an act of war? Australians fear French move to new nuclear test site', *Alternatives: Perspectives on Science, Technology and the Environment*, 14: 70–71

— (1992a) 'Tourism in Antarctica: activities, impacts, and management', *Journal of Tourism Research*, 30(4): 2–9

— (1992b) *Wasteland to World Heritage: Preserving Australia's wilderness*, Melbourne University Press, Carlton.

— (1993) 'Ecotourism in the Australian and New Zealand Sub-Antarctic Islands', *Tourism Recreation Research*, 18(2): 13–21.

— (2000) 'The tourist and economic significance of Antarctic travel in Australian and New Zealand Antarctic gateway cities', *Tourism and Hospitality Research: The Surrey Quarterly Review*, 2(2): 157–69.

Hall, C.M. and McArthur, S. (1993) 'Case-study: ecotourism in Antarctica and adjacent Sub-Antarctic islands: development, impacts, management and prospects for the future', *Tourism Management*, 14: 117–22.

Hall, C.M., McArthur, S. and Spoelder, P. (1992) 'Ecotourism in Antarctica and adjacent sub-Antarctic islands: development, impacts, management and prospects for the future', in B. Weiler (ed.) EcoTourism, Canberra: Bureau of Tourism Research.

Hall, C.M. and Piggin, R. (2002) 'Tourism business knowledge of World Heritage sites: a New Zealand case study,' *International Journal of Tourism Research*, 4(5): 401–11.

Hall, C.M. and Wouters, M. (1994) 'Managing nature tourism in the Sub-Antarctic islands', *Annals of Tourism Research*, 21(2): 355–74.

Headland, R.K. (1994) 'Historical development of Antarctic tourism', *Annals of Tourism Research*, 21(2): 269–80.

Higham, T. (ed.) (1991) *New Zealand's Sub-Antarctic islands – a guidebook*, Invercargill: Department of Conservation.

Hughes, J. (1994) 'Antarctic historic sites: the tourism implications', *Annals of Tourism Research*, 21(2): 281–94.

Ingham, R.J. and Summers, D. (2002) 'Falkland Islands cruise ship tourism: an overview of the 1999–2000 season and the way forward', *Aquatic Conservation: Marine and Freshwater Ecosystems*, 12(1): 145–52.

Lamers, M., Haase, D. and Amelung, B. (2008) 'Facing the elements: analysing trends in Antarctic tourism', *Tourism Review*, 63(1): 15–27.

Landau, D. (2007) 'Tourism in polar regions and the sub-Antarctic islands', *Papers and Proceedings of the Royal Society of Tasmania*, 141(1): 173–80.

Levich, S.V. and Fal'kovich, N.S. (1987) 'Recreation and tourism in the Southern Ocean and Antarctica', *Izvestiya Vsesoyuznogo Geograficheskogo Obshchnestva*, 119(2): 168–74.

McKee, R. (2009) South Georgia 2009, reports to 20th Annual General IAATO Meeting, June 2009, Providence, Rhode Island. Stanley: Government of South Georgia and the South Sandwich Islands.

Molenaar, E.J. (2005) 'Sea-borne tourism in Antarctica: avenues for further intergovernmental regulation', *The International Journal of Marine and Coastal Law*, 20(2): 247–95.

Molloy, L.F. and Dingwall, P.R. (1990) 'World Heritage values of New Zealand islands', in D. Towns, C. Daugherty and I. Atkinson (eds.) *Ecological Restoration of New Zealand Islands*, Conservation Sciences Publication No.2, Wellington: Department of Conservation.

O'Connor, K.F. and Simmons, D.G. (1990) 'The use of islands for recreation and tourism: changing significance for nature conservation', in D. Towns, C. Daugherty and I. Atkinson (eds.) *Ecological Restoration of New Zealand Islands*, Conservation Sciences Publication No.2, Wellington: Department of Conservation.

Pasteur, L. and Walton, D.W. (2006) *South Georgia: Plan for progress. Managing the Environment: 2006 – 2010.* Cambridge: British Antarctic Survey and the Government of South Georgia and the South Sandwich Islands.

Pfeiffer, S. and Peter, H. (2004) 'Ecological studies toward the management of an Antarctic tourist landing site (Penguin Island, South Shetland Islands)', *Polar Record*, 40(215): 345–53.

Poncet, S. (2003) *South Georgia Land and Visitor Management Report. Report to the Government of South Georgia and the South Sandwich Islands*, Technical Report No. EBS03/2, 1–73. Stanley: Government of South Georgia and the South Sandwich Islands.

Poncet, S. and Crosbie, K. (2006) *A Visitors Guide to South Georgia.* Maidenhead: Wild Guides.

Poncet, S. and Poncet, J. (1991) *Southern Ocean Cruising Handbook*, Stanley: Government Printing Office, Falkland Islands.

Powell, R.B., Kellert, S.R. and Ham, S.H. (2008) 'Antarctic tourists: ambassadors or consumers?' *Polar Record*, 44: 233–41.

Ramsar Secretariat (2009) *The List of Wetlands of International Importance, 30 September 2009.* Gland: Ramsar Secretariat.

Rounsevell, D. and Copson, G. (1985) 'Southern Ocean sanctuary', *UNESCO Review*, 10: 9–11.

Sanson, L. (1994) 'An ecotourism case study in Sub-Antarctic islands', *Annals of Tourism Research*, 21(2): 344–55.

Selkirk, P.M., Seppelt, R.D. and Selkirk, D.R. (1990) *Sub-Antarctic Macquarie Island – Environment and Biology*, Cambridge: Cambridge University Press.

Swithinbank, C. (1993) 'Airborne tourism in the Antarctic', *Polar Record*, 29(169): 103–10.

Tasmanian Parks and Wildlife Service (TPWS) (2005) *Guidelines for Tourist Operations and Visits to Macquarie Island Nature Reserve World Heritage Area.* Hobart: Tasmanian Parks and Wildlife Service, Department of Tourism, Parks, Heritage and the Arts.

— (2006) *Macquarie Island Nature Reserve and World Heritage Area Management Plan 2006.* Hobart: Tasmanian Parks and Wildlife Service, Department of Tourism, Parks, Heritage and the Arts.

Tracey, P. (2007) 'Tourism management on the southern oceanic islands', in J. Snyder and B. Stonehouse (eds) *Prospects for Polar Tourism.* Wallingford: CABI.

Tristan da Cunha Government and the Tristan da Cunha Association (2009) Visits Section, the Tristan da Cunha website, Online. Available HTTP: http://www.tristandc.com/visits.php (accessed 1 October 2009).

Udvardy, M.D.F. (1975) *A Classification of the Biogeographical Provinces of the World,* IUCN Occasional Paper No.18, Morges: IUCN.

UNESCO MAB Secretariat (2009) *Biosphere Reserves World Network.* Paris: UNESCO MAB Secretariat.

de Villiers, M.S., Cooper, J., Carmichael, N., Glass, J.P..Liddle, G.M., McIvor, E., Micol, T. and Roberts, A. (2005) 'Conservation management at Southern Ocean Islands: towards the development of best-practice guidelines', *Polarforschung,* 75(2–3): 113–31.

Walton, D.W.II. (1985) 'The Sub-Antarctic islands', in W. Bonner and D. Walton (eds.) *Key Environments: Antarctica,* Oxford: Pergamon Press.

West, C. (2005) *New Zealand Subantarctic Islands Research Strategy,* Invercargill: Southland Conservancy, Department of Conservation.

White, K.J. (1994) 'Tourism and the Antarctic economy', *Annals of Tourism Research,* 21(2): 245–68.

World Heritage Centre (2009) World Heritage List. Online. Available HTTP: http://whc.unesco.org/en/list (accessed 1 October 2009).

World Wildlife Fund (WWF) (2009) *Are We On Track? Marine Protected Areas for Antarctica and the Southern Ocean.* Sydney: WWF.

Wouters, M.M. (1993) Promotion or protection: managing the paradox – the management of tourist visitation to Antarctica and the Sub-Antarctic islands, the New Zealand situation as a case study, unpublished masters thesis, Massey University, Palmerston North.

Wouters, M. and Hall, C.M. (1995a) 'Managing tourism in the Sub-Antarctic islands', in C.M. Hall and M. Johnston (eds.) *Polar Tourism: Tourism in Arctic and Antarctic Regions,* Chichester: John Wiley.

— (1995) 'Tourism and New Zealand's Sub-Antarctic islands', in C.M. Hall and M. Johnston (eds.) *Polar Tourism: Tourism in Arctic and Antarctic Regions,* Chichester: John Wiley.

16 Contested Place and the Legitimization of Sovereignty Claims through Tourism in Polar Regions

Dallen J. Timothy

Introduction

Countries have a tradition of zealously guarding every metre of national territory for a variety of reasons, including the resources that might lie beneath, the valuable agricultural land above, or to be able to control shipping routes and ocean resources. For these same reasons, countries have a long tradition of occupying and annexing lands beyond their traditional borders. While much of this type of activity has diminished in the modern world as most of the earth has now been explored and come under the sovereign control of nearly 200 nation states, there are some land areas still in dispute between two or more vying polities, most of which lie in extreme peripheral zones or are comprised of seemingly insignificant islets or rocky outcrops in the seas, as well as marine areas under the Law of the Sea. Claimant countries have devised a variety of ways to assert their territorial claims, including establishing scientific research stations, creating human settlements, and initiating economic activities.

Of particular interest in this chapter, however, is states' use of tourism as an instrument to shore up international recognition and support for declarations of sovereignty, an issue of growing importance in the polar regions (see chapter 1). This chapter examines the notion of sovereignty and how countries use various means to declare their sovereignty over disputed lands and waters, with particular emphasis on the role of tourism in these efforts. Empirical examples are provided from Antarctica, Svalbard, and Canada to illustrate the various tourism-related mechanisms being exploited for the political purpose of legitimising state claims to contested territories in the north and south polar regions of the world.

Sovereignty and International Law

The most prized possession a state can have is sovereignty, which generally refers to absolute control of national territory and the right to exercise power over that territory and its people, resources, and interests without interference from other states (Joyner 1992; Philpott 1995; Glassner and Fahrer 2004). The concept also entails certain responsibilities and duties of the state over territory. For sovereignty to exist, this totality of responsibilities and rights must be recognised by the global community and international law. To exercise power over state territory, countries have waged bitter wars to expand their boundaries, sometimes even around seemingly small tracts of land for a variety of reasons, including resource extraction, protecting the rights of ethnic minorities, or simply the desire to expand national space.

International law generally recognises the expansion of territorial sovereignty through one of several different processes (Joyner 1992; Glassner and Fahrer 2004). The first process is occupation of *terra nullius*, or the occupation of unclaimed (belonging to no one) or uninhabited lands. European colonialism forwarded this notion, and even though many lands, such as in the Arctic, that were annexed between the 14th and 19th centuries were inhabited by indigenous peoples, they were seen from the Eurocentric viewpoint as unclaimed by legitimate sovereign states (Fogelson 1985).

The second process of territorial acquisition is prescription, or the surrender of territory that is occupied by a neighbouring state. When the territory of one country has been possessed and used extensively by a neighbouring country for a long period of time, functionally as though it is part of its own space, the land can potentially be absorbed into the national territory of the state that has been using it. An Arctic example of this includes the Petsamo region of Finland, which was occupied by the Soviet Union between 1939 and 1946, at which time Finland ceded the land to the Soviets.

Third, territorial sovereignty can also be expanded by voluntary cession, whereby one state transfers territory to another state by formal agreement. Although this is rare today, it was not uncommon in the past, particularly as territories were traded or exchanged between neighbouring countries for pragmatic reasons.

Conquest and annexation are a fourth important, albeit less prevalent, process in the contemporary world. The Soviet Union's (now Russia's) occupation of some of the Kuril Islands, which Japan also claims, is a current example.

Finally, accretion, or the gradual deposition of soil, changes the shape of the state. This is most common in areas where borders are located in rivers. In these cases, depending on the original boundary treaties, most political borders remain in their original position even if the river changes course, thereby dismembering pieces of land on the riverbank, as has happened on the Finnish–Swedish and Finnish–Norwegian riverine borders in the Arctic zone. Such changes may become more significant in polar areas in the longer term as climate change leads to wider environmental change in river systems as well as the potential effects of sea-level rise on some boundaries (see chapter 2).

As the above paragraphs denote, there are several ways in which national space can be acquired. However, nearly all large-scale territorial claims today are grounded in the idea of occupation of *terra nullius*. As noted earlier, international law recognises that sovereignty over land requires the establishment of a state presence, government functions, and the carrying out of prescribed responsibilities. According to the international view of *terra nullius*, a claimant state must demonstrate minimum conditions: that the territory in question is capable of supporting human habitation, that there is a history of effective occupation, and that it exercises state functions over the area in question (Triggs 1986; Joyner 1992). Some of the most commonly acknowledged state functions include issuing currency, posting and maintaining flags, establishing border controls, enabling outside access and transportation capabilities, providing various public services to inhabitants, operating police and security functions, levying taxes, and establishing postal services.

There are several 20th-century cases in which the law of *terra nullius* was made effective and sovereignty granted to states through international agreement; in most of these cases, there were overlapping claims and disputes{—}all being based on occupation of *terra nullius*. For example, Eastern Greenland (which Norway also claimed) was granted to Denmark in 1933.

In the polar regions, sovereignty and rights of jurisdiction have long been contested and are regularly the focal point of geopolitical analysis (Rothwell 1996; Dodds 1997; Collis 2004; Charron 2005). The Law of the Sea and its ocean-based economic and control zones have been at the heart of these discussions and conflicts. The Arctic and Antarctic regions are trickier to analyse than other parts of the world, because of the presence of ice and the invisibility of land under the South Pole. Some observers (e.g. Hoffecker *et al.* 1993; McGhee 2005) have noted that the polar regions are probably unable to support true or sustained human habitation, because of physiographic and climatic conditions, and are thus not subject to sovereignty, although this assertion has been variously rejected (Triggs 1986). The primary difference between Antarctica and the Arctic is that much of the latter is an ice shelf, whereas the former is primarily land overlaid by ice. These definitional differences have important legal ramifications as questions arise regarding whether or not territorial sovereignty can be acquired over ice and icebergs (Kratochwil *et al.* 1985).

Tourism and claims to territorial sovereignty

Territorial disputes exist all over the world at both a national and subnational level. At an international level, there are countless conflicting claims to sovereign control over portions of the Earth (Allcock *et al.* 1992). While the roots of these conflicts are diverse, tourism is linked directly or indirectly to many of them. Examples include China and Russia, where the common boundary is ill defined in the Amur River, an area that is becoming a significant cross-border travel area (Timothy 2001).

Some claimant states have attempted to use tourism as a mechanism to assert legal ownership and jurisdiction over disputed areas (Hall 1994; Timothy 2001). Nation states in conflict argue that a functioning tourism industry fulfils the three legal requisites for international recognition and acceptance: the place can support human habitation, there exists a history of claimant-state occupation, and state functions/responsibilities are being exercised. Probably the best known example today is the Spratly Islands, which are an archipelago of some 230 small islands, minute atolls, and rocky outcrops in the South China Sea. Together they total only

5 km² of exposed land, and only 25 or so of the islands are even somewhat substantial. Only a couple of the islets can be seriously considered inhabitable. Tourism has also been used similarly in the Arctic and Antarctic regions by Canada and Norway in the north and by several claimant parties in Antarctica.

Antarctica

Seven states claim sovereign rights over most of Antarctica: Argentina, Australia, Chile, France, New Zealand, Norway and the United Kingdom. Joyner (1992) provides a succinct overview of each of the claimant's positions and claims to its wedge of the continent. Argentina asserts its Antarctic rights based on historical 'occupation' of Laurie Island's (South Orkneys) weather station since 1904, the country's independence from Spain, and its geographical proximity to Antarctica. Chile's Territorio Chileno Antarctico is similar to that of Argentina's, and includes assertions that Chile is geologically connected to Antarctica. France's territory, Terra Adelie, is the smallest claim on the continent. France's claim is based upon discovery, especially the expedition of Dumont d'Urville in 1840 and subsequent 20th-century voyages of Charcot. The French claims were administered by the Governor of Madagascar until 1955, but now the French Southern and Antarctic Territories are governed by the Ministry of Overseas France in Paris. Australia claims approximately 6.24 million km² of Antarctica{—}the largest claim on the continent. The legal bases for Australia's claim are twofold: discovery by British and Australian explorers, starting with Captain James Cook in 1770–75 and Sir Douglas Mawson in 1910. Secondly, Australia boasts a continuous occupation, purposeful administration, and effective control of its Antarctic Territory. The Ross Dependency is New Zealand's territorial claim. Like Australia's portion, Ross Dependency was originally claimed by the United Kingdom but transferred to New Zealand following its independence from the UK. The core of New Zealand's legal basis is also founded on British exploration and discovery, including Admiral James Ross in 1841 and Robert Scott in 1901. The British claim is based on historical exploration, like its former colonies, Australia and New Zealand. The Norwegian territory is known as Dronning Maud Land. Its petition is based on early exploration and 'geographical work' (exploring and mapping) carried out in the 1800s and early 1900s, but focuses more on continued occupation and use of Antarctic waters for commerce (i.e. whaling). Additional claims were made over Antarctic islands in 1928 and 1931.

To boost international acceptance, the claimant states have carried out significant efforts to demonstrate effective control and occupation, inhabitation, and provision of services (Triggs 1986; Glassner and Fahrer 2004; Collis 2004, 2007). Property (border) markers have been erected, plaques and monuments constructed, post offices opened and staffed, stamps minted especially for use in Antarctica, stamps and maps issued that depict Antarctic territories as integral parts of the state, holding legislative/cabinet meetings on the continent, appointing magistrates and coroners, sending pregnant women to give birth in Antarctica, promoting wedding ceremonies, establishing civilian settlements or colonies, constructing administrative buildings, building research stations, establishing ministries over Antarctic affairs, and declaring national Antarctic holidays (Joyner 1992). Some claimants (Australia, France, New Zealand, UK) have organised their claims as colonial territories. Others (Chile and Argentina) have integrated their claims into their national territory. Despite these claims, no state has recognised legal claim to Antarctic sovereignty, although the UK, New Zealand, and Norway agreed to recognise each other's territorial claims in 1938 (Joyner 1992).

Because of growing conflict over territorial claims, growing interest in occupying Antarctica, and tensions over the use of the continent's natural resources, 12 nations established the Antarctic Treaty in 1959, which came into force in 1961. The original signatories were the countries active in Antarctica during the International Geophysical Year of 1957–58, which accepted a US invitation to the meeting at which the treaty was negotiated. These countries were the ones with significant interests in Antarctica at the time: Argentina, Australia, Belgium, Chile, France, Japan, New Zealand, Norway, South Africa, the Soviet Union, the United Kingdom and the United States. As of the time of writing the Treaty had been signed by 46 countries. According to the Treaty,

- Antarctica will be used only for peaceful purposes; military activities are prohibited
- The freedom to conduct scientific research and cooperation will continue
- There will be a free exchange of information and personnel
- Radioactive waste and nuclear explosions are forbidden
- Observers from signatory states may visit any area and may inspect all stations, equipment, and installations, with proper advanced notice
- Jurisdiction over observers and scientists resides with these people's own states
- The Antarctic region includes all land and ice shelves south of latitude 60°S
- Treaty signatories shall meet regularly and often to consult about issues in the region, such as environmental conservation
- These meetings shall be accessible to contracting parties that conduct extensive research on the continent
- Member states will discourage activities by any country that defies the treaty
- Disputes must be settled peacefully between concerned parties, or ultimately by the International Court of Justice
- No prior territorial claims are recognised, disputed, or established, and no new claims can be made while the treaty is in force (Secretariat of the Antarctic Treaty 2009).

The most critical of these articles for the present discussion is the final one. The Treaty does not require any country to renounce its claims, but it does suggest that no new claims can be made or enlarged.

Tourism is actively being used as a tool for substantiating territorial claims in Antarctica, despite the fact that the treaty restricts economic activities as a basis for asserting, supporting or denying a claim. Chile, Argentina and Australia are the most ardent in their tourism-cum-claim to sovereignty efforts.

In 1984, Chile hosted the first group of tourists to spend the night on shore in Antarctica and has since continued hosting tourists at its base at Teniente Marsh. Argentina's encouragement of couples to travel with their wedding parties to Antarctica to be married is an interesting and unusual example. While probably not a feasible option, Argentina even considered building a brand-name hotel on its territorial claim (Glassner and Fahrer 2004). Official policy in Canberra, Australia, in the 1990s regarding tourism in Antarctica includes the use of tourism as a means to 'preserve its sovereignty over the [Australian Antarctic Territory], including rights over the adjacent offshore areas' (quoted in Hall 1994: 88). Cruises, overflights, and visits to scientific bases are lauded as coalescing elements to sovereignty claims (Scott 2001). Because scientific stations are government sponsored and under the control of treaty states, national centres of scientific research become national centres of tourism, thus fuelling the assertion of state jurisdiction. Heritage sites and wildlife also promote nationalism in the claimant territories, and visits to such places are sometimes viewed by contending countries as justifiable grounds for basing claims on heritage, or a history of exploration.

The non-existence of sovereign state control in Antarctica has a number of important implications from many perspectives, including tourism. The uncertain legal status of facilities and ambiguous legal jurisdiction over the continent is of grave concern to the tourism industries (Enzenbacher 1995; ATCM 2006). One of the most pressing matters today related to a dearth of sovereignty is the environment. While many international regulations are in place that pertain to environmental protection (i.e. the Kyoto Protocol), there is a lack of state authority in Antarctica to enforce controls or international regulations and laws (Auburn 1982; Davis 1999; Kriwoken and Rootes 2000; Bastmeijer and Roura 2004). Ecological standards and codes of conduct have been set for tourism in the region, and discussions have taken place regarding limiting Antarctic tourism, but without sovereign control there is a lack of standardisation and enforcement. With no governing body to administer environmental conservation regulations, the ecological well-being of the region is left to the honesty and prudence of tour operators, cruise companies, and the tourists themselves (Hall 1992; Witte 2006).

Related to ecological management concerns are pressing issues of a cultural heritage nature (see chapter 10). Past discussions in the United Nations focused on Antarctica as a common World Heritage Site that should be preserved for the shared patrimony of humankind. Such efforts require some sort of oversight regime, which some observers believe should be assigned to the UN (Herber 1991). There are more than 60 recognised heritage sites in Antarctica, and various natural areas, all agreed upon by multilateral treaties, with some falling under the jurisdiction of national preservation laws that can help protect them. Many of the locations are designated Sites of Special Scientific Interest. Periodic checks are made of these heritage sites by national inspection teams, but there is no uniform set of criteria upon which conservation, interpretation, and site management can be based (US Department of State 1994).

There are also salient concerns about safety and security. Whenever cruise ships ply Antarctic waters or planes conduct flyovers, there is a danger of ships running aground or airplanes crashing. Like pollution and environment conventions, there is no single authority or formal mechanism to regulate tourism security beyond each country's domestic laws and law enforcement (Glassner and Fahrer 2004). Instead, when planes crash and ships are grounded, rescue efforts are usually left to scientific station staff and icebreaker operators at great expense and inconvenience (Auburn 1982; Murray and Jabour 2004; Snyder and Prokosch 2007).

Jurisdiction over environmental and safety controls lies with the country of the ship or airliner's registry, and the global tourism sector is beginning to demand that cruise and airline companies are self-policing in their ecological impacts and security mechanisms (Landau 2001), just as cruise ships are self-monitoring on the high seas. Many cruise ships are registered in countries that are not party to the Antarctic Treaty, and therefore the edicts established in the treaty have little direct control over these vessels. Likewise, voyages cannot be prohibited or regulated (Auburn 1982; Murray and Jabour 2004)

Svalbard

Another interesting example is Svalbard, an Arctic archipelago located halfway between Norway and the North Pole. In 1925, sovereignty over Svalbard was given to Norway in the 1920 International Treaty Concerning Spitsbergen (the former name for Svalbard). More than 40 countries have signed the treaty approving and recognising Norwegian sovereignty over the islands. Nonetheless, this is a unique example of recognised sovereignty in that there are some salient restrictions on Norway's jurisdiction there. Among these are that the territory can be used only for peaceful activities (it must remain demilitarised) and treaty signatories have the right to undertake commercial activities there, such as coal mining and fishing (Smedal 1931; Ulfstein 1995). Currently only Russia and Norway have coal-mining operations in Svalbard, and Poland operates a scientific research station.

Because of the concept of full Norwegian sovereignty with limited jurisdiction, there has been some friction with Russia over local governance, mining, fishing and public services. Currently there are three permanent settlements in Svalbard and a handful of scientific research stations. One of the current settlements, Barentsburg, is a Russian village of several hundred Russian and Ukrainian miners, employed by Arkitugol, a state-owned Russian coal company. This locale illustrates well the idea of sovereignty versus jurisdiction. Barentsburg and Pyramiden, another Russian settlement that was abandoned in 1998, have traditionally resembled Russian outliers on Norwegian soil, functionally, though not legally, part of Russia. Arkitugol mints its own coinage in St Petersburg for circulation in the two communities (nowadays alongside Norwegian currency). Until postal services were provided to Barentsburg and Pyramiden by Norway in 1990, mail to and from the settlements bore Soviet stamps and was postmarked

Murmansk. There is a Russian consulate in Barentsburg, and most food imports still come from Russia rather than Norway. Likewise, most of the children are oriented toward Russia in their pursuits of higher education, and everyday life focuses on Russian social structure and community traditions (Capelotti 2000; Umbreit 2005). Because miners were seen as national heroes during the Soviet era, Barentsburg was famous in the USSR, and its people were patriotic to the motherland. Today there are still remnants of that nationalism, with communist symbols, such as busts of Lenin, scattered throughout the village.

During the Cold War, the USSR held tightly to its settlements in Svalbard to shore up its claims to offshore resources; it was also toward the end of the Cold War (in the 1970s and 1980s) that Norway began to put its sovereignty over Svalbard into practice more earnestly. In the 1970s, Norway started implementing state functions, such as a post office in the archipelago's capital, Longyearbyen, and the appointment of a governor to the islands. During the 1980s and 1990s, Norway asserted its sovereign rights even further in the Russian settlements by installing Norwegian traffic signs, telephone networks, and post offices in locations that had until then been *de facto* administered from Moscow and Murmansk (Ulfstein 1995). With increased pressure from the Soviet Union, and subsequently Russia, and its counterclaims, Norway began to consider tourism as a potential tool for reinforcing its sovereignty over Svalbard and its continental shelf. Thus, beginning in the 1990s, the Norwegian government began emphasising tourism as an alternative economy to the declining fishing and mining sectors, not only to fulfil economic ends but also to reaffirm its legal rights to Svalbard (Ulfstein 1995).

Most tourism in the islands focuses on nature (e.g. polar bear viewing), although culture and the interesting heritage of the region are also part of the tourist appeal (Viken 1995; Viken and Jørgensen 1998). Another primary attraction is the remoteness and uniqueness for people who 'collect' unique and unusual destinations and who can claim that they have been somewhere extraordinary (Timothy 1998). Svalbard has become a cruise destination for dozens of ships each year, while many other tourists fly in and take local boats and snowmobiles or dog sleds in winter to get around.

International treaties concerning Svalbard, however, strongly influence one of the main travel-related functions of a state: passport and visa controls. Norway is part of the Schengen area; it shares a common visa with other Schengen members, and passports are not required when travelling between Norway and other Schengen states. However, Svalbard, despite being part of Norway, is not part of the Schengen area, primarily because of the open immigration policy established for the archipelago by the International Treaty Concerning Spitsbergen. The accord stipulates that citizens and companies from all Spitsbergen Treaty nations enjoy the same right of access to and residence in Svalbard (Governor of Svalbard 2008). Visitors entering the territory directly from anywhere in the world are not required to possess a Norwegian (or Schengen) visa and have traditionally not had to show passports upon arrival in Svalbard, even if they arrive from countries outside Norway (Baldacchino 2006; Governor of Svalbard 2008). Because

Svalbard lies outside the Schengen area, however, in December 2008, the Norwegian Ministry of Justice began requiring passports from all travellers arriving in Svalbard from mainland Norway, even for Norwegian citizens (Solholm 2008).

Canadian Arctic

Several countries, including Norway, Denmark and Russia, claim sovereignty over the northern Arctic regions of the world. Canada, too, has long maintained claims to sovereignty over the northern Arctic region, including territorial waters, extending to the North Pole, arguing that its continental shelf extends that far and that acts of discovery by English and French explorers constitute discovery and subsequent occupation of *terra nullius* (Rothwell 1996; Lineback and Lineback Gritzner 2007; Mifflin 2007). The international community, however, does not recognise any state's ownership of the North Pole and the waters (including ice) that surround it. The USA and the European Union contend that the Arctic waters are international waters. According to the US Department of State, 'we cannot accept the assertion of a Canadian claim that the Arctic waters are internal waters of Canada{...}Such acceptance would jeopardise the freedom of navigation essential for United States naval activities worldwide' (quoted in Carnaghan and Goody 2006: 4).

One of the most pressing issues for Canada is the Northwest Passage, an Arctic Ocean sea route through the Canadian Arctic archipelago. It connects the Atlantic and Pacific Oceans in the north and has significant transshipment potential. Canada claims the passage is internal waters based on the location of Canadian islands and the tenets of the Law of the Sea, while some members of the international community, namely the USA and the European Union, argue that the route constitutes an international passage (Charron 2005; Elliot-Meisel 1999). While the route clearly lies within the normal boundaries of Canadian waters, either in the 24-nautical-mile Contiguous Zone or within the 200-nautical-mile Exclusive Economic Zone, the argument for its being an international strait is based largely on two legal premises: that it connects two bodies of the high seas (Atlantic and Pacific Oceans) and that it is a functional route for ship navigation that has experienced significant numbers of transits (Pharand 1988). Although 'there has not yet been a sufficient number of transits to qualify it as a "useful route for international maritime traffic"' (Carnaghan and Goody 2006: 4), Canada fears that its claims to the internal waterway status of the corridor could be seriously challenged if enough vessels ply the Northwest Passage without seeking permission from Canada. All of these concerns rest upon the accepted notion that as the polar ice continues to melt, the Northwest Passage will be open to increasingly more shipping activity, which could challenge Canada's Arctic claims even further (Carnaghan and Goody 2006; Stewart and Draper 2006; chapter 2).

Canada is also involved in a dispute with Denmark over a small (1.3 km²) piece of land, Hans Island, which lies in the Arctic halfway between Ellesmere Island, Canada and Greenland (Denmark). Since the early 1970s Denmark has argued that the international boundary is just west of the rocky outcrop, while Canada claims it lies just to the east, thereby placing the island completely in Canada. However, based on more accurate satellite imagery, the boundary probably runs through the middle of the island (Canadian Press 2007). Control of Hans Island is important for Canada as well as Denmark because it is indicative of the country's ability to exercise sovereignty over its Arctic claims and sends a salient message to other states that counterclaim Arctic territory or that question Canada's jurisdiction there (Timothy and Olsen 2001; Carnaghan and Goody 2006).

To solidify its declaration of sovereignty over its Arctic territories and waters, Canada uses tourism and tourism-related mechanisms. One of the most prominent is national parks. According to Hall and Johnston (1995), Canada's establishment of virtually inaccessible national parks in the far northern reaches of Ellesmere Island and Baffin Island, such as Aulavik, Quttinirpaaq and Sirmilik, may be viewed as a way of reinforcing its territorial claims to the Arctic archipelago and surrounding waters. A trickle of adventure tourists visit these isolated parks each year, lending additional support to Canada's assertion of occupation and administration (see chapter 12) Another mechanism is indigenous people. While this does not always relate directly to tourism, it often does in the far north. As citizens of Canada, the indigenous people of the north play an important role in personifying stewardship, use and occupancy over the Arctic lands and waters. The northern First Nations play a crucial role in tourism development in the Arctic territories, and the Canadian Government supports the northern peoples in this regard by offering lucrative incentives and emphasising native-based tourism development efforts.

The development of deep-water ports for transportation of goods and to facilitate cruises is achieving momentum in government and economic circles. The Government of Canada announced in 2007 that it would spend over three billion dollars on new ships to patrol the Arctic for commercial and military purposes. This will no doubt smooth the progress of increasing northern cruises. These efforts are in line with the Prime Minister's statement that 'Canada has a choice when it comes to defending our sovereignty over the Arctic{...}we either use it or lose it' (Lin 2007: n.p.).

Conclusions

This chapter highlights some of the efforts of states to assert and justify their territorial claims in the north and south polar regions. Although according to international law, states may increase their geographical extent through several recognised methods of accruing territory, the most common approach is the occupation of *terra nullius*, or unclaimed land. For such claims to be recognised legally by the international community, a country must demonstrate that the place is able to support human tenancy, that there has been a history of effectual habitation, and that the state is practising active stewardship (i.e. functions) over the area in question.

Since the 1960s, most states that have declared sovereignty over lands and seas in the northern and southern polar regions have targeted tourism to underscore their claims. From their perspective, tourism and all the humans it involves (destination-based employees, tour operators, guides, cruise operators, tourists) are a strong indicator of inhabitability and human occupation of *terra nullius*. Likewise, government sponsorship of events and tourism programmes, the facilitation of access, security protection, and the construction of monuments and tourism-related structures are treated by claimants as equivalent to providing state functions.

Questions continue to arise, however, that might thwart claimant states' assertions. For example, are the Arctic and Antarctic lands truly capable of supporting human habitation? Can tourism and tourist visits be seen legally as 'human habitation' since they are temporary in nature, and can a history of effective human occupation be shown through tourism? Significantly, there are legal precursors in other parts of the world where sovereignty has been acquired via temporary migration and sporadic occupation. Such was the case of Eastern Greenland in 1933 noted above. Are tourism-related policies based on national tour operators and flag carriers sufficient to demonstrate an exercise of state functions in polar regions? Before the 1960s, all of the legal requirements for sovereignty were being justified by claimant states through a history of resource extraction (e.g. mining and fishing), exploration, and scientific research. However, in the post-industrial world, tourism has also come to the fore in geopolitics, essentially replacing extractive economies with service economies as a foundation for territorial claims. It remains to be seen how well tourism will be accepted by the international community as a basis for recognising sovereignty over the disputed polar portions of the globe.

References

Allcock, J.B., Arnold, G., Day, A.J., Lewis, D.S., Poultney, L., Rance, R. and Sagar, D.J. (1992) *Border and Territorial Disputes*, 3rd edn. London: Longman.

Antarctic Treaty Consultative Meeting (ATCM) (2006) *Strategic Issues Posed by Commercial Tourism in the Antarctic Treaty Area*. Edinburgh: ATCM.

Auburn, F.M. (1982) *Antarctic Law and Politics*. London: C. Hurst.

Baldacchino, G. (2006) 'Innovative development strategies from non-sovereign island jurisdictions? A global review of economic policy and governance practices', *World Development*, 34(5): 852–67.

Bastmeijer, K. and Roura, R. (2004) 'Regulating Antarctic tourism and the precautionary principle', *American Journal of International Law*, 98(4): 763–81.

Canadian Press (2007) Satellite imagery moves Hans Island boundary: report. CBCNews. com. Online. Available HTTP: http://www.cbc.ca/technology/story/2007/07/26/hans-technology.html (accessed December 15, 2008).

Capelotti, P.J. (2000) *The Svalbard Archipelago: American Military and Political Geographies of Spitsbergen and Other Norwegian Polar Territories, 1941–1950*. Jefferson, NC: McFarland.

Carnaghan, M. and Goody, A. (2006) *Canadian Arctic Sovereignty*. Ottawa: Library of Parliament.

Charron, A. (2005) 'Canada, the United States, and the Northwest Passage: sovereignty to the side', *Polar Geography*, 29(2): 139–55.

Collis, C. (2004) 'The proclamation island moment: making Antarctica Australian', *Law Text Culture*, 8: 1–18.

— (2007) 'Mawson and Mirnyy Stations: the spatiality of the Australian Antarctic Territory, 1954–61', *Australian Geographer*, 38(2): 215–31.

Davis, P.B. (1999) 'Beyond guidelines: a model for Antarctic tourism', *Annals of Tourism Research*, 26(3): 516–33.

Dodds, K. (1997) *Geopolitics in Antarctica: Views from the Southern Ocean Rim*. Chichester: Wiley

Elliot-Meisel, E.B. (1999) 'Still unresolved after fifty years: the Northwest Passage in Canadian-American relations, 1946–98', *American Review of Canadian Studies*, 29(3): 407–30.

Enzenbacher, D.J. (1995) 'The regulation of Antarctic tourism', in C.M. Hall and M.E. Johnston (eds) *Polar Tourism: Tourism in the Arctic and Antarctic Regions*. Chichester: Wiley.

Fogelson, N. (1985) 'The tip of the iceberg: the United States and international rivalry for the Arctic, 1900–925', *Diplomatic History*, 9(2): 131–48.

Glassner, M.I. and Fahrer, C. (2004) *Political Geography*, 3rd edn. Hoboken, NJ: Wiley.

Governor of Svalbard (2008) Entry and residence. Online. Available HTTP: http://www.sysselmannen.no/hovedEnkel.aspx?m = 45270 (accessed 19 December, 2008).

Hall, C.M. (1992) 'Tourism in Antarctica: activities, impacts, and management', *Journal of Travel Research*, 30(4): 2–9.

— (1994) *Tourism and Politics: Policy, Power and Place*. Chichester: Wiley.

Hall, C.M. and Johnston, M. (eds) (1995) 'Pole to pole: tourism issues, impacts and the search for a management regime in polar regions', in C.M. Hall and M. Johnston (eds), *Polar Tourism: Tourism in the Arctic and Antarctic Regions*. Chichester: Wiley.

Herber, B.P. (1991) 'The common heritage principle: Antarctica and the developing nations', *American Journal of Economics and Sociology*, 50(4): 391–406.

Hoffecker, J.F., Powers, W.R. and Goebel, T. (1993) 'The colonization of Beringia and the peopling of the New World', *Science*, 259: 46–53.

Joyner, C.C. (1992) *Antarctica and the Law of the Sea*. Dordrecht: Martinus Nijhoff.

Kratochwil, F., Rohrlich, P. and Mahajan, H. (1985) *Peace and Disputed Sovereignty: Reflections on Conflict over Territory*. Lanham, MD: University Press of America.

Kriwoken, L.K. and Rootes, D. (2000) 'Tourism on ice: environmental impact assessment of Antarctic tourism', *Impact Assessment and Project Appraisal*, 18(2): 138–50.

Landau, D. (2001) Antarctic tourism: what are the limits? Paper presented at the World Tourism Convention—Striking a New Balance—Exploring New Horizons, Hobart, Tasmania, 31 October-02 November.

Lin, W. (2007) 'Canada to be forced to boost Arctic security, expert says', *Ottawa Citizen*, 15 September: 13.

Lineback, N. and Lineback Gritzner, M. (2007) '*Claiming the Arctic Ocean*', *Perspective*, 36(2): 9, 14.

McGhee, R. (2005) *The Last Imaginary Place: A Human History of the Arctic World*. Chicago: University of Chicago Press.

Mifflin, M. (2007) 'Arctic sovereignty: a view from the north', *Policy Options*, May: 55–58.

Murray, C. and Jabour, J. (2004) 'Independent expeditions and Antarctic tourism policy,' *Polar Record*, 40(4): 309–17.

Pharand, D. (1988) *Canada's Arctic Water in International Law*. Cambridge: Cambridge University Press.

Philpott, D. (1995) 'Sovereignty: an introduction and brief history', *Journal of International Affairs*, 48(2): 352–68.

Rothwell, D.R. (1996) *The Polar Regions and the Development of International Law*. Cambridge: University of Cambridge.

Scott, S.V. (2001) 'How cautious is precautious? Antarctic tourism and the precautionary principle', *International and Comparative Law Quarterly*, 50: 963–71.

Secretariat of the Antarctic Treaty (2009) Antarctic Treaty System. Online. Available HTTP: http://www.ats.aq/e/ats/htm (accessed March 20 2009).

Smedal, G. (1931) *Acquisition of Sovereignty over Polar Areas*. Oslo: Gyldendal Forlag.

Snyder, J. and Prokosch, P. (2007) *Tourism in Polar Regions: The Sustainability Challenge*. Geneva: United Nations Environment Programme.

Solholm, R. (2008) 'Passport control for Svalbard travellers', *The Norway Post*, 19 December. Online. Available HTTP: http://www.norwaypost.no/News/Passport-control-for-Svalbard-travellers/menu-id-26.html (accessed December 20, 2008)

Stewart, E.J. and Draper, D. (2006) 'Sustainable cruise tourism in Arctic Canada: an integrated coastal management approach', *Tourism in Marine Environments*, 3(2): 77–88.

Timothy, D.J. (1998) 'Collecting places: geodetic lines in tourist space', *Journal of Travel and Tourism Marketing*, 7(4): 123–29.

— (2001) *Tourism and Political Boundaries*. London: Routledge.

Timothy, D.J. and Olsen, D.H. (2001) 'Challenges and opportunities of marginality in the Arctic: a case of tourism in Greenland', *Tourism*, 49(4): 299–308.

Triggs, G. (1986) *International Law and Australian Sovereignty in Antarctica*. Sydney: Legal Books.

Ulfstein, G. (1995) *The Svalbard Treaty: From Terra Nullius to Norwegian Sovereignty*. Oslo: Scandinavian University Press.

Umbreit, A. (2005) *Spitsbergen: The Bradt Travel Guide*. Chalfont St Peter: Bradt Travel Guides.

US Department of State (1994) *Handbook of the Antarctic Treaty System*. Washington, DC: US Department of State.

Viken, A. (1995) 'Tourism experiences in the Arctic: the Svalbard case', in C.M. Hall and M.E. Johnston (eds), *Polar Tourism: Tourism in the Arctic and Antarctic Regions*. Chichester: Wiley.

Viken, A. and Jorgensen, F. (1998) 'Tourism on Svalbard', *Polar Record*, 34: 123–28.

Witte, B. (2006) 'March of the tourists: officials debate limits on travel to Antarctica', *News and Observer*, 05 November: 11.

17 Last Chance to See? Future Issues for Polar Tourism and Change

C. Michael Hall and Jarkko Saarinen

Introduction

The question 'Isn't the weather strange lately?' seems to be increasingly asked in these days of conjecture about the effects of climate change. Although individual weather events cannot be specifically connected to climate change they do act as indicators of a potential future for high-latitude climates as well as being potential evidence for some of the greater variability of weather events that has been forecast as part of climate change. Since the commencement of the International Polar Year (IPY) in 2007 to just prior to the Copenhagen climate conference in December 2009 a number of notable anomalies have occurred:

- Alaska (2007–08): second highest winter snowfall in 30 years
- Northern hemisphere snow cover extent (January 2008): largest January snow cover extent on record
- Arctic sea ice (September 2007): all-time lowest extent on record in September, surpassed previous record set in 2005 by 23%
- Arctic sea ice (September 2009): second lowest extent on record behind September 2007
- Fenno-Scandinavia (2008): warmest winter ever recorded in most parts of Norway, Sweden and Finland
- Eurasian snow cover extent (January 2008): largest January extent on record and smallest extent during March, April, and boreal spring
- Antarctic ozone hole (2008): a maximum 27.2 million km² in September; fifth largest recorded (McMullen and Jabbour, 2009).

Such events have served to focus the attention of governments and other stakeholders not only on the influence of climate change in polar regions but also because of its synergies with natural and political systems. For example, the decline in Arctic sea ice extent is inseparable from the increased interest in maritime access to the polar seas for fishing, mineral exploration and exploitation, trade and tourism, and concerns over political sovereignty. However, one of the great lessons of climate change is that the Earth behaves as a single, self-regulating system comprised of physical, chemical, biological and human components. This means that what happens in the polar regions also has implications throughout the world in terms of environmental and other futures and that human activities, including those elsewhere in the world, are affecting high latitudes. Of the nine tipping elements considered as Earth System components vulnerable to climate change by Lenton *et al.* (2008), five are directly polar related:

Arctic summer sea ice: as sea ice melts it exposes darker ocean, which absorbs more heat than ice does, causing further warming (possible time frame: by 2020, temperature increase 0.2–2°C).

Boreal forests: Longer growing seasons and dry periods increase vulnerability to fires and pests (possible time frame: by 2060, temperature increase 3–5°C).

Atlantic Ocean thermohaline circulation: Regional ice melt will freshen North Atlantic water; this could shut down the ocean circulation system, including the Gulf Stream, which is driven by the sinking of dense saline water in this region (possible time frame: by 2100, temperature increase 3–5°C).

Greenland ice sheet: As ice melts, the height of surface ice decreases, so the surface is exposed to warmer temperatures at lower altitudes, which accelerates melting that could lead to ice-sheet break up (possible time frame: by 2300, temperature increase 1–2°C).

West Antarctic ice sheet: Ice sheet is frozen to submarine mountains, so high potential for sudden release and collapse as oceans warm (possible time frame: by 2300, temperature increase 3–5°C).

Yet the likelihood of such changes occurring is also related to the actions that humankind makes with respect to anthropogenic influence on climate change, which is in itself connected to responses to knowledge and forecasts of change and response to events as they occur. Undoubtedly, there are many uncertainties in forecasts of climate change but by their nature the consensus characteristics of IPCC reports has meant that they are inherently conservative perspectives on change. For example, the 2007 IPCC stated that 'Sea ice is projected to shrink in both the Arctic and Antarctic under all SRES scenarios [Special Report on Emissions Scenarios]. In some projections, arctic late-summer sea ice disappears almost entirely by the latter part of the 21st century' (IPCC 2007: 15). Yet just 2 years after the IPCC report was released there is recognition that Arctic sea ice is likely to disappear in a timescale of decades.

In 2007 the sea ice in the Arctic Ocean shrank to its smallest extent on record, 24% less than the previous record set in 2005 and 34% less than the average minimum extent between 1970 and 2000. Arctic sea ice coverage in 2008 finished with the second-lowest minimum extent in the satellite record, 9% above the 2007 minimum (Haas *et al.* 2008). On 12September 2009 sea ice extent dropped to 5.10 million km^2 (1.97 million miles^2). This appears to have been the lowest point of the year, as sea ice has now begun its annual cycle of growth in response to autumn cooling. The 2009 minimum is the third-lowest recorded since 1979, 580,000 square kilometers (220,000 miles^2) above 2008 and 970,000 km^2 (370,000 miles^2) above the record low in 2007 (National Snow and Ice Data Center [NSIDC] 2009). The 2009 minimum is 1.61 million km^2 (620,000 miles^2) below the 1979–2000 average minimum and 1.28 million km^2 (490,000 miles^2) below the 30-year 1979–2008 average minimum. Although the 2009 minimum is less than 2008, the second-lowest year on record, when the minimum sea ice extent was 4.52 million km^2, there is no indication that the long-term trends are reversing (Schiermeier 2009).

Arctic sea ice cover also has more extensive proportions of first- and second-year ice. In 1988, 21% of the sea ice cover was 7+ years old and 31% was 5+ years old. In 2007, only 5% was 7+ years old and 10% was 5+ years old. Such issues are important as first-year ice is thinner and prone to melt more quickly than thicker multiyear ice. In 2009, ice older than 2 years accounted for less than 10% of the ice cover at the end of February (NSIDC 2009). Less ice means more open water exposed to shortwave solar radiation that is absorbed and transformed into heat, therefore providing a strong positive feedback that further accelerates the melting of Arctic sea ice (sea ice areas covered with snow have a high albedo that reflects 80% of the incoming solar radiation back into space; in contrast the open ocean has a low albedo that reflects only 20% of solar radiation, absorbing the other 80%) (Dmitrenko *et al.* 2008; Dickson 2009). Such a situation led a group of scientists associated with the IPY (2009) to conclude

> …that there is a very low probability that Arctic sea ice will ever recover. As predicted by all IPCC models, Arctic sea ice is more likely to disappear in summer in the near future. However it seems like this is going to happen much sooner than models predicted…The entire Arctic system is evolving to a new super interglacial stage seasonally ice free, and this will have profound consequences for all the elements of the Arctic cryosphere, marine and terrestrial ecosystems and human activities. Both the atmosphere and the ocean circulation and stratification (ventilation) will also be affected. This raises a critical set of issues, with many important implications potentially able to speed up melting of the Greenland ice sheet, accelerating the rise in sea-levels and slowing down the world ocean conveyor belt (THC) [thermohaline circulation]. That would also have a lot of consequences on the ocean carbon sink…and ocean acidification. Permafrost melting could also accelerate during rapid Arctic sea-ice loss due to an amplification of Arctic land warming 3.5 times greater than secular 21st century climate trends [Lawrence *et al.* 2008]. This permafrost evolution would have important consequences and strong impacts on large carbon reservoirs and methane releases, either in the ocean and/or on land.

One of the key points that arises from the loss of Arctic sea ice is that it is not just the ocean that is then subject to change but also the coastline and the hinterland. The larger heat transfer from the ocean to the atmosphere (the maritime effect) will help moderate autumn and winter cold temperatures. As ice retreats from shorelines, 'winds gain a longer fetch over open water, resulting in stronger waves and increased shore erosion. The rapid retreat of Arctic sea ice could accelerate rapid warming 1,500 km inland throughout Alaska, Canada, and Russia. During rapid ice retreat, the rate of inland warming could be more than three times that previously suggested by global climate models' (McMullen and Jabbour 2009: 19).

Given such concerns it is perhaps not surprising that some polar destinations and tourism companies are looking to promote climate change tourism (Salt 2006; chapter 1 [this volume]) as part of a 'Last chance to see' also referred to as 'doom tourism' (UK MSN Travel 2009). 'The world has never travelled to the Arctic like now. Aided by global warming – that's opening up areas never before visited – but tinged by a quiet urgency, it's here the world gets a live demonstration of how our world is changing' (Destinations of the World News 2008: 2). Round's (2008: 46) observation that, 'The plight of the region has become such a part of our contemporary background that it's no wonder demand for the region has become so high. The message is quite clear: come quickly or you'll miss it', is something of a moot point, but it is one shared by a number of travel writers and commentators (e.g. E The Environmental Magazine 2002; Egan 2005; Margolis 2006).

As highlighted in chapter 1, the numbers of tourists travelling in the Arctic region is substantial, of the order of over five million visitors per year. Such figures run counter to the perspectives of Frigg Jorgensen, general secretary of the AECO, who commented, 'Passengers are usually highly educated people that understand the importance of conservation. Secondly, our regulations and those of Arctic countries protect sites. Thirdly, operators are responsible for managing them properly and it's in their interests to maintain the pristine environment they are selling. Finally, compared to national parks in Alaska where many thousands visit, for example, the number of Arctic tourists are minimal' (quoted in Round 2008: 47). Similarly, Round (2008: 46) states, 'do we need just a little more perspective? Only a few thousand travelers visit the Arctic every year compared to the hundreds of thousands of people that cross the manicured grass of New York's Central Park everyday'. Apart from the geographical challenge of not including Alaska as part of the Arctic, there still remains the issue that the number of tourists is continuing to increase and represents a significant figure in relation to permanent populations and concentration in a small number of accessible areas in space and time. For example, the number of fly-in tourists per year now exceeds the population of Greenland, with the number of cruise guests already being over half. A similar situation of number of visitors per year in relation to permanent population also exists in Iceland, Svalbard, and northern Norway, Sweden and Finland above the Arctic Circle (see chapter 1).

Given the number of visitors to the Arctic it should therefore be of no surprise that tourism is regarded as such a key component of the economy, along with fisheries and mineral and energy development. Climate change, rather than having a negative impact on the regional economy, is regarded as being a major beneficiary along with maritime transport generally as access to many northern areas is improved (ACIA 2005; Snyder 2007, 2009). Similarly, Antarctica and the sub-Antarctic are also receiving increasing numbers of tourists, which although not on the scale of the Arctic, also has significant economic benefits both for the small number of sub-Antarctic communities as well as the gateway communities in Australia, New Zealand and South America (Hall 2000). Given the much smaller amount of visitor access to ice-free areas, tourism is arguably of proportionally even greater significance in terms of direct environmental impact in the Antarctic than the Arctic (see chapter 2). Nevertheless, despite the importance of tourism as both a potential means of economic adaptation to the effects of climate change as well as being a direct source of environmental impact and change and a significant contributor to GHG emissions its potential role in the future of the economic and environmental transition of high latitudes to a new set of climatic, environmental, socioeconomic and political states is not well understood.

Although there have been a number of notable analyses and reviews of tourism in polar regions (e.g. Hall and Johnston 1995; Bauer 2001; Stewart *et al*. 2005; Snyder and Prokosch 2007; Snyder and Stonehouse 2007) such work has often occurred in isolation from broader research on response to environmental and social change in polar regions (c.g. Anisimov *et al*. 2001, 2007; AHDR 2004; Chapin *et al*. 2004, 2006; ACIA 2005; Instanes *et al*. 2005; Slaymaker and Kelly 2007). There has not only been a gap between those undertaking research in the physical and biological sciences in polar regions and those studying tourism, but even between students of tourism and other social scientists. This has meant that the nature and role of tourism in high-latitude economies has not been adequately appreciated in studies of climate change (e.g. Anisimov *et al*. 2007), nor its positive and negative contributions to biodiversity conservation in polar regions (see chapter 2). For example, because of the extent to which tourism provides an economic justification for transport infrastructure that existing population sizes may not justify alone, tourism therefore becomes extremely important in providing connectivity for peripheral high-latitude communities to major settlements. This may take the form of increased numbers of connections (i.e. flights), improved connections (i.e better quality of road, or speed of transport available), or whether there is a connection or no connection at all. Tourism's role in polar economic development when well planned and managed therefore goes well beyond that of tourism alone as it provides a major 'enabling' role via transport, accommodation and other infrastructure that may also contribute to local quality of life.

There is therefore a need to better integrate tourism into the broader understanding of climate and environmental change in polar regions and for greater dialogue of those who study tourism with other disciplines. One way in which this can be advanced is by recognising the role that tourism plays in the proposals for future research of the IPCC, some of which has already begun to be addressed as an outcome of the IPY (of which this book is a part). Tourism's potential role in the IPCC research agenda is identified in Table 17.1. This is especially important given tourism's economic role in polar regions for both indigenous and non-indigenous populations. An issue recognised by Anisimov *et al*. (2007: 676) is the need to examine the economic impacts of climate change 'which are difficult to address at present due to the dearth of information'. However, in addition to a greater integrative dimension of tourism research with other fields and regional research projects there are also a number of tourism-specific issues that need to be addressed in terms of the development of a more substantial knowledge base (Stewart *et al.* 2005; Hall 2008). These include

- tourism entrepreneur and organization perceptions of climate change and their adaptation and mitigation strategies to climate and environmental change
- tourist perception of the effects of climate change on polar destination attractiveness
- the extent to which polar tourism experiences create environmental advocates from those who participate in them
- the impacts of environmental change on place promotion
- the effectiveness of tourism codes of conduct in managing operator and tourist behaviour
- the role of tourism as a vector for the introduction of invasive species
- the potential environmental impacts of cruise ships in polar regions
- the role of tourism in polar governance and sovereignty issues
- the role of tourism in the sociocultural resilience of indigenous peoples and remote communities in the Arctic
- the role of tourism in economic development and diversification

Although tourism has been regarded by some as inappropriate in high-latitude regions because of the potential environmental and, to an extent in the Arctic, sociocultural impacts there is 'increasing recognition that responsible tourism is an appropriate and legitimate activity' (Splettstoesser 2000: 54). Given that tourism is such a significant economic activity and, as Stewart *et al.* (2005: 383) noted, even a 'desired industry in some communities', it is clearly vital that a deeper understanding of the complexity of polar tourism be achieved in terms that are useful for policy-makers, especially when tourism is also integral to climate and environmental change adaptation and mitigation.

At the conclusion of the first book on polar tourism the authors proclaimed the hope that the volume would 'provide a basis on which some of the critical policy and management decisions will be based' (Hall and Johnston 1995: 311). We would like to think that many of the chapters in the present volume would have a similar usefulness or at least be able to contribute to the wider knowledge base for polar region management and decision-making of which tourism is an important part. When interviewed as to the challenge of climate change for tourism Miriam Geitz, Climate Change Officer, WWF International Arctic Programme, commented

> ...the most interesting question is how will tour operators respond to climate change themselves. For instance will they visit new areas as soon as they open up, or will they take charge and forgo those areas – that may be sensitive

Table 17.1: Tourism's role in key uncertainties and related scientific recommendations and approaches identified by the IPCC (2007)

Uncertainty	Recommendation and approach	Role of tourism
Detection and projection of changes in terrestrial, freshwater and marine Arctic and Antarctic biodiversity and implications for resource use and climatic feedbacks	Further development of integrated monitoring networks and manipulation experiments; improved collation of long-term data sets; increased use of traditional knowledge and development of appropriate models	• Tourism as a source of change in biodiversity as a result of the introduction of invasive species • Tourism as an economic justification for biodiversity conservation
Current and future regional carbon balances over Arctic landscapes and polar oceans, and their potential to drive global climate change	Expansion of observational and monitoring networks and modelling strategies	• Tourism's impacts on carbon balance
Impacts of multiple drivers (e.g., increasing human activities and ocean acidity) to modify or even magnify the effects of climate change at both poles	Development of integrated bio-geophysical and socio-economic studies	• Tourism's overall contribution to climate change • tourism as a human activity in polar regions, particularly with respect to the potential to introduce invasive species
Fine-scaled spatial and temporal variability of climate change and its impacts in regions of the Arctic and Antarctic	Improved downscaling of climate predictions, and increased effort to identify and focus on impact 'hotspots'	• impact of climate change on tourist activities
The combined role of Arctic freshwater discharge, formation/melt of sea ice and melt of glaciers/ice sheets in the Arctic and Antarctic on global marine processes including the thermohaline circulation	Integration of hydrologic and cryospheric monitoring and research activities focusing on freshwater production and responses of marine systems	
The consequences of diversity and complexity in Arctic human health, socio-economic, cultural and political conditions; interactions between scales in these systems and the implications for adaptive capacity	Development of standardised baseline human system data for circumpolar regions; integrated multidisciplinary studies; conduct of sector-specific, regionally specific human vulnerability studies	• Tourism's role in Arctic human health, socio-economic, cultural and political conditions • Tourism as an element of adaptive capacity
Model projections of Antarctic and Arctic systems that include thresholds, extreme events, step-changes and non-linear interactions, particularly those associated with phase-changes produced by shrinking cryospheric components and those associated with disturbance to ecosystems	Appropriate interrogation of existing long-term data sets to focus on nonlinearities; development of models that span scientific disciplines and reliably predict non-linearities and feedback processes	• Tourism's role as a potential source of ecosystem disturbance
The adaptive capacity of natural and human systems to cope with critical rates of change and thresholds/tipping points	Integration of existing human and biological climate-impact studies to identify and model biological adaptive capacities and formulate human adaptation strategies	• Tourism's role in natural and human systems and contribution to adaptive capacity and resilience as well as contribution to change

Source: IPCC key uncertainties and related scientific approaches and recommendations from Anisimov et al. (2007): 677.

to visitor pressure – to protect them?…Any human activity, not only from tourism, is a stress factor and should be carefully considered for its consequences.

We have seen tourism as the natural ally of nature and local cultures. The people who come to the region come mainly for the experience, are fairly considerate to preservation. Through their visit, hopefully, they are changed by the experience, connect with the region and become ambassadors to the rest of the world.

(in Round 2008: 51).

These are also important issues and concerns for those researching polar tourism. Tourism, when sustainably planned and managed, undoubtedly has much to contribute to polar economies, cultures and science. Yet, Round's (2008: 48) observation with respect to the Greenland and Svalbard Arctic that 'whether you are for or against tourism…there is no doubt that climate change is transforming the region and future visitors will have a very different experience from those of today' will certainly hold true for the polar regions at current rate of change. We certainly do not wish polar tourism to become 'the last chance to see', yet without appropriate adaptation and mitigation by the tourism industry both globally and at high latitudes, and broader changes in humankind's unsustainable consumption of natural capital, it is becoming increasingly likely that the polar attractions of today will be but a dim memory retained on film by the end of this century.

References

Anisimov, O., Fitzharris, B.B., Hagen, J.O., Jefferies, B., Marchant, H., Nelson, F., Prowse, T. and Vaughan, D. (2001) 'Polar regions (Arctic and Antarctic)', in J.J. McCarthy, O.F. Canziani, N.A. Leary, D.J. Dokken and K.S. White (eds.) *Climate Change 2001: Impacts, Adaptation, and Vulnerability. Contribution of Working Group II to the Third Assessment Report of the Intergovernmental Panel on Climate Change*, Cambridge: Cambridge University Press.

Anisimov, O.A., Vaughan, D.G., Callaghan, T.V., Furgal, H., Marchant, H., Prowse, T.D., Vilhjálmsson, H. and Walsh, J.E. (2007) 'Polar regions (Arctic and Antarctic)', in M.L. Parry, O.F. Canziani, J.P. Palutikof, P.J. van der Linden and C.E. Hanson (eds) *Climate Change 2007: Impacts, Adaptation and Vulnerability*, Cambridge: Cambridge University Press.

Arctic Climate Impacts Assessment (ACIA) (2005) *Impacts of a Warming Arctic: Arctic Climate Impacts Assessment*, Cambridge: Cambridge University Press.

Arctic Human Development Report (AHDR) (2004) *Arctic Human Development Report*, Akureyri: Stefansson Arctic Institute.Bauer, T. (2001) *Tourism in the Antarctic: opportunities, constraints and future prospects*. London: The Haworth Hospitality Press.

Chapin, F.S., III, Hoel, M., Carpenter, S.R., Lubchenko, J., Walker, B., Callaghan, T.V., Folke, C., Levin, S.A., Mäler, K.-G., Nilsson, C., Barrett, S., Berkes, F., Crépin, A.-S., Danell, K., Rosswall, T., Starrett, D., Xepapadeas, A. and Zimov, S.A. (2006) Building resilience and adaptation to manage Arctic change. *AMBIO: A Journal of the Human Environment*, 35(4): 198–202.

Chapin III, F.S., Peterson, G. Berkes, F., Callaghan, T.V., Angelstam, P., Apps, M., Beier, C., Bergeron, Y., Crépin, A.-S., Danell, K., Elmqvist, T., Folke, C., Forbes, B., Fresco, N., Juday, G., Niemelä, J., Shvidenko, A. and Whiteman, G. (2004) 'Resilience and vulnerability of northern regions to social and environmental change', *AMBIO: A Journal of the Human Environment*, 33: 342–47.

Destinations of the World News (2008) 'Contents', *Destinations of the World News*, 21(March): 2.

Dickson, B. (2009) 'Securing the legacy of the IPY', *Nature Geoscience*, 2: 374–76.

Dmitrenko, I., Polyakov, I.V., Kirillov, S., Timokhov, L., Frolov, I.E., Sokolov, V.T., Simmons, H.L., Ivanov, V.V. and Walsh, D. (2008) 'Towards a warmer Arctic Ocean: spreading of the early 21st Century Atlantic water warm anomaly along the Eurasian Basin margins', *Journal of Geophysical Research* 113, C05023, doi:10,1029/2007JC004158.

E The Environmental Magazine (2002) 'Last chance to see it? Visiting the pristine Arctic National Wildlife Refuge', *E The Environmental Magazine*, 13(2)(March/April). Online. Available HTTP: http://www.emagazine.com/view/?542 (accessed 20 September 2009).

Egan, T. (2005) 'The race to Alaska before it melts', *The New York Times*, 26 June. Online. Available HTTP: http://travel2.nytimes.com/2005/06/26/travel/26alaska.html?ex = 1277438400&en = e88a719ca3494a76&ei = 5090&partner = rssuserland&emc = rss (accessed 20 September 2009).

Haas, C., Pfaffling, A., Hendricks, S., Rabenstein, L., Etienne, J.L. and Rigor, I. (2008) 'Reduced ice thickness in Arctic Transpolar Drift favors rapid ice retreat', *Geophysical Research Letters*, 35(17), L17501, doi:10.1029/2008GL034457.

Hall, C.M. (2000) 'The tourist and economic significance of Antarctic travel in Australian and New Zealand Antarctic gateway cities', *Tourism and Hospitality Research: The Surrey Quarterly Review*, 2(2): 157–69.

—— (2008) 'Tourism and climate change: knowledge gaps and issues', *Tourism Recreation Research*, 33: 339–50.

Hall, C.M and Johnston, M.E. (eds.) (1995) *Polar Tourism: Tourism in the Arctic and Antarctic Regions*, Chichester: John Wiley & Sons.

Instanes, A., Anisimov, O., Brigham, L., Goering, D., Ladanyi, B., Larsen, J.O. and Khrustalev, L.N. (2005) 'Infrastructure: buildings, support systems, and industrial facilities', in C. Symon, L. Arris and B. Heal (eds) *Arctic Climate Impact Assessment, ACIA*, Cambridge: Cambridge University Press.

Intergovernmental Panel on Climate Change (IPCC) (2007) 'Summary for policymakers', in S. Solomon, D. Qin, M. Manning, Z. Chen, M. Marquis, K.B. Averyt, M.Tignor and H.L. Miller (eds) *Climate Change 2007: The Physical Science Basis. Contribution of Working Group I to the Fourth Assessment Report of the Intergovernmental Panel on Climate Change*, Cambridge: Cambridge University Press.

International Polar Year (IPY) (2009) International Polar Year 2007–9. February 19, Online. Available HTTP: http://www.ipy.org/index.php?/ipy/detail/ arctic_sea_ice_will_probably_not_recover/

Lawrence, D.M., Slater, A.G., Tomas, R.A., Holland, M.M. and Deser, C. (2008) 'Accelerated Arctic land warming and permafrost degradation during rapid sea ice loss' [Preview], *Geophysical Research Letters*, 35, 11506

Lenton, T.M., Held, H., Kriegler, E., Hall, J.W., Lucht, W., Rahmstorf, S. and Schellnhuber, H.J. (2008) Tipping elements in the Earth's climate system. *Proceedings of the National Academy of Sciences,* 105(6): 1786–93.

Margolis, M. (2006) 'The rush to see it before it's gone. Tourists threaten many of the world's great tourism sites', Newsweek, 17 April Online. Available HTTP: http://www. newsweek.com/id/46018 (accessed 20 September 2009).

McMullen, C.P. and Jabbour, J. (2009) *Climate Change Science Compendium 2009*, Nairobi: United Nations Environment Programme, EarthPrint.

National Snow and Ice Data Center (NSIDC) (2009). Arctic Sea Ice News and Analysis. National Snow and Ice Data Centre (NSIDC) Online. Available HTTP: http://nsidc.org/ arcticseaicenews (accessed 19 September 2009).

Round, A. (2008) 'Paradise Lost', *Destinations of the World News*, issue 21(March): 44–51.

Salt, D. (2006) 10 wonders to visit before they disappear. Cosmos, December. Online. Available HTTP: http://www.cosmosmagazine.com/node/3026/full (accessed 20 September 2009)

Schiermeier, Q. (2009) Arctic sea ice levels third-lowest on record, Nature, 18 September, doi:10.1038/news.2009.930. Online. Available HTTP: http://www.nature.com/ news/2009/090918/full/news.2009.930.html (accessed 19 September 2009).

Slaymaker, O. and Kelly, R.E.J. (2007) *The Cryosphere and Global Environmental Change*. Oxford: Blackwell.

Snyder, J.M. (2007) 'Economic roles of polar tourism', in J. Snyder and B. Stonehouse (eds) *Prospects for Polar Tourism*, Wallingford: CABI.

— (2009) 'Arctic Tourism: A Growing Presence in an Ice Diminishing Region', paper presented at 3rd Symposium on the Impacts of an Ice-Diminishing Arctic on Naval and Maritime Operations, June 9–11, 2009, US Naval Academy, Alumni Center, Annapolis, Maryland.

Snyder, J. and Prokosch, P. (2007) *Tourism in Polar Regions: The Sustainability Challenge*. Geneva: United Nations Environment Programme.

Snyder, J. and Stonehouse, B. (eds.) (2007) *Prospects for Polar Tourism*. Wallingford: CABI.

Splettstoesser, J. (2000) 'IAATO's stewardship of the Antarctic environment: a history of tour operator's concern for a vulnerable part of the world', *International Journal of Tourism Research*, 2: 47–55.

Stewart, E.J., Draper, D. and Johnston, M.E. (2005) 'A review of tourism research in the polar regions', *Arctic*, 58(4): 383–94.

UK MSN Travel (2009) Last chance to see…UJ MSN Travel, 10 September. Online. Available HTTP: http://travel.uk.msn.com/inspiration/photos.aspx?cp-documentid = 149582681 (accessed 20 September 2009).

Index

MIX
Paper from
responsible sources
FSC® C013056

Printed and bound in Great Britain by
TJ International Ltd, Padstow, Cornwall